The Major Religions

The Major Religions

An Introduction with Texts

Second Edition

T. Patrick Burke

Blackwell
Publishing

BLACKWELL PUBLISHING LTD
350 Main Street, Malden, MA 02148-5020, USA
108 Cowley Road, Oxford OX4 1JF, UK
550 Swanston Street, Carlton, Victoria 3053, Australia

First edition published 1996 by Blackwell Publishing Ltd
Second edition published 2004

Library of Congress Cataloging-in-Publication Data

Burke, T. Patrick (Thomas Patrick), 1934–
    The major religions : an introduction with texts / T. Patrick Burke.—
2nd ed.
        p. cm.
Includes bibliographical references and index.
    ISBN 1-4051-1049-X (pbk. : alk. paper)
    1. Religions. I. Title.

    BL80.3.B87 2004
    200—dc22
                                        2003014807

A catalogue record for this title is available from the British Library.

Set in 10.5/12.5pt Galliard
by Graphicraft Limited, Hong Kong
Printed and bound in the United Kingdom
by TJ International, Padstow, Cornwall

For further information on
Blackwell Publishing, visit our website:
http://www.blackwellpublishing.com

Contents

Illustrations

Maps

Preface to Second Edition

The terrorist attacks carried out on the United States by radical Muslims on September 11, 2001, and the response of the United States and its allies against the Taliban regime in Afghanistan and against that of Saddam Hussein in Iraq, have raised urgent new questions about the ethical teachings of the major religions, especially their attitude towards war and the use of violence, as well as about their relationship to the modern world.

In consequence, in this new edition, two new sections have been added to most of the chapters, one on ethics and the other on modern developments. The former gives special attention to the question of war, especially whether a distinction has been developed in the tradition between just and unjust wars. The latter asks about the relationship of the religion to such aspects of the modern world as science, democracy, and the capitalist economy. A further section has been added to the chapter on Islam, discussing Muslim terrorism.

In addition, since some less well-known religions from other parts of the globe can now be encountered routinely in the urban centers of the West, an attempt has been made to at least begin to respond to this by including an entire new chapter on Sikhism, with its accompanying selection of texts.

In the first edition, the method of marking off the original texts from the author's comments was not entirely happy and sometimes led to confusion. A new method is used in this edition, which it is hoped will obviate the problem.

Comments from users of the first edition have been very helpful in preparing this new one, and readers are again encouraged to send in any suggestions for the improvement of the book.

The Transcription of Foreign Languages

In general, the traditional systems, or those best known to the public at large, are used in this book to transcribe foreign languages, rather than those currently employed by scholars. Thus for Chinese we continue to use the Wade–Giles system; however, the Pinyin form of many words is given in parentheses. For Islam current usage is no longer entirely consistent, since in recent years it has become common to use the Arabic for some words, such as Muslim, while continuing to use the Urdu for others, such as Mohammed, Mecca and Medina. In this edition we attempt to follow common usage, giving the alternative, whether Urdu or Arabic, in parentheses on the first use of the term. For Hebrew the Sephardic spelling, or the spelling which is commonly taken to represent the Sephardic pronunciation, seems to have become further entrenched since the earlier edition.

Preface to First Edition

This is a modest book with a modest aim. It is intended for short introductory courses in world religions where there is not sufficient time to cover the full range of material that would otherwise be of interest. The book developed out of my experience in teaching during summer sessions, lasting usually only six or seven weeks. While such courses can be useful to the beginning student in providing a preliminary orientation and a sense of direction in a vast and complex field, there is often a danger that the student will be overwhelmed by the quantity of material that needs to be mastered in such a short time. My students have constantly remarked that the textbooks available contain too much material, even where limited sections were designated for class work. The aim of this book is to fill this need, by focusing on just a few essentials in each religion, deliberately omitting much which could be treated with more time or which the more advanced student might find helpful. My purpose has been to provide all but only what is needed for such a short introductory course, so that the student will have the clear feeling that the course work is manageable.

A second purpose has been to focus a little more on the worldview of each religion, on the beliefs and values that make the religions meaningful to their followers, rather than on their history, as some texts in world religions do. While some knowledge of the historical development of each religion is indispensable, and an attempt is made here to provide that, the beginning student in my experience is helped more by understanding what gives each religion its rationale, what makes it attractive to its followers and secures their loyalty. In general, historical material has been included only where it was felt to be necessary to illuminate the worldview of the religion. Consequently, more attention is paid to historical development in some religions, such as Hinduism, where successive eras have left markedly different emphases, than in others, such as the Chinese religions.

As part of this aim a section has been included at the beginning of each chapter on the spirit of that religion. This is usually a story or poem from a primary source, selected because, in the highly subjective opinion of the author, it captures in a special way something of the mood and atmosphere that in the mind of its followers characterizes that religion.

A special effort has been made to highlight clearly the main ideas in each religion and distinguish them from one another, by devices such as paragraph headings and indentation. Although at times these may give the text the appearance of being a mere list, I have found that they improve markedly the beginning student's comprehension of the material.

Introductory textbooks on world religions usually have to be supplemented by a collection of readings. Yet for the typical short introductory course a whole book of readings again contains too much material. In order to provide the small quantity of readings useful in a short course, a few judged most enlightening by the author are included at the end of each chapter. The translations have been chosen and edited more for readability than for scholarly exactitude. The author regrets this, but has found that the best scholarly translations are not always the clearest for the beginning student.

To help the student, a number of study aids are also provided at the end of each chapter: (a) a brief summary of the religion, (b) questions for discussion, which can be expected to elicit different responses, (c) sample test questions, and (d) recommendations for additional reading. A combined glossary is included at the end of the book, to provide for students who may be unsure to which religion a term belongs.

A word should perhaps be said about the order in which the religions are treated. In general I have found it a good rule to begin students with the religions most different from the one they are chiefly familiar with, and to leave that one till last. In this way they acquire a broader perspective, a larger framework, within which to view their own religion. The majority of my students have come from a Christian background, and as a result the chapter on Christianity is placed last, in some defiance of the historical order, which would place Islam last. Instructors whose classes have a different constitution may wish to consider using the chapters in a different order.

When an attempt is made to convey such complex realities as the major religions to beginning students, there will inevitably be some oversimplification, which will need to be corrected in more advanced courses. While every effort has been made to avoid statements that are simply false, of course, to introduce all the qualifications necessary to give the full truth would sometimes overburden the beginning student, who is better served by having at the start a definite foundation, a clear framework of ideas, which he can later modify as he acquires more detailed information. The author begs the indulgence of his professional colleagues for statements which have been oversimplified for this pedagogic purpose.

Any comments which may help to improve the book will be welcomed.

Acknowledgments

The author and publisher gratefully acknowledge the permission granted to reproduce copyright material in this book:

Martin Buber, *Tales of the Hadism*, trans. Olga Marx, Schocken Books, 1947.

E. W. Burlingame, from the "Anguttara Commentary", *Buddhist Parables*, Yale University Press, 1922.

Ch'u Ta-Kao, *Tao Te Chin*, Allen & Unwin, 1937. Copyright © Ch'u Ta-Kao 1937. Reprinted by permission of HarperCollins Publishers Ltd.

Edward Conze (ed.), *Buddhist Texts through the Ages*, Philosophical Library, 1954 and Harper Torchbooks, 1964.

N. J. Dawood (trans.), *The Koran*, Penguin Classics, 1956. © 1956 by N. J. Dawood. Reproduced by permission of Penguin Books Ltd.

W. T. De Bary et al., "Simile of a Chariot," in *Sources of Indian Tradition*. Copyright © 1958 Columbia University Press. Reprinted with the permission of the publisher.

W. T. De Bary, Wing-tsit Chan, and Burton Watson, *Sources of Chinese Tradition*, vol. 1. Copyright © 1964 Columbia University Press. Reprinted with the permission of the publisher.

W. T. De Bary and W. E. Soothill (trans.), "The Lotus of the Good Law," in E. A. Burtt (ed.), *The Teachings of the Compassionate Buddha*, New American Library, 1982.

W. A. C. H. Dobson, *Mencius*, University of Toronto, 1963.

Driss Chaibi, *Heirs to the Past*, trans. Len Ortzen, Heinemann Educational Books, 1971.

G. W. F. Hegel, from *Lectures on the Philosophy of Religion*, Routledge & Kegan Paul, 1962.

Arthur Hertzberg (ed.), *Judaism: The Key Spiritual Writings of the Jewish Tradition*. Washington Square Press, 1970. Copyright © 1991 by Arthur Hertzberg. Reprinted with permission of Simon & Schuster Adult Publishing Group.

T. J. Hopkins (trans.), from *The Hindu Religious Tradition*, Dickenson Publishing Company, 1971.

Ibn Ishaq, "*Sirat Rasul Allah*", trans. by Alfred Guillaume, *The Life of Muhammad*, Oxford, Oxford University Press, 1955.

New English Bible © Oxford University Press and Cambridge University Press, 1961, 1971.

Swami Prabhavananda and Christopher Isherwood (trans.), *Bhagavad-Gita*, New American Library, 1954.

Swami Prabhavananda and Frederick Manchester (trans.), *The Upanishads, Breath of the Eternal*, New American Library, 1957.

Sirdar Iqbal Ali Shah, *The Lights of Asia*, London, Arthur Barker, 1934.

Nikki-Guninder Kaur Singh (trans.), *The Name of my Beloved: Verses of the Sikh Gurus*. HarperSanFrancisco, 1995.

E. J. Thomas, *Early Buddhist Scriptures*, Routledge & Kegan Paul, 1913. Reprinted with permission.

Arthur Waley (ed. and trans.), *The Book of Songs*, Allen & Unwin, 1937. Reprinted with permission of the Arthur Waley Estate.

Burton Watson (trans.), *The Complete Works of Chuang Tzu*. Copyright © 1968 Columbia University Press. Reprinted with the permission of the publisher.

Wing-tsit Chan, from *A Sourcebook in Chinese Philosophy*. Copyright © 1963 (renewed 1991) Princeton University Press. Reprinted by permission of Princeton University Press.

R. C. Zaehner (trans.), from *Hindu Scriptures*, Dent, 1966.

Heinrich Zimmer, *Myths and Symbols in Indian Art and Civilization*, ed. Joseph Campbell, Harper & Row, 1962.

Every effort has been made to trace copyright holders and to obtain their permission for the use of copyright material. The publisher apologizes for any errors or omissions in the above list and would be grateful if notified of any corrections that should be incorporated in future reprints or editions of this book.

I particularly wish to thank several scholars who have given me the benefit of their comments: Khalid Blankinship, Murray Friedman, Charles Wei-hsin Fu, Thomas Selover, Arvind Sharma, Jacob Staub, Leonard Swidler, Linwood Urban, Bibhuti Yadav, and Blackwell's reviewers, whose names are unknown to me. I have a very special debt of gratitude to James Dunaway, who on his own initiative provided me with many pages of detailed comments on most of the book, as well as a large number of study questions.

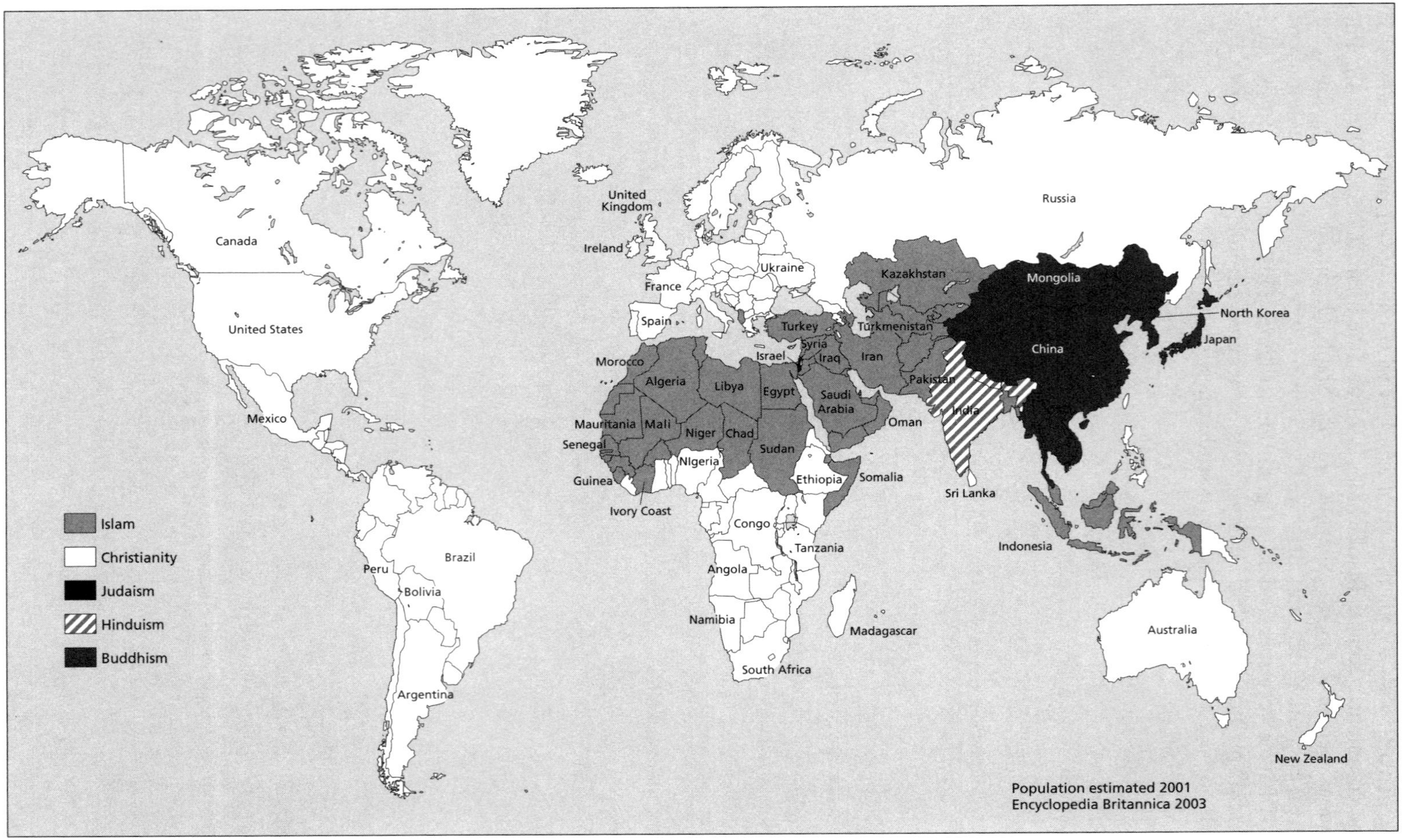
Canada
United States
Mexico
Peru
Brazil
Bolivia
Argentina
United Kingdom
Ireland
France
Spain
Ukraine
Russia
Kazakhstan
Mongolia
North Korea
Japan
China
Turkey
Turkmenistan
Syria
Israel
Iraq
Iran
Pakistan
India
Morocco
Algeria
Libya
Egypt
Saudi Arabia
Oman
Mauritania
Mali
Niger
Chad
Senegal
Sudan
Nigeria
Guinea
Ethiopia
Somalia
Sri Lanka
Ivory Coast
Congo
Tanzania
Indonesia
Angola
Namibia
Madagascar
South Africa
Australia
New Zealand
Islam
Christianity
Judaism
Hinduism
Buddhism
Population estimated 2001
Encyclopedia Britannica 2003

Distribution of religions in the world

Introduction

The Significance of Religion

Some people find religion puzzling. They do not see any grounds to believe that it is true, they do not observe that it fulfills any very useful function, and they do not understand why it should arouse the ardent passions that it often does. It seems to them to be merely an eccentricity, a form of emotional self-indulgence and self-delusion unjustified by the hard facts of life. Religious people appear to them to be largely hypocrites, preaching loftier ideals than others but rarely leading better lives.

To gain an understanding of religion and its role in human life, perhaps one place to start might be with what we may call the *spiritual dimension* of life. Although it is not easy to describe this in words, it is the aspect of life that rises above our usual preoccupation with our individual selves, transcending our personal needs and desires. Our outlook on life is spiritual when we look at things from a broader, a less self-centered, a more impartial or universal perspective, where we become detached from our ego and are no longer concerned with our own personal fate, at least in this life. The spiritual dimension of life is sometimes described as having the perspective of eternity, because when we are inclined to get wrapped up in some urgent present concern, such as achieving a promotion or obtaining possession of some material object, it asks us to disengage ourselves from the present moment and consider how important this particular thing will be in a hundred years, or perhaps a thousand. Even those most skeptical about religion often see the nobility of such a state of detachment from the narrow confines of the self. For a mature person the spiritual side of life is more important than the material.

Another way of putting this is to say that religion has to do with the *soul*. This does not necessarily mean an independent substance, living on perhaps after death, but rather that deep dimension of each person's identity and character where he

1

takes up his most fundamental stance towards life. A person's soul is not something that can be discovered under a microscope. The body can be healthy, but the soul twisted and diseased. As one religious leader has reminded us, it is possible to gain the whole world, yet lose one's soul. Our soul in this sense represents the most important aspect of us, what makes us uniquely ourselves.

This does not mean that all religions are automatically good for the soul. Just as the medical profession may make mistakes about what is good for our physical health, so religions can make enormous and grotesque errors about our spiritual health. Some religions have practiced human sacrifice, some have distorted human values grossly in other ways. But religion is characterized by concern for the soul, just as medicine is characterized by concern for our bodily welfare.

The realm of the soul and the spirit is also the realm of *meaning*. Religion has to do with the overall meaning of our lives, with the significance of human existence, and especially with the significance of the negative experiences of suffering and evil, since these are what most threaten our sense of meaning in life.

We each know only too well that our existence is not always plain sailing. Although sometimes things go well, there are other occasions when life crushes our hopes, frustrates our labors, and inflicts pain, loss, sorrow, dismay, and terror. Even worse than the experience of bodily pain may be the callousness, unkindness, and outright injustice of others. We are forever at the mercy of chance and absurdity. We live our lives at the edge of a precipice, and we can never tell when the ground will not give way beneath our feet. One day, though we may not like to think about the fact, life will push us over that cliff, and our story, so far as we can see, will come to an end. Our highest feelings, our most intense desires, our noblest aspirations, our very being will, apparently, come to nothing.

Why is this so? How are we to respond to it? If we have asked ourselves such questions, we are in a frame of mind when the religions of mankind may speak to us.

Each of the major religions has a message about the human condition; each points to something that it views as fundamentally wrong and unsatisfactory about our ordinary existence; each offers a diagnosis of the cause of that unsatisfactoriness and points to a possible remedy. By doing this religions provide a framework of meaning for human life. Every event in our lives and every action that we take have some kind of relationship to that framework, which tells us what its ultimate significance is for us. As a result the framework carries with it an overarching set of values, indicating where we ought to set our priorities, what we ought to hold important and what we ought to regard as trivial.

The transcendent

The diagnoses which the major religions provide, and the remedies toward which they point, do not lie within the field of ordinary human experience, but are transcendent, that is, they point to a realm of being beyond our ordinary experience, a realm which can often be described as supernatural. However closely they may pay attention to the details of human living, it is the realm of the transcendent which ultimately concerns them. This marks them off from diagnoses of the human condition made solely in terms of this life and this world, such as Marxism, which are therefore not included here, even though there may be some superficial resemblances.

In the preface to his *Lectures on the Philosophy of Religion* the German philosopher Hegel says:

> Religion is the loftiest object that can occupy human beings; it is the absolute object. It is the region of eternal truth and eternal virtue, the region where all the riddles of thought, all contradictions, and all the sorrows of the heart are resolved, the region of the eternal peace through which the human being is truly human . . .
>
> All other aims go back to this final end; though previously valid for themselves, they disappear in the face of it, no other aim holds out against it, and all are resolved in it. Occupation with this object is fulfilling and satisfying by itself, and desires nothing else but this. Hence it is the abolutely free occupation, the absolutely free consciousness . . .
>
> Religion holds this position for all peoples and persons. Everywhere this concern is regarded as the sabbath of life, in which finite aims, limited interests, toil, sorrow, unpleasantness, earthly and finite cares . . . waft away in devotion's present feeling or hope . . . the whole realm of temporality passes away into eternal harmony.

The meaning of the word "religion"

Like many words having to do with human affairs, such as "art" or "science," the word "religion" can have two different kinds of meaning. In one, it refers to a set of historical facts, namely what a certain group of people actually have done or typically do, as when we speak of "the religion of the Greeks." This factual sense can include references to errors and moral failures.

In the second sense "religion" and related words refer to a set of ideals, which may perhaps never be fully carried out. When the word is used in this sense it would be out of place to include references to errors or moral failures. If a Christian were to remark of another person that "he is a true Christian," this is intended in the sense of something inherently praiseworthy.

The Families of Religions

In this book we shall be examining eight major religions: Hinduism, Buddhism, Sikhism, Confucianism, Taoism, Judaism, Christianity, and Islam. These religions are not isolated traditions, unrelated to one another. Rather, each is a member of a family of religions, sharing with the other members of its family many if not most of the fundamental categories and conceptions by which it interprets the world. This happens in some instances because one religion has given rise to another, or because a number of religions have developed side by side within the same culture. Different religions belonging to the same family may employ their common conceptions in different ways, but the differences within each family are to a certain extent like variations on the same theme in a piece of music. The theme, the distinctive approach of each family of religions, varies with the culture.

The major religions occur in three such families:

- the religions of Indian origin, which include Hinduism, Buddhism, and Sikhism, as well as Jainism which will not be examined here;
- those of Chinese origin, embracing Confucianism and Taoism, and also Chinese Buddhism;
- and those of Semitic origin, including Judaism, Christianity, and Islam.

Taking them overall, it might be said that within each family the resemblances between one religion and another are for the most part more striking than the differences, while between religions belonging to different families the differences typically stand out more strongly. These three families of religions can be viewed as offering three fundamentally different alternatives in the understanding of human life and the world.

Summarizing briefly, and at the risk of oversimplification, we may say that the religions of Indian origin in their developed forms focus in a distinctive way on the themes of Suffering, the Ego, and Liberation:

- Religion arises out of human need – rather than from a divine command, for example, as in the case of the religions of Semitic origin. The religions of India agree that human existence left to itself is an unending cycle of birth, death and rebirth, *samsara*, condemning us to an eternal destiny of suffering and limitation. Religion provides us with the means of overcoming and ending that cycle, and transcending the deficiencies of existence, if we are wise enough to take advantage of it.
- The cycle of birth, death, and rebirth is caused fundamentally not by the external objective world or nature, but by our own subjective egos, by self-centered desire.
- It is possible to overcome and abandon this egocentricity by attaining to a transcendent and universal viewpoint which will liberate the spirit from the confines of the individual ego: *moksha* or *nirvana*. Once this transcendent condition has been attained, the cycle of birth, death, and rebirth will be brought to an end.

These features give the religions of Indian origin a singularly spiritual and idealistic quality.

The religions of Chinese origin, by contrast, emphasize especially such ideas as Harmony and Nature:

- The religions of Chinese origin do not emphasize the deficiencies of human existence as strongly as do the religions of Indian or Semitic origin. It may be said that they take their point of departure from the widespread failure of human life to run smoothly and successfully – understanding "success" in a broad sense, as the flourishing of the human enterprise.
- Their diagnosis is that this unsuccessfulness is caused by a lack of harmony with the natural order of things.
- Their aim, as a result, is to regain the lost harmony with the natural order, and so make human life more successful, in a very broad sense of the term. Their conception of this natural order differs, Taoism emphasizing what might be called cosmic nature, and Confucianism stressing human nature, but both share an emphasis on the natural order of things.

The religions of Semitic origin, lastly, are forms of ethical monotheism, interpreting human life largely in terms of such concepts as God, Creation, Revelation, Law, Sin, and Judgement:

- There is a single divine Being, personal in nature.
- He created the world as a reality distinct from Himself.
- Religion begins not with man's need, but with a revelation from this God.
- He gives a law which must govern men's relations with Him and with one another.
- Men will be judged by God according to their obedience to this law.

These features give the religions of Semitic origin a stronger focus on moral or ethical concerns than many other religions.

Places of worship

Corresponding to these differences, as well as to the differences between their cultures, the three families of the major religions have different kinds of places of worship. Those of the religions of Indian origin in their original or standard form are not places for an assembly to gather, but are rather designed for individual worship and frequently resemble a cave. Those of Chinese origin take the form of a garden containing a number of pavilions. Those of Semitic origin are essentially communal, places for an assembly to gather. This latter description applies also to Sikhism, which, though of Indian origin, has been influenced by Islam in some respects.

Religions and cultures

These families of religions are cultural families. A religion tends to reflect the mentality, the basic attitudes, concerns and values, of the culture in which it originates – without being simply reducible to an expression of the culture.

Consequently, to encounter a religion is to encounter a culture, a broader reality which provides in a sense the framework within which the religion exists. When one religion encounters another, especially when they belong to different families, this is also an encounter between cultures. This is perhaps one of the reasons why it is usually difficult and unusual to change from one religion to another.

Belief and action

Religion consists above all in action. Although the action usually arises out of theoretical presuppositions, religions are not in the first instance theoretical undertakings, but aim to accomplish something. To be religious means above all to do certain kinds of things, not merely to think about them. To understand a religion, therefore, it is necessary to become familiar with what is done in it. The format of a written book, however, such as this textbook, lends itself more easily to the description of belief than of action. For this reason it is recommended that this book be supplemented by other kinds of instructional material, such as films, and especially by the living experience of the religions as they are practiced by their followers, so far as that is possible. Students are encouraged to visit temples, churches, synagogues, mosques and gurdwaras, attend their ceremonies, and meet and talk with their adherents. Not all will be immediately hospitable to the stranger, but many will.

Some Categories of Religions

In studying religions it may happen that we wish to ask in what ways they resemble and differ from one another, and in this regard there are some categories or classifications that we may find useful to bear in mind. These categories should not be understood too rigorously, since most religions are complex and present exceptions to almost every rule we try to impose on them, but simply as indications of the direction in which a religion or some portion of it tends. While these categories can sometimes be enlightening, their application to a particular case may often not be simple.

Universal and particular

Some religions understand themselves as addressed to the whole human race; their aim is to embrace all of mankind and they actively desire converts. These are sometimes called universal religions. This is not to imply that they actually do embrace all human beings, which is obviously not true, but that this is their ideal. Buddhism, Christianity, and Islam are universal religions in this sense.

Other religions have no such universal aim, but understand themselves as existing only for a particular people, tribe, or nation. They usually do not especially desire converts. These religions may be called communal, tribal, ethnic, or national religions. Judaism and Hinduism are examples. Not all religions fit easily into this distinction: the Confucian and Taoist traditions, for example, neither aim explicitly to embrace the whole of mankind, nor consider themselves in principle restricted to the Chinese people: historically they have been identified with Chinese culture, but the main elements in them seem, in principle, capable of being adopted by others outside of that culture.

Ethical and mystical

Some religions place special emphasis on the way people treat one another. For example, both Judaism and Christianity emphasize the Ten Commandments, one of which is: You shall not steal. Concepts such as justice and injustice presuppose that human beings have distinct identities, that I am not you, and you are not me. These are ethical religions. (The term does not refer to the actual behavior of their adherents, but to the role their beliefs allot to ethical considerations.)

Other religions, however, do not make this supposition, but instead see everything as one. On the level of reality, in their view, there is only one undifferentiated being or reality. Differences and distinctions belong then only to the world of appearances, the phenomenal world. These are mystical religions. A view is mystical when it emphasizes the oneness of things underlying all appearances of individuality and distinctness, or even sees and experiences a single, sole reality. For example, as we shall see, the form of religion set forth in the Upanishads holds such a view. If everything is fundamentally one, then the distinctions between individual identities that are necessary for ethics do not really exist. At bottom, what we call "you" and what we call "me" are the one identical being. In mystical religions ethical values tend to have a subordinate place, and ethical religions tend to be in some measure hostile to mysticism.

Saviorist and pelagian

Again, some religions emphasize that human beings are incapable of saving themselves and require to be saved by a savior. These may be called, not surprisingly, saviorist religions. Christianity and some forms of Mahayana Buddhism are examples of this.

Other religions, by contrast, stress that it is possible for the individual to do whatever is necessary to attain salvation without the special assistance of any external power. We do not possess a suitable word to designate these religions. Here they may be called religions of self-liberation or self-power, or we may sometimes use the term "pelagian" (after Pelagius, an ancient Christian believed to have taught this doctrine; the term is purely descriptive, and should not be taken with the pejorative connotation it has had in the mainstream Christian tradition). Theravada Buddhism is of this type. Again, some religions, such as the Chinese traditions and Judaism, do not fit neatly into this distinction. And sometimes different strands within a tradition will have different emphases, as in the case of Catholic and Protestant Christianity (see below, pp. 336–8).

Civil and personal

It may also be useful to distinguish between personal and civil religion. By civil religion is meant a form of religion that addresses primarily the needs of a civil society such as a nation. This would be true of traditional Chinese religion and the Confucian tradition, for example. Personal religion, by contrast, is concerned more with the needs and feelings of the individual, as is the case with devotional Hinduism and Buddhism. Again, these categories do not necessarily apply straightforwardly to every religion, but it can be helpful to bear them in mind.

Modern Developments

The major religions emerged in the ancient world, or, in the case of Sikhism, several centuries ago, before the development of science, representative democracy, the free market economy, and modern technology. In the twentieth century, especially since the Second World War, the encounter with these features of modern life has subjected the traditional religions to intense pressures and has sometimes led to significant changes. An attempt will be made here to indicate the more prominent of these briefly in each case.

The Role of Value Judgements in the Study of Religions

The phenomenological approach

Religion is an emotional subject: it easily arouses strong agreements and disagreements. The student of religions will find many things which may offend his sensibilities. For this reason it has become common for specialists in the subject to lay it down as a condition of successful work in the field that all value judgements be set aside, "bracketed," or postponed indefinitely. The aim of the study of religions, in this view, is simply to arrive at a knowledge and understanding of the historical facts, whatever they may be. Our study aims not only at knowledge, in the sense of knowing the external facts, but understanding, that is, grasping with some degree of empathy the reasons for them, why people have believed and acted as they have in their religious life. Following this approach, a person will not refer to a belief as "superstitious," for example, because that implies a value judgement on it. This way of approaching the study of religions is often called "phenomenological," from a Greek word meaning "the study of appearances."

However, this approach is not without difficulties. It seems to imply that all beliefs are equally valid and all practices equally good, which it would be folly to believe, and which arguably no one does believe. A complete relativism is extremely difficult to adopt consistently, and can scarcely be maintained indefinitely.

Current debate

From its inception the study of religions as a discipline has generally endeavored to follow a middle path between theology, on the one hand, which is committed to belief in a particular religion, and the social sciences such as anthropology, which, although they preserve scientific detachment, are not concerned with the specifically religious character of religious phenomena, but with their social dimension. In recent years, however, the view has been put forward that the study of religions in its traditional form by its very nature inevitably implies some degree of commitment to religion: if not to a particular religion, at least commitment to the value of religion as such and in general. No one will bother to study religions who feels that they are entirely valueless. The tendency of this argument is to propose in effect that the study of religions should be more like anthropology.

This view has been accused by its opponents of being reductionist, that is, of assuming that everything in religion can be explained in terms of non-religious factors, such as psychological or sociological ones. Religion, they maintain, is *sui generis*, its essence is special to itself, and it can be understood only if it is approached on that basis.

The approach of this book

This book does not assume that the study of religions necessarily presupposes commitment to their truth or value. Our aim is simply to enable the student to become familiar with the basic information about the main religious traditions. Each reader can then decide for him- or herself what is of value. For this reason we have avoided all value judgements in the body of the chapters.

As a general rule it is wise to suspend judgement until we are certain we understand the matter sufficiently. This applies to the theological beliefs, of course, but also to such matters as the Hindu caste system, or the fact that the major religions traditionally favor the male gender. The initial approach of the student should be to try to understand the reasons that may have led to the features he finds difficult to accept.

On the other hand, we do not think that the question of evaluation should be entirely swept under the rug, as if everything taught and practiced by all religions was right and good. This is obviously not the case. Some religions, to take an extreme example, have practiced human sacrifice, and however much we may try to understand with some degree of sympathy the thought processes that led to such practices, at the end of the day we are obliged as human beings with a conscience to condemn them. It is inevitable that readers will make value judgements, and it can scarcely be maintained that they have no right to do so. One of the important reasons why people study religions is to help form their own views. On the other hand, the moral principles that we bring to bear on such a question do not arise specifically from within the study of religions, but from our general sense of right and wrong, so there is a sense in which evaluational questions, however important and necessary they may be, are not precisely an integral part of the study of religions. For this reason, while avoiding value judgements in the body of the chapter, we have included evaluational questions at the end of each chapter in the questions for discussion. Instructors who do not wish to use these need not do so.

For those who do, it is recommended that they try to bring out in the discussion both sides of each question, so that neither side wins a victory merely by default. It is important that students learn to make value judgements in a fair-minded and unprejudiced way, taking into account all the relevant factors.

Gender and class

A good example of this is perhaps the question of the attitude of the traditional religions towards gender and class. It is possible, and perhaps even probable, that preoccupation with social equality may be chiefly a phenomenon of societies which are predominantly middle class. The development of a predominantly middle-class society may be a prerequisite for the emergence of a functioning democracy, as well as for a strong sense of egalitarianism. If that is the case, it will not be surprising that to societies which consist of an aristocracy and a peasantry, as many traditional societies do, and which possess little or no middle class, any extensive idea of social equality may seem unrealistic, if not ludicrous. Unsurprisingly, traditional societies tend to favor the traditional division of labor between the sexes, assigning to men the public sphere, which includes religion in all its social manifestations, and to women the domestic sphere and submission to the authority of the male. Similarly, it will not be surprising that traditional societies do not typically have strong objections to class distinctions. While this acceptance of inequality in traditional societies runs counter to widespread conceptions current in Western societies, which are predominantly middle class, the student of religions would do well initially to suspend his own value assumptions and approach it as he approaches other questions, such as those of belief and ritual, by trying to understand the reasons for it. This does not preclude, however, but rather suggests an eventual discussion of the topic in class.

Personal faith and the study of religions

It is possible for the study of other religions to have the effect, in the mind of the student, of relativizing all religions, since, as remarked above, all are placed on the same level and given the same respect. If a student has grown up as an adherent of one religion, it can come to appear merely as one among many, and to be placed in question by them, as it in turn places the others in question. The study of religions *can* lead to a sense of disillusionment with one's own religion, and with all religion.

However, this outcome of relativization is not inevitable. On the contrary, it is possible to study other religions in such a way that one's appreciation of one's own religion is enhanced rather than diminished. The effect of the study of religions ought to be that we acquire a better understanding both of other people's religion and also of our own, if we already have one.

The perspective from which the study of religions is conducted in this book is not from the inside, the viewpoint of the believer, but from the outside, that of an external, neutral observer. Unavoidably this misses a great deal, perhaps the most important thing about any religion. The study of religion might perhaps be compared to that of political parties. The task of a political scientist is to study a political party objectively, from the viewpoint not of its dedicated members but of a detached onlooker. Inevitably he misses what really animates and motivates the party, its soul, because he does not, and as a scientist cannot, share in the enthusiasm of the members for its distinctive programme; he is not personally moved by what moves them. Something similar is true of science. A historian studying the development of the science of physics can say what theories were accepted and what discarded, but he is not in a position to make the crucial scientific judgement that the acceptance or rejection of a theory is adequately supported by the evidence, and so a process that is the epitome of rationality can come, when viewed from the outside, to seem irrational.

The student who begins the study of other religions as a practicing adherent of one is encouraged not to draw premature conclusions about truth and validity, but rather to postpone such reflections till he is in a position to think the question through with the thoroughness it deserves.

A supermarket of religions?

In the past most people knew little about religions other than their own. But over the last thirty years knowledge of the major religions has spread widely and is now almost a commonplace among more educated people. Sometimes this new situation is referred to as presenting us with a "supermarket of religions."

However, this image can be misleading as a guide to the nature of religions. In a supermarket we pick and choose: what we choose is a matter of our personal preference. But while some religions see themselves as what a wise and prudent person would choose (for example, Theravada Buddhism), other religions see themselves rather as representing an objective claim which lays on us an obligation to choose in a certain way (for example, Christianity or Islam). The Christian or Muslim does not consider religion to be just a matter of his own personal preference. Instead it is a matter of responding to a call, a summons, which comes to him from outside himself. From this perspective the choice of a religion is not only a question of its adequacy in regard to our needs or our experience of life, but involves questions of truth.

The seriousness and frivolity of studying religions

A word should be said about the seriousness, and by the same token the frivolity, of the study we are about to begin. A religion – any religion – is like a whole world. It encompasses everything. To understand a world, you must live in it, and to understand it properly, you must live in it a long time, perhaps a lifetime. It is not enough merely to dip our toes into it. Being devoutly religious is like being in love: it goes to the depths of our being. Everything may stay the same, yet everything is changed by it.

Studying a new religion each new week is a little like falling head over heels in love with a different person each week, or changing our native culture each week. Properly speaking, it cannot be done. A religion's hold on a person, if genuine, is too deep to be lightly adopted or discarded. And to study a religion is to give it some hold on one, or at least to open onself up to the possibility of its acquiring a hold.

Because making the acquaintance of a religion is such a serious undertaking and potentially profound experience, a course that promises to introduce you to some eight religions in one semester is essentially a frivolous affair. That does not mean it cannot be useful. Even frivolity has its uses. But we should at least be aware that the study we are embarking upon is not without danger: the danger of superficializing our deeper selves.

It is all the more important, then, that the study of a book like this be accompanied by the practical activity of personally visiting, witnessing, and if possible taking part in at least some of the services of one or more of these religions. This may not save us from superficiality, but it will, perhaps, confront us a little more vividly with the question.

Test questions

1   Arrange the major religions in their families.

2   What is meant by a "universal" religion?

3   What is meant by a religion of "self-liberation"?

4   What is meant by the phenomenological approach to the study of religions? What are the reasons for it, and what objections can be raised against it?

Part I

The Religions of Indian Origin

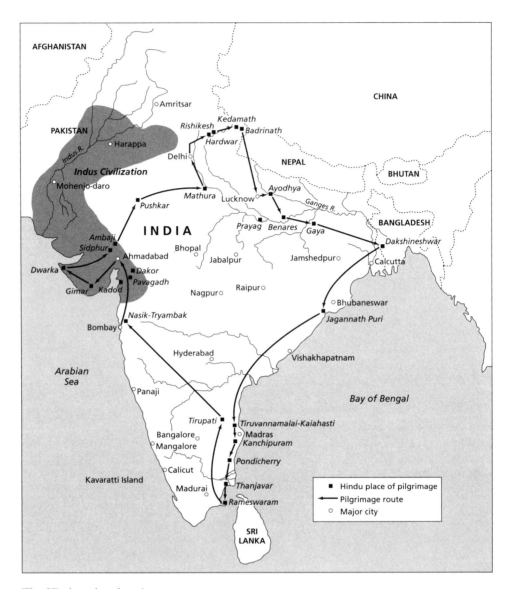

The Hindu cultural region

1

Hinduism

The Spirit of Hinduism

Through prolonged austerities and devotional practices the sage Narada won the grace of the god Vishnu. The god appeared before him in his hermitage and granted him the fulfillment of a wish. "Show me the magic power of your Maya," Narada prayed. The god replied, "I will. Come with me," but with an ambiguous smile on his lips.

From the shade of the hermit grove, Vishnu led Narada across a bare stretch of land which blazed like metal under the scorching sun. The two were soon very thirsty. At some distance, in the glaring light, they perceived the thatched roofs of a tiny village. Vishnu asked, "Will you go over there and fetch me some water?" "Certainly, O Lord," the saint replied, and he made off to the distant group of huts.

When Narada reached the hamlet, he knocked at the first door. A beautiful girl opened to him, and the holy man experienced something of which he had never up to that time dreamed: the enchantment of her eyes. They resembled those of his divine Lord and friend, Vishnu. He stood and gazed, simply forgetting what he had come for. The girl, gentle and candid, bade him welcome. Her voice was a golden noose around his neck. As though moving in a trance, he entered the hut.

The occupants of the house were full of respect for him, and received him honorably, but almost as if he were an old friend whom they had not seen for a long time. Narada was impressed by their cheerful and noble bearing, and felt entirely at home. Nobody asked him what he had come for. He just seemed to belong to the family. After a certain period, he asked the father for permission to marry the girl, which was no more than everyone in the house was expecting. He became a member of the family, sharing with them the age-old burdens and simple delights of a peasant household.

Twelve years passed; he had three children. When his father-in-law died, he became head of the household, inheriting the estate and managing it, tending the cattle and cultivating the fields. The twelfth year, the rainy season was extraordinarily violent: the streams swelled, torrents poured down from the hills, and the little village was inundated by a sudden flood. In the night the straw huts and the cattle were swept away, and everybody fled.

With one hand supporting his wife, with the other leading two of his children, and bearing the smallest on his shoulder, Narada set forth hastily. Forging ahead through the pitch darkness and lashed by the rain, he waded through the slippery mud, staggering through the swirling waters. The burden was more than he could manage. He stumbled, and the child slipped from his shoulder and disappeared in the roaring night. With a desperate cry, Narada let go the older children to catch at the smallest, but he was too late. Meanwhile the flood carried off the other two, and even before he could realize the disaster, ripped from his side his wife, swept his own feet from under him, and flung him headlong into the torrent. Unconscious, he was stranded eventually on a little cliff. When he returned to consciousness, he opened his eyes and saw only a vast sheet of muddy water. He could only weep.

"Child!" He heard a familiar voice, which nearly stopped his heart. "Where is the water you went to fetch for me? I have been waiting for more than half an hour."

Narada turned round. Instead of the water he beheld the brilliant desert in the midday sun, and the god standing at his shoulder. "Do you comprehend now the secret of my Maya?"

(Heinrich Zimmer, *Myths and Symbols in Indian Art and Civilization*, ed. Joseph Campbell, New York, Harper & Row, 1962)

This story, told by the Bengali saint, Sri Ramakrishna, is based on earlier stories from the classical period of Hinduism.

Questions for discussion

1 What is Maya?

2 Why does Vishnu have an ambiguous smile on his lips? (See p. 25 below, "The Later Upanishads.")

The Hindu View of Life

What we call "Hinduism" is not a unified and single entity, but the sum total of the traditional religious beliefs and practices of the Indian people, a colorful, diverse, and complex set of traditions inherited from a long history, and sometimes only loosely related to one another. Each period of Indian history has left its mark and is embodied in its own distinctive writings. This diversity allows individuals a good deal of liberty in choosing a form of religious life suitable to their needs.

If there is one theme that runs through these different traditions, summing up perhaps what is most typical of Hinduism as a whole, it is a feeling of the inherent presence of the divine in every being. Everywhere he looks, the devout Hindu sees God. A feeling very much like this has been described by the great English poet, William Wordsworth:

> And I have felt
> A presence that disturbs me with the joy
> Of elevated thoughts; a sense sublime
> Of something far more deeply interfused,
> Whose dwelling is the light of setting suns,
> And the round ocean, and the living air,
> And the blue sky, and in the mind of man:
> A motion and a spirit, that impels
> All thinking things, all objects of all thought,
> And rolls through all things.
>
> (*Tintern Abbey*)

Since God is what is most real, the Hindu tends to see all the varied manifestations of the world as essentially one, as merely different aspects of the same fundamental reality. You and I are like waves on the ocean of being. The waves come and go, but the vast ocean of eternal being remains.

Pre-Vedic Religion

The earliest strands of Hinduism that we have knowledge of date back to about the year 2000 BC, to a mysterious civilization which developed in the northwest of India near the Indus river, in what is now Pakistan. Centered on the two cities of Harappa and Mohenjo-Daro (see Map on p. 14), this civilization was in some respects surprisingly advanced. The cities were laid out geometrically, had bathing and sewage systems better than anything India was to see again until modern times, and even the working classes had better accommodations than many in India possess today.

Our knowledge of their religion comes mainly from figurines and some 2,000 engraved seals used for business purposes. Although no one has yet succeeded in deciphering the writing on the seals, we can learn a certain amount from the pictures engraved on them. In these images we can see already elements of the rich mythological life that has since characterized India.

As with many agricultural societies, the religion of the Harappan people focused on fertility, and it did so in ways which we still recognize as typically Indian. The Harappans worshipped a Mother Goddess, familiar to Indians today under the title of Devi. They had various sacred plants and animals, as Indians still have, notably the sacred bull, now known as Nandi, the Joyous. They had statues of nude men reminiscent of the somewhat stiff statues of the saints now honored by the Jains. But perhaps the most surprising figure is that of a god bearing a striking resemblance to the god Shiva, who now plays such a large role in the religious life of India. This deity, depicted on a number of seals, is shown with buffalo horns rising out of his head, a fierce look on his face, sitting nude in what can only be the posture of a yogi, with a prominent phallus, the symbol of sexual potency, and surrounded by wild animals, including two deer (as in the later representations of the Buddha preaching his first sermon in the Deer Park in Benares). This divinity has been called Proto-Shiva. The Shiva known to later Hinduism, though he plays many roles, is perhaps above all the god of fertility, but at the same time he is the great yogi, the supreme ascetic, and one of his titles is Pasupati, the Lord of Beasts.

Around 1700 BC the Harappan civilization came to a mysterious end. Its cities were abandoned and its people fled. We do not know why; perhaps because of armed invasion, possibly because of a very prolonged drought. Nor are we certain what happened to the people; perhaps they migrated towards South India, and became merged with what is now the Dravidian population there. During the period which immediately followed, the Vedic period, we see few traces of the Harappan religion, but much of it was evidently preserved, for after the Vedic period ended we find the Harappan divinities mentioned above still alive and well in the religion of the Indian people.

Vedic Religion

The Aryans Around 1500 BC a group of tribes migrated into India from the northwest. They were relatively light-skinned and had tamed the horse, which they used in chariots. They spoke an early version of the Sanskrit language, a member of the Indo-European family of languages which includes Greek, Latin, and English, and called themselves Aryans, a word meaning "noble." Other branches of the same race migrated southwards into Iran and westwards into Europe, eventually making up the bulk of the population there.

The Vedas The priests of these newcomers had developed a highly advanced poetry, in which they composed the hymns to be sung at their sacrifices. Over a thousand of these hymns were handed down very carefully for many centuries by word of mouth, and eventually they were written down and collected into a book, which is called the Rig Veda. The word "Veda," which is related to English words like "vision" and "video," means "knowledge." In addition to the Rig Veda, which is the oldest, there are three other Vedas: the Sama Veda, a compilation of some of the hymns of the Rig Veda, the Yajur Veda, containing sacrificial formulas, and the Atharva Veda, which contains mainly magical spells and incantations. Attached to each of these collections are treatises called Brahmanas, which explain the ritual of the sacrifices. These four Vedas, including some later additions to them called the Upanishads, comprise the sacred scriptures of Hinduism. An orthodox Hindu is one who recognizes the authority of the Vedas.

The Vedic gods   The religion of the Vedas can be summarized, for the most part, as a buoyant, robust, and self-confident nature-worship. The gods to whom the hymns of the Rig Veda are addressed are chiefly male and embody natural forces, especially forces associated with the sky. The general term for them is *devas*, a word which is related to the English words "divinity" and "deity," and which means the same thing. The highest god is Dyauspitr, the Sky-Father (*dyaus* = sky, *pitr* = father), known to the Romans as Jupiter; like many high gods, however, he receded into the background and was little worshipped in practice.

Although the Aryans worshipped many gods, they frequently prayed to a particular god as if only he existed. This practice, which has been called kathenotheism, can be confusing to the modern reader unless it is recognized.

The god who receives the most attention is Indra. Indra is associated with storm, thunder, and lightning, by which he destroys his enemies. As the chief god of power he is also the god of battles and warriors: it is he who leads his people to victory. Indra slew the evil dragon Vritra, who had held back the waters of the sky, thus bringing rain again to the crops and herds. Like many a warrior, Indra is also somewhat rambunctious, not above getting a little drunk and throwing his weight around.

Several gods are associated with the sun. Surya rides across the sky in a flaming chariot. Vishnu is also connected with the sun and covers the earth in three paces, though in the Vedas he has none of the outstanding importance that he comes to possess later in classical Hinduism. Savitri is another sun-god, distinguished by the fact that a special verse, called the Gayatri, of a hymn to him is considered the most sacred portion of the Rig Veda:

> Let us think on the lovely splendour
> of the god Savitri,
> that he may inspire our minds.

Agni (a word which means simply "fire" and is related to the English word "ignition") is the god of fire, and this leads him to play many roles. Since the sacrifices were offered with fire, Agni is the god of the priestly caste. As each home centers around the hearth, Agni is also the god of the household. He is present in the lightning and in the fire-stick.

Soma was originally a plant from which a narcotic drink was prepared during the sacrifices; it induced vivid hallucinations. From this Soma was elevated to the status of a god, to whom a special collection of hymns in the Rig Veda is dedicated. Since the growth of plants was thought to be associated with the moon, Soma was later identified with that heavenly orb.

Perhaps the most impressive of the Vedic gods is Varuna.* His name is possibly related to that of the Greek heaven-god Uranus. Varuna is the creator of

---

* The accent is on the first syllable since the "u" is short.

An image of Agni, the god of fire, on a temple at Khajuraho (Ann & Bury Peerless)

the cosmos. Ethically he is the highest of the Vedic gods, and the closest to the Judaeo-Christian conception of God. He is present everywhere and knows all the actions of men. Whereas the other Vedic gods are expressions of the physical forces of nature, essentially cheerful sorts, relatively easy to stay on good terms with by offering the occasional sacrifice, and are not always models of virtue, Varuna is holy and demands holiness from men. He detests sin, such as lying and injustice, and punishes it. When the evil die, he condemns them to the "House of Clay," where they live a depressing, shadowy life, in great contrast to the bright "World of the Fathers," to which the good go. But Varuna forgives those who repent. When the worshipper approaches Varuna, he puts on sack-cloth and ashes.

Varuna has created and maintains a cosmic order, called *Rta*, which represents perhaps the highest conception to be found in the Rig Veda. Rta includes the physical order of nature, such as the order of the seasons, but it also includes the moral order. Perhaps the best translation of it might be "the natural law," in both the physical and the moral senses of that term. In the figure of Varuna Indian thought came close to developing the kind of ethical monotheism achieved by the Hebrew people, which would have greatly transformed Indian religion. But instead, as we shall see, it took a different direction.

20

There are many other Vedic gods: Mitra, the assistant and messenger of Varuna, who is especially concerned with promises and contracts; Yama, the lord of the dead; Tvashtri, the god of the volcano, related to the Greek god Hephaistos; Aryaman, guardian of marriage and other contracts; Vayu, the wind-god, and others. A number of goddesses are also mentioned, though they play no role in the sacrifices. Several beautiful hymns are addressed to Usas, the goddess of the dawn.

Sacrifice   The Vedic gods were worshipped by sacrifice (*yajna*), which included animal sacrifice and was the central activity of Vedic religion. The chief purpose was to give pleasure to the gods, and thereby obtain blessings from them. Most of the gods were good-natured, and it was apparently not particularly difficult to stay in their good graces. There is little mention of sacrifice for sin or guilt, as with the ancient Israelites. The sacrifices were paid for by the wealthy and required numerous priests, who alone knew the rituals which had power with the gods.

Brahman   The Rig Veda mentions frequently a mysterious power called *Brahman*, which gives the sacrifice its efficacy. The reason why the ritual, performed in one place at one time, is capable of influencing what happens at another place and time, is that there is a power which pervades the cosmos, linking everything that is, and by tapping into it human beings can come into communication with the divine.

At its height the religion of the Aryans, like that of the ancient Greeks, Romans, and Germans, took a positive view of nature and of human existence. It is filled with vigor, courage, and optimism. In this it contrasts markedly with what was to come.

The last hymns to be included in the Vedas already sound a different note, of questioning and doubt. How do we know that things really are as they are portrayed in the ancient hymns? Where did the universe really come from? Is there perhaps only one God rather than many? Does even he have all the answers? Who knows?

The Vedic period lasted for about a thousand years, from about 1500 BC to about 600 BC. Since that time, although the Vedas remain the sacred scripture of Hinduism and the test of orthodoxy, and although their hymns are still recited in rituals, the Vedic gods have departed from the religious life of the Indian people. What is prized in the Vedas today is the religion of a set of later additions included in the Vedas, known as the Upanishads.

The Worldview of the Upanishads

The term Upanishad means literally "a session," sitting at the feet of a master who teaches secret doctrines. Altogether the Upanishads comprise about 200 documents, some long, some short, written from about the seventh century BC

21

and subsequently appended to the Vedas. About a dozen are considered classical. They recount the beliefs which developed among the Aryan peoples as they spread further east and south into Indian territory, interacting more and more with the indigenous peoples who preceded them. By the seventh century BC there emerged an important body of religious practitioners, the hermits or *munis*, who lived in the forest and practiced asceticism and meditation. These hermits, who in time came to play as important a role as the priests in the spiritual life of the people, developed elaborate techniques for inducing mystical ecstasy, and at the same time complex philosophical systems to interpret their mystical experiences. Initially their purpose was mainly to obtain magical powers, for it was believed that the mortification of the body created a store of physical power in the individual, rather like electricity, which could be put to practical uses such as disposing of one's enemies. With some hermits, however, this self-centered utilitarianism was overcome in a genuine spirituality, and the religious viewpoint which they achieved is widely considered, not only by Hindus, as one of the great spiritual accomplishments of the human race.

The central focus in this new vision is the concept of Brahman. In the hymns of the Rig Veda, as indicated above, this word means the magic power of the sacrifice, which can move the gods and the universe to grant what the worshipper desires. In the early Upanishads it undergoes a great extension. It comes to mean a supreme, infinite, impersonal Reality which is present throughout the universe, in all the objects of ordinary experience, and which constitutes the true identity of every being. Brahman is Pure Being, Pure Consciousness, Pure Bliss. Brahman is Absolute Reality.

The true Brahman, according to this view, is *nirguna* Brahman, Brahman "without attributes or predicates." Although for the sake of convenience we may speak of Brahman in terms of certain concepts, such as being, consciousness, or personhood, in truth Brahman transcends all our concepts and all our understanding. In attempting to refer to Brahman all language fails. Brahman is "not this, not that." We identify individual beings by their name and form, but Brahman is above all name and form. Every category of human thought is a restriction, and Brahman surpasses all restrictions. For religious purposes we may think of Brahman as if It were a person, for example, but in actuality the concept of personhood is inadequate and misleading as an expression of the reality of Brahman (this is reinforced by the grammatical fact that the word "Brahman" is neuter). The Brahman we can understand is not the true Brahman.

> The Self is not this, not that (neti, neti). It is incomprehensible, for it is not comprehended. It is indestructible, for it is never destroyed. It is unattached, for it does not attach itself. It is unfettered. It does not suffer. It is not injured.
>
> (Brihadaranyaka 3.9.26, trans. Hopkins)

What is the relation, then, between Brahman and the gods? Brahman is not a god, but is above all the gods. The gods no doubt exist, but they derive their being and their power from Brahman.

At the same time the sages of the Upanishads are concerned to discover the true identity of man. They ask, what is our real self? Is it our body? That is our external self, but we also have an inner self. To refer to this inner self they employ the ordinary Sanskrit reflexive pronoun, *atman*, "self."

The answer at which they eventually arrive is that the inner self, the Atman, is nothing less than Brahman. This is the outstanding thesis of the Upanishads. The true identity of each person and thing in the universe is the Eternal Power, the Absolute Reality, Brahman itself.

This leads the Upanishads to make a distinction between the True Self of beings and their merely apparent self. The apparent self is what can be observed by the senses, what we encounter in ordinary experience. Our apparent self is what we normally think of as ourselves: not only our body, with its sensations, but also our mind and will, our feelings and desires, our thoughts and intentions, everything that we usually and ordinarily experience of ourselves. This apparent self is subject to time and change, to suffering and sorrow, to decay and death. "What is other than the Self suffers" (Brihadaranyaka 3.5). Our True Self, by contrast, that is, our Atman, being nothing less than Brahman, is infinite and eternal; it does not grow old, it does not suffer pain or sorrow, it does not die.

> He is the unseen seer, the unheard hearer, the unthought thinker, the ununderstood understander. No other Seer than He is there, no other hearer than He, no other thinker than He, no other understander than He. He is the Self within you, the Inner Controller, the Immortal. What is other than He suffers.
>
> (Brihadaranyaka 3.7.23, trans. Zaehner)

My Self is not something distinct from your Self, and your Self is not something distinct from my Self. Although to all appearances you and I are separate beings, this separation is only an appearance. In our inner selves we are one. It is not just that we are similar, that our natures are alike, but that there is only the one being, the one existent reality. This reality takes on one appearance and becomes what we call "you," and it takes on another appearance and becomes what we call "me." In our innermost self you and I are one identical being. The same applies to all beings in the universe. The religion of the Upanishads is a form of monism. "Brahman alone is, nothing else is." The person who grasps this truth will see and love nothing but Brahman.

> It is not for love of a husband that a husband is dearly loved.
> Rather it is for the love of the Self that a husband is dearly loved.
> It is not for the love of a wife that a wife is dearly loved.
> Rather it is for the love of the Self that a wife is dearly loved.
> It is not for the love of sons that sons are dearly loved.
> Rather it is for love of the Self that sons are dearly loved.
> It is not for love of contingent beings that contingent beings are dearly loved.
> Rather it is for the love of the Self that contingent beings are dearly loved.
>
> (Brihadaranyaka 2.4.5, trans. Zaehner)

The effect of this view is to bring profound peace of mind. There can be no true grounds for conflict with others, since they are ultimately identical with myself, nor for dissatisfaction with life.

> Therefore one who knows this, becoming pacified, controlled, at peace, patient, full of faith, should see the Self in the Self alone. He looks upon everyone as it. Everyone comes to be his Self; he becomes the Self of everyone. He passes over all evil; evil does not pass over him. He subdues all evil; evil does not subdue him. He is free from evil, free from age, free from hunger, free from thirst, a Brahman, whoever possesses this knowledge.
>
> (Brihadaranyaka 4.4.28, trans. Hopkins)

The path to salvation from sorrow and suffering lies in obtaining sacred knowledge, that is, the knowledge of Brahman, the knowledge that our True Self is nothing less than Brahman.

The authors of the Upanishads came to accept a further doctrine, of uncertain origin, reincarnation. At death the body dies, but the soul, the *jiva* or *jivatman*, which is part of the apparent self, is born again into a new body. This belief may have been suggested by the cycle of growth in crops, with the emergence of agriculture: "Like corn a man ripens and falls to the ground; like corn he springs up again in his season" (Katha Upanishad).

The new body may again be that of a human being, but it may also be that of a higher form of existence, such as a god, or a lower one, such as that of an animal (according to some, even a plant). This reincarnation takes place as a verdict on the individual's conduct, to reward the good and punish the wicked. It takes place automatically, in virtue of the "Law of Karma," a law which is part of the fabric of the universe, a judgement without a judge.

Instead of a straightforward if mysterious existence in the "House of Clay" or the "World of the Fathers," as described in the Vedic hymns, the individual was now faced with the prospect of an endless cycle of births, deaths, and rebirths: the wheel of Samsara. As this doctrine took hold, the religious mood changed, from one of buoyancy and optimism to one of world-weariness and pessimism. It was not enough to achieve entrance into Heaven, for even the gods were subject to death and reincarnation. One Indra would be replaced by another Indra, and he by another, in an endless round. It was necessary to find some way to get off the wheel altogether.

The doctrine of the identity of the Atman with Brahman provided the solution to this problem. The wheel of Samsara belongs to the world of *maya*. When the veil of maya is pierced, and Brahman is revealed as the sole existent Reality, release will be obtained from the wheel of Samsara. This is moksha, or liberation; after it there will be no more rebirth. Later it was also called nirvana, "extinction," meaning "of craving and suffering."

How does it come about that we are separated from Brahman? Why is it that the world appears to us to be a genuine reality? The answer given by the Upanishads is that we are deceived because of our self-centeredness, our egocentricity. We are in a state of ignorance, an ignorance created by selfish desire. If we could once divest ourselves of ourselves, if we could rid ourselves of self-centered desire, if we could attain to a point of view which was completely impersonal and universal, and no longer wrapped up in the isolation of our ego, then the illusion would fall away, our merely apparent self would be shed, as a growing snake sheds its skin, and Brahman alone would reign. The "sacred knowledge" then, the knowledge of Brahman, is not merely a theoretical knowledge, but depends on our becoming detached from our individual selves.

The hermits who wrote the early Upanishads proclaimed that it is indeed possible to obtain that sacred knowledge, by practicing meditation and the discipline of asceticism. Through meditation one learns to focus one's attention on Brahman, on the Eternal and the One, and to leave behind the transitory world of the individual self.

Asceticism means deliberate self-mortification, self-deprivation. The ascetic abandons all worldly possessions and all desire for them. He practices depriving himself of bodily comfort, for example, sleeping on a hard floor. He practices fasting, eating and drinking only what is necessary to sustain life, without being concerned about the taste of food or drink. He does not marry, for the experience of sexual intercourse is a pleasure. He does not wish to have children, for children are a possession. "There is no difference between a desire for sons and a desire for riches; and there is no difference between a desire for riches and a desire for states of being: all of them are nothing more than desire." He deprives himself of the company of others and lives in silence. Thus he becomes detached from his individual self.

> From the unreal lead me to the real,
> From darkness lead me to light,
> From death lead me to immortality.
> (Brihadaranyaka)

The Later Upanishads

In the later Upanishads these views undergo some modification and further development. One far-reaching alteration takes place in the understanding of Brahman. In the early Upanishads, as we have seen, Brahman was thought of as nirguna, "without attributes," above "name and form," "not this, not that." In the later Upanishads, however, the conception of Brahman becomes more personal. Brahman is now no longer "It," but "He," "the Lord." This conception is sometimes called "*saguna* Brahman," Brahman with attributes or qualities, or Ishvara. This is a very significant change, for with this it becomes possible to pray to Brahman in human terms and to hope for an answer from him to one's prayers. In the Svetasvatara Upanishad, for example, Brahman is identified with the god Rudra or Shiva. Shiva is now no longer just one god among many, but is Brahman himself, creator and ruler of the universe. Salvation consists in knowledge of the Lord.

A further development takes place in the understanding of the universe of ordinary experience. The universe as we experience it is fundamentally deceptive, for it conceals its true nature from us. In truth the world is Brahman, the One, the Lord. Yet it presents itself to us as multiple and limited. This deceptive character of the world is expressed by saying that the world is maya, which means a conjuror's trick, a work of misleading magic. (The word "maya" may possibly be related etymologically to the word "magic.") Salvation consists in piercing through the veil of maya, and reaching the truth and reality of the Godhead concealed within it. When salvation is achieved, the illusory world of maya will fall away, and Brahman or Divinity alone will be seen to exist.

A third development took place in the later Upanishads in regard to the method of attaining salvation. In the early Upanishads, as we have seen, this is attained through sacred knowledge, the living awareness of one's identity with Brahman. In the later Upanishads this is developed by means of the concept of *yoga*. This word, which is etymologically related to the English word "yoke," means "a setting to work" or "the pursuit of a goal," and can perhaps be translated as a "path" or "discipline." Yoga in general means the pathway which leads to spiritual liberation, the breakup and dissolution of the individual ego. The yoga described in the later Upanishads consists in certain exercises designed to establish control over the body and mind. They begin with control of the breath and the bodily posture, which is meant to lead to quietness and control of the senses, and by this means one could eventually hope to gain control of the mind. By practicing ever greater discipline of the mind it would be possible to focus it to such a pitch of concentration that the distinction between the mind and its object of thought would be eliminated, and there would remain only pure unitary consciousness, which would be Brahman or the Lord himself.

Classical Hinduism

The period of the Upanishads was followed by the rise and predominance of Buddhism, which sprang from similar sources and lasted for several hundred years. Eventually, however, the religious synthesis which may properly be called Hinduism emerged and grew in strength till it won over the allegiance of the Indian people. Buddhism gradually disappeared as a separate religion, many of its ideas being assimilated into Hinduism.

The religion of the Vedas and Upanishads was centered in the Aryan north of India. Classical Hinduism, however, developed largely out of influences from the Dravidian south. The trend towards a personal conception of the Godhead, begun in the later Upanishads, intensified dramatically. Religion became fervently, even ecstatically, devotional.

Classical Hinduism is enshrined especially in two sets of books, the Epics and the Puranas. The Epics in question are two long poems, the *Mahabharata*, which describes a feud between two ancient clans, and the *Ramayana*, which

Shiva Nataraja, Lord of the Dance: his dance preserves but also destroys the world
(Circa Photo Library)

narrates the story of Rama, an incarnation of Vishnu. The Puranas are extensive
collections of stories about the gods and their incarnations.

Vishnu and Shiva   The conception of the one, ultimate Godhead as a person to
be worshipped by the intense devotion of the heart was embodied especially in
two divine figures: Vishnu and Shiva. (A third, Brahma – not to be confused
with Brahman – was originally also important, but is no longer much worshipped.)

Vishnu had received a passing mention in the Vedas, but no more. Now he
became the most popular of the gods. To his devotee (termed a Vaishnavite),
Vishnu is the ultimate reality, the source of the universe. He sleeps in the
primeval ocean, on a thousand-headed snake. While he sleeps a lotus grows out
of his navel, and in the lotus is born the god Brahma, who creates the world.
When the world has been created Vishnu awakes and takes his place as its ruler

A cave shrine to Shiva (Circa Photo Library)

on high. He is usually shown in images as a dark-blue man wearing a crown and possessing four arms, each of which holds an object specially associated with him: a conch shell, a discus, a mace, and a lotus. Vishnu is deeply concerned for the welfare of mankind.

In order to help men Vishnu is believed to have become incarnate in various forms, several of which are animals, and about which many stories are told. His two chief incarnations (*avataras*), however, are as men: Rama and Krishna. Rama, often shown carrying a bow and arrow, is the embodiment of ideal manhood: a brave leader, a just king, and a gentle and faithful husband to his wife Sita, who is herself the ideal of womanhood. The story of Rama and Sita is told especially in the ancient epic poem, the *Ramayana*.

The principal incarnation of Vishnu is Krishna ("black" or "dark"). In the stories told about him Krishna plays a great variety of roles: in some he is a child, playing childish pranks; in others he is a warrior, in yet others he is a youth who seduces the wives and daughters of his cowherds, his favorite being the beautiful Radha. These latter stories are clearly erotic, but are interpreted by his devotees in the sense of a religious allegory of the love between God and the soul.

An image of Durga carried during a festival in her honor (Ann & Bury Peerless)

Shiva bears a marked resemblance to the paradoxical deity of fertility and asceticism we have already encountered in pre-Vedic religion (see above, pp. 17–18). Unlike Vishnu, Shiva has a ruthless, intolerant, and ferocious aspect. He is "the Destroyer." This is now usually explained by his devotees as meaning that he destroys moral evil, but originally perhaps he signified the awesome destructive power of nature. He wears a necklace of skulls, inhabits burning-grounds and battlefields, and is accompanied by ghosts and demons. He is the god of death and of time, which destroy all things.

By the same token he is the great ascetic and yogi, that is, he is the symbol of the great creative power of nature, and the patron of ascetics and yogis. He sits on a tiger's skin, sunk in meditation, high on the Himalayan mountains, and by his meditation he preserves the world. He is depicted with a third eye in his forehead, as a sign of his wisdom. He is the lord of snakes, which cover his limbs. His body is covered with ashes, in token of detachment. He is the Lord of the Dance (*Nataraja*), and his eternal dance animates the universe – or destroys it.

Lakshmi, the goddess of wealth (Circa Photo Library)

Shiva is usually depicted with four arms, with each hand holding an emblem: a trident, an antelope, a noose for binding his enemies, and a drum. He wears a tiger's skin around his loins. The special symbol of Shiva, often taking the place of his image in temples, is the lingam, a stylized phallic-shaped object, usually of stone. A devotee of Shiva is termed a "Shaivite."

The goddess: shakti As we have seen, the Mother Goddess was worshipped in India from prehistoric times. With the emergence of the Hindu gods, each god was assigned a goddess as wife. This divine spouse is referred to as the god's *shakti*, a term which means "power," the theory being that the god was transcendent and inactive, above human concerns, but his divine wife (who was ultimately identical with him) projected his power into the world and acted on his behalf. Although many of these goddesses have little actual significance, three are important in the devotional life of Hinduism.

The most prominent is the wife of Shiva, who has many characters and is known by many names. As Parvati she is young, beautiful, and kind, the goddess of beauty; as Durga or Kali she is a hag, with fangs and a blood-red tongue protruding from her mouth. The special symbol of Shiva's shakti is the *yoni*, a stylized form of the female sexual organ, usually found together with the *lingam* of Shiva. (Hindus often have difficulty in accepting the suggestion of scholars that the lingam and yoni represent sexual organs.)

Ganesha (Ann & Bury Peerless)

Lakshmi ("Fortune") or Sri, the wife of Vishnu, is the goddess of wealth and prosperity. She is usually shown sitting on a lotus and is a popular divinity.

Sarasvati is the wife of Brahma and the patroness of art, music, speech, and literature. She rides on a peacock and carries a musical instrument, the vina, and a book. She is said to have invented the Sanskrit language and is worshipped especially by students, writers, and musicians.

A god especially beloved by all Hindus is Ganesha, or Ganapati, the second son of Shiva and Parvati. A cheerful and benevolent deity, he has the head of an elephant, with one tusk broken, and a prominent belly, and was probably originally a non-Aryan elephant god. He is the "Lord of Obstacles" and is worshipped at the beginning of all enterprises, such as journeys or business ventures, to overcome difficulties.

Classical Hinduism is a polytheistic religion. Hindus do not necessarily assume, however, that polytheism is incompatible with monotheism. Some versions of Hinduism (which we do not have the space to treat here) are explicitly monotheistic. Even apart from them, it is widely accepted that the individual divinities are expressions or representations of a single ultimate Godhead. (Something similar was true of the ancient Greeks and Romans.) The Gita explains that for many people it is easier to focus the mind and heart on the image of a particular deity who is thought of as possessing human-like features than on the impassive and abstract conception of Brahman.

Puja Whereas the Vedic gods were venerated by sacrifice (yajna), the Hindu gods are venerated by worship (*puja*). This is directed to an image of the god, which is sanctified by a special ritual, so that the god is considered to inhabit it as his home. The purpose of puja is not so much to ask for favors as to offer the deity homage and entertainment. For the purposes of the ritual the image is treated as if it were the god himself. He is offered flowers, and water to wash his feet. In the morning he is awakened by music and the ringing of bells. He is washed, dried, and dressed. He is fed with rice and fruit. In the temple he is fanned by the attendants and may even be entertained by dancing girls. The god presents himself to his devotees for ritual viewing, called *darshana*, sometimes being carried through the streets for that purpose, and the devotee brings the god food, termed *prasada*.

The four classes (Varnas)

Religious duties are not the same for everyone. From the time of the Aryan migrations Indian society has been divided into four great classes according to the main occupations of the people: Brahmins, the priestly class; Kshatriyas, the warriors; Vaishyas, the peasants, merchants, and craftsmen; and Shudras, the laborers. Each class has its own duties. The Brahmin must always maintain ritual purity and therefore must not eat meat or drink alcohol, for example, since these are ritually unclean, while the Shudra may do both. The Brahmin may study the scriptures while the Shudra may not, being typically in a state of ritual impurity. The *Bhagavad-Gita* teaches that it is better to carry out the duties of one's own class badly rather than those of another class well.

These duties are described in detail in various writings of classical Hinduism, especially the Laws of Manu. The chief duty of the Brahmin is to study and teach, to sacrifice, and to give and receive gifts. The duty of the Kshatriya is to protect the people. The duty of the Vaishya is to breed cattle and till the earth, to pursue trade and to lend money. The duty of the Shudra is to serve the other three. A provision of the Laws of Manu states that the class system exists only for the good of the people, and that if it should lose the support of the people, it may be abolished.

At about the age of eight a Brahmin boy undergoes the ancient ceremony of initiation (*upanayana*), when, clothed as an ascetic and carrying a staff in his hand, he is invested with a sacred cord, hung over his left shoulder and under his right arm, which he must wear constantly for the rest of his life, on pain of severe penance. He is now formally an Aryan, and is described as "twice-born" (*dvija*). Theoretically this applies to all three of the upper classes, but in practice the Kshatriyas and Vaishyas largely neglect it. The Shudra is excluded from this rite and does not become a full Aryan.

Beneath the four classes are the Outcastes or Untouchables. These are groups who are judged, usually because of their typical patterns of behavior, to be altogether outside the pale of so-called proper Hindu society: for example, because they hunt and eat meat.

Children, ascetics, and widows fall outside the class system.

The castes (Jatis)

As their names imply, the four Varnas are function or activity groupings, and do not necessarily rule out intermarriage; in earlier times intermarriage was not uncommon. The Varnas are subdivided, however, into several thousand smaller divisions properly called castes or *Jatis*, which typically rule out intermarriage. The castes originated in different ways – some were based on occupation, others on geographic region, while yet others derived from the incorporation of aboriginal tribes or other ethnic or religious groups into Hinduism – and as a result there is a great deal of diversity between them. Membership is by birth ("jati" means birth). The castes are related hierarchically to one another: each is either superior or inferior to its neighbors, and they are often further divided into subcastes.

Each caste or subcaste lays down detailed rules for its own members regarding food, marriage, and occupation. Often members of a higher caste may not accept food cooked by members of a lower caste, for example. In economic life, each caste is recognized as possessing a monopoly of its own occupation, other castes not being allowed to compete against it.

This caste and class system forms an integral part of traditional Hinduism, which considers it sacred, a part of the cosmic order. The person who lives a good life will be reborn into a higher caste, while one who has lived an evil life will return in a lower caste. Although officially the caste system was banned by the constitution when India attained independence in 1947, it still remains an important factor in the national life. It has been argued that in its time it was essentially a humane system, simply a realistic recognition of the differences that existed between the members of the society, and that it has kept an immensely diverse people, with the potential for serious conflict, stable and at peace over several thousand years.

The Four Ends of Man

Human pursuits can be guided by four different kinds of motive or purpose. We can do something because it is right, it is our duty, it is what we ought to do. This is the First End of Man: Duty, *Dharma*. Or we can do it for the sake of securing some material gain, such as money or power. This is the Second End of Man: *Artha*. Or we can do it in order to obtain pleasure, which is the Third End of Man: *Kama*. Finally, we can do it in order to achieve spiritual liberation, release from the everlasting cycle of birth, death, and rebirth. This is the Fourth End of Man: *Moksha*.

Duty is the first because it is the most fundamental, the most indispensable. We must fulfill our obligations. To be motivated by a sense of duty means not only to fulfill our general moral obligations towards others, but also to observe the duties especially associated with one's class, as a Brahmin, Kshatriya, Vaishya, or Shudra, with one's caste and subcaste, and with one's stage in life.

In the Hindu view there is nothing wrong with the Second End, the search for material gain. It is a necessary part of life. But it must be guided and regulated by the requirements of duty. If there should be a conflict between duty on the one hand and the desire for power or possessions on the other, duty must always win out.

Similarly there is nothing objectionable about the Third End, the pursuit of pleasure. Pleasures are of very different kinds: some are refined and noble, such as the pleasure aroused by beautiful music, art, or literature. But again, the quest for pleasure must be controlled by the demands of duty. If conflict should arise between the requirements of duty and the quest for pleasure, we must follow the path that duty dictates.

The fourth goal, liberation, Moksha, is the highest. It is the goal towards which the wise man ultimately directs all his actions.

The four stages of life (Ashramas)

Just as religious duties are different for each class, so also are they different for each stage of life. Classical Hinduism recognized four stages, each with its own responsibilities.

On being invested with the sacred cord, the Brahmin boy enters the first stage, that of the *Brahmacarin*, the celibate student, when his chief duty is to study the Vedas, living in the house of his teacher.

When his education is finished he returns home, marries, and becomes a *Grihastha*, a householder. His principal duty during this time is to care for the welfare of his family.

When his hair turns white and he sees his sons' sons, according to the Sacred Law he should retire into the forest and live the life of a hermit, a *Vanaprastha*, either leaving his children to the care of his wife or taking his wife with him, and spending his days in meditation and devotion.

Beyond this there is a further and final stage, that of the *Sannyasin*. This is a homeless wanderer, who cuts off all ties to his family, even changing his name, and gives up all possessions except a staff, a begging bowl, and a few pieces of clothing. The Sannyasin is beyond all the religious duties laid down in the Sacred Law. Even today it is not unusual for elderly men to follow this path.

The Sannyasin is not the only figure in Hindu society to practice asceticism. In addition, there is a recognized class of wandering ascetics, called Sadhus or holy men, who may be of any age or class.

The Song of God: the Bhagavad-Gita

This poem, a portion of the *Mahabharata* mentioned above, is the great document of classical Hinduism. In the eyes of many it is India's supreme contribution to the literature of the spirit. Whereas the Upanishads had confined the pathway of spiritual liberation to those few who gave up life and action in the world, who lived the arduous life of the ascetic, practicing full-time the physical and mental exercises designed to give control over the mind and senses, the Gita opens it up to all, to men and women, to rich and poor, to high caste and low caste. The message of the Gita is that it is not necessary to give up the life of action in the world: there is another road. This new road is the path of selfless action (*karma*), achieved through devotion (*bhakti*) to the Divine Person.

Selfless action means doing what needs to be done, but doing it without attachment to its success or failure. "Do the work for the sake of the work, not for the sake of the fruits of the work." On every person duties are incumbent by reason of the place he occupies in society. (See pp. 32–3 above on the four classes.) He must carry these duties out, not abandon them; but he must perform them in a spirit of personal detachment, not allowing himself to be carried away by good fortune or cast down by adversity.

> A man should not hate any living creature. Let him be friendly and compassionate to all. He must free himself from the delusion of "I" and "mine." He must accept pleasure and pain with equal tranquillity. He must be forgiving, ever-contented, self-controlled . . .
>
> He neither molests his fellow men, nor allows himself to become disturbed by the world. He is no longer swayed by joy and envy, anxiety and fear . . .
>
> He does not desire or rejoice in what is pleasant. He does not dread what is unpleasant, or grieve over it. He remains unmoved by good or evil fortune.
>
> His attitude is the same toward friend and foe. He is indifferent to honor and insult, heat and cold, pleasure and pain.
>
> A man's own natural duty, even if it seems imperfectly done, is better than work not naturally his own, even if this is well performed.

How is this spiritual self-possession to be attained? By attachment to the Supreme Person. "Perform every action with your heart fixed on the Supreme Lord." The Supreme Person in the form of the god Vishnu is depicted as saying: "Mentally resign all your action to me. Regard me as your dearest loved one. Know me to be your only refuge. Be united always in heart and consciousness with me. United with me, you shall overcome all difficulties by my grace."

Although the doctrine of the *Bhagavad-Gita* is framed in terms of devotion to the god Vishnu, it has been understood by Hindus as applicable to all the gods, understood as images or manifestations of the One Supreme Reality, Brahman.

Hindu festivals

The Hindu calendar has many festivals, varying from place to place, and only a few of the chief ones can be mentioned here.

Makar Sakranti, celebrated usually around the middle of January, marks the entrance of the sun into the sign of Capricorn or Makar, considered astrologically auspicious.

Vasant Panchami, held not long after Makar Sakranti, is a festival in honor of spring, when students lay books and writing materials at the feet of the goddess of learning, Sarasvati.

Shivarat, the night of Shiva, is celebrated around the middle or end of February, when Shiva is worshipped with flowers during the whole night.

Holi is a carnival, held in February or March, and a very popular occasion. Bonfires are lit the preceding night, to celebrate the destruction of evil, and on the day of the festival crowds fill the streets, throwing red or yellow powder or colored water over passers-by.

Janam Ashtami, in July or August, celebrates the birth of Krishna.

Ganesh Chaturthi is a festival in honour of Ganesha, held around the end of August.

Dassehra is a ten-day festival celebrated in September or October, symbolizing the triumph of good over evil, and dedicated largely to the goddess Durga.

Divali is the Festival of Lights, celebrated in October or November. Oil lamps made of clay (or often electric lights now) are placed in the windows of houses or set afloat on rivers or the sea to welcome Lakshmi, the goddess of wealth and prosperity.

Kumbha Maha Mela is a great religious gathering held once every twelve years at a number of sacred places.

Hindu Ethics

Perhaps the feature of traditional Hindu ethics which the Western observer is most likely to find striking is its acceptance of, and even emphasis on, human inequality rather than equality. Ethics tends traditionally to be understood in Hinduism to a large extent as the fulfillment of class and caste duties, which differ from person to person and from one stage of life to another, as explained above. The classes and castes are not merely different from one another but deeply unequal in their moral dignity; some being morally superior to others and others morally inferior. For the effect of the doctrine of reincarnation is to assert not merely that justice will be done in a future life, but that the present life, with all its inequalities as reflected in one's class and caste, represents a just judgement on one's previous life.

At the same time, however, the Hindu tradition also recognizes that there are duties common to all human beings (*samanya* or *sadharana dharma*). The ideal of *ahimsa*, non-injury to men and animals, though primarily a Buddhist and Jain doctrine, has played a significant role in Hindu thinking ever since the time of the emperor Ashoka (*c.*270 BC). This ideal inculcates respect for all forms of conscious life, since reincarnation is possible under any such life-form. It finds special expression in the universal veneration of the cow, which must everywhere be allowed free passage. Ahimsa is widely taken to imply vegetarianism.

Interestingly, however, ahimsa has never been understood to exclude war. Unlike the West, India never developed a doctrine of the just war or the concept of an unjust war. Indian thinkers, like those in most non-Western societies, have almost universally accepted war as simply something that rulers and governments do. The dharma or class duty of the Kshatriya class is to engage in warfare. On the other hand, given that wars take place, rules were developed for their just conduct.

The renowned scholar of things Indian, A. L. Basham, has written that in ancient India "inequality of birth was given religious sanction, and the lot of the humble was generally hard. Yet our overall impression is that in no other part of the ancient world were the relations of man and man, and of man and the state, so fair and humane. In no other early civilization were slaves so few in number, and in no other ancient lawbook are their rights so well protected as in the *Arthasastra* . . . To us the most striking feature of ancient Indian civilization is its humanity . . . India was a cheerful land, whose people, each finding a niche in a complex and slowly evolving social system, reached a higher level of kindliness and gentleness in their mutual relationships than any other nation of antiquity" (*The Wonder that was India*, pp. 8–9).

Modern Developments

The story of the Hindu religion over the last hundred years has been dominated above all by the figure of Mohandas Gandhi (1869–1948). Gandhi elevated the traditional moral doctrine of *ahimsa*, non-violence, into a political weapon of great power by organizing peaceful demonstrations of civil disobedience against the laws and policies of the British government of India in a quest, ultimately successful, to achieve political independence for India. It should be conceded that this outcome was possible only because he was dealing with a government that allowed a large role to conscience. The subsequent division of the sub-continent into the two countries of India, intended to be a secular state, and Pakistan, a state specifically for Muslims, however, led to enormous loss of life and continuing belligerency between them.

In a reflection of modern Western values, Gandhi also championed the cause of the Untouchables, whom he called *harijans*, or children of God, with the consequence that although discrimination based on class and caste has been an all-pervasive feature of Hindu life for millenniums, it was declared illegal in 1950 by the new Indian Constitution. In practice, however, caste remains a powerful force in Hindu life. In a sense it has even been given a new lease of life by the fact that it is now accepted in law as a basis of political and legal identity or entitlement. It remains a factor in questions of marriage and occupation, though without the unquestioning acceptance it once enjoyed. For over 50 years now India has been a functioning democracy, and this has strengthened the sense of human equality among Hindus.

On the other hand Gandhi also turned the moral weight of religion against modern capitalism and the industrial economy. The Hindu religion has not traditionally been opposed to commerce. On the contrary, the doctrine of the Four Ends of Man explicitly recognizes the acquisition of material wealth as legitimate, and Indian communities outside of India have typically prospered. But Gandhi preached a doctrine of a return to the simple life, and of individual and national self-sufficiency, which had the effect of greatly retarding economic development in India. Recent years, however, have seen a reaction against this and a return to a more positive view of capitalism.

Also in recent years there has been a marked resurgence of militant Hindu nationalism (*Hindutva*). This is a movement to reassert the rights of Hindus and the values of the Hindu tradition against what it views as encroachments from Islam and the West. In particular, militant Hindu nationalism is a protest against the special privileges given to Muslims in Indian law and society. For example, the Indian Constitution gives Muslim but not Hindu men the right of non-judicial divorce (see below, pp. 278–9). It has its own political party, the Bharatiya Janata (Indian People's) party, which has become a formidable force on the Indian political scene, and at the time of writing controls the federal government. Some Hindu nationalists have perpetrated acts of great violence, especially against Muslims, but also against Christians, Sikhs, and other minorities.

Summary of Hinduism

1 Pre-Vedic religion worshipped a Proto-Shiva and the Mother Goddess.

2 Vedic religion was a form of nature worship, in which the powers of nature, especially of the sky, were personified in divinities, worshipped by animal sacrifices.

3 The Upanishads teach that there is a supreme or absolute Reality, Brahman, which constitutes the true identity, the Atman, of every being. Spiritual liberation or moksha, bringing release from the endless cycles of birth, death, and rebirth, Samsara, is attained through the realization of this identity.

4 In Classical Hinduism the concept of Brahman becomes more personal. He is worshipped in the forms of the gods, especially Vishnu and Shiva, and their Shaktis. Moksha may be attained by following the path of selfless action through devotion.

Questions for discussion

1 What considerations might lead you to believe that the worldview of the Upanishads is valid?

2 What considerations might lead you to reject it as mistaken?

3 To what extent would it be possible to abandon the class and caste system, yet retain the essential beliefs and values of Hinduism?

4 Would you expect the doctrines of the Upanishads or of classical Hinduism to have any consequences for the political life of India? How could they affect its economic life?

Test questions

1 Identify: Indra, Agni, Varuna, Rta.

2 Explain what is meant by the following terms: Brahman, Atman, maya, moksha, Samsara, yoga.

3 Outline the worldview of the Upanishads.

4 Identify: Vishnu, Shiva, Sarasvati, Kali.

5 What is the principal message of the *Bhagavad-Gita*?

6 What are the Four Ends of Man?

7 What are the four stages of life?

8 What are the four Varnas?

Additional reading

Dasgupta, S. N., *Hindu Mysticism*, New York, Frederick Ungar, 1959 (1st pub. 1927). A classic study of the varieties of Hindu mysticism.

Deussen, Paul, *The Philosophy of the Upanishads*, New York, Dover Publications, 1966 (1st pub. 1906). Despite its age, a very thorough and still useful examination of the philosophical beliefs of the Upanishads.

Hopkins, Thomas J., *The Hindu Religious Tradition*, Encino, CA, Dickenson, 1971. An excellent historical introduction.

Klostermaier, Klaus K., *A Survey of Hinduism*, Albany, NY, SUNY, 1989. Undertakes to explain Hinduism as a coherent and self-consistent body of traditions; an especially good glossary and bibliography.

Radhakrishnan, Sarvepalli, *The Hindu View of Life*, London, Allen & Unwin, 1974 (1st pub. 1927). An explanation and defense of Hinduism as seen from the "inside" by a noted Hindu author.

Sharma, Arvind, *Classical Hindu Thought: An Introduction*, New Delhi, Oxford University Press, 2000.

Zaehner, R. C., *Hinduism*, New York, Oxford University Press, 1966. A book likely to be appreciated by students who already possess some background knowledge.

Zimmer, Heinrich, *Philosophies of India*, ed. Joseph Campbell, Princeton, Princeton University Press, 1974 (1st pub. 1951). A very readable classic.

Hinduism: Texts

The Katha Upanishad

This Upanishad is a dialogue between Nachiketa and Yama, the King of Death. The question it discusses is whether there is a life after death, the question presented as Nachiketa's third request.

> When a man dies, there is this doubt: Some say he is (that is, he continues to exist after death); others say, he is not. Taught by you, I would know the truth.

Before Nachiketa can obtain an answer to this question, however, he must first go through a spiritual preparation. The question of life after death, the King of Death implies, like other religious topics, cannot be approached in a purely objective fashion, as if it were simply a matter of grasping a factual truth. We must be spiritually ready to receive the answer, otherwise it will be lost on us. Yama therefore first puts Nachiketa to the test, by refusing to answer his question.

> Nay, even the gods were once puzzled by this mystery. Subtle indeed is the truth regarding it, not easy to understand. Choose some other boon, O Nachiketa.

When Nachiketa is not put off, but insists on an answer, Yama tries to distract him with other tempting offers. He will give him wealth, or political power, or the delights of sexual intercourse. But Nachiketa stands firm.

These things endure only till the morrow...How shall he desire wealth,
O Death, who once has seen your face?...Knowing well the vanity of the
flesh, how shall I wish for long life?...No other boon will I ask.

Nachiketa shows that he has already acquired a certain degree of detachment
from himself, so he passes the test, and Yama, satisfied, begins to teach him.

His teaching, in a nutshell, is that the question about a life after death is
misguided, for it rests on a twofold mistaken presupposition, namely that
we truly exist as distinct individuals in what we are pleased to call this life,
and that the prolongation of this existence will be a good thing. A being
can continue to exist only if it already existed previously. In truth, however,
there are two aspects to us: we possess two selves. One of them is our True
Self and the other is a mere illusion. Our True Self, our Atman, is nothing
less than the eternal and infinite Brahman, always in existence and incapable of dying. Our merely apparent self is the individual self or identity
that we attribute to ourself when we normally think of "ourself," the being
who dwells in this body and thinks with this mind. This apparent self is
the source of all our misery and our aim must be to get rid of it, to dispel
the illusion it represents.

We achieve this by attaining the knowledge of Brahman, through meditation. We must purify our mind of all self-centered desire, attaining a
standpoint where we are utterly unconcerned about our personal fate. And
since the question about life after death is an expression of self-centered
desire, it follows, presumably, that we must give up asking for it!

If we do not attain this purification of the mind and knowledge of
Brahman, we will remain mired in illusion. That illusion, of our individual
existence, will then be continued after death into reincarnation, either as a
human being or as some other form of life.

Of those ignorant of the Self, some enter into beings possessed of wombs,
others enter into plants – according to their deeds and the growth of their
intelligence. [See p. 49 below.]
If a man fail to attain Brahman before he casts off his body, he must again
put on a body in the world of created things. [See p. 50 below.]

In other words, life after death is not, as we usually assume, something
desirable, but merely a prolongation of ignorance and misery.

Brahman is "neither cause nor effect" of the world, for the world does
not truly exist. As the Hindu philosopher Shankara was to explain centuries
later, what we call "the world" arises because we in our minds "super-
impose" on the only truly existent reality, Brahman, an appearance or
illusion of individuality and multiplicity. The Upanishadic view of the world
is therefore fundamentally different from that of the religions of Semitic
origin, for example, which see the world as created by God, and therefore
real, though its reality is subordinate.

Om . . .
May Brahman protect us,
May he guide us,
May he give us strength and right understanding.
May love and harmony be with us all.
OM . . . Peace – peace – peace.

On a certain occasion Vajasrabasa, hoping for divine favor, performed a rite which required that he should give away all his possessions. He was careful, however, to sacrifice only his cattle, and of these only such as were useless – the old, the barren, the blind, and the lame. Observing this niggardliness, Nachiketa, his young son, whose heart had received the truth taught in the scriptures, thought to himself: "Surely a worshipper who dares bring such worthless gifts is doomed to utter darkness!" Thus reflecting, he came to his father, and cried:

"Father, I too belong to you: to whom do you give me?"

His father did not answer; but when Nachiketa asked the question again and yet again, he replied impatiently: "I give you to Death!"

Then Nachiketa thought to himself: "Of my father's many sons and disciples I am indeed the best, or at least of the middle rank, not the worst; but of what good am I to the King of Death?" Yet, being determined to keep his father's word, he said:

"Father, do not repent your vow! Consider how it has been with those that have gone before, and how it will be with those that now live. Like corn, a man ripens and falls to the ground; like corn, he springs up again in his season."

Having thus spoken, the boy journeyed to the house of Death.

But the god was not at home, and for three nights Nachiketa waited. When at length the King of Death returned, he was met by his servants, who said to him:

"A Brahmin, like to a flame of fire, entered your house as guest, and you were not there. Therefore must a peace offering be made to him. With all accustomed rites, O King, must you receive your guest, for if a householder show not due hospitality to a Brahmin, he will lose what he most desires – the merits of his good deeds, his righteousness, his sons, and his cattle."

Then the King of Death approached Nachiketa and welcomed him with courteous words.

"O Brahmin," he said, "I salute you. You are indeed a guest worthy of all reverence. Let, I pray you, no harm befall me! Three nights have you passed in my house and have not received my hospitality; ask of me, therefore, three boons – one for each night."

"O Death," replied Nachiketa, "so let it be. And as the first of these boons I ask that my father be not anxious about me, that his anger be appeased, and that when you send me back to him, he recognize me and welcome me."

"By my will," declared Death, "your father shall recognize you and love you as heretofore; and seeing you again alive, he shall be tranquil of mind, and he shall sleep in peace."

Then said Nachiketa: "In heaven there is no fear at all. You, O Death, are not there, nor in that place does the thought of growing old make one tremble. There, free from hunger and from thirst, and far from the reach of sorrow all rejoice and are glad. You know, O King, the fire sacrifice that leads to heaven. Teach me that sacrifice, for I am full of faith. This is my second wish."

Whereupon, consenting, Death taught the boy the fire sacrifice, and all the rites and ceremonies attending it. Nachiketa repeated all that he had learned, and Death, well pleased with him, said:

"I grant you an extra boon. Henceforth shall this sacrifice be called the Nachiketa Sacrifice, after your name. Choose now your third boon."

And then Nachiketa considered within himself, and said:

"When a man dies, there is this doubt: Some say, he is; others say, he is not. Taught by you, I would know the truth. This is my third wish."

"Nay," replied Death, "even the gods were once puzzled by this mystery. Subtle indeed is the truth regarding it, not easy to understand. Choose some other boon, O Nachiketa."

But Nachiketa would not be denied.

"You say, O Death, that even the gods were once puzzled by this mystery, and that it is not easy to understand. Surely there is no teacher better able to explain it than you – and there is no other boon equal to this."

To which, trying Nachiketa again, the god replied:

"Ask for sons and grandsons who shall live a hundred years. Ask for cattle, elephants, horses, gold. Choose for yourself a mighty kingdom. Or if you can imagine aught better, ask for that – not for sweet pleasures only but for the power, beyond all thought, to taste their sweetness. Truly, the supreme enjoyer will I make you of every good thing. Celestial maidens, beautiful to behold, such indeed as were not meant for mortals – even these, together with their bright chariots and their musical instruments, will I give unto you, to serve you. But for the secret of death, O Nachiketa, do not ask!"

But Nachiketa stood fast, and said: "These things endure only till the morrow, O Destroyer of Life, and the pleasures they give wear out the senses. Keep horses and chariots, keep dance and song, for yourself! How shall he desire wealth, O Death, who once has seen your face? Nay, only the boon that I have chosen – that only do I ask. Having found out the society of the imperishable and the immortal, as in knowing you I have done, how shall I, subject to decay and death, and knowing well the vanity of the flesh – how shall I wish for long life?

"Tell me, O King, the supreme secret regarding which men doubt. No other boon will I ask."

Whereupon the King of Death, well pleased at heart, began to teach Nachiketa the secret of immortality.

KING OF DEATH

The good is one thing; the pleasant is another. These two, differing in their ends, both prompt to action. Blessed are they that choose the good; they that choose the pleasant miss the goal.

Both the good and the pleasant present themselves to men. The wise, having examined both, distinguish the one from the other. The wise prefer the good to the pleasant; the foolish, driven by fleshly desires, prefer the pleasant to the good.

You, O Nachiketa, having looked upon fleshly desires, delightful to the senses, have renounced them all. You have turned from the miry way wherein many a man wallows.

Far from each other, and leading to different ends, are ignorance and knowledge. You, O Nachiketa, I regard as one who aspires after knowledge, for a multitude of pleasant objects were unable to tempt you.

Living in the abyss of ignorance yet wise in their own conceit, deluded fools go round and round, the blind led by the blind.

To the thoughtless youth, deceived by the vanity of earthly possessions, the path that leads to the eternal abode is not revealed. This world alone is real, there is no hereafter – thinking thus, he falls again and again, birth after birth, into my jaws.

To many it is not given to hear of the Self. Many, though they hear of it, do not understand it. Wonderful is he who speaks of it. Intelligent is he who learns of it. Blessed is he who, taught by a good teacher, is able to understand it.

The truth of the Self cannot be fully understood when taught by an ignorant man, for opinions regarding it, not founded in knowledge, vary one from another. Subtler than the subtlest is this Self, and beyond all logic. Taught by a teacher who knows the Self and Brahman as one, a man leaves vain theory behind and attains to truth.

The awakening which you have known does not come through the intellect, but rather, in fullest measure, from the lips of the wise. Beloved Nachiketa, blessed, blessed are you, because you seek the Eternal. Would that I had more pupils like you!

Well I know that earthly treasure lasts but till the morrow. For did not I myself, wishing to be King of Death, make sacrifice with fire? But the sacrifice was a fleeting thing, performed with fleeting objects, and small is my reward, seeing that only for a moment will my reign endure.

The goal of worldly desire, the glittering objects for which all men long, the celestial pleasures they hope to gain by religious rites, the most sought-after of miraculous powers – all these were within your grasp. But all these, with firm resolve, you have renounced.

The ancient, effulgent being, the indwelling Spirit, subtle, deep-hidden in the lotus of the heart, is hard to know. But the wise man, following the path of meditation, knows him, and is freed alike from pleasure and from pain. The man who has learned that the Self is separate from the body, the senses, and the mind, and has fully known him, the soul of truth, the subtle principle – such a man verily attains to him, and is exceeding glad, because he has found the source and dwelling place of all felicity. Truly do I believe, O Nachiketa, that for you the gates of joy stand open.

NACHIKETA

Teach me, O King, I beseech you, whatsoever you know to be beyond right and wrong, beyond cause and effect, beyond past, present, and future.

KING OF DEATH

Of that goal which all the Vedas declare, which is implicit in all penances, and in pursuit of which men lead lives of continence and service, of that will I briefly speak. It is – OM. This syllable is Brahman. This syllable is indeed supreme. He who knows it obtains his desire. It is the strongest support. It is the highest symbol. He who knows it is reverenced as a knower of Brahman. The Self, whose symbol is OM, is the omniscient Lord. He is not born. He does not die. He is neither cause nor effect. This Ancient One is unborn, imperishable, eternal: though the body be destroyed, he is not killed. If the slayer think that he slays, if the slain think that he is slain, neither of them knows the truth. The Self slays not, nor is he slain. Smaller than the smallest, greater than the greatest, this Self forever dwells within the hearts of all. When a man is free from desire, his mind and senses purified, he beholds the glory of the Self and is without sorrow. Though seated, he travels far; though at rest, he moves all things. Who but the purest of the pure can realize this Effulgent Being, who is joy and who is beyond joy. Formless is he, though inhabiting form. In the midst of the fleeting he abides forever. All-pervading and supreme is the Self. The wise man, knowing him in his true nature, transcends all grief.

The Self is not known through study of the scriptures, nor through subtlety of the intellect, nor through much learning; but by him who longs for him is he known. Verily unto him does the Self reveal his true being. By learning, a man cannot know him, if he desist not from evil, if he control not his senses, if he quiet not his mind, and practice not meditation. To him Brahmins and Kshatriyas are but food, and death itself a condiment.

Both the individual self and the Universal Self have entered the cave of the heart, the abode of the Most High, but the knowers of Brahman and the house-holders who perform the fire sacrifices see a difference between them as between sunshine and shadow.

May we perform the Nachiketa Sacrifice which bridges the world of suffering. May we know the imperishable Brahman, who is fearless, and who is the end and refuge of those who seek liberation.

Know that the Self is the rider, and the body the chariot; that the intellect is the charioteer, and the mind the reins.

The senses, say the wise, are the horses; the roads they travel are the mazes of desire. The wise call the Self the enjoyer when he is united with the body, the senses, and the mind.

When a man lacks discrimination and his mind is uncontrolled, his senses are unmanageable, like the restive horses of a charioteer. But when a man has discrimination and his mind is controlled, his senses, like the well-broken horses of a charioteer, lightly obey the rein.

He who lacks discrimination, whose mind is unsteady and whose heart is impure, never reaches the goal, but is born again and again. But he who has discrimination, whose mind is steady and whose heart is pure, reaches the goal, and having reached it is born no more.

The man who has a sound understanding for charioteer, a controlled mind for reins – he it is that reaches the end of the journey, the supreme abode of Vishnu, the all-pervading.

The senses derive from physical objects, physical objects from mind, mind from intellect, intellect from ego, ego from the unmanifested seed, and the unmanifested seed from Brahman – the Uncaused Cause.

Brahman is the end of the journey. Brahman is the supreme goal.

This Brahman, this Self, deep-hidden in all beings, is not revealed to all; but to the seers, pure in heart, concentrated in mind – to them is he revealed.

The senses of the wise man obey his mind, his mind obeys his intellect, his intellect obeys his ego, and his ego obeys the Self.

Arise! Awake! Approach the feet of the master and know that. Like the sharp edge of a razor, the sages say, is the path. Narrow it is, and difficult to tread! Soundless, formless, intangible, undying, tasteless, odorless, without beginning, without end, eternal, immutable beyond nature, is the Self. Knowing him as such, one is freed from death.

THE NARRATOR

The wise man, having heard and taught the eternal truth revealed by the King of Death to Nachiketa, is glorified in the heaven of Brahma.

He who sings with devotion this supreme secret in the assembly of the Brahmins, or at the rites in memory of his fathers, is rewarded with rewards immeasurable!

KING OF DEATH

The Self-Existent made the senses turn outward. Accordingly, man looks toward what is without, and sees not what is within. Rare is he who, longing for immortality, shuts his eyes to what is without and beholds the Self.

Fools follow the desires of the flesh and fall into the snare of all-encompassing death; but the wise, knowing the Self as eternal, seek not the things that pass away. He through whom man sees, tastes, smells, hears, feels, and enjoys is the omniscient Lord.

He, verily, is the immortal Self. Knowing him, one knows all things.

He through whom man experiences the sleeping or waking states is the all-pervading Self. Knowing him, one grieves no more.

He who knows that the individual soul, enjoyer of the fruits of action, is the Self – ever present within, lord of time, past and future – casts out all fear. For this Self is the immortal Self.

He who sees the First-Born – born of the mind of Brahma, born before the creation of waters – and sees him inhabiting the lotus of the heart, living among physical elements, sees Brahman indeed. For this First-Born is the immortal Self.

That being who is the power of all powers, and is born as such, who embodies himself in the elements and in them exists, and who has entered the lotus of the heart, is the immortal Self.

Agni, the all-seeing, who lies hidden in fire sticks, like a child well guarded in the womb, who is worshiped day by day by awakened souls, and by those who offer oblations in sacrificial fire – he is the immortal Self.

That in which the sun rises and in which it sets, that which is the source of all the powers of nature and of the senses, that which nothing can transcend – that is the immortal Self.

What is within us is also without. What is without is also within. He who sees difference between what is within and what is without goes evermore from death to death.

By the purified mind alone is the indivisible Brahman to be attained. Brahman alone is – nothing else is. He who sees the manifold universe, and not the one reality, goes evermore from death to death.

That being, of the size of a thumb, dwells deep within the heart. He is the lord of time, past and future. Having attained him, one fears no more. He, verily, is the immortal Self.

That being, of the size of a thumb, is like a flame without smoke. He is the lord of time, past and future, the same today and tomorrow. He, verily, is the immortal Self.

As rain, fallen on a hill, streams down its side, so runs he after many births who sees manifoldness in the Self.

As pure water poured into pure water remains pure, so does the Self remain pure, O Nachiketa, uniting with Brahman.

To the Birthless, the light of whose consciousness forever shines, belongs the city of eleven gates. He who meditates on the ruler of that city knows no more sorrow. He attains liberation, and for him there can no longer be birth or death. For the ruler of that city is the immortal Self.

The immortal Self is the sun shining in the sky, he is the breeze blowing in space, he is the fire burning on the altar, he is the guest dwelling in the house; he is in all men, he is in the gods, he is in the ether, he is wherever there is truth; he is the fish that is born in water, he is the plant that grows in the soil, he is the river that gushes from the mountain – he, the changeless reality, the illimitable!

He, the adorable one, seated in the heart, is the power that gives breath. Unto him all the senses do homage.

What can remain when the dweller in this body leaves the outgrown shell, since he is, verily, the immortal Self?

Man does not live by breath alone, but by him in whom is the power of breath.

And now, O Nachiketa, will I tell you of the unseen, the eternal Brahman, and of what befalls the Self after death.

Of those ignorant of the Self, some enter into beings possessed of wombs, others enter into plants – according to their deeds and the growth of their intelligence.

That which is awake in us even while we sleep, shaping in dream the objects of our desire – that indeed is pure, that is Brahman, and that verily is called the Immortal. All the worlds have their being in that, and no one can transcend it. That is the Self.

As fire, though one, takes the shape of every object which it consumes, so the Self, though one, takes the shape of every object in which it dwells.

As air, though one, takes the shape of every object which it enters, so the Self, though one, takes the shape of every object in which it dwells.

As the sun, revealer of all objects to the seer, is not harmed by the sinful eye, nor by the impurities of the objects it gazes on, so the one Self, dwelling in all, is not touched by the evils of the world. For he transcends all.

He is one, the lord and innermost Self of all; of one form, he makes of himself many forms. To him who sees the Self revealed in his own heart belongs eternal bliss – to none else, to none else!

Intelligence of the intelligent, eternal among the transient, he, though one, makes possible the desires of many. To him who sees the Self revealed in his own heart belongs eternal peace – to none else, to none else!

NACHIKETA

How, O King, shall I find that blissful Self, supreme, ineffable, who is attained by the wise? Does he shine by himself, or does he reflect another's light?

KING OF DEATH

Him the sun does not illumine, nor the moon, nor the stars, nor the lightning – nor, verily, fires kindled upon the earth. He is the one light that gives light to all. He shining, everything shines.

This universe is a tree eternally existing, its root aloft, its branches spread below. The pure root of the tree is Brahman, the immortal, in whom the three worlds have their being, whom none can transcend, who is verily the Self.

The whole universe came forth from Brahman and moves in Brahman. Mighty and awful is he, like to a thunderbolt crashing loud through the heavens. For those who attain him death has no terror.

In fear of him fire burns, the sun shines, the rains fall, the winds blow, and death kills.

If a man fail to attain Brahman before he casts off his body, he must again put on a body in the world of created things.

In one's own soul Brahman is realized clearly, as if seen in a mirror. In the heaven of Brahma also is Brahman realized clearly, as one distinguishes light from darkness. In the world of the fathers he is beheld as in a dream. In the world of angels he appears as if reflected in water.

The senses have separate origin in their several objects. They may be active, as in the waking state, or they may be inactive, as in sleep. He who knows them to be distinct from the changeless Self grieves no more.

Above the senses is the mind. Above the mind is the intellect. Above the intellect is the ego. Above the ego is the unmanifested seed, the Primal Cause.

And verily beyond the unmanifested seed is Brahman, the all-pervading spirit, the unconditioned, knowing whom one attains to freedom and achieves immortality.

None beholds him with the eyes, for he is without visible form. Yet in the heart is he revealed, through self-control and meditation. Those who know him become immortal.

When all the senses are stilled, when the mind is at rest, when the intellect wavers not – then, say the wise, is reached the highest state.

This calm of the senses and the mind has been defined as yoga. He who attains it is freed from delusion.

In one not freed from delusion this calm is uncertain, unreal: it comes and goes. Brahman words cannot reveal, mind cannot reach, eyes cannot see. How then, save through those who know him, can he be known?

There are two selves, the apparent self and the real Self. Of these it is the real Self, and he alone, who must be felt as truly existing. To the man who has felt him as truly existing he reveals his innermost nature.

The mortal in whose heart desire is dead becomes immortal. The mortal in whose heart the knots of ignorance are untied becomes immortal. These are the highest truths taught in the scriptures.

Radiating from the lotus of the heart there are a hundred and one nerves. One of these ascends toward the thousand-petaled lotus in the brain. If, when a man comes to die, his vital force passes upward and out through this nerve, he attains immortality; but if his vital force passes out through another nerve, he goes to one or another plane of mortal existence and remains subject to birth and death.

The Supreme Person, of the size of a thumb, the innermost Self, dwells forever in the heart of all beings. As one draws the pith from a reed, so must the aspirant after truth, with great perseverance, separate the Self from the body. Know the Self to be pure and immortal – yea, pure and immortal!

THE NARRATOR

Nachiketa, having learned from the god this knowledge and the whole process of yoga, was freed from impurities and from death, and was united with Brahman. Thus will it be with another also if he know the innermost Self.

OM . . . Peace peace peace.

(*The Upanishads, Breath of the Eternal,* trans.
Swami Prabhavananda and Frederick Manchester,
New York, New American Library, 1957)

Questions for discussion

1   What is Nachiketa's question?

2   What is the King of Death's answer?

3   What is meant by "The good is one thing, the pleasant is another"?

4   Why does the King of Death describe Brahman as "neither cause nor effect"?

5   What is meant by saying that "Brahman alone is – nothing else is"?

6   What is meant by saying that "There are two selves, the apparent self and the real Self"?

The *Bhagavad-Gita*

In its present form the Gita is an episode in a much longer poem, the *Mahabharata*, which tells the story of a war between two clans. As the Gita opens, the two armies are drawn up on the field of battle. The leader of one side, Arjuna, faces a dilemma. By an irony of war, the opposing army contains not only enemies, but also his own relatives, teachers, and friends. Which would be worse, to lose the battle or to win it? "If we kill them, none of us will wish to live." He turns for advice to his charioteer, who is none other than Krishna, the incarnation of the god Vishnu. Krishna uses the situation as an opportunity to give Arjuna some instruction. This somewhat artificial set-up is a pretext for the author to convey religious and ethical ideas.

Krishna, that is, Vishnu, begins by teaching Arjuna the doctrine of the Upanishads (which we have seen above), that mortal life and death belong to the world of appearances, not to reality. The true reality of every being, the Atman, is indestructible. This applies not only to Krishna, but also to Arjuna and the opposing camps. "There was never a time when I did not exist, nor you, nor any of these kings. Nor is there any future in which we shall cease to be." The Atman is "unborn, undying, never ceasing, never beginning, deathless, birthless, unchanging for ever." "Therefore, you should never mourn for anyone." Arjuna's cause is just, the war is righteous, his caste duty as a Kshatriya is to fight. He should be utterly indifferent to victory or defeat, life or death. If he does not fight he could be accused of cowardice.

Krishna proceeds to teach Arjuna about the various pathways to attain this state of indifference, this realization of the Eternal Self. These paths are comprised under the heading of yoga.

SANJAYA (THE NARRATOR)

Then his eyes filled with tears, and his heart grieved and was bewildered with pity. And Sri Krishna spoke to him, saying:

SRI KRISHNA

Arjuna, is this hour of battle the time for scruples and fancies? Are they worthy of you, who seek enlightenment? Any brave man who merely hopes for fame or heaven would despise them.

What is this weakness? It is beneath you. Is it for nothing men call you the Foe-consumer? Shake off this cowardice, Arjuna. Stand up.

ARJUNA

Bhisma and Drona are noble and ancient, worthy of the deepest reverence. How can I greet them with arrows, in battle? If I kill them, how can I ever enjoy my wealth, or any other pleasure? It will be cursed with blood-guilt. I would much rather spare them, and eat the bread of a beggar.

Which will be worse, to win this war, or to lose it? I scarcely know. Even the sons of Dhritarashtra stand in the enemy ranks. If we kill them, none of us will wish to live.

Is this real compassion that I feel, or only a delusion? My mind gropes about in darkness. I cannot see where my duty lies. Krishna, I beg you, tell me frankly and clearly what I ought to do. I am your disciple. I put myself into your hands. Show me the way.

Not this world's kingdom,
Supreme, unchallenged,
No, nor the throne
Of the gods in heaven,
Could ease this sorrow
That numbs my senses!

SANJAYA

When Arjuna, the foe-consuming, the never-slothful, had spoken thus to Govinda (another name for Krishna), ruler of the senses, he added: "I will not fight," and was silent.

Then to him who thus sorrowed between the two armies, the ruler of the senses spoke, smiling:

SRI KRISHNA

Your words are wise, Arjuna, but your sorrow is for nothing. The truly wise mourn neither for the living nor for the dead.

There was never a time when I did not exist, nor you, nor any of these kings. Nor is there any future in which we shall cease to be.

Just as the dweller in this body passes through childhood, youth and old age, so at death he merely passes into another kind of body. The wise are not deceived by that.

Feelings of heat and cold, pleasure and pain, are caused by the contact of the senses with their objects. They come and they go, never lasting long. You must accept them.

A serene spirit accepts pleasure and pain with an even mind, and is unmoved by either. He alone is worthy of immortality.

That which is non-existent can never come into being, and that which is can never cease to be. Those who have known the inmost Reality know also the nature of is and is not.

That Reality which pervades the universe is indestructible. No one has power to change the Changeless.

Bodies are said to die, but That which possesses the body is eternal. It cannot be limited, or destroyed. Therefore you must fight.

Some say this Atman
Is slain, and others
Call It the slayer:
They know nothing.
How can It slay
Or who shall slay It?

Know this Atman
Unborn, undying,
Never ceasing,
Never beginning,
Deathless, birthless,
Unchanging for ever.
How can It die
The death of the body?

Knowing It birthless,
Knowing It deathless,
Knowing It endless,
For ever unchanging,
Dream not you do
The deed of the killer,
Dream not the power
Is yours to command it.

Worn-out garments
Are shed by the body:
Worn-out bodies
Are shed by the dweller
Within the body.
New bodies are donned
By the dweller, like garments.

Not wounded by weapons,
Not burned by fire,
Not dried by the wind,
Not wetted by water:
Such is the Atman,

Not dried, not wetted,
Not burned, not wounded,
Innermost element,
Everywhere, always,
Being of beings,
Changeless, eternal,
For ever and ever.

This Atman cannot be manifested to the senses, or thought about by the mind. It is not subject to modification. Since you know this, you should not grieve.

But if you should suppose this Atman to be subject to constant birth and death, even then you ought not to be sorry.

Death is certain for the born. Rebirth is certain for the dead. You should not grieve for what is unavoidable.

Before birth, beings are not manifest to our human senses. In the interim between birth and death, they are manifest. At death they return to the unmanifest again. What is there in all this to grieve over!

There are some who have actually looked upon the Atman, and understood It, in all Its wonder. Others can only speak of It as wonderful beyond their understanding. Others know of Its wonder by hearsay. And there are others who are told about It and do not understand a word.

He Who dwells within all living bodies remains for ever indestructible. Therefore, you should never mourn for any one.

Even if you consider this from the standpoint of your own caste-duty, you ought not to hesitate; for, to a warrior, there is nothing nobler than a righteous war. Happy are the warriors to whom a battle such as this comes: it opens a door to heaven.

But if you refuse to fight this righteous war, you will be turning aside from your duty. You will be a sinner, and disgraced. People will speak ill of you throughout the ages. To a man who values his honor, that is surely worse than death. The warrior-chiefs will believe it was fear that drove you from the battle; you will be despised by those who have admired you so long. Your enemies, also, will slander your courage. They will use the words which should never be spoken. What could be harder to bear than that?

Die, and you win heaven. Conquer, and you enjoy the earth. Stand up now, son of Kunti, and resolve to fight. Realize that pleasure and pain, gain and loss, victory and defeat, are all one and the same: then go into battle. Do this and you cannot commit any sin.

I have explained to you the true nature of the Atman. Now listen to the method of Karma Yoga. If you can understand and follow it, you will be able to break the chains of desire which bind you to your actions.

In this yoga, even the abortive attempt is not wasted. Nor can it produce a contrary result. Even a little practice of this yoga will save you from the terrible wheel of rebirth and death.

In this yoga, the will is directed singly toward one ideal. When a man lacks this discrimination, his will wanders in all directions, after innumerable aims. Those who lack discrimination may quote the letter of the scripture, but they are really denying its inner truth. They are full of worldly desires, and hungry for the rewards of heaven. They use beautiful figures of speech. They teach elaborate rituals which are supposed to obtain pleasure and power for those who perform them. But, actually, they understand nothing except the law of Karma, that chains men to rebirth.

Those whose discrimination is stolen away by such talk grow deeply attached to pleasure and power. And so they are unable to develop that concentration of the will which leads a man to absorption in God.

The Vedas teach us about the three gunas and their functions. You, Arjuna, must overcome the three gunas. You must be free from the pairs of opposites. Poise your mind in tranquillity. Take care neither to acquire nor to hoard. Be established in the consciousness of the Atman, always.

When the whole country is flooded, the reservoir becomes superfluous. So, to the illumined seer, the Vedas are all superfluous.

You have the right to work, but for the work's sake only. You have no right to the fruits of work. Desire for the fruits of work must never be your motive in working. Never give way to laziness, either.

Perform every action with your heart fixed on the Supreme Lord. Renounce attachment to the fruits. Be even-tempered in success and failure; for it is this evenness of temper which is meant by yoga.

Work done with anxiety about results is far inferior to work done without such anxiety, in the calm of self-surrender. Seek refuge in the knowledge of Brahman. They who work selfishly for results are miserable.

In the calm of self-surrender you can free yourself from the bondage of virtue and vice during this very life. Devote yourself, therefore, to reaching union with Brahman. To unite the heart with Brahman and then to act: that is the secret of non-attached work. In the calm of self-surrender, the seers renounce the fruits of their actions, and so reach enlightenment. Then they are free from the bondage of rebirth, and pass to that state which is beyond all evil.

When your intellect has cleared itself of its delusions, you will become in-different to the results of all action, present or future. At present, your intellect is bewildered by conflicting interpretations of the scriptures. When it can rest, steady and undistracted, in contemplation of the Atman, then you will reach union with the Atman.

ARJUNA

Krishna, how can one identify a man who is firmly established and absorbed in Brahman? In what manner does an illumined soul speak? How does he sit? How does he walk?

SRI KRISHNA

He knows bliss in the Atman
And wants nothing else.
Cravings torment the heart:
He renounces cravings.
I call him illumined.

Not shaken by adversity,
Not hankering after happiness:
Free from fear, free from anger,
Free from the things of desire.
I call him a seer, and illumined.
The bonds of his flesh are broken.
He is lucky, and does not rejoice:

He is unlucky, and does not weep.
I call him illumined.

The tortoise can draw in his legs:
The seer can draw in his senses.
I call him illumined.

The abstinent run away from what they desire
But carry their desires with them:
When a man enters Reality,
He leaves his desires behind him.
Even a mind that knows the path
Can be dragged from the path:

The senses are so unruly.
But he controls the senses
And recollects the mind
And fixes it on me.
I call him illumined.

Thinking about sense-objects
Will attach you to sense-objects;
Grow attached, and you become addicted;
Thwart your addiction, it turns to anger;
Be angry, and you confuse your mind;
Confuse your mind, you forget the lesson of experience;
Forget experience, you lose discrimination;
Lose discrimination, and you miss life's only purpose.

When he has no lust, no hatred,
A man walks safely among the things of lust and hatred.
To obey the Atman
Is his peaceful joy:
Sorrow melts
Into that clear peace:
His quiet mind
Is soon established in peace.

The uncontrolled mind
Does not guess that the Atman is present:
How can it meditate?
Without meditation, where is peace?
Without peace, where is happiness?

The wind turns a ship
From its course upon the waters:
The wandering winds of the senses
Cast man's mind adrift

And turn his better judgment from its course.
When a man can still the senses
I call him illumined.

The recollected mind is awake
In the knowledge of the Atman
Which is dark night to the ignorant:
The ignorant are awake in their sense-life
Which they think is daylight:
To the seer it is darkness.

Water flows continually into the ocean
But the ocean is never disturbed:
Desire flows into the mind of the seer
But he is never disturbed.
The seer knows peace:
The man who stirs up his own lusts
Can never know peace.
He knows Peace who has forgotten desire.
He lives without craving:
Free from ego, free from pride.

This is the state of enlightenment in Brahman.
A man does not fall back from it
Into delusion.
Even at the moment of death
He is alive in that enlightenment:
Brahman and he are one.

(*Bhagavad-Gita*, trans. Swami Prabhavananda
and Christopher Isherwood, New York,
New American Library, 1954)

Questions for discussion

1   Why does Krishna tell Arjuna to fight?

2   What is the Karma Yoga which Krishna explains to Arjuna?

3   What is your reaction to the statement, "He knows peace who has
forgotten desire"?

The Gita II

In this section Krishna explains that there is an alternative to the arduous path of the hermit which the Upanishads had preached: the path of selfless action, resulting from devotional attachment to Krishna himself.

XII The Yoga of Devotion

ARJUNA

Some worship you with steadfast love. Others worship God the unmanifest and changeless. Which kind of devotee has the greater understanding of yoga?

SRI KRISHNA

Those whose minds are fixed on me in steadfast love, worshipping me with absolute faith. I consider them to have the greater understanding of yoga.

As for those others, the devotees of God the unmanifest, indefinable and changeless, they worship that which is omnipresent, constant, eternal, beyond thought's compass, never to be moved. They have all the senses in check. They are tranquil-minded, and devoted to the welfare of humanity. They see the Atman in every creature. They also will certainly come to me.

But the devotees of the unmanifest have a harder task, because the unmanifest is very difficult for embodied souls to realize.

Quickly I come
To those who offer me
Every action,
Worship me only,
Their dearest delight,
With devotion undaunted.

Because they love me
These are my bondsmen
And I shall save them
From mortal sorrow
And all the waves
Of Life's deathly ocean.

Be absorbed in me,
Lodge your mind in me;
Thus you shall dwell in me,
Do not doubt it,
Here and hereafter.

If you cannot become absorbed in me, then try to reach me by repeated concentration. If you lack the strength to concentrate, then devote yourself to works which will please me. For, by working for my sake only, you will achieve perfection. If you cannot even do this, then surrender yourself to me altogether. Control the lusts of your heart, and renounce the fruits of every action.

Concentration which is practiced with discernment is certainly better than the mechanical repetition of a ritual or a prayer. Absorption in God – to live with Him and be one with Him always – is even better than concentration. But renunciation brings instant peace to the spirit.

A man should not hate any living creature. Let him be friendly and compassionate to all. He must free himself from the delusion of "I" and "mine." He must accept pleasure and pain with equal tranquillity. He must be forgiving, ever-contented, self-controlled, united constantly with me in his meditation. His resolve must be unshakeable. He must be dedicated to me in intellect and in mind. Such a devotee is dear to me.

He neither molests his fellow men, nor allows himself to become disturbed by the world. He is no longer swayed by joy and envy, anxiety and fear. Therefore he is dear to me.

He is pure, and independent of the body's desire. He is able to deal with the unexpected: prepared for everything, unperturbed by anything. He is neither vain nor anxious about the results of his actions. Such a devotee is dear to me.

He does not desire or rejoice in what is pleasant. He does not dread what is unpleasant, or grieve over it. He remains unmoved by good or evil fortune. Such a devotee is dear to me.

His attitude is the same toward friend and foe. He is indifferent to honor and insult, heat and cold, pleasure and pain. He is free from attachment. He values praise and blame equally. He can control his speech. He is content with whatever he gets. His home is everywhere and nowhere. His mind is fixed upon me, and his heart is full of devotion. He is dear to me.

This true wisdom I have taught will lead you to immortality. The faithful practice it with devotion, taking me for their highest aim. To me they surrender heart and mind. They are exceedingly dear to me.

(*Bhagavad-Gita*, trans. Swami Prabhavananda and Christopher Isherwood)

Questions for discussion

1   What does Krishna mean by saying "Renounce the fruits of every action"?

2   What attitude of mind is meant by "not desiring or rejoicing in what is pleasant"?

2

Buddhism

The Spirit of Buddhism

The Parable of the Mustard Seed

Gotami was her name, but because she tired easily, she was called Kisa Gotami, or Frail Gotami. She was reborn at Savatthi in a poverty-stricken house. When she grew up, she married, going to the house of her husband's family to live. There, because she was the daughter of a poverty-stricken house, they treated her with contempt. After a time she gave birth to a son. Then they accorded her respect.

But when that boy of hers was old enough to play and run hither and about, he died. Sorrow sprang up within her. Thought she: Since the birth of my son, I, who was once denied honor and respect in this very house, have received respect. These folk may even seek to cast my son away. Taking her son on her hip, she went about from one house door to another, saying: "Give me medicine for my son!"

Wherever people encountered her, they said, Where did you ever meet with medicine for the dead? So saying, they clapped their hands and laughed in derision. She had not the slightest idea what they meant.

Now a certain wise man saw her and thought: This woman must have been driven out of her mind by sorrow for her son. But medicine for her, no one else is likely to know – the Possessor of the Ten Forces alone is likely to know. Said he: "Woman, as for medicine for your son, there is no one else who knows – the Possessor of the Ten Forces, the foremost individual in the world of men and the world of the Gods, resides at a neighboring monastery. Go to him and ask."

The man speaks the truth, thought she. Taking her son on her hip, when the Tathagata sat down in the Seat of the Buddhas, she took her stand in the outer circle of the congregation and said, "O Exalted One, give me medicine for my son!"

The Teacher, seeing that she was ripe for conversion, said: "You did well, Gotami, in coming hither for medicine. Go enter the city, make the rounds of the entire city, beginning at the beginning, and in whatever house no one has ever died, from that house fetch tiny grains of mustard seed."

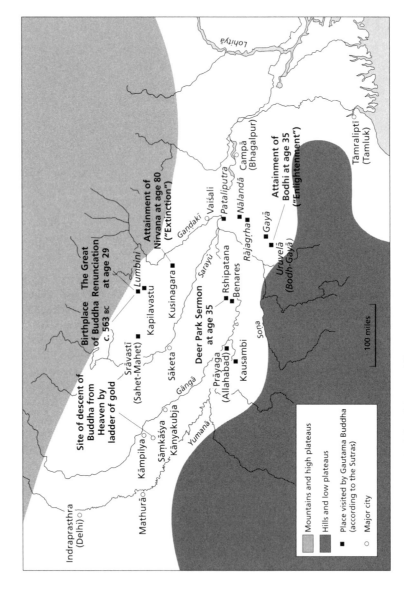

Places and events in the life of the Buddha

"Very well, reverend sir," she said. Delighted in heart, she entered within the city, and at the very first house said; "The Possessor of the Ten Forces bids me fetch tiny grains of mustard seed for medicine for my son. Give me tiny grains of mustard seed."

"Alas, Gotami," said they, and brought and gave to her.

"This particular seed I cannot take. In this house some one has died!"

"What say you, Gotami! Here it is impossible to count the dead!"

"Well then, enough! I'll not take it. The Possessor of the Ten Forces did not tell me to take mustard seed from a house where any one has ever died."

In this same way she went to the second house, and to the third. Thought she: In the entire city this must be the way! This the Buddha, full of compassion for the welfare of mankind, must have seen! Overcome with emotion, she went outside of the city, carried her son to the burning-ground, and holding him in her arms, said: "Dear little son, I thought that you alone had been overtaken by this thing which men call death. But you are not the only one death has overtaken. This is a law common to all mankind." So saying, she cast her son away in the burning-ground. Then she uttered the following stanza:

> No village law, no law of market town,
> No law of a single house is this.
> Of all the world and all the world of gods
> This only is the Law, that all things are impermanent.

Now when she had so said, she went to the Teacher. Said the Teacher to her: "Gotami, did you get the tiny grains of mustard seed?"

"Done, reverend sir, is the business of the mustard seed! Only give me a refuge!"

(From the Anguttara Commentary, in E. W. Burlingame, *Buddhist Parables*, New Haven, Yale University Press, 1922, pp. 92–4)

Question for discussion

1 One commentator remarks that two of the Buddha's most important doctrines are taught in this story. Can you deduce what they might be? See below, pp. 62, 66.

The Buddhist View of Life

As we shall see, Buddhism is not a single, unified religion, but exists in a variety of forms. All these forms, however, have at least one thing in common: an emphasis on the transitoriness of human life as we know it. Although in our hearts we may long for eternity, the unavoidable fact is that we are only temporary beings, and true spirituality begins with acknowledging that. All the varieties of Buddhism would agree with Shakespeare's Prospero:

> We are such stuff as dreams are made on,
> And our little life is rounded with a sleep.
>
> (*The Tempest*)

Siddhartha Gautama of the Shakyas

Towards the close of the sixth century BC there was a teacher who founded an order of yellow-robed monks and nuns, and was called by them the *Buddha*, "He who is Awake, or Enlightened."*

We know little for certain about the historical facts of his life and teaching. The traditional stories about him were written much later, and the Buddhist scriptures which purport to give his teaching are often of doubtful authenticity.†

We can be reasonably sure of some things. His name was Siddhartha Gautama (this is its Sanskrit form; *Siddhattha Gotama* in the dialect of the earliest Buddhist texts, Pali), and he was the son of a chief of the Shakya tribe which lived not far from the city of Kapilavastu (see map on p. 62). He became an ascetic and teacher, and his doctrines attracted many disciples. He spent a long life teaching in the region north of the Ganges, and died around 486 BC at the age of 80. For the rest, we must be content with the stories told by his followers.

The Four Passing Sights and the Great Going Forth

Buddhist tradition has embellished the bare facts of Gautama's life with dramatic stories. While he was still in the womb, his mother had a dream which was interpreted by wise men, that she had conceived a remarkable child, who would become either a Universal Emperor or a Universal Teacher. If he saw four signs of the world's suffering, he would become a Universal Teacher. His father determined that this should not happen, and from the time of his birth rigorously secluded him from the life of the society in order to prevent him ever experiencing sorrow. But the gods had other plans: as he was being driven around the royal park, a god took on the disguise of a man bowed down with age, where Siddhartha could not avoid seeing him. Siddhartha asked his charioteer what this was, and, on being told that all men must grow old, he was greatly distressed. In a similar way he saw three other signs: a very ill man, covered with sores and shivering with fever; a corpse being carried to the burning-ground; and a wandering religious beggar, whose countenance was filled with peace and joy.

These experiences made him resolve to become also a wandering beggar. In the middle of the night he rode out of the palace, the gods cushioning the

---

* "Buddha" is the past participle of the verb *budh*, to be awake, to come to consciousness, to notice or understand.

† The Buddhist scriptures are known as the Three Baskets, the Tripitaka: one "basket" contains the rules of conduct (Vinaya), another (the largest) the sermons attributed to the Buddha (Sutta), and the third metaphysics (Abhidhamma).

sound of his horse's hooves. This was the "Great Going Forth." He took up the life of a beggar for a time, but soon retired into the forest as a hermit.

In the forest he made the acquaintance of other hermits, who taught him various doctrines of the Upanishads, about the Atman and the quest for the sacred knowledge. For six years he followed this path, eventually practicing the most extreme austerities in the company of five other ascetics. But at last he came to the conclusion that the path of extreme asceticism was mistaken and abandoned it, whereupon his companions left him.

The Great Awakening

One day he sat down beneath a large pipal tree near the town of Gaya, and vowed not to rise until he had solved the problem of suffering. For 49 days he sank deeper and deeper into meditation. Mara, the evil spirit, foreseeing what might happen, tried one means after another to distract him, but he remained unmoved. On the forty-ninth day he saw the truth: why there is suffering, and what must be done to overcome it. He had attained Enlightenment, he had woken up, and would henceforth be known as the Awakened One, the Buddha. He continued meditating for another seven weeks under the Tree of Enlightenment (Bodhi).

At first he thought it would be impossible to teach others what he had discovered. But the god Brahma descended from heaven to persuade him not to keep his insight to himself. Rising, he travelled to the Deer Park near Benares, where his five former companions were now living. To them he preached his first sermon, on the Four Noble Truths and the Eightfold Path. They became his disciples, the first of many.

He fashioned his followers into an order of monks, the Sangha or Society, giving them the Ten Precepts as a rule of life. He spent some 40 years walking the roads of India with them, preaching his message to all who would listen. At the age of 80 he became ill after eating a meal and, feeling his end approaching, gave them his last teaching: "Be lamps unto yourselves. Rely on yourselves, and do not rely on external help." "Decay is inherent in all compounded things: work out your salvation with diligence." He died, and his body was cremated according to Indian custom.

Buddhism emerged during the period of the Upanishads, and from a milieu very similar in some respects to that which produced them (see above, pp. 21–2). While the doctrines of the Upanishads were accepted by the Brahmins as compatible with the orthodoxy of the Vedas, the Buddhist teachings were not. This may indicate that perhaps they stem more from pre-Vedic sources.

Buddhism today is not so much one religion as two. After the Buddha's death his followers divided into several different sects, of which only two remain today. Although these two have some important things in common, the differences that divide them are profound. One is named Theravada, which means "the Way of the Elders." It is also sometimes called the Hinayana, which means "the Lesser Vehicle," although Western scholars do not now use this name very

Buddha preaching, Sarnath (Ann & Bury Peerless)

frequently because of what they consider its pejorative connotation. The other is named Mahayana, "the Great Vehicle." The language of the Theravada scriptures is Pali, that of the Mahayana, Sanskrit.

Theravada Buddhism

Theravada is the form of Buddhism predominant in Sri Lanka (or Ceylon), Burma, Thailand, Cambodia, and Laos.

The four noble truths

In meditation beneath the Bodhi Tree, as we have seen, the Buddha discovered the truth about suffering: what gives rise to it, and what must be done to overcome it. What was the secret he discovered? He announced it to his five disciples in his first sermon in the ancient Deer Park at Benares. His announcement follows the traditional formula in which Indian physicians made a diagnosis of a disease. There are four truths, and each can be summarized in one word, but a word which needs much explanation to make it clear.

1 The first is a statement of the problem, of the affliction that must be remedied. It is *Dukkha*: "suffering" or "sorrow." The problem is that human life is pervaded by suffering. This problem needs to be understood. It is not that there is no such thing as pleasure, or that we constantly experience physical pain. Of course, some unfortunate people do experience a great deal of physical pain and mental anguish. Physical pain was no doubt more prevalent in the Buddha's time than it is now, when so much has been done to alleviate the ancient burdens of life such as infectious disease and bodily labor. But that is not exactly what is meant here, Buddhists tell us. Fortunately, there can also be a great deal of pleasure and joy in human life: there can even be moments of exaltation and of ecstasy. None of this is denied, but we are asked to examine our moments of joy and gladness a little more closely.

Over even our greatest joys there hangs a sword of Damocles: the passage of time. We are transient beings, and even our best experiences are transient. Our most intense joys will pass away and never return. This is not merely an objective fact about them: it also infects them inwardly, for it is a fact of which we are always conscious in some degree, even when we would most like to forget it. We can never really enjoy anything fully, because we are always at least subconsciously aware that it is limited and fleeting. Human existence is permeated by sadness, a sadness that is no less real because it is often partly unconscious.

A more fundamental explanation of the sorrow of existence will be given below, in the discussion of the Five Groups of Grasping (see pp. 72–3).

2 What is the cause of this state of affairs? That is the second truth discovered by the Buddha. The reason why human existence is pervaded through and through by sorrow is *Tanha*: "thirst, craving, desire." This statement also needs explanation. It would have been possible for the Buddha to locate the cause of human sadness in the *external* conditions of human life, in the lack of the *objective* means of happiness. If we have a broken leg, the cause of the pain is not far to seek. We might think: it lies in the objective fact that the leg is broken. Social scientists today similarly sometimes point to external, objective factors as the causes for a person's condition, explaining his emotional condition perhaps by his poverty, or the behavior of his parents when he was a child. But the Buddha deliberately refused to take this route. Instead he located the source of human sorrow within the subjective ego. We suffer because we desire.

It is a common human experience that the things we love the most make us suffer the most. The persons we love best are the ones who cause us the most intense sorrow. Love makes us vulnerable to pain. The Buddha generalizes this, and says, in effect, that whenever we experience pain or sorrow, it is because we have an excessive emotional attachment to the person or thing causing our suffering.

Having taken this step, the Buddha then takes another, telling us that the fundamental reason why we are emotionally attached to other persons and things is because we are attached to ourselves. If we suffer at the loss of someone or something dear to us, it is because at bottom we are excessively fond of ourselves, we are egocentric.

However, the Buddha tells us, this ego of which we are so fond is a fiction, a fiction both created by desire and which reinforces desire. There is desire, and there is suffering. But there is no underlying being that desires and suffers. "There is suffering, but no sufferer." Instead, there is merely a bundle of forces, which we think of as our "self," and which is temporary and transient. It has no stable or permanent identity, but the forces which make it up come together for a while, in what we think of as our existence, and then separate. Desire gives rise to thought, to the thought that there is an "I," and that some things are "mine," but this thought is a delusion. This delusion lies at the heart of suffering; without it there would be no pain or distress. Especially, without the fiction of a permanent "I" there would be no reason for distress over the passage of time.

That suffering is caused by excessive attachment to our (imaginary) ego is true, in the Buddhist view, even for physical pain, such as the agony caused by the broken leg. The story is told of the philosopher Bertrand Russell that once, when he was in the dentist's chair, the dentist, investigating a pain, asked him "Where does it hurt?" Russell responded: "In my mind, of course!" To use a modern term, physical pain is psychological in origin: it arises out of the mind, and it would not occur but for the mind's determination to maintain itself in existence. The broken leg by itself would not cause pain, for it is possible to have a broken leg and yet not feel pain in it. A Buddhist may point out that instances of this have been known to occur, for example, when a person is distracted by a greater concern.

3   The third truth states the remedy. Self-centered desire can be extinguished, and with it suffering. If the cause of sadness is egocentricity, emotional attachment to ourselves, maintaining the fiction of the Self, the remedy is to abolish the fiction, to abandon the idea of the Self. This is the truth of *Nirvana*: "extinction." It is possible, asserts the Buddha, to attain to a state of total selflessness, that is, a state in which we realize fully and adequately, not only in thought but also in deed, that our ego does not in fact have any objective existence, that we have been indulging in a delusion. It is possible, he maintains, to achieve "the cessation of desire, without a remainder."

4   Now this might seem to be an extravagant confidence. How is it possible to attain to such a state? That is the fourth truth, *Marga*: "the Path." The Buddha spells out a concrete way of living which, he maintains, if followed

conscientiously, will eventually lead to the goal of Nirvana. This Path contains eight strands: not steps or stages, as if they were to be trodden one after the other, but concurrent programs to be carried out simultaneously.

The Eightfold Path

The Eightfold Path is described by the Buddha as a "Middle Way" between extreme asceticism and self-indulgence. There is nothing magical about it. It consists essentially in not causing harm, and in practicing self-awareness and meditation.

The first two elements or programs in the Path are usually classified by Buddhists under the heading of Wisdom (*Panna, Prajna*):

1   Right Understanding. This consists in comprehending the first three Noble Truths.
2   Right Thought. This consists in fostering in oneself thoughts of non-violence and love. "All that we are," says the *Dhammapada*, "is the result of what we have thought." Thoughts lead to action, so that if we wish to reform our behavior, we must begin by reforming our thoughts.

The third, fourth, and fifth programs are classified together under the heading of ethical conduct (*Sila*). The most fundamental principle of Buddhist ethics is not to cause harm: ahimsa, often translated as "non-violence."

3   Right Speech. This is speech which causes no harm: not lying, not slandering, not giving offense, not gossiping or talking idly. One should speak pleasantly and benevolently, or not speak at all.
4   Right Conduct. This is in the first instance behavior which causes no harm: not taking life, not stealing, not defrauding. One should do what one can to help others.
5   Right Livelihood. There are some ways of earning a living which have the effect of causing harm, even if the individual person is not directly the cause of it, such as dealing in arms or selling intoxicating drinks. These professions should be avoided.

The final three programs are classified under the heading of Meditation or Mental Discipline (*Samadhi, Samatha*):

6   Right Effort. This is the determined effort to eliminate and prevent bad states of mind, and to cultivate good and wholesome states of mind.
7   Right Mindfulness. This is perhaps the most interesting for a modern Westerner, and it will be explained in a little more detail. It consists in becoming aware of what is happening within one's body and mind. Sometimes it happens that a person may have feelings of which he is unconscious. For example, it is possible to feel angry, yet not realize that one is angry. The

same is true of thoughts and beliefs: we may make an assumption without realizing we are making it. It is perhaps especially true of our motives: it is easy for us to conceal from ourselves our true motives in undertaking an action. It is even true for objective states and for actions. A person may be tired, yet not realize it, or may be drumming his fingers on the table, yet not be aware of the fact because his mind is elsewhere.

Although these thoughts, emotions, motives, and actions are unconscious, they can still have a strong influence on our behavior. If we are to become genuinely detached from ourselves, we must secure control not only over our conscious desires but also our unconscious ones, and the prerequisite for that is to bring them up into consciousness.

The practice of mindfulness is often begun with the exercise of paying close attention to one's breathing. The eventual aim is to learn to give the mind fully to whatever one is doing.

8   Right Concentration. This is the practice of deep meditation. The initial aim is to root out turbulent desires and emotions, thus attaining peace of mind. Gradually, through a number of stages, negative feelings are abandoned, then intellectual activities, and finally even positive feelings such as joy and happiness, so that the "still point" of the mind is reached, a state of perfect equanimity. The ultimate goal is to arrive at a state of mind in which all distinction between the mind and objects disappears.

The rule of right conduct is made more concrete for daily practice by the Ten Precepts which the Buddha gave to his disciples. In everyday living these receive more attention than the Eightfold Path:

1   Not to destroy life.
2   Not to steal.
3   Not to commit adultery.
4   Not to tell lies.
5   Not to take intoxicants.
6   Not to eat at forbidden times (i.e. after midday).
7   Not to dance, sing, play music, or act on the stage.
8   Not to use perfumes or jewelry.
9   Not to use a high or broad bed.
10   Not to receive gold or silver (i.e. not to handle money).

Monks and laity

In Theravada Buddhism there is a marked difference between the monks and the laity. To be a true, dedicated Buddhist in the Theravadin sense one must become a monk. The term *Sangha*, meaning the Buddhist community, refers only to the monks, not to the laity. It will be evident that it would be difficult for lay persons to observe the last five of the Ten Precepts, especially the tenth, and so they are allowed as a concession to follow only the first five. The traditional role of the laity consists largely in providing for the needs of the monks, especially food.

The Three Jewels (Pali, Tiratana; Sanskrit, Triratna)

Not long after the Buddha's death his followers began to recite a threefold utterance called the "Three Jewels," which is repeated every day by all Buddhists, both monks and laity:

> I take refuge in the Buddha.
> I take refuge in the Dharma.
> I take refuge in the Sangha.

In Buddhism the term "Dharma," which we encountered in the chapter on Hinduism in the sense of "duty," has a different meaning: the teaching of the Buddha.

Buddhist theory

One of the most remarkable statements attributed to the Buddha is that "the Buddha is free from all theories." Buddhism understands itself to be a thoroughly practical religion. Once when a monk came to him asking whether the world is eternal, whether a person continues to live after death, and a number of similar questions, the Buddha replied that such theoretical questions are a waste of time. It is, he said, as if a man has been pierced with an arrow, but will not let it be taken out until he receives answers to a list of questions: Who shot the arrow? Was he tall or short? What color was his skin? Was he from the town or the country? The man will die, said the Buddha, before his questions are answered. "The religious life does not depend on the doctrine that the world is eternal, or that the world is not eternal. Whether the doctrine obtain that the world is eternal, or that the world is not eternal, there still remain birth, old age, death, sorrow, lamentation, misery, grief, and despair, for the extinction of which in the present life I am prescribing."

Despite this, however, Buddhism surprisingly has some theories. These can be summed up in the three related ideas of Impermanence, No Self, and the Five Aggregates.

Impermanence (Pali, Anicca; Sanskrit, Anitya)

This is the doctrine that all things, without any exception, are impermanent and pass away in the course of time. "Decay is inherent in all compounded things." Not only does nothing last for ever in this world, but neither is there anything eternal in any other world. The reason for this state of affairs is given in the next doctrine.

Do not vainly lament, but wonder at the rule of transience and learn from it the emptiness of human life. Do not cherish the unworthy desire that the changeable might become unchanging.

No self (*Pali,* Anatta; *Sanskrit,* Anatman)

This is the doctrine that there is no such thing anywhere as a self or a substance. There is no such thing as being, there is only becoming. Nothing has a genuine identity. There are simply forces or energies.

This is true in the first instance of human beings, as we have seen above in discussing the Second Noble Truth. Our impression that we possess an objective self, a unique identity which makes us the individual that we are, is a delusion. There is no ego. There is no soul which could survive the death of this body and be reincarnated in another one. A human being is simply a transient bundle of forces, which come together briefly and then part.

By the same token there is no God. There is no divine substance or entity, no Brahman. The Upanishads are mistaken: there is no Atman.

The same is true of animals and plants, of everything. Nothing has an identity. Everywhere there are only forces or energies.

> There is suffering but no sufferer,
> There is the deed but no doer,
> Extinction is, but none who is extinct,
> There is no walker, but the Way.
>
> (Buddhaghosa, 5th cent. AD, trans.
> Hans Wolfgang Schumann,
> *Buddhism*, 1974, p. 90)

These two doctrines explain why it is that desire causes suffering. Even if we should obtain what we desire, it will pass away – or else our desire for it will.

The five aggregates (*Pali,* Khandhas; *Sanskrit,* Skandhas)

This doctrine explains in a little more detail what a human being consists of. According to the doctrine the forces or energies that make up what we call a human being are divided into five groups, or bundles, or "aggregates." These energies are all energies of "attachment," that is, they are just different manifestations of craving or desire, and hence they are referred to as "Groups of Grasping." The five groups are:

Matter What we call matter is not a substance, but a bundle of energies, forces, desires, strivings, cravings, grasping, or attachments. All these words have the same meaning. The human body is included in this category.

Sensations Every sensation is a form of attachment or craving. A sensation in this sense is what happens in the eye, for example, when it sees an object, or in the ear when it hears a sound. According to Buddhist theory the senses include the mind, so there are six senses rather than five. The mind is not a distinct, spiritual entity, as other philosophies have taught, but just another organ of sensation, like the eye or ear, except that it responds to ideas rather than to physical objects. Buddhists do not make a distinction between spirit and matter.

Perception Similarly, every perception is a form of attachment or craving. A perception is the recognition of an external object by one of the six senses.

Mental formations The word "mental" here means having to do with inclinations and emotions. It is a broad term and includes such things as paying attention, having confidence, and feeling repugnance. All such things are forms of attachment or craving.

Consciousness Again, every instance of consciousness is a form of attachment or craving. (Consciousness in Buddhist theory can arise only where the other four groups have arisen; it is material and cannot exist separately from matter. Also, consciousness as it is understood by Buddhists does not necessarily imply consciousness of any particular object. It is possible, they believe, in the higher levels of meditation, to have a consciousness that is not a consciousness of anything.)

Thus, when the Buddhist looks at the universe, what he sees is a gigantic bundle of energies. These energies are never at rest, but are constantly changing. None of their formations is permanent. He does not see, as many Hindus believe they do, a mere illusion. The universe is real, for the energies that make it up are real. But it is not substantial.

The Five Groups of Grasping are the very essence of sorrow and suffering, of Dukkha, for craving is sorrow, and the universe is nothing but craving. The Five Groups also make clear why the individual human person has no substantial existence and must inevitably pass away.

Dependent origination or conditioned genesis (*Pali*, Paticca-samuppada; *Sanskrit,* Pratitya-Samutpada)

The doctrine of Dependent Origination is another way of conveying the idea that there is no "I." How is it that this delusion arises? It occurs as part of an entire web of ignorance, desire and delusion, in which one regrettable thing gives rise to another and each reinforces the other.

1	Ignorance gives rise to karmic or self-centered Actions.
2	Karmic actions give rise to Consciousness.
3	Consciousness gives rise to Name and Form (the identification of mental and physical phenomena).

4	Name and Form give rise to the six faculties of Sense (the five sense organs and the mind).
5	The six faculties of Sense give rise to Contact (with bodies).
6	Contact gives rise to Feeling.
7	Feeling gives rise to Craving (thirst, Tanha).
8	Craving gives rise to Grasping.
9	Grasping gives rise to Becoming.
10	Becoming gives rise to Birth.
11 and 12	Birth gives rise to old age, death, grief, lamentation, pain, affliction, and despair – which in turn give rise to ignorance.

But from the utter fading out and ending of Ignorance comes also the ending of Actions;
from the ending of Actions comes also the ending of Consciousness;
from the ending of Consciousness comes the ending of Name and Form;
from the ending of Name and Form comes the ending of Sense;
from the ending of Sense comes the end of Contact;
from the ending of Contact comes the ending of Feeling;
from the ending of Feeling comes the ending of Craving;
from the ending of Craving comes the ending of Grasping;
from the ending of Grasping comes the ending of Becoming;
from the ending of Becoming comes the ending of Birth;
from the ending of Birth comes the ending of Age-and-death, Sorrow and Grief, Woe, Lamentation, and Despair. Such is the ending of all this mass of Ill.

(Attrib. to Buddha, trans. F. L. Woodward)

Rebirth

Buddhists accept the general Indian belief in rebirth. Yet as normally understood, for example by Hindus, as we have seen, it presupposes that there is a soul which departs from the dying body and is reborn in another body. Since Buddhism rejects belief in a soul, how can it maintain its belief in rebirth?

The Buddhist answer to this is to compare it to lighting one candle from another. It is not that there is a substance which passes over from the one to the other, but there is causal continuity: the first instigates or initiates or en-kindles the other. At the end of life, our desires and attachments are a karmic spark which ignites a new round of desires and attachments, and with them a new ego-illusion. Nirvana literally means a "blowing out," the extinction of this entire process by extinguishing the desire which gives rise to it.

The many Buddhas

Although Siddhartha Gautama was the Buddha to whom we in this cycle of the world owe the preaching of the truth, he is not the only Buddha to have lived.

There have been many cycles of the world, each with its own Buddha. Everyone who attains Enlightenment or Nirvana by his own efforts and insight, and who dedicates himself to teaching others, as Siddhartha did, is a Buddha. A person who attains Nirvana but without dedicating himself to teaching others is a saint or arhat (Pali, *arahant*).

It will be evident to the reader that Theravada Buddhism is a religion of self-liberation, what we have called a pelagian religion (see above, p. 7). Only the individual can dismantle his own ego. As we saw above, the Buddha taught: "Be lamps unto yourselves. Rely on yourselves, and do not rely on external help"; "Decay is inherent in all compounded things: work out your salvation with diligence."

Mahayana Buddhism

When we turn from Theravada to Mahayana Buddhism, we enter another world, for in the Mahayana the most fundamental conceptions of Buddhism are dramatically transformed. The "Three Jewels," the Buddha, the Dharma (the Buddha's teaching), and the Sangha (the Buddhist community), are retained, yet understood very differently. The result is a different picture of the universe and of human existence. Mahayana is the form of Buddhism predominant in China, Japan, and Korea.

Like the Theravada, the Mahayana is based upon the Four Noble Truths: that existence is inherently sorrowful, that sorrow is caused by self-centered desire, that this can be extinguished, and that there is a path which leads to that goal. But in the course of time a twofold development occurred. On the one hand, it came to be felt that the scope or range of the Buddhist community was unnecessarily restricted. As we have just seen, the path of Theravada Buddhism can be followed seriously only by taking up the life of a monk or nun. But this limits it to a very small number of people. The Mahayana proposed an understanding of Buddhism which opens it up to everybody. That is the reason for the name "Mahayana," "the Great Vehicle."

What made this opening up possible was a new understanding of the nature of Buddhahood. In the Theravada, as we have seen, the Buddha is simply a man who came to a profound understanding of human life, taught this to others, and then passed away into Nirvana, leaving his disciples to struggle as he did for liberation from desire and its attendant suffering. For the Mahayana, the Buddha Siddartha Gautama is a manifestation of the Eternal Buddha, who is boundless compassion:

Do not think that the compassion of the earthly Buddha is only for the present life; that was only a manifestation of the timeless compassion of the eternal Buddha that has been operative since mankind first went astray from ignorance. The eternal Buddha ever appears before people in most friendly forms and brings to them the wisest methods of relief . . . The task of Buddhahood is as everlasting as human life is everlasting; and as the depth of ignorance is bottomless, so Buddha's compassion is boundless.

(*The Teaching of Buddha*, Tokyo, Bukkyo Dendo Kyokai, 1971, p. 15)

Followers of the Mahayana sometimes illustrate the difference between their view and that of the Theravada by pointing out that on achieving Enlightenment under the Bodhi Tree, Siddhartha could have simply entered into his own private nirvana, but instead walked the roads of India for some 40 years, trying to communicate to others the remedy he had found for the ills of human existence. His life was not simply a private quest for Enlightenment, Nirvana, and the end of sorrow for himself: it was above all an expression of compassion, of concern for the welfare of others.

The eternal Buddha manifests this compassion by taking on various forms, of which Siddhartha was one, in order to liberate all sentient beings from suffering. In Mahayana Buddhism the Buddha not only teaches, but saves.

The Bodhisattva

In the Mahayana the primacy of compassion and concern for others is expressed especially in the figure of the *Bodhisattva*. Literally this term means "Enlightenment Being, a being whose essence is bent on attaining enlightenment." Initially it was applied to Siddhartha Gautama during the period before he attained Enlightenment and became a Buddha. But in Mahayana usage the term was extended to mean any person who has pursued the path to Enlightenment steadfastly and thoroughly, and who has accumulated sufficient merits or karma to enter Nirvana. He now stands on the threshold of Nirvana. But instead of entering, he turns his back on it and delays his entry into it in order to lead all sentient beings, all beings that can experience suffering, across this world's ocean of misery to the peaceful shore of Nirvana. He can accomplish this by transferring to them some of his own inexhaustible supply of merit. More than that: in order to achieve the salvation of other beings, he is willing to take on himself the burden of their suffering. (The text of the vow said to be taken by the Bodhisattva is given in the section of Buddhist texts following this chapter; see pp. 95–6.) The Bodhisattva is the embodiment of a compassion which is heroic.

Nirvana and Samsara

The Bodhisattva turns his back on Nirvana. But precisely *by* the act of turning his back on it, he achieves spiritual perfection and total selflessness. This state can be nothing else but Nirvana! Paradoxically, then, by rejecting Nirvana the Bodhisattva attains it.

The Nirvana that the Bodhisattva attains, however, needs to be understood somewhat differently from the way it is understood in the Theravada. In the

Theravada, Nirvana is simply the absence of self-centeredness, and so the absence of suffering and sorrow. Nirvana in the sense of the Mahayana retains this interpretation, but also includes something else: the state of spiritual perfection, of total compassion and concern for others. Followers of the Mahayana view their concept of Nirvana as having a more altruistic character than for the Theravada.

This difference shows itself in another respect. In the Theravada there is a gulf between Nirvana and Samsara. The two are simply opposites. To be in Samsara is by definition not to be in Nirvana, and to be in Nirvana is not to be in Samsara. To attain Nirvana one must leave the world of birth and rebirth behind. But in the Mahayana this cannot be the case. The Bodhisattva attains Nirvana, but does so only by immersing himself in Samsara, taking upon himself again and again the suffering of others, which is almost the definition of Samsara. It was the Buddha's action in devoting himself to others that set the seal on his attainment of Enlightenment and Nirvana, and he devoted himself to others by remaining in Samsara, by walking the roads of India and preaching his message to all who would listen.

For the Mahayana, then, Nirvana is in Samsara and Samsara is in Nirvana. It can even be said that in a certain sense Nirvana is Samsara and Samsara is Nirvana, for the difference between them proves on examination to be a mere appearance, not a reality. In the Mahayana, to attain Nirvana means, not leaving the world of Samsara behind, but seeing and experiencing it differently – without attachment.

The Eternal Buddha

For the Mahayana, the Buddha nature is an eternal reality which is not born and does not die, and is nothing less than absolute Truth and ultimate Reality. It is pure compassion, pure altruism. The world of time and change, by comparison, is only a transient appearance cloaking this great reality. To liberate the world from its suffering, the Eternal Buddha became incarnate as the historical Gautama, and has sent countless other embodiments of himself into the world of appearances down through the ages.

The Eternal Buddha nature is pure compassion. But where is the Buddha nature to be found? Is it encountered only in the incarnate Buddhas? The response of the Mahayana is that the Buddha nature is present within everything that exists.

Since it is possible for every person to attain Enlightenment and Nirvana, every person must be a potential Buddha. But that implies that each person already possesses the Buddha nature, except that we do not realize it. And this must be true of all sentient beings, of all beings capable of experiencing suffering (for in Buddhist thought, as in Indian thought generally, there is no distinction between humans and animals, since people can be reborn as animals). The eternal Buddha nature is the true identity of every being. But if that is the case, we must distinguish the true identity of things from their merely apparent identity.

The apparent identity of things, their nature as this particular individual, Tom Smith or Sally Jones, can only be a mere appearance. And this must apply to the whole empirical world, the entire world of ordinary experience. In comparison to the transcendent reality of the Buddha nature, the world is merely an appearance. The Eternal Buddha nature is the sole true reality. Mahayana Buddhism is thus a form of monism.

We have returned, then, to a doctrine which is surprisingly similar in some respects to the concept of Brahman, the Atman, and Maya.

Emptiness (Sunyata)

What is the nature of the Eternal Buddha? It is pure compassion, pure altruism, we said, and also pure reality. But these are only human words for something that goes far beyond our ability to grasp it. Our human minds, our concepts and words, belong to the empirical world, the world of ordinary experience, which we have just seen is essentially only an appearance. To try to grasp ultimate Reality by means of a mere appearance can only be futile. It is not possible, then, to give any true description of the Eternal Buddha. If we think we have understood the Buddha, it is not the Buddha.

This train of thought was expressed by means of the concept of Emptiness, a term used in several senses. The Buddha nature is empty (*sunya*), in the sense that it cannot be described, and that it has no ego. In addition, all the phenomena, all the appearances of the world, all the elements of things are empty, in the sense that they are mere appearances.

We saw above that the Bodhisattva is the embodiment of compassion (*karuna*). Here we must add that he is also the embodiment of wisdom (*prajna*), that is, insight into Emptiness.

Liberation, grace, merit, and the Law of Karma

As we saw above, Theravada Buddhism is entirely a religion of self-liberation, where each person is considered to possess within himself or herself the power to attain salvation. It is up to the individual to save himself or herself, by following the Eightfold Path and the Ten Precepts. There is no concept of grace, or of the transfer of merit (at least, not officially; popular religion can be a little different). The Law of Karma reigns supreme, which ensures that each person's fate is decided by his or her own actions.

In the Mahayana, however, the situation is more complicated. The individual *qua* individual is only an appearance. On one level, the level of absolute truth, we can say that each person is already liberated, since his true identity is the eternal Buddha nature. On the level of appearances, however, ignorance and sorrow still remain, and liberation is still necessary. If this ignorance and sorrow are overcome, that can happen only by the power and compassion of the Eternal Buddha. Consequently, Mahayana Buddhism can be considered as at least potentially a saviorist religion. This is especially evident in its devotional forms, which emphasize that the merits of one person, such as a Buddha or Bodhisattva, can be transferred to another. This has the effect, to all intents and purposes, of abolishing the Law of Karma, or at least of making it very much more elastic, for there is no longer any strict connection between what a person deserves and what he or she obtains.

Meditation

Mahayana Buddhism has developed in two main forms. One of these takes aim directly at the mind, seeking to achieve Enlightenment through the practice of meditation, for the illusion of individual identity is seen as a trick that the mind plays on us, which can be overcome by defeating the mind. Meditational Mahayana holds that, in truth, we are already saved, but in our normal condition we do not realize it. The aim of meditation is to achieve the realization that our true nature is nothing less than the Buddha nature. This kind of meditation may occupy eight or more hours a day, making meditational Buddhism a full-time occupation. It is practiced especially by monks or nuns living a monastic life.

Since in our inmost nature we are already liberated, it is not necessary to try to achieve liberation. Our salvation does not depend on following the Eightfold Path or the Ten Precepts. Instead, a person's orderly life becomes a sign of the fact that he or she is already saved. In practice the Path and the Precepts are less important in all forms of the Mahayana than in the Theravada: they are no longer the central focus of the religion.

How, then, does the Mahayana explain the fact that the Buddha undoubtedly taught the Eightfold Path and the Ten Precepts? It regards these as educational devices, "skillful means," a kind of benevolent deception that the Buddha used at first, because his first hearers were not able to absorb his true message.

Since the version of meditational Mahayana which is best known today developed in China, we shall return to it in more detail in the chapter on Chinese religion (see Chapter 4).

Devotion

The other kind of Mahayana Buddhism turns for aid to the Buddhas and Bodhisattvas, much as Catholic Christians turn to the saints, praying to them and worshipping them in private prayer and public ceremony, in order not only to attain Nirvana, but also to obtain help with the trials of this life. This devotional Buddhism is the form of Mahayana most widely practiced by lay people. It makes use of temples, altars, and statues, and is organized by priests.

These two forms of Mahayana, the meditational and the devotional, do not oppose but rather complement one another, for they share the same fundamental understanding of the Buddha nature. It is not unusual for a layman who otherwise practices devotional Buddhism to spend some time in a monastery learning the skills and mental discipline of meditation.

The remainder of this chapter will be concerned especially with devotional Mahayana.

Some Buddhas and Bodhisattvas

Mahayana theory recognizes countless Buddhas and Bodhisattvas: as many as there are who have attained Enlightenment and Nirvana. Some are Earthly or human, some are Celestial or transcendent. Devotional Buddhism worships especially some 20 or so of these, who bring assistance to people in various ways, comparable to the many gods of Hinduism or the saints of Catholic Christianity. The most popular Buddha is Amitabha (known in Japan as Amida.) He has created a paradise, called the Pure Land or the Western Paradise, described in the Sukhavativyuha Sutra, and everyone who invokes his name even once in faith will be reborn there. The Pure Land is not Nirvana, but it is much easier to reach Nirvana from there.

Each Bodhisattva personifies an aspect of the Buddha nature. Manjusri represents wisdom. An especially popular Bodhisattva is Avalokiteshvara ("he who looks down in mercy") – often depicted with a thousand arms to symbolize his willingness to help – who can suspend the Law of Karma, and who even descends into hell to bring relief to those in torment. He takes special care of those in danger from fire, water, demons, the sword, and enemies. When his cult spread to China he was transformed into a female, Kuan Yin (see p. 199).

Some Mahayana Buddhists also worship the future or messianic Buddha, Maitreya, who will banish suffering from the earth and restore the original teaching of the Buddha. This belief, like the similar Jewish belief in a messiah, may owe some of its inspiration to Persian influence.

The threefold body of the Buddha

In order to clarify the relationships between the various Buddhas and Bodhisattvas, the Mahayana developed the doctrine of the Threefold Body of the Buddha. According to this doctrine the Buddha has three bodies or aspects. One is earthly or human, called the "Manifest" Body (*Nirmanakaya*); the Buddhas and Bodhisattvas who have lived on earth, such as Siddhartha Gautama, share in this body and suffer the misery of old age, illness, and death as he did. The second body of the Buddha is heavenly or transcendent, called the "Enjoyment" Body (*Sambhogakaya*); the Buddhas and Bodhisattvas who share in this belong entirely to the spiritual world, cannot be seen by human senses, and are not subject to bodily ills. The third body of the Buddha is the "Truth" Body (*Dharmakaya*). This is the Eternal Buddha, Absolute Reality, which is immanent in all things. On this absolute level there is only one Buddha.

The historical Buddha

What then of Siddhartha Gautama? As we have seen, the Theravada already accepted the existence of many Buddhas. For the Mahayana the historical

The Bodhisattva Avalokiteshvara, "he who looks down in mercy" (Circa Photo Library)

Siddhartha is even less unique than for the Theravada. He was only one embodiment of the eternal Buddha nature, one incarnation of the Eternal Compassion, out of many. He was essentially an appearance which the eternal Buddha nature projected into the world of appearances to liberate sentient beings from suffering.

Faith

How is the grace and mercy of the Buddha brought to bear on us individually? For devotional Mahayana it is not through our actions, but through our faith, our trust in the Buddha. Thus devotional Mahayana Buddhism developed a doctrine of salvation by faith alone. Strictly speaking, nothing more is necessary than faith in the Buddha.

As a result, in several versions of the Mahayana simply the utterance of the Buddha's name in faith is all that is necessary. Some versions of Mahayana go even further and teach that everyone will be saved, not only the good but also the wicked. Indeed, Shinran, founder of Jodo Shinshu Buddhism, declared: "If even the good are saved, how much more the wicked!"

The Sangha

Since, according to Mahayana Buddhism, each human person in his true, inner nature is identical with the eternal Buddha nature and has the power to realize this, this form of Buddhism breaks down the barrier between monks and laity, between men and women, and between social classes. It is a Buddhism for everybody. Although there are many orders of monks and priests in the Mahayana, the Sangha is not restricted to them, but includes all believers.

Buddhist festivals

The main festivals celebrated by Buddhists commemorate events in the life of the Buddha: his Birthday, Enlightenment Day, and Nirvana Day. Mahayanists celebrate these on three separate days. The Birthday of the Buddha is commemorated on April 8, known as Flower Day, because according to Mahayana tradition he was born on that date in a flower garden. The Buddha's enlightenment is celebrated on December 8, and his death and entry into Nirvana on February 15.

The Theravadins celebrate all three events on the one day, Full Moon Day, which occurs on the day of the full moon in the Indian month of Vaishakha (Hindi, Baisakh), around April–May in the Western calendar, since the Theravada tradition ascribes his birth to that day.

Buddhist Ethics

While Buddhism encourages many virtues, Buddhist ethics is guided above all by compassion for suffering. In our dealings with others, the indispensable minimum is not to use violence or cause suffering or harm to any living thing (*ahimsa*). As far as possible we should help and benefit others, showing love (*metta*) and goodwill towards all living things, joy (*mudita*) for those who are happy, and compassion (*karuna*) for all beings that suffer.

In a classic Buddhist scripture the Buddha advises a young man to show sacred respect in "six directions" – towards his parents, his teacher, his wife and children, his friends, his servants or employees, and monks – it being understood that these also have reciprocal responsibilities (*Digha-nikaya*).

Buddhism encourages people to strive within reasonable limits for happiness in this world. This includes such things as caring for the life of the mind, intellectually and culturally, having virtuous friends, practicing a profession well, improving one's economic condition, earning sufficient income and spending wisely. Buddhism takes a positive attitude towards economic development.

The most distinctive feature of Buddhist ethics is its rejection of the concept of justice. Buddhism is opposed to the punishment of crime, for the reason that punishment by its nature inflicts suffering. The attempt to eradicate crime through punishment is viewed as futile. This means that Buddhism essentially rejects law and government as these are customarily practiced, for they depend on the use or threat of justice and punishment. In the Buddhist view, crime should be remedied by remedying its causes, such as poverty. By the same token, Buddhism encourages respect for human rights but rejects the attempt to enforce them through the use of coercion.

A fortiori, Buddhism rejects the concept of a just war. No war is justified, even in self-defense, since war necessarily involves violence. A Buddhist authority writes that Buddhism "does not approve of any violence or destruction of life. According to Buddhism there is nothing that can be called a 'just war'. . . Who decides what is just or unjust? The mighty and victorious are 'just,' and the weak and defeated are 'unjust'" (W. Rahula.)

In practice, however, this reluctance to discriminate between just and unjust uses of force has sometimes led to acquiescence in both, and even to enthusiastic support for war. (See below, p. 276, for a further discussion of this in the context of East Asia.)

Modern Developments

The Buddhist world has been as yet little affected by the rise and success of science, with its emphasis on empirical verification. Many consider that Theravada Buddhism is in an especially advantageous position in this regard, since its analysis of the human mind and soul as a cluster of forces rather than a special substance is just what science would seem to suggest, though the same cannot be said for the belief in reincarnation.

Similarly, Buddhism has been little affected by the rise of democratic forms of government, since it is not tied to any particular governmental order. By the same token, however, nor does it seem to provide any particular intellectual support for democracy, since, as we have just seen, it rejects in principle the use of punishment, and therefore of coercion, law, justice, and government, as illegitimate. From this perspective it would seem that there is little to choose between one form of government and another.

In regard to capitalism and the market economy, Buddhism has traditionally favored economic development, as we have just seen, while discouraging materialism and greed.

Neo-Buddhism

In 1956, shortly before his death, the Indian social reformer B. R. Ambedkar, who had long championed the cause of the Untouchables (now called Dalits), and had built up a large following among them, announced his conversion to Buddhism, but to a form of Buddhism which rejects certain traditional beliefs such as reincarnation. Several million Dalits have followed him in this, largely as a protest against the inequalities of the Hindu class and caste system, and the name Neo-Buddhism has been given to this movement.

Summary of Buddhism

1 Buddhism exists in two very different forms: Theravada and Mahayana.

2 In Theravada Buddhism the Buddha is a teacher; his teaching is contained especially in the Four Noble Truths, the Eightfold Path, and the Ten Precepts.

3 Theravada Buddhism is a religion of self-liberation.

4 Theravada is predominantly monastic.

5 Mahayana Buddhism is open to all.

6 For the Mahayana the historical Buddha, Siddhartha Gautama, is a manifestation of the Eternal Buddha, whose nature is infinite compassion.

7 The compassion of the Eternal Buddha takes heroic form in the Bodhisattvas, who renounce Nirvana in order to help others, and by that renunciation enter Nirvana.

8 The eternal Buddha nature is the true identity of each living thing. It is the ultimate reality, in comparison with which the things of this world are mere appearances. The Buddha nature is characterized by Emptiness.

9 Mahayana Buddhism exists in two different but related forms, the meditational and the devotional.

10 Meditational Mahayana teaches that in our inmost being we are already identical with the Buddha nature, and therefore liberated from suffering, and we need only to realize the fact.

11 Devotional Mahayana seeks the aid of the Buddhas and Bodhisattvas in achieving liberation and in overcoming the trials of this life.

Questions for discussion

1 What considerations might incline you to accept the worldview of Theravada Buddhism as valid?

2 What considerations might incline you to reject it as mistaken?

3 Would you expect the doctrines of Theravada Buddhism to have any (a) social consequences, (b) political consequences, and (c) economic consequences?

4 Would you expect the doctrines of Mahayana Buddhism to have any (a) social consequences, (b) political consequences, and (c) economic consequences?

5 What similarities and dissimilarities do you see between the two kinds of Buddhism, on the one hand, and the religion of the Upanishads?

Test questions

1 Summarize the story of the Buddha's life.

2 What are the Four Noble Truths?

3 Explain the elements of the Eightfold Path.

4 What are the Ten Precepts?

5 Explain the doctrine of No Self.

6 What is a Bodhisattva?

7 Explain the relationship between Nirvana and Samsara for the Mahayana.

8 What is meant by the "Buddha nature"?

9 What is meant by "emptiness"?

Additional reading

Ch'en, Kenneth K. S., *Buddhism: The Light of Asia*, Woodbury, NY, Barron's Educational Series, 1968.

Conze, Edward, *Buddhism: Its Essence and Development*, New York, Harper & Row, 1959. One of many books on Buddhism by a recognized expert.

Coomaraswamy, A. K., *Buddha and the Gospel of Buddhism*, New York, Harper & Row, 1964 (1st pub. 1916). An older work but still useful.

Rahula, Walpola, *What the Buddha Taught*, New York, Grove Press, 1974 (1959). Probably the best current introduction to Theravada Buddhism, by one of its monks.

Schumann, Hans Wolfgang, *Buddhism*, Madras, Theosophical Publishing House, 1974.

Appendix to Buddhism

Readers of Buddhist literature may encounter references to the following:

The Five Eyes of the Buddha:
  The Physical Eye,
  The Heavenly Eye through Concentration,
  The Wisdom Eye,
  The Law Eye,
  The Buddha Eye.

The Six Supernatural Powers of the Buddha:
   Instantaneous view of all existence,
   Ability to hear sound everywhere,
   Ability to know other minds,
   Ability to know former existence,
   Ability to be everywhere and to do anything,
   Supernatural consciousness of the waning of defilements.

The Four Wisdoms of the Buddha:
   Magnificent Great Mirror Wisdom,
   Wisdom of Equanimity,
   Wisdom of Great Observation,
   Wisdom of All-accomplishment.

The Six Perfections:
   Charity, discipline, patience, effort, calmness, and wisdom.

The Ten Powers of the Buddha:
   The power to know what is right and wrong in every condition,
   to know the karma of all beings,
   to know all stages of concentration and liberation through wisdom,
   to know the faculties of all beings,
   to know the desires of all beings,
   to know the actual conditions of all beings,
   to know the directions and consequences of all laws,
   to know all causes of life and death and good and evil,
   to know the end of all beings,
   and to know the destruction of all delusions.

> (From William Theodore De Bary, Wing-tsit Chan,
> and Burton Watson, *Sources of Chinese Tradition*, vol. 1,
> New York, Columbia University Press, 1964, p. 357)

Buddhism: Texts

Theravada Buddhism

The sermon at Benares

This is the classic statement of the Four Noble Truths and the Eight-fold Path. It culminates in the Buddha's exultant cry: "This is my last existence; now there is no rebirth!" In addition, it also states the doctrine of impermanence: whatever comes into existence must eventually go out of existence.

The many repetitions in these documents were probably a device to aid memory.

The gods Buddhists do not necessarily disbelieve in gods, but they also have no special respect for them. In Buddhism, it is no great thing to be a god. The gods are more powerful than human beings, and sometimes they can be of help, as they helped Siddhartha, but they are also less enlightened, because they do not possess the teachings of the Buddha. To be reborn as a god is a sign that one has not yet achieved Enlightenment.

Thus have I heard: at one time the Lord dwelt at Benares at Isipatana in the Deer Park. There the Lord addressed the five monks: "These two extremes are not to be practiced by one who has gone forth from the world. What are the two? That conjoined with the passions and luxury, low, vulgar, common, ignoble, and useless; and that conjoined with self-torture, painful, ignoble, and useless. Avoiding these two extremes the Tathagata has gained the enlightenment of the Middle Path, which produces insight and knowledge, and tends to calm, to higher knowledge, enlightenment, Nirvana.

"And what is the Middle Path, of which the Tathagata has gained enlightenment, which produces insight and knowledge, and tends to calm, to higher knowledge, enlightenment, Nirvana? This is the noble Eightfold Way: namely, right view, right thought, right speech, right action, right livelihood, right effort, right mindfulness, right concentration. This is the Middle Path, of which the Tathagata has gained enlightenment, which produces insight and knowledge, and tends to calm, to higher knowledge, enlightenment, Nirvana.

"(1) Now this is the noble truth of pain: birth is painful, old age is painful, sickness is painful, death is painful, sorrow, lamentation, dejection, and despair are painful. Contact with unpleasant things is painful, not getting what one wishes is painful. In short the five groups of grasping are painful.

"(2) Now this, monks, is the noble truth of the cause of pain: the craving, which tends to rebirth, combined with pleasure and lust, finding pleasure here and there; namely, the craving for passion, the craving for existence, the craving for non-existence.

"(3) Now this, monks, is the noble truth of the cessation of pain, the cessation without a remainder of craving, the abandonment, forsaking, release, non-attachment.

"(4) Now this, monks, is the noble truth of the way that leads to the cessation of pain: this is the noble Eightfold Way; namely, right views, right intention, right speech, right action, right livelihood, right effort, right mindfulness, right concentration.

"'This is the noble truth of pain': Thus, monks, among doctrines unheard before, in me sight and knowledge arose, wisdom arose, knowledge arose, light arose.

"'This noble truth of pain must be comprehended.' Thus, monks, among doctrines unheard before, in me sight and knowledge arose, wisdom arose, knowledge arose, light arose.

"'It has been comprehended.' Thus, monks, among doctrines unheard before, in me sight and knowledge arose, wisdom arose, knowledge arose, light arose. [Repeated for the second truth, with the statement that the cause of pain must be abandoned and has been abandoned, for the third truth that the cessation of pain must be realized and has been realized, and for the fourth that the Way must be practiced and has been practiced.]

"As long as in these four noble truths my due knowledge and insight with the three sections and twelve divisions was not well purified, even so long, monks, in the world with its gods, Mara, Brahma, its beings with ascetics, brahmins, gods, and men, I had not attained the highest complete enlightenment. This I recognized.

"And when, monks, in these four noble truths my due knowledge and insight with its three sections and twelve divisions was well purified, then monks . . . I had attained the highest complete enlightenment. This I recognized. Knowledge arose in me, insight arose that the release of my mind is unshakeable: this is my last existence; now there is no rebirth."

Thus spoke the Lord, and the five monks expressed delight and approval at the Lord's utterance. And while this exposition was being uttered there arose in the elder Kondanna the pure and spotless eye of the doctrine that whatever was liable to origination was all liable to cessation.

(E. J. Thomas, *Early Buddhist Scriptures*, London,
Routledge & Kegan Paul, 1913)

Questions for discussion

1   What is meant by saying that suffering is caused by thirst or craving?

2   Why does the Buddha's sermon on the Four Noble Truths lead Kondanna to see the truth of impermanence, that whatever is liable to origination is all liable to cessation?

The simile of the chariot

> This famous passage from *The Questions of King Menander* illustrates the Theravadin Buddhist view that we possess no substantial identity, but are only temporary conglomerations of elements. The King raises the powerful objection that if that were the case, nobody would be responsible for his actions, since there would be no center to which personal responsibility could be attributed. In reply Nagasena says in effect that nonetheless his doctrine is correct. Just as a chariot is not a substance, but merely an assemblage of parts, so also, he maintains, are we.
>
> Menander was a Greek, ruler of a Greek kingdom set up by Alexander the Great in the northwest of India. Some scholars have thought that this dialogue shows traces of the influence of Plato.

Then King Menander went up to the Venerable Nagasena, greeted him respectfully, and sat down. Nagasena replied to the greeting, and the King was pleased at heart. Then King Menander asked: "How is your reverence known, and what is your name?"

"I'm known as Nagasena, your Majesty, that's what my fellow monks call me. But though my parents may have given me such a name . . . it's only a generally understood term, a practical designation. There is no question of a permanent individual implied in the use of the word."

"Listen, you five hundred Greeks and eighty thousand monks!" said King Menander. "This Nagasena has just declared that there's no permanent individuality implied in his name!" Then, turning to Nagasena, "If, Reverend Nagasena, there is no permanent individuality, who gives you monks your robes and food, lodging and medicines? And who makes use of them? Who lives a life of right-eousness, meditates, and reaches Nirvana? Who destroys living beings, steals, fornicates, tells lies, or drinks spirits? . . . If what you say is true, there's neither merit nor demerit, and no fruit or result of good or evil deeds. If someone were to kill you there would be no question of murder. And there would be no masters or teachers in the (Buddhist) Order and no ordinations. If your fellow monks call you Nagasena, what then is Nagasena? Would you say that your hair is Nagasena?"

"No, your Majesty."

"Or your nails, teeth, skin, or other parts of your body, or the outward form, or sensation, or perception, or the psychic constructions, or consciousness? Are any of these Nagasena?"

"No, your Majesty."

"Then are all these taken together Nagasena?"

"No, your Majesty."

"Or anything other than they?"

"No, your Majesty."

"Then for all my asking I find no Nagasena. Nagasena is a mere sound! Surely what your Reverence has said is false!"

Then the Venerable Nagasena addressed the King.

"Your Majesty, how did you come here – on foot, or in a vehicle?"

"In a chariot."

"Then tell me what is the chariot? Is the pole the chariot?"

"No, your Reverence."

"Or the axle, wheels, frame, reins, yoke, spokes, or goad?"

"None of these things is the chariot."

"Then all the separate parts taken together are the chariot?"

"No, your Reverence."

"Then is the chariot something other than the separate parts?"

"No, your Reverence."

"Then for all my asking, your Majesty, I can find no chariot. The chariot is a mere sound. What then is the chariot? Surely what your Majesty has said is false! There is no chariot! . . ."

When he had spoken, the five hundred Greeks cried "Well done!" and said to the King, "Now, your Majesty, get out of that dilemma if you can!"

"What I said was not false," replied the King. "It's on account of all these various components, the pole, axle, wheels, and so on, that the vehicle is called a chariot. It's just a generally understood term, a practical designation."

"Well said, your Majesty! You know what the word 'chariot' means! And it's just the same with me. It's on account of the various components of my being that I'm known by the generally understood term, the practical designation Nagasena."

(W. T. De Bary et al. (eds), *Sources of Indian Tradition*, Vol. I,
New York, Columbia University Press, 1970)

Question for discussion

1 Can Nagasena's view of human identity be reconciled with the King's concerns for moral responsibility?

Where is the Buddha? Or, what is Nirvana?

> This passage contains the well-known Buddhist fourfold negation. A person who has attained Nirvana neither exists, nor does not exist, nor does he both exist and not exist, nor does he neither exist nor not exist. Although this rules out all the logical possibilities, it is implied that it does not exhaust the actual possibilities.
>
> The term Dhamma (Pali), or Dharma (Sanskrit), is used in Buddhism for the teaching of the Buddha.

"If a fire were blazing in front of you, Vaccha, would you know that it was?"

"Yes, good Gotama."

"And would you know the reason for its blazing?"

"Yes, because it had a supply of grass and sticks."

"And would you know if it were to be put out?"

"Yes, good Gotama."

"And on its being put out, would you know the direction the fire had gone to from here – east, west, north, south?"

"This question does not apply, good Gotama. For the fire blazed because it had a supply of grass and sticks; but when it had consumed this and had no other fuel, then, being without fuel, it is reckoned as gone out."

"Even so, Vaccha, that material shape, that feeling, perception, those impulses, that consciousness by which one, in defining the Tathagata,* might define him – all have been got rid of by the Tathagata, cut off at the root, made like a palm-tree stump that can come to no further existence in the future. Freed from reckoning by material shape, feeling, perception, the impulses, consciousness, is the Tathagata; he is deep, immeasurable, unfathomable, as is the great ocean. 'Arises' does not apply, nor does 'does not arise,' nor 'both arises and does not arise', nor 'neither arises nor does not arise'."

(*Majjhima-nikaya*, I, 487–8, in Edward Conze (ed.), *Buddhist Texts through the Ages*, Harper Torchbooks, 1964, p. 106)

---

* *Tathagata* is a somewhat mysterious term the Buddha uses in referring to himself and other Buddhas. It means, literally, "the Thus-come," and is sometimes translated as "the one who has come to the truth."

Since a Tathagata, even when actually present, is incomprehensible, it is inept to say of him – of the Uttermost Person, the Supernal Person, the Attainer of the Supernal – that after dying the Tathagata is, or is not, or both is and is not, or neither is nor is not . . .

(*Samyutta-Nikaya*, III, 118, in Conze (ed.), *Buddhist Texts*, p. 106)

The king said: "Did you, revered Nagasena, see the Buddha?"

"No, sire."

"Then did your teachers see the Buddha?"

"No, sire."

"Well, then, Nagasena, there is not a Buddha."

"But have you, sire, seen the Himalayan river Uha?"

"No, sir."

"Then did your father ever see it?"

"No, sir."

"Well then, sire, there is not a river Uha."

"There is, sir. Even if neither my father nor I have seen it, there is the river Uha all the same."

"Even so, sire, even if neither my teachers nor I have seen the Lord, there is the Lord all the same."

"Very good, Nagasena. But is the Buddha pre-eminent?"

"Yes, sire."

"But how do you know, Nagasena, when you have not seen him in the past, that the Buddha is pre-eminent?"

"What do you think about this, sire? Could those who have not already seen the great ocean know that it is so mighty, deep, immeasurable, unfathomable, that although these five great rivers – the Ganges, Jumna, Aciravati, Sarabhu, and the Mahi – flow into it constantly and continually, yet is neither its emptiness nor its fullness affected thereby?"

"Yes, they could know that."

"Even so, sire, having seen great disciples who have attained Nirvana, I know that the Lord is pre-eminent."

"Very good. Is it then possible to know this?"

"Once upon a time, sire, the Elder named Tissa was a teacher of writing. Many years have passed since he died. How is it that he is known?"

"By his writing."

"Even so, sire, he who sees Dhamma sees the Lord; for Dhamma, sire, was taught by the Lord."

"Very good, Nagasena. Have you seen Dhamma?"

"Sire, disciples are to conduct themselves for as long as life lasts with the Buddha as guide, with the Buddha as designation."

"Very good, Nagasena. But is there a Buddha?"

"Yes, sire, there is a Buddha."

"But is it possible, Nagasena, to point to the Buddha as being either here or there?"

"Sire, the Lord has attained Nirvana in the Nirvana-element that has no groups of existence still remaining. It is not possible to point to the Lord as being either here or there."

"Make a simile."

"What do you think about this, sire? When some flame in a great burning mass of fire goes out, is it possible to point to the flame as being either here or there?"

"No, sir. That flame has ceased to be, it has disappeared."

"Even so, sire, the Lord has attained Nirvana in the Nirvana-element that has no groups of existence still remaining. The Lord has gone home. It is not possible to point to him as being here or there. But it is possible, sire, to point to the Lord by means of the Dhamma-body; for Dhamma, sire, was taught by the Lord."

"Very good, Nagasena."

(*Questions of King Menander*, in E. Conze (ed.), *Buddhist Texts through the Ages*, New York, Philosophical Library, 1954, pp. 106–7, 113, 119)

Question for discussion

1   If it is inappropriate to say that the Buddha after death is, or that he is not, or that he both is and is not, or that he neither is nor is not, how are we to think of him?

Mahayana Buddhism

The Bodhisattva's vow of universal redemption

The first part of this passage argues that a truly noble person is not concerned merely for himself, but also for others, and therefore would never be content to enter Nirvana by himself, but would spare no effort to share its blessings with others. This is a criticism of the Theravadin ideal, which it designates as the Pratyeka-buddha or solitary Buddha.

The second part contains the celebrated vow of the Bodhisattva to redeem all beings by taking on himself their suffering.

THE LORD: "What do you think, Sariputra, does it occur to any of the Disciples and Pratyeka-buddhas to think that 'after we have known full enlightenment, we should lead all beings to Nirvana, into the realm of Nirvana which leaves nothing behind'?"

SARIPUTRA: "No indeed, O Lord."

THE LORD: "One should therefore know that this wisdom of the Disciples and Pratyeka-buddhas bears no comparison with the wisdom of a Bodhisattva. What do you think, Sariputra, does it occur to any of the Disciples and Pratyeka-buddhas that 'after I have practiced the six perfections, have brought beings to maturity, have purified the Buddhafield, have fully gained the ten powers of a Tathagata, his four grounds of self-confidence, the four analytical knowledges and the eighteen special dharmas of a Buddha, after I have known full enlightenment, I shall lead countless beings to Nirvana'?"

SARIPUTRA: "No, O Lord."

THE LORD: "But such are the intentions of a Bodhisattva. A glowworm, or some other luminous animal, does not think that its light could illuminate the Continent of Jambudvipa [a name for India], or radiate over it. Just so, the Disciples and Pratyeka-buddhas do not think that they should, after winning full enlightenment, lead all beings to Nirvana. But the sun, when it has risen, radiates its light over the whole of Jambudvipa. Just so a Bodhisattva, after he has accomplished the practices which lead to the full enlightenment of Buddhahood, leads countless beings to Nirvana."

(Conze (ed.), *Buddhist Texts*, p. 119)

THE LORD: "Suppose, Subhuti, that there was a most excellent hero, very vigorous, of high social position, handsome, attractive and most fair to behold, of many virtues, in possession of all the finest virtues, of those virtues which spring from the very height of sovereignty, morality, learning, renunciation, and so on. He is judicious, able to express himself, to formulate his views clearly, to substantiate his claims; one who always knows the suitable time, place, and situation for everything. In archery he has gone as far as one can go, he is successful in warding off all manner of attack, most skilled in all arts, and foremost, through his fine achievements, in all crafts . . . He is versed in all the treatises, has many friends, is wealthy, strong of body, with large limbs, with all his faculties complete, generous to all, dear and pleasant to many. Any work he might undertake he manages to complete, he speaks methodically, shares his great riches with the many, honors what should be honored, reveres what should be revered, worships what should be worshipped. Would such a person, Subhuti, feel ever-increasing joy and zest?"

SUBHUTI: "He would, O Lord."

THE LORD: "Now suppose, further, that this person, so greatly accomplished, should have taken his family with him on a journey, his mother and father, his sons and daughters. By some circumstance they find themselves in a great, wild forest. The foolish ones among them would feel fright, terror, and hair-raising fear. He, however, would fearlessly say to his family: 'Do not be afraid! I shall soon take you safely and securely out of this terrible and frightening forest. I shall soon set you free!' If then more and more hostile and inimical forces should rise up against him in that forest, would this heroic man decide to abandon his family, and to take himself alone out of that terrible and frightening

94

forest – he who is not one to draw back, who is endowed with all the force of firmness and vigor, who is wise, exceedingly tender and compassionate, courageous and a master of many resources?"

SUBHUTI: "No, O Lord. For that person, who does not abandon his family, has at his disposal powerful resources, both within and without. On his side forces will arise in that wild forest which are quite a match for the hostile and inimical forces, and they will stand up for him and protect him. Those enemies and adversaries of his, who look for a weak spot, who seek for a weak spot, will not gain any hold over him. He is competent to deal with the situation, and is able, unhurt and uninjured, soon to take out of that forest both his family and himself, and securely and safely will they reach a village, city, or market town."

THE LORD: "Just so, Subhuti, is it with a Bodhisattva who is full of pity and concerned with the welfare of all beings, who dwells in friendliness, compassion, sympathetic joy, and evenmindedness."

(Conze (ed.), *Buddhist Texts*, pp. 128–9)

"Although the son of Jina has penetrated to this immutable true nature of dharmas, yet he appears like one of those who are blinded by ignorance, subject as he is to birth, and so on. That is truly wonderful. It is through his compassionate skill in means for others that he is tied to the world, and that, though he has attained the state of a saint, yet he appears to be in the state of an ordinary person. He has gone beyond all that is worldly, yet he has not moved out of the world; in the world he pursues his course for the world's weal, unstained by worldly taints.

"As a lotus flower, though it grows in water, is not polluted by the water, so he, though born in the world, is not polluted by worldly dharmas. Like a fire, his mind constantly blazes up into good works for others; at the same time he always remains merged in the calm of the trances and formless attainments.

"Through the power of his previous penetration (into reality), and because he has left all discrimination behind, he again exerts no effort when he brings living things to maturity. He knows exactly who is to be educated, how, and by what means, whether by his teaching, his physical appearance, his practices, or his bearing. Without turning towards anything, always unobstructed in his wisdom, he goes along, in the world of living beings, boundless as space, acting for the weal of beings.

"When a Bodhisattva has reached this position, he is like the Tathagatas, insofar as he is in the world for the sake of saving beings. But as a grain of sand compares with the earth, or a puddle in a cow's footprint with the ocean, so great still is the distance of the Bodhisattvas from the Buddha."

(Conze (ed.), *Buddhist Texts*, pp. 130–1)

A Bodhisattva resolves: I take upon myself the burden of all suffering, I am resolved to do so, I will endure it. I do not turn or run away, do not tremble, am not terrified, nor afraid, do not turn back or despond.

And why? At all costs I must bear the burdens of all beings. In that I do not follow my own inclinations. I have made the vow to save all beings. All beings I must set free. The whole world of living beings I must rescue, from the terrors of birth, of old age, of sickness, of death and rebirth, of all kinds of moral offense, of all states of woe, of the whole cycle of birth and death, of the jungle of false views, of the loss of wholesome dharmas, of the concomitants of ignorance – from all these terrors I must rescue all beings . . .

I walk so that the kingdom of unsurpassed cognition is built up for all beings. My endeavors do not merely aim at my own deliverance. For with the help of the boat of the thought of all-knowledge, I must rescue all these beings from the stream of Samsara, which is so difficult to cross; I must pull them back from the great precipice, I must free them from all calamities, I must ferry them across the stream of Samsara. I myself must grapple with the whole mass of suffering of all beings. To the limit of my endurance I will experience in all the states of woe, found in any world system, all the abodes of suffering. And I must not cheat all beings out of my store of merit. I am resolved to abide in each single state of woe for numberless aeons; and so I will help all beings to freedom, in all the states of woe that may be found in any world system whatsoever.

And why? Because it is surely better that I alone should be in pain than that all these beings should fall into the states of woe. There I must give myself away as a pawn through which the whole world is redeemed from the terrors of the hells, of animal birth, of the world of Yama; and with this my own body I must experience, for the sake of all beings, the whole mass of all painful feelings. And on behalf of all beings I give surety for all beings, and in doing so I speak truthfully, am trustworthy, and do not go back on my word. I must not abandon all beings.

And why? There has arisen in me the will to win all knowledge, with all beings for its object, that is to say, for the purpose of setting free the entire world of beings. And I have not set out for the supreme enlightenment from a desire for delights, not because I hope to experience the delights of the five sensualities, or because I wish to indulge in the pleasures of the senses. And I do not pursue the course of a Bodhisattva in order to achieve the array of delights that can be found in the various worlds of sense desire.

And why? Truly no delights are all these delights of the world. All this indulging in the pleasures of the senses belongs to the sphere of Mara [the evil spirit; see above, p. 60].

(Conze (ed.), *Buddhist Texts*, pp. 131–2)

Question for discussion

1   What is the relationship between the Bodhisattva and the Buddha?

The parable of the lost son

If the Mahayana is correct, with its exalted conception of the true nature of every being as nothing less than the infinite and eternal Buddha nature, how do we account for the fact that the historical Buddha taught the contrary doctrines of Impermanence and No Self?

The Mahayana response is that these doctrines were a necessary but temporary subterfuge on the part of the Buddha, because his first hearers were not capable of absorbing the lofty truth of their own dignity. The Buddha had at first to conceal from them their true nature, out of compassion, and he allowed them to know the full truth only when they were ready to receive it. This is expressed in the following parable, which bears a striking resemblance to the New Testament story of the Prodigal Son. Like that story, it highlights the compassion of the father, who in this case is the Buddha. It reaches its climax in the statement that "We are all as the Buddha's sons . . . and such things as Buddha-sons should obtain, we have all obtained."

A man parted from his father and went to another city; and he dwelt there many years . . . The father grew rich and the son poor. While the son wandered in all directions [begging] in order to get food and clothes, the father moved to another land, where he lived in great luxury . . . wealthy from business, money-lending, and trade. In the course of time the son, wandering in search of his living through town and country, came to the city in which his father dwelt. Now the poor man's father . . . forever thought of the son whom he had lost . . . years ago, but he told no one of this, though he grieved inwardly, and thought: "I am old, and well advanced in years, and though I have great possessions I have no son. Alas that time should do its work upon me, and that all this wealth should perish unused . . . It would be bliss indeed if my son might enjoy all my wealth!"

Then the poor man, in search of food and clothing, came to the rich man's home. And the rich man was sitting in great pomp at the gate of his house, surrounded by a large throng of attendants, . . . on a splendid throne, with a footstool inlaid with gold and silver, under a wide awning decked with pearls and flowers and adorned with hanging garlands of jewels; and he transacted business to the value of millions of gold pieces, all the while fanned by a fly whisk . . . When he saw him the poor man was terrified . . . and the hair of his body stood on end, for he thought that he had happened on a king or on some high officer of state, and had no business there. "I must go," he thought, "to the poor quarter of the town, where I'll get food and clothing without trouble. If I stop here he'll seize me and set me to do forced labor, or some other disaster will befall me!" So he quickly ran away . . .

But the rich man . . . recognized his son as soon as he saw him; and he was full of joy . . . and thought: "This is wonderful! I have found him who shall enjoy my riches. He of whom I thought constantly has come back, now that I am old and full of years!" Then, longing for his son, he sent swift messengers, telling them to go and fetch him quickly. They ran at full speed and overtook him; the poor man trembled with fear, the hair of his body stood on end . . . and he uttered a cry of distress and exclaimed, "I've done you no wrong!" But they dragged him along by force . . . until . . . fearful that he would be killed or beaten, he fainted and fell on the ground. His father in dismay said to the men, "Don't drag him along in that way!" and, without saying more, he sprinkled his face with cold water – for though he knew that the poor man was his son, he realized that his estate was very humble, while his own was very high.

So the householder told no one that the poor man was his son. He ordered one of his servants to tell the poor man that he was free to go where he chose . . . And the poor man was amazed [that he was allowed to go free], and he went off to the poor quarter of the town in search of food and clothing. Now in order to attract him back the rich man made use of the virtue of "skill in means." He called two men of low caste and of no great dignity and told them: "Go to that poor man . . . and hire him in your own names to do work in my house at double the normal daily wage; and if he asks what work he has to do tell him that he has to help clear away the refuse dump." So these two men and the poor man cleared the refuse every day . . . in the house of the rich man, and lived in a straw hut nearby . . . And the rich man saw through a window his son clearing refuse, and was again filled with compassion. So he came down, took off his wealth and jewels and rich clothes, put on dirty garments, covered his body with dust, and, taking a basket in his hand, went up to his son. And he greeted him at a distance and said, "Take this basket and clear away the dust at once!" By this means he managed to speak to his son. [And as time went on he spoke more often to him, and thus he gradually encouraged him. First he urged him to] remain in his service and not take another job, offering him double wages, together with any small extras that he might require, such as the price of a cooking-pot . . . or food and clothes. Then he offered him his own cloak, if he should want it . . . And at last he said: "You must be cheerful, my good fellow, and think of me as a father . . . for I'm older than you and you've done me good service in clearing away my refuse. As long as you've worked for me you've shown no roguery or guile . . . I've not noticed one of the vices in you that I've noticed in my other servants! From now on you are like my own son to me!"

Thenceforward the householder called the poor man "son," and the latter felt towards the householder as a son feels towards his father. So the householder, full of longing and love for his son, employed him in clearing away refuse for twenty years. By the end of that time the poor man felt quite at home in the house, and came and went as he chose, though he still lived in the straw hut.

Then the householder fell ill, and felt that the hour of his death was near. So he said to the poor man: "Come, my dear man! I have great riches . . . and am very sick. I need someone upon whom I can bestow my wealth as a deposit, and you must accept it. From now on you are just as much its owner as I am, but you must not squander it." And the poor man accepted the rich man's wealth . . . but personally he cared nothing for it, and asked for no share of it, not even the price of a measure of flour. He still lived in the straw hut, and thought of himself as just as poor as before.

Thus the householder proved that his son was frugal, mature, and mentally developed, and that though he knew that he was now wealthy he still remembered his past poverty, and was still . . . humble and meek . . . So he sent for the poor man again, presented him before a gathering of his relatives, and, in the presence of the king, his officers, and the people of town and country, he said: "Listen, gentlemen! This is my son, whom I begot . . . To him I leave all my family revenues, and my private wealth he shall have as his own."

(W. T. De Bary et al. (eds), *Sources of Indian Tradition*,
Vol. I, pp. 163–6)

When the poor son heard these words of his father, great was his joy at such unexpected news, and he thought: "Without any mind for, or effort on my part, these treasures now come of themselves to me" . . .

The very rich elder is the Tathagata, and we are all as the Buddha's sons. The Tathagata has always declared that we are his sons . . . Because of the three sufferings, in the midst of births and deaths we have borne all kinds of torments, being deluded and ignorant and enjoying our attachment to trifles. Today the World-honoured One has caused us to ponder over and remove the dirt of all diverting discussions of inferior things. In these we have hitherto been diligent to make progress, and have got, as it were, a day's pay for our effort to reach Nirvana. Obtaining this, we greatly rejoiced and were contented, saying to ourselves: "For our diligence and progress in the Buddha-law, what we have received is ample." But the World-honoured One, knowing beforehand that our minds were attached to low desires and took delight in inferior things, let us go our own way, and did not discriminate for us, saying: "You shall yet have possession of the treasure of Tathagata-knowledge" . . . The Buddha, knowing that our minds delighted in inferior things, by his tactfulness taught according to our capacity, but still we did not perceive that we were really Buddha-sons . . . From of old we are really sons of Buddha, but have only taken pleasure in minor matters . . . But now the Great Treasure of the King of the Law has of itself come to us, and such things as Buddha-sons should obtain, we have all obtained.

(*The Lotus of the Good Law*, trans. William Theodore De Bary and
W. E. Soothill, in E. A. Burtt, *Teachings of the Compassionate Buddha*,
New York, New American Library, 1982, pp. 150, 162)

Question for discussion

1   How does this story illustrate the distinctive teachings of the Mahayana?

3

Sikhism

The Spirit of Sikhism

There is One Being

Truth by Name

Primal Creator

Without fear

Without enmity

Timeless in form

Unborn

Self-existent

The grace of the Guru.

MEDITATE

Truth before time

Truth throughout time

Truth here and now

Says Nanak, Truth is evermore.

(Morning prayer, *Jap*, Adi Granth)

The Sikh View of Life

The supreme reality is the one, eternal, all-pervading God. Men are separated from God by their self-love, which casts them into rebirth after rebirth. By overcoming their self-love and loving God they are liberated from the cycle of rebirth and are united with God.

100

The Sikh religion grew out of devotional (bhakti) Hinduism (see above, p. 35), with its emphasis on personal love for the divine, retaining the Hindu belief in reincarnation and liberation, but, perhaps as a result of influence from Islam, rejecting the many gods of Hindu polytheism with their myths, and also rejecting the inequalities of the Hindu caste system. In place of these Sikhism teaches the oneness of God and also the oneness of humanity.

At the same time Sikhism rejects what it considers the legalism and violence of Islam. Its message is one of intense personal love for God.

Guru Nanak

Sikhism was established in the Punjab region of northern India during the fifteenth and sixteenth centuries AD, when most of India was governed by Muslim rulers, the Mughals, or Moguls. Although they constituted the ruling class, the Muslims were a minority among the Hindu population. Despite the deep differences between the overall traditions of Hinduism and Islam – Islam rejecting both the numerous gods of Hinduism and also its caste system as well as its belief in reincarnation – there were nonetheless certain forms of each religion that shared some similarities: both devotional or bhakti Hinduism, on the one hand, and Sufism on the other (see below, p. 280), emphasized a personal, devotional love of God. A number of religious movements and leaders emerged during this period who placed devotional love of God at the center of their lives, and it is largely out of this movement, sometimes called the sant tradition, that Sikhism developed.

Its founder was Nanak. He was born in 1469 into an orthodox Hindu family, but appears at an early age to have begun to question both the multitude of Hindu gods and the caste system. When he was 30 years old, Nanak went to the river as usual one day to make his morning prayers (a common Hindu custom) but did not return. Since his clothes were discovered near the river, it was assumed that he had drowned, and the river was dragged to find his body, without success. Three days later he reappeared, saying nothing. The next day he made the famous utterance, "There is neither Hindu nor Muslim; so whose path shall I follow? I shall follow God's path. God is neither Hindu nor Muslim, and the path I follow is God's."

This event seems to have marked a turning point in his life. After it he became acknowledged as a *Guru* (originally a Sanskrit word meaning "weight," and then a weighty person, an authority), and gave up the observance of Hindu caste practices, which otherwise play such a ubiquitous role in Indian life. He set out with a Muslim companion and musician, Mardana, on travels across India to preach his message.

The Message of Nanak

God

The central theme of Nanak's message is God and union with God.

> What terrible separation it is to be separated from God and what blissful union to be united with Him.
>
> (*Maru* 1, Adi Granth, p. 989)

The God of whom Nanak speaks is, first, a single God, one only, "and there is no other." He is self-existent and eternal, and cannot be grasped in human language or measured by human concepts. He is supremely good. He is a personal God, who bends towards man in grace, and to whom man's response must be love. God is the creator of the world and his being pervades the world. He is the creator of man and he dwells within man's being. Not only has he made everything that is, but he sustains it in existence at every moment of time and watches over it.

The bhakti Hinduism practiced in Nanak's environment focused on devotion to the God Vishnu and his avatars or incarnational figures, Rama and Krishna.* As we have seen above (p. 25), Hindu theory considers these figures as aspects of *saguna* Brahman, "Brahman with attributes", Brahman considered as if possessing particular qualities, especially personhood, so that prayer, worship, and love for the divine become possible. The real Brahman, however, so to speak, remains *nirguna* Brahman, "Brahman without attributes", the supreme reality which transcends all particular qualities, and so transcends personhood. It does not make sense to pray to nirguna Brahman or worship It or love It.

In place of this conception of an ultimate reality which is not personal, but treated in the imagination as if it were, Nanak teaches that the ultimate divine reality itself is fully personal, and that there is only the one divine person, who is supremely good, who has created and sustains the world, and whom it is right to pray to, worship, and above all love. This conception of God is very similar to that in the religions of Semitic origin (see below, p. 221), which has led many scholars to believe that Nanak must have been influenced by the Islam of the Mughal ruling class.

Nanak's God is both immanent and transcendent. He is immanent in the world and in man, so that he exists and reveals himself and can be reached everywhere in his creation. "Wherever I look, there Thou art." At the same time he infinitely transcends and surpasses his creation; the world gives us no more than a glimpse of his true glory. In himself he is beyond all forms, all limits, He is the Formless One. "Thou hast thousands of forms and yet no form."

For Nanak, the most natural expression of religious feeling is the hymn of praise to the unimaginable greatness of God.

---

* The term *Vaishnava*, from Vishnu, is applied to this form of Hinduism.

God reveals himself to man within the human heart, in the depths of the soul. This revelation Nanak terms "the Word" (*Sabad*). If man responds to this Word through love, he becomes one with God. Nanak uses several other terms with largely similar meanings: God is "the Name" (*Nam*), and the Truth (*Sach*). As the source of the True Word, God is the chief of all Gurus, the *Satguru*.

God also reveals himself by his Will (*Hukam*), which creates the world, not only the physical universe but also the moral order. "By Thy Will Thou didst create all forms." God's Will creates the law of karma, according to which those who die separated from God are destined to return to this life, but those who die united with God are taken up into the reality of God and released from the cycle of rebirths.

Union with God in love and release from the cycle of rebirths does not occur without man's will, which must therefore be free. But the larger role is played by God's grace (*Nadar*), which takes the initiative and reaches out to man.

Man

The natural condition of man as he is born into the world is one of self-centeredness and self-love, summed up in the term *haumai*. In this condition man exists in "duality": he is separated from God, and is a victim of maya, the delusion that the world is what is truly important and real (see above, pp. 15, 26).* As long as he continues in this state, man experiences rebirth after rebirth. The remedy for haumai is absorption in the love of God.

Religion

True religion for Nanak is the interior religion of the heart. It consists in one thing only, a deep, intense, personal love of God. This is achieved by meditation on the goodness and greatness of God.

The religion practiced in Nanak's environment appears to have been largely a matter of external observances, such as those imposed by the Hindu class and caste system.** These practices are very numerous and affect almost everything in the daily life of an observant Hindu, governing the food he can eat, whom he can marry, and how he can earn a living. They are important in Hinduism because they mark off one class and caste from another, and the class and caste one is born into represent a divine judgement on one's previous life, the immediate goal of the practice of religion being to move up to a higher level in one's next life.

Nanak, however, rejects the religion of external practices, and with it the entire Hindu caste and class system. "Caste and status are futile, for the One

---

*   In Nanak's usage maya does not have quite as strong a sense of cosmic illusion as in Hinduism, and is perhaps better translated as delusion.
** An exception to this statement must be made for the Vaishnava bhakti and the Sufi and sant traditions, which are, however, all few in numbers.

watches over all." Caste practices as mere superstition and a distraction from the true religious life of love for God. This and this alone is what enables a person to make spiritual progress from one life to the next.

Similarly, Nanak rejects ascetic practices, such as abandoning the world to live the life of a hermit or a mendicant monk. "He who eats what he has earned by his own labour and gives some (to others) – Nanak, he it is who knows the true way" (Adi Granth, p. 1245, in McLeod, *Guru Nanak*).

Nanak sometimes makes fun of Hindu ceremonies. For example, the story is told of how, one day, he came across Brahmins throwing water eastwards towards the rising sun as a form of worship on behalf of ancestors (pitra puja); he then began to throw water towards the west. When they asked him why he did this, he answered, "If your water can reach your ancestors, I am sure mine can reach my fields near Lahore which is barely a stone's throw from here!" (Cole and Sambhi, *The Sikhs*, p. 12).

In place of the divisions of Hindu society into class and caste, which were dominated by the power and prestige of the Brahmins, Nanak preached the oneness of mankind in the sight of God. As a powerful symbol of this oneness, he instituted the practice of the "Common Kitchen," the *langar*. Of all the traditional Hindu caste regulations, the ones regarding the preparation and eating of food were among the most divisive. Nanak laid down that after worship a common meal should always be served for all those taking part, which compels them to put aside all caste differences. The meal is an integral part of the service.

The Sikh community

Human beings, enmeshed in self-love, need the guidance and example of a Guru to lead them to the experience of God. The Guru is the leader of the Sikh community. He is the bearer of the Word. The chief Guru is God, the Satguru. The word "Sikh" means disciple or follower, namely of the Guru, and especially of the Satguru.

> The Guru is the ladder, the dinghy, the raft by means of which one reaches God.
> Without the Guru there can be no bhakti, no love . . .
> Without the Guru one blindly engages in futile endeavour;
> But with the Guru one is purified, for one's filth is purged by the Word.

Nanak died in 1539. Shortly before his death he installed an ardent follower, Lehna, as the second Guru, changing his name to Angad (a "limb" or part of Nanak's body).

Guru Gobind Singh (b. 1666, Guru 1675–1708)

The movement created by Nanak had not only religious but also political significance. Nanak spoke and wrote in the Punjabi language, and gave the people of the Punjab a voice, which became a voice for political independence from the Muslim Mughal government ruling northern India. The Mughal rulers responded with severe repression, which led the Sikh community to form an army to defend itself. These developments reached a peak under the tenth and last Guru, Gobind Singh.

In 1699 Guru Gobind created within the Sikh community a special group or order known as the *Khalsa*, or Pure. These were to be Sikhs absolutely devoted to their cause, willing to lead the Sikh life in the fullest way and to shed their blood for their religion. He inaugurated the order in a dramatic scene. Before the public assembly, standing in front of his tent, he asked for men to come forward who would give him their heads. The request was greeted with stunned silence. Eventually one man came forward and went with the Guru into his tent. The Guru emerged with a blood-stained sword. Four more men volunteered themselves and also went into the tent, and three more times the Guru emerged with blood on his sword. But the last time he came out with all five alive. They became, with him, the first members of the Khalsa, known as the "Beloved Five" (*panj pyare*).

To mark their entrance into the Khalsa, Guru Gobind created a ceremony, usually called baptism. While hymns were sung, he dissolved sugar in water in an iron bowl, stirring it with a two-edged dagger, and then gave them the mixture (*amrit*, nectar) to drink, drinking it himself afterwards. Others then joined, who came from many different castes and from the ranks of the Untouchables.

For the new order Gobind laid down certain rules. They were not to use tobacco or alcohol, eat meat slaughtered according to the Muslim ritual (*halal*), or molest Muslim women. They were to wear five symbols: uncut hair (*kes*), a comb (*kangha*) in the hair to keep it tidy, a steel wrist guard (*kara*), a sword (*kirpan*), and short trousers (*kach*). These are known as the Five Ks (*kakas*).

Guru Gobind laid down further that all men initiated into the ranks of the Khalsa should receive a new surname, Singh, meaning a lion, in place of their former names, and he himself did this, becoming Guru Gobind Singh. At the same time he decreed that women could be admitted to the Khalsa, and would receive the surname Kaur, princess.

The Granth

Before he died, Guru Gobind Singh announced that the line of the Gurus, of whom there had been 10 altogether, would come to an end with him. In its stead for the future he placed the sacred book of the Sikh community, the Adi Granth (*Granth* being the Punjabi word for a book, *adi* meaning first). From that time on, the Adi Granth has also been known as the Guru Granth Sahib (*sahib* is a title of respect, meaning Lord).

The Granth is essentially a book of poetry. It is a large, standardized volume, which contains always 1,430 pages. Most of the poems were composed by Guru

Interior of Golden Temple, Amritsar (Ann & Bury Peerless)

Exterior of Golden Temple, Amritsar (Photo © Blaine Harrington III/CORBIS)

Nanak, but others are from a variety of authors, including both Hindu and Muslim saints. The collection was put together by Guru Gobind Singh, but although he was renowned as a poet, none of his poems are included in the Granth, being collected instead in the Dasam Granth.

Worship and the Gurdwara

The Sikh place of worship is termed a *gurdwara* (in English sometimes spelt "gurudwara"), a word meaning the dwelling (literally, "door") of the Guru. Sikhs do not have a special day of worship, nor a priesthood. Nor do worship services traditionally begin at certain published times. Rather, since one ought always to have God in mind, worship is considered something to be done daily, and Sikhs are encouraged to spend as much time in the gurdwara as feasible. In many gurdwaras, especially in the larger villages and towns, some prayer activity typically takes place fairly constantly throughout the day, rising to a peak at times when more people are able to come. In India worship services are usually held in the morning and especially in the evening after work, but in Sikh communities in Western countries, for reasons of convenience, the custom has developed of holding the worship service on Sundays.

The focal point of the gurdwara is the book, the Guru Granth Sahib, which is treated with profound respect, being now the actual Guru of the community. It is placed on a lectern on a dais under a canopy, above the level of the congregation, who typically sit on the floor. Before entering the gurdwara, shoes must be removed and the head covered. Upon entering a Sikh first goes up to the dais, bows down before the Granth Sahib, forehead touching the floor, and makes an offering of money or food. Men usually sit on the right side, women on the left. The service consists largely of hymn-singing (*kirtan*), usually led by musicians (*ragis*), together with prayers, sermons, and stories.

An essential part of worship is the common meal, the langar (see above), in which all should take part. Every gurdwara is equipped with a kitchen. This practice has the effect of annulling, at least for the time being, the differences of class and caste which are otherwise a marked feature of Hindu society and which typically prohibit eating together. The Indian custom according to which men and women do not eat together is generally observed, however.

Daily Life

A Sikh, particularly a member of the Khalsa, should begin each day by rising early, taking a bath in running water, and singing or chanting morning prayer from the Guru Granth. Before beginning the day's work he should take part in singing prayers in the gurdwara. At sunset another selection of prayers should be recited, and a further set just before going to bed. Before prayer, shoes should be removed and the head covered.

Male Sikhs must wear a turban. Although some others in India also wear the turban, it is the special symbol of Sikh identity. When a boy reaches the age of 11 or 12, in many families there will be a ceremony, conducted in the gurdwara, in which his first turban is tied.

Marriage is a religious ceremony, carried out in the gurdwara, and Sikhs practice monogamy.

Sikh Ethics

Sikhism places a special emphasis on three virtues: loving meditation on God, honest work, and generosity to those in need. Manual work is highly esteemed. No Sikh should earn his living by begging. Guru Nanak stated, "He alone has found the right way who eats what he has earned through toil and shares his earnings with others."

Sikhism accepts the concept of the just war. Guru Gobind Singh wrote:

> When all efforts to restore peace prove useless and no words avail,
> Lawful is the flash of steel, it is right to draw the sword.

But, he taught, war should always be defensive, the Sikh should never commit aggression.

Many Sikhs are vegetarians, following the widespread Indian custom, but Sikhism does not prohibit the eating of meat. To accommodate those who do not eat it, however, meat is not served in the langar.

From the beginning Sikhism has affirmed the equality of the sexes. The Gurus rejected the practices, common in India, of female infanticide, dowries, and seclusion. Women are not required to wear a veil, can read the Guru Granth Sahib in public and lead the worship service, as well as be members of the Khalsa.

Guru Nanak established a leprosarium, and wherever they go Sikhs have created charitable institutions such as hospitals, schools, and orphanages. Many gurdwaras in India contain a pharmacy.

Modern Developments

Like the other religions of India, Sikhism has been as yet little touched by the kinds of questions raised for Judaism and Christianity by the rise and success of science, since its theology is not dependent on particular historical narrations.

Sikhism is a democratic religion, and is not threatened by the rise of democratic systems of civil government. However, many Sikhs would still like to see the Punjab, the Sikh home territory, obtain political unity and independence. At the partition of India and Pakistan in 1947, an important part of the Punjab, which contained many historic sites and shrines of Sikhism, was incorporated into Pakistan and has thus become inaccessible to the Sikh community.

Sikhism, although originally the religion of a farming community in India, has had little difficulty adjusting to the modern capitalist economy. On the contrary, the Punjab is the most prosperous area of India, and Sikh communities in Western countries have been generally able to take full advantage of the opportunities they offer. No doubt this is because of the esteem in which hard work, individual responsibility, and personal discipline are held.

Summary of Sikhism

1   Sikhism is an offshoot of devotional Hinduism.

2   It is monotheistic; and accepts the doctrine of rebirth.

3   Its message focuses on a deep personal love of God.

4   Founded by Nanak, its historic leaders are the Ten Gurus.

5   Its sacred scripture is the Adi Granth, now recognized as Guru.

6   A special place is accorded the order of the Khalsa.

7   Sikh ethics emphasizes meditation, work, and charity.

Question for discussion

1   Does Sikhism have anything to offer people of other cultures?

Test questions

1   Summarize the story of Guru Nanak's life.

2   What are the main elements in his teaching?

3   Describe the historic significance of Guru Gobind Singh.

4   What is the langar?

5   What is the Khalsa? What are its symbols?

Additional reading

The most objective and also the most detailed books are in general those by
    Hew McLeod, especially *Sikhism*, Penguin Books, 1997. See also:
Guru Nanak and the Sikh Religion, Oxford, Clarendon Press, 1968.

Textual Sources for the Study of Sikhism, Manchester, Manchester University Press, 1984.

Cole, W. Owen and Sambhi, Piara Singh, *The Sikhs*, London, Routledge & Kegan Paul, 1978. An excellent work.

Singh, Khushwant, *A History of the Sikhs*, 6th edn, 2 vols., Oxford, Oxford University Press, 2001. The best history from the Sikh viewpoint.

Sikhism: Texts

Jap

This is the Sikh morning prayer, composed in verse by Guru Nanak, ideally to be said at dawn, the "ambrosial hour." The first half of the prayer, which consists of 38 sections altogether, is given below. This translation is by Nikky-Guninder Kaur Singh. It commences with the text given at the beginning of Chapter 3 (see p. 100), and continues as follows.

1   Thought cannot think,
          nor can a million thoughts.
    Silence cannot silence,
          nor can seamless contemplation.
    Greed is not made greedless,
          not by the wealth of all the world.
    Though a thousand mental feats become a million,
          not one can go with us.
    How then to be true?
          How then to break the wall of lies?
    By following the Will.
    Says Nanak, this is written for us.

2   By the divine Will, all forms were created;
          what that Will is, no one can say.
    By that Will, all life is formed
          and, by that Will, all are exalted.
    The Will determines what is high and what is low;
          the Will grants all joy and suffering.

Some are blessed by the Will,
      others migrate from birth to birth.
All are within the Will, none stands apart.
Says Nanak, by recognizing the Will,
      we silence our ego.

3   Filled with might, they sing praise of the Might,
Seeing the signs, they sing praise of the Bounty,
Perceiving the virtues, they sing praise of the Glory.
Some sing praise through high philosophy,
Some sing praise of the power that creates and destroys,
Some sing in awe of the giving and taking of life.
Some sing of the thereness, the utter transcendence,
Some sing of the hereness, the close watch over all.
Stories and stories add one to another,
Preaching and preaching lead nowhere.
The Giver gives, the receivers tire of receiving;
Age upon age they eat and eat the gifts.
All are directed by that Will;
Says Nanak, the Carefree is ever in bliss.

4   The True Sovereign, Truth by Name,
      infinite love the language.
Seekers forever seek gifts
      and the Giver gives more and more.
What can we offer for a glimpse of the Court?
What can we say to win divine love?
In the ambrosial hour, exalt and reflect upon the True Name.
Through actions each is dressed in a body,
      but liberation comes only from the Gaze of grace.
Says Nanak, know the Absolute thus.

5   That One cannot be moulded or made,
Alone immaculate and self-existent.
Those who serve receive honours.
Nanak says, sing of the Treasure of virtues,
Sing, listen, and hold love in the heart
So sorrow is banished, joy ushered in.
Through the Guru comes the sacred Word,
      through the Guru comes the scripture,
      through the Guru, That One is experienced in all.
The Guru is Shiva, the Guru is Vishnu, the Guru is Brahma,
      the Guru is Parvati, Lakshmi and Sarasvati.*

---

*   The cycle of existence is represented through the Hindu trinity of the gods of creation, preservation, and destruction and their respective consorts, the goddesses of knowledge, prosperity, and energy (translator's note).

Were I to comprehend, I'd still fail to explain,
      for That One is beyond all telling.
Guru, let me grasp this one thing:
All creatures have one Provider,
      may I not forget this.

6   I would bathe at a pilgrimage site only to please That One;
      without approval what is the use?
I see the expanse of creation,
      how could it be without divine favour?
Hearing a single teaching from the Guru,
      the mind shines with jewels, rubies and pearls.
Guru, let me grasp this one thing:
All creatures have one Provider,
      may I not forget this.

7   If we were to live four ages, or even ten times four,
If we were known in the nine continents,
      and hailed as leader by all,
If we were to win good name, glory and fame
      throughout the world,
But were denied the loving Gaze, we would be cast out,
      Treated as the lowest of worms, accused as criminals.
Says Nanak, the wicked are made virtuous,
      and the virtuous granted more virtue,
But it is unthinkable that anyone could grant virtue to That One.

8   By hearing, we are graced like saints and gods,
By hearing, we fathom the earth, underworld and skies,
By hearing, we know the nine continents,
      the many worlds and underworlds,
By hearing, we are freed from the clutches of death.
Says Nanak, the devout enjoy eternal bliss,
Hearing banishes all suffering and sin.

9   By hearing, we become as Shiva, Brahma and Indra,
By hearing, the corrupt open their mouths in praise,
By hearing, ways of meditation and mysteries of the body are revealed,
By hearing, treatises and scriptures are illumined.
Says Nanak, the devout enjoy eternal bliss,
Hearing banishes all suffering and sin.

10 Hearing leads to truth, contentment and knowledge,
Hearing bathes us in the sixty-eight sacred sites,
Hearing wins scholarly repute,

Hearing inspires peaceful contemplation.
Says Nanak, the devout enjoy eternal bliss,
Hearing banishes all suffering and sin.

11 Hearing the Word, we plumb the depths of virtue,
Hearing the Word, we rise to the status of sages and kings,
Hearing the Word, the path is lit for the blind,
Hearing the Word, the fathomless is fathomed.
Says Nanak, the devout enjoy eternal bliss,
Hearing the Word banishes all suffering and sin.

12 No words can speak of remembrance,
Attempts to explain are later regretted.
No paper, pen or scribe can describe,
Nor any philosophizing help to realize,
So wondrous is the immaculate Name,
It is known only by those who hold It in their mind.

13 Remembering, our mind and intellect awaken,
Remembering, we learn of all the worlds;
Remembering, we are safe from blows and pain;
Remembering, we part company with death.
So wondrous is the Immaculate Name,
It is known only by those who hold It in their mind.

14 Remembering, we walk on a clear path,
Remembering, we advance in honour and glory,
Remembering, we do not stray down lanes and byways,
Remembering, we keep to righteousness.
So wondrous is the immaculate Name,
It is known only by those who hold It in their mind.

15 Remembering, we find the door to liberation,
Remembering, our family is liberated too,
Remembering, we swim and lead our companions to the shore,
Remembering, says Nanak, we need not beg in circles for freedom.
So wondrous is the Immaculate Name,
It is known only by those who hold It in their mind.

16 The chosen win approval, they are the chosen ones,
The chosen receive honours in the Court,
The chosen shine splendidly at the royal Gate,
The chosen meditate on the one and only Guru.
To speak or think of the Creator's deeds
Is beyond calculation.

The bull that bears the earth is righteousness,
      child of compassion,
Its rope is contentment, holding the earth in balance.
All who see, live the life of truth.
How heavy the weight borne by the bull,
For there is not one earth but many more above and beyond.
Who stands beneath supporting all?
This diversity of creatures, castes and colours
Has all been written in a single stroke of the Pen.
Who knows to write this infinite Writ?
What an infinite Writ to write.
What power and beauty of form.
How to estimate the gift,
This expanse from a single command,
Millions of rivers flowing forth at once.
How can I express the Primal Power?
I cannot offer myself to You even once,
Only that which pleases You is good.
You are for ever constant, Formless One.

17   Countless are the ways of meditation,
        and countless the avenues of love,
    Countless the ways of worship,
        and countless the paths of austerity and sacrifice.
    Countless the texts, and countless the Vedic reciters,
    Countless the yogis turning away from the world,
    Countless the devout reflecting on virtue and knowledge,
    Countless the pious, and countless the patrons,
    Countless the warriors, faces scarred by iron
    Countless the sages sunk in silent trance.
    How can I express the Primal Power?
    I cannot offer myself to you even once.
    Only that which pleases You is good.
    You are for ever constant, Formless One.

18   Countless the fools lost in pitch dark,
    Countless the thieves living off others,
    Countless the tyrants bullying their way,
    Countless the killers with blood on their hands,
    Countless the sinners trailing misdeeds behind them,
    Countless the liars spinning in lies,
    Countless the perverts devouring filth,
    Countless the slanderers bent by their burden.
    After thought, lowly Nanak says this,
    I cannot offer myself to you even once.

> Only that which pleases You is good.
> You are for ever constant, Formless One.

19 Countless are Your names and countless Your places,
    Unreachable and unfathomable are Your countless spheres.
    Declaring them "countless" we increase our burden.
    Yet, by words we name, by words we acclaim,
    By words we know and sing and praise,
    By words we speak and by words we write,
    By words we communicate and unite,
    By words all our actions are written.
    But who writes is above all writing.
    As it is spoken, so are all allotted.
    As expansive the creation, so too the Name,
    There is no place without the Name.
    How can I express the Primal Power?
    I cannot offer myself to you even once.
    Only that which pleases You is good.
    You are for ever constant, Formless One.

Ardas (Petition)

This is the prayer recited by Sikhs most frequently. It is said as a conclusion to both morning and evening prayer, and to most Sikh rituals. It is recited standing up. An individual leads it, and the rest of the congregation joins in with the exclamation *Vaheguru*.

There is One Being, all victory belongs to the Wonderful Guru,
May the divine Might help us.
The Tenth Guru's Ode to the divine Might.

First remember the divine Might, then think of Guru Nanak,
Next Gurus Angad, Amar Das and Ram Das,
    may they stand by us.
Gurus Arjan, Hargobind and Har Rai,
Think of Guru Harkrishan, that sight dispels all suffering.
Remember Guru Tegh Bahadur,
    who brings the nine treasures to our home.
May they support us everywhere.
May the Tenth Guru, Gobind Singh, support us everywhere.
The light of the Ten Gurus shines in the Guru Granth Sahib,

Consider its sacred word, envisage its sacred sight,
    And proclaim: *Vaheguru*, the Wonderful Guru!

The heroic deeds of the five beloved ones, the four princes,
    the forty who attained liberation,
The determined, the devout and the self-denying,
They who contemplated the Name, shared their earnings,
    established free kitchens, prepared for battle,
They who forgave others their faults,
Remember the purity and goodness of their deeds, Khalsaji,
    Proclaim: *Vaheguru*, the Wonderful Guru!

The Sikh men and women who gave their heads for their religion,
Whose limbs were cut off one by one,
Who were scalped, broken on the wheel, and sawn in pieces,
Who sacrificed their lives to serve the gurudwaras,
Their faith triumphed.
They served the Sikh religion with uncut hair to their last breath,
Remembering their steadfast faith, Khalsaji,
    Proclaim: *Vaheguru*, the Wonderful Guru!

Remember the five takhts, and all gurudwaras, Khalsaji,
    And proclaim: *Vaheguru*, the Wonderful Guru!

First of all, the Khalsa prays for remembrance of the
    Wonderful Guru, *Vaheguru, Vaheguru, Vaheguru*!
May this remembrance bring peace and happiness to all.
Wherever the Khalsa be, may Your protection and favour be there,
May our supplies in the kitchen and battlefield never fail,
May You uphold the honour of Your devotees,
May You grant victory to the Sikh community,
May the Sword aid us,
May the words of the Khalsa ever be exalted.
    Proclaim: *Vaheguru*, the Wonderful Guru!

Grant Your Sikhs the gift of the Sikh religion,
The gift of uncut hair, of good conduct and of knowledge,
The gift of trust, the gift of faith,
The gift of gifts, devotion to the Name,
And a bath in the sacred pool of Amritsar.
May the choirs that glorify You, the flags which herald You,
    and the places where we learn of You endure for ever.
May righteous action ever triumph.
    Proclaim: *Vaheguru*, the Wonderful Guru!

May Sikhs lower their egos, and raise their wisdom,
You Yourself are the Sustainer of wisdom,
    Vaheguru, the Wonderful Guru!

Primal Being, eternal Sustainer of Your community,
May the Khalsa freely behold and serve Nankana Sahib
    and the other gurudwaras and all sacred places
From which we have been exiled.

Honour of the honourless, Power of the powerless,
    Shield of the shieldless,
Our true Parent, *Vaheguru*, the Wonderful Guru!
We humbly offer our prayers in Your presence.

[*At this point personal or communal prayers are said, for example:*]
May we be free of lust, anger, greed, attachment and pride.

Overlook our flaws in reading and reciting the sacred text.
May everyone's actions be fulfilled.
Join us with the faithful who inspire remembrance of Your Name.
Says Nanak, may Your Name be ever ascendant.
And, through Your Will,
    may everyone in the world fare well.

The Khalsa belongs to the Wonderful Guru,
Victory belongs to the Wonderful Guru!

Part II

The Religions of Chinese Origin

Emerging within the same ancient culture, the three religions of Chinese origin, despite important differences, share significant common features. They emphasize especially the idea of nature, and their goal can be described as harmony, especially harmony with nature. They are concerned more with human well-being in this present life than with a future one. This gives them a noticeably different atmosphere from that of the religions of Indian origin.

What differentiates them from one another is the meaning they attach to the idea of nature. For the Confucian tradition the focus of attention is on human nature; the goal of the Confucianist is to become more fully human. For Taoism the focus is on what we might perhaps call by contrast cosmic nature; the Taoist's goal is to attain harmony with the fundamental forces of the universe. For Chinese Buddhism, nature is a mystical fusion of the nature of the self, the nature of the cosmos, and the Buddha nature.

In the past these three traditions have sometimes been mutually antagonistic, and today their officials are still quite conscious of their differences from one another, typically considering them to be mutually exclusive. However, this is not the case with the broad mass of the Chinese people, who, for the most part, do not maintain a special allegiance to one tradition rather than another, and commonly make use of all three, moving between them with ease.

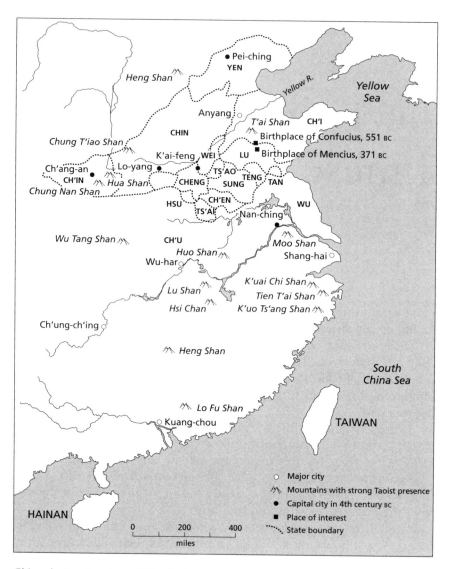

China during the time of Confucius

4

Traditional Chinese Religion and Confucianism

The Spirit of Traditional Chinese Religion

> Thick grows the star-thistle;
> We must clear away its prickly clumps.
> From of old, what have we been doing?
> We grow wine-millet and cooking-millet,
> Our wine-millet, a heavy crop;
> Our cooking-millet doing well.
> Our granaries are all full,
> For our stacks were in their millions,
> To make wine and food,
> To make offering, to make prayer-offering,
> That we may have peace, that we may have ease,
> That every blessing may be vouchsafed . . .
> Very hard have we striven
> That the rites might be without mistake.
> The skillful recitant conveys the message,
> Goes and gives it to the pious son:
> "Fragrant were your pious offerings,
> The Spirits enjoyed their drink and food.

In the Wade–Giles system of transcription used here, if the initial consonant is followed by an apostrophe, the consonant is pronounced as it is written. (In English, these consonants are pronounced with a slight puff of air like an "h", an aspiration, which is represented in Wade–Giles by the apostrophe.) If it is not followed by an apostrophe, it is pronounced as a "unaspirated" consonant, that is, without the slight puff of air; for example, K'uei is pronounced with an initial K, but Kuei is pronounced almost as if it were Guei. Thus Ti is pronounced roughly as Di, Tao is roughly Dao, and so on.

They assign to you a hundred blessings.
According to their hopes, to their rules,
All was orderly and swift,
All was straight and sure.
For ever they will bestow upon you good store;
Myriads and tens of myriads."
(Ode 209, *The Book of Songs*, trans. and ed.
Arthur Waley, London, Allen & Unwin, 1937)

Questions for discussion

1 This was a hymn associated with sacrifice. What does it tell us about the concerns of early Chinese religion?

2 Why does the hymn emphasize that the message is given to the son? (See below, pp. 127, 134.)

Traditional Chinese Religion

Traditional Chinese religion was fundamentally different from both Indian and Semitic religion in that it was not in the first instance personal religion, but what we may call civil religion, the religion of the civil society, concerned for the well-being of the society. Religion was a function of government. It had no separate priestly caste. Initially it was the religion of the family as a unit, and it was only the male head of the family who carried out its rituals. As the family grew into a tribe, a people, and a nation, only the head of these larger units, that is, the king, and those designated by him, could perform the central religious rites.

The nearest analogy to a priestly caste was the class of scholars and administrators, the Ju, who were the experts in the performance and interpretation of the rituals, and the transmitters of the higher learning. It was to this class that Confucius belonged, and it was they who became the custodians of his doctrine.

Although the imperial sacrifices are no longer offered, many of the conceptions of ancient Chinese religion are preserved in the popular religion today, and they form an indispensable background for understanding the Confucian tradition.

The Religion of the Shang Dynasty (*c.*1500–1100 BC)

The Shang is the earliest Chinese dynasty of which we have historical records. The mass of the Shang people were peasants, who did not have their own land, but worked on their master's land under his direction. The land was owned and the people governed by a city-dwelling aristocracy who were already far advanced in many aspects of civilization. They produced pottery and bronzes of great beauty, with delicate yet vigorous decoration. They apparently invented the Chinese script. On the other hand, they still practiced human sacrifice, burying alive with their dead kings the wives and retainers who had accompanied them during life, so that they could continue to be with them after death.

The ancestors

From the beginning perhaps the most distinctive feature of Chinese religion in comparison with the religions of Indian and Semitic origin is the attention paid to ancestors, the inclusion of the spirits of the dead ancestors in the human community. The ancestors of a family, ascending to Heaven as good spirits, or *shen*, after death, are an integral part of the family, and remain active on its behalf, continuing in death the functions they had performed in life, of ensuring its fertility, bringing success in the hunt, and protecting it against harm. It is vital to have the ancestors' approval. To this day traditional Chinese homes have an ancestral shrine, containing the Spirit Tables of the ancestors, pieces of wood on which their names are inscribed.

Spirits

For the early Chinese, as for most of their descendants today, the spirit world was of great importance. The religion of the Shang was dominated by concern for the life beyond the grave. After death the spirit of man lingers for a while near the corpse or tomb, as a *kuei* (Pinyin, *gui*), then, as the corpse disintegrates, the spirit is absorbed back into the earth, for the earth contains within itself the source of the energy which animates living beings. The *kuei* can be harmful to the living if it does not receive sustenance, so it must be provided with food and drink. Although the art of embalming had not been developed in China as it had in Egypt, every effort was made by the Shang to preserve the corpse, since that preserved the spirt of the deceased in existence. Furthermore, the existence of the spirit could be prolonged by sacrifices carried out by the eldest son.

In addition to the *kuei* there are also good spirits, *shen*, which ascend to Heaven, and among which the spirits of the ancestors were typically considered to belong. Later the view developed that the human soul consisted of two parts, one of which, the *p'o*, was earthly by nature and turned into a *kuei* at death, while the other, the *hun*, was heavenly by nature and became a *shen*. When sacrifice is offered, the *shen* descend from Heaven to be present at it.

Gods

In addition to the spirits there are gods of various kinds, especially of the land. Each piece of land has its own god, the *T'u Ti* (Pinyin, *Tu di*), whose task it is to care for the inhabitants of that particular area. These gods are arranged in a hierarchy of importance, reflecting the size and significance of their territories. Each family or local farm, each town or village, each larger division of the land, or county, and each state has its own god, the gods of the larger units being the superiors of those of the intermediary ones, and the gods of the inter-mediary areas being the superiors of those of the smaller ones. Finally each country has its own *T'u Ti*. Thus the empire has a celestial administration which mirrors its earthly one.

The Chinese conception of a god is quite different from that found in the religions of Indian or Semitic origin. The Chinese gods were, and are typically to this day, not always gods, but were originally notable human beings, such as kings or generals or other outstanding people, who were elevated to the status of a god after their death because of their achievements. By the same token, they can also be dismissed from their position if they fail to do their job properly in caring for the needs of those entrusted to them.

While the spirits of the ancestors were worshipped at the shrine in the home, the gods of the soil were worshipped at earth altars in the open air. Beside each earth altar stood a tree which represented the god. In addition to the gods of the soil there are many other gods, of grain, of rivers and mountains, of wind and rain. The dragon is a rain god and is essentially benevolent.

Ti (*Pinyin*, **Di**)

The spirit of the ancestral ruler not only ascends to Heaven as a *shen*, but becomes a god. In particular, the ancestors of the Shang at their death became gods, known as *Ti*. Above all the lesser *Ti* is the original or Great Ancestor of the Shang clan, the supreme *Ti*. The lesser gods form a divine hierarchy, analogous to the hierarchy of officials who administer the kingdom, and the supreme *Ti* presides over them as the king does over his ministers and officials.

Divination

There are various ways to discover whether the gods and spirits look favorably on an undertaking. One of these is the use of oracle bones, others are the use of sticks and divination pieces.

The Shang oracle bones are one of our chief sources of information about them. We possess some 100,000, excavated mainly near the site of the Shang capital at An Yang. On many of the bones a question was inscribed, and heat then applied so that the bone cracked. The shape of the crack was taken to give the answer to the question.

Ritual or Li

Man will prosper if he is in harmony with Heaven and Earth. The chief task of the king is to maintain this harmony by carrying out the proper ritual. If the kingdom suffers disaster, even natural catastrophes such as flood or fire, there is a presumption that the king has not carried out his duties conscientiously. The lives of the noble families likewise are regulated by rituals designed to preserve harmony with Heaven and Earth, and they are liable to share in the blame if things go awry.

Power or Te (*Pinyin,* De)

This is the magical power which the gods and spirits possess. It can be good or bad. It is also a quality of the great man or king, which enables him to overcome his enemies, win the support of the people, and achieve influence and authority, whether for good or ill.

 These conceptions of Shang religion remain largely alive still today in popular Chinese religion.

The Religion of the Chou Dynasty (*c.*1100–500 BC)

Around the year 1100 BC the Chou clans overthrew the Shang government and set up their own. This political revolution brought about a religious one, for the Chou undertook to give a public explanation for their action, and in so doing introduced a new, theological conception of government based on new principles of morality and religion. They kept the Shang ceremonies, but transformed their meaning.

The High God, Shang Ti (Pinyin, Shang Di)

If they had followed the usual custom the Chou would have replaced the Great Ancestor of the Shang, *Ti*, with their own Great Ancestor. However, manifesting a liberal and conciliatory outlook, they did not do this. Instead, they not only preserved *Ti*, but elevated him from the position of Supreme Ancestor of the Shang clan to that of an independent High God, under the name Shang Ti or *Ti* "on high." Shang Ti is no longer an ancestor, even a deified one, but simply God, concerned not merely for the welfare of a particular clan, but of all. He deigns, however, to associate the ancestors with himself on high, and when he descends to the sacrifice they descend with him.

Heaven, T'ien (*Pinyin,* Tian)

In their own tradition the Chou referred to God as *T'ien*, Sky or Heaven (whom they had probably worshipped together with Earth in an early fertility cult). They now identified *T'ien* with Shang Ti. But the two names retained slightly different connotations, Shang Ti being clearly thought of as personal, but *T'ien* less clearly so.

 At the same time the conception of the deity became much more moral. As we have seen, moral considerations did not play a large role in Shang religion.

For the Chou, by contrast, moral principles were of fundamental importance. Shang Ti or *T'ien* is not merely powerful, but also just and righteous, and expects justice and righteousness from men. He cares deeply about virtue. Especially, he demands good government, that is, just government.

The mandate of Heaven, T'ien Ming

It is this conception of a just God that provided the foundation for the Chou explanation of their revolution. The Shang government had become morally corrupt. It had thereby lost the support of Shang Ti, or T'ien, and because of that it had lost its legitimacy as a government, it had lost the right to rule. Rule passed to the Chou only because the Chou believed in justice. Apart from that, the Chou were nobodies; they were merely a small collection of tribes from the fringe of the civilized world. If it had not been for the fact that Shang Ti had chosen them as his instrument, they could never have overthrown the Shang government.

According to this view, rulership depends not merely on the ability to wield superior force, or on the possession of a hereditary title, but above all on moral right or title. The ruler rules only by the will of God, and God gives his mandate only to the just. Thus any government that becomes unjust automatically loses its right to govern, no matter how strong its hereditary claim to the throne might be, or how powerful the armies it can muster to defend it. And, the Chou implied, this applied not only to the Shang, but also to themselves: if the time ever came when they were morally corrupt, they would also lose their right to govern. "The favour of Heaven is not easily preserved."

Virtue, Te

Under the Shang, *te* had meant magical power, whether good or bad. With the Chou it came to mean moral power, the power of the king used to bring justice and prosperity to the land. It can now be translated as "virtue" or "goodness." Heaven is virtuous, it possesses *te*, and men must also. *Te* is the very foundation of the majesty of Heaven. It is the *te* of a government which obtains for it the mandate of Heaven. And if the king has *te*, it will flow out to the people.

Filial piety, Hsiao (*Pinyin,* Xiao)

One of the chief virtues is filial piety, the reverence and obedience which the son owes to his father, *hsiao*.

> The king said: "Great criminals should be detested, but how much more those who lack filial pity and brotherly love: the son who does not reverently attend to his father's needs, and wounds the heart of his ancestors."
>
> (Shu Ching: K'ang Kao 16)

126

The Son of Heaven, T'ien Tzu (*Pinyin,* Tian Zi)

The relationship of the ruler to God is analogous to that of a son to his father. The ruler is the Son of Heaven. This is not meant as a mythological conception, that is, as if Heaven gave direct physical birth to the ruler, but an ethical one. To be the Son of Heaven is to have the same obligations of reverence and obedience towards Heaven that an earthly son has to his father. Thus the concept of the Son of Heaven implies the concept of just government.

The organization of religion

As with the Shang, there is no separate priestly caste or community. It is always the civil authority that functions as the priest.

The Period of the Warring States (*c.*500–221 BC)

During this time the authority of the central government collapsed, and the country descended into anarchy. The kingdom broke up into numerous independent states, which made constant war on one another. Great calamities descended on the people, typhoons, fires, famine, and flood, leading many to lose faith in Heaven.

> Compassionate Heaven rages in fury, sending down death and afflicting with famine. The people wander about and perish. Everywhere destruction reigns.
>
> (*Classic of Poetry,* 3: 3; 11, 1)

> It is right that sinners should be punished for their crimes, but why should innocent people be overwhelmed with ruin?
>
> (2: 4; 10, 1)

> August Heaven is unpitying. Disorders have no end.
>
> (2: 4; 7, 5–6)

The state ceremonies and sacrifices were continued, but became largely mechanical. The name Shang Ti, implying a personal God, came to be supplanted by the more impersonal term, Heaven, *T'ien.*

During this period numerous thinkers attempted to speak to the problems the people were experiencing. From the viewpoint of subsequent history the most significant of these thinkers was Confucius, but there were many others, including Mo Tzu, Confucius' chief rival, who taught that love should be universal rather than focused especially on the family, as Confucius did; Mencius, the most noted follower and interpreter of Confucius; Hsün Tzu, a follower of Confucius, but one whose outlook was more naturalistic and humanistic, and who believed, in contrast to the mainstream Confucian tradition inspired by Mencius, that human nature is evil; Han Fei Tzu, a disciple of Hsün Tzu, who emphasized the strict enforcement of the civil law; not to mention the various Taoist thinkers whose acquaintance we shall make in Chapter 5. As a result, this era is known as the Age of the Hundred Philosophers. It was the Confucian viewpoint, however, which won the allegiance of the Chinese people.

The Five Classics

During this period a number of books were compiled which are considered the classics of Chinese civilization. These "Five Classics" provide an important part of the background for the Confucian system:

The Classic of Changes, *I Ching*, a book of divination containing striking images.
The Classic of History, *Shu Ching*, which contains, among other things, the Chou theology.
The Classic of Poetry, *Shih Ching*, a collection of some 300 poems, many very beautiful, dealing with a wide range of themes, including love poetry.
The Book of Ritual, *Li Chi*.
The Spring and Autumn Annals, *Ch'un Ch'iu*.

Originally there was also a sixth, the Classic of Music, which has been lost. These books continued to be edited after Confucius' death, and their present versions contain some later material.

Confucianism

The spirit of the Confucian tradition

Once Confucius and his disciples on the side of Mount T'ai heard a woman wailing in mourning. Confucius approached her and asked the reason why she wept. She replied, "My husband's father was killed here by a tiger, my husband too, and now my son has met the same fate."

"Then why then do you stay in this dreadful place?" Confucius asked.

"Because there is no oppressive ruler here," she replied.

Confucius turned to his disciples and said: "Learn from this that an oppressive rule is crueller than a tiger."

The Confucian view of life

Heaven has given us our nature as human beings. Our pathway to a good and successful life lies in carrying out the will of Heaven, and we do that by living according to our human nature. This means especially developing our sense of humanity, cultivating in our hearts and in our actions a sense of fellow-feeling with other human beings, the feeling that for all our differences they share our

Confucius (Ann & Bury Peerless)

essential nature. The place where we chiefly learn this fellow-feeling for others is within the family, which therefore has the first claim on us.

Confucius (K'ung Fu Tzu) (552–479 BC) (Pinyin, Kongfuzi)

We know little for certain about the life of Confucius. He was probably born in 552 BC, during the era known as the Spring and Autumn period, in the small independent state of Lu. His father died when he was young, and his mother was left impoverished. Despite this, he must have received a good education. From an early age he began to study the history of his people intensely, becoming an expert on their ancient writings. He made a living by giving the sons of gentlemen an education that would prepare them to take government office in one of the many Chinese kingdoms. He himself ardently desired to be employed by some prince so that he could put his own teachings on the right way to

129

govern into effect, and for that purpose he travelled from one state to another, but it is doubtful that he ever succeeded in obtaining such a position. He returned to Lu, and died in 479 BC, at the age of 73.

Confucius himself seems to have written little. While he may have edited some of the Classics, he did not write down his own doctrines. His teachings were compiled and published by his followers, with numerous additions. In time they became more and more widely accepted, and were finally adopted as the official philosophy of the Chinese empire.

The teachings of Confucius and his followers must be understood against the background of the collapse and barbarization of civil society, the decline of ethical standards among the ruling classes, and the people's consequent loss of faith in Heaven, which had begun during the Spring and Autumn era when Confucius lived, and which became worse during the period of the Warring States which followed. He responded to this by emphasizing *virtue*, or character, as the foundation of civilized society. In his view the best understanding of this, and of the nature of things in general, was to be found in the worldview of the early Chou sages, so he did not see himself as teaching anything new, but merely advocating a return to their wisdom.

From a Western perspective the Confucian tradition is perhaps better described as a religious philosophy than as a fully-fledged religion. Confucius did not create "a religion" in the sense that the Buddha, Jesus, or Mohammed did, a movement for the masses. His aim was to transform the governing class in its outlook and conduct, and his doctrines, viewed in isolation, may appear to be in the main only a system of ethics. But for Confucius ethics has religious significance, because it is mandated by Heaven, and our relationship to Heaven is governed by how we conduct ourselves. This is especially true of the ethics of the governing class. His doctrines assume the framework of traditional Chinese religion. As we have seen, Chinese religion was a function of government, the governing class was the nearest thing to a priesthood, and so the philosophy of the governing class was an integral part of the religion. Confucius created a philosophy and a set of values which in its broad outlines was adopted by the Chinese scholarly and administrative class for some 2,000 years.

The teachings of Confucius were expanded and developed by his followers over several centuries. The chief of these was Meng Tzu, or Mencius, who lived about a century after Confucius, from about 390 to 305 BC, and who developed explicitly the thesis, which had remained implicit with Confucius, that human nature is inherently good.

The Four Books

The teachings ascribed to Confucius can be found chiefly in the "Four Books":

- The *Analects*, the earliest and most reliable collection of his thoughts. Since it was compiled a considerable time after his death, however, it is doubtful whether many of the statements given there record Confucius' actual words.

- *The Doctrine of the Mean*, written by an early follower, which develops especially the religious aspects of Confucius' views; it forms a chapter of the Book of Ritual.
- *The Great Learning*, a short treatise on moral education; it also forms a chapter of the Book of Ritual.
- *Mencius*, a collection of the teachings of Confucius' outstanding disciple, Meng Tzu.

These four books, together with the Five Classics mentioned above (p. 128), are sometimes referred to as the scriptures of Confucianism.

The main ideas of the Confucian philosophy are as follows.

Heaven, T'ien (*Pinyin*, Tian)

Heaven is for Confucius the same transcendent moral power that it was for the Chou sages. Presiding over the world is a divine power which endows all beings with their natures, sees the thoughts and actions of men, and sets the standards for their behavior. Man must live according to the Will of Heaven, and that will is shown to us clearly in our nature as human beings. To be in harmony with Heaven we must strive to become fully human. "What Heaven imparts to man is called human nature. To follow our nature is called the Way" (*The Doctrine of the Mean*, 1).

Confucius is wary of claiming detailed knowledge about the motives or intentions of Heaven, since it does not reveal them to us. Heaven does not intervene in the world to work miracles, but governs all things by virtue of the eternal law it has written in their natures.

Heaven is humane. Although its ways are often hidden from us, it is concerned for the welfare of man, and points out to him through his nature the path to follow. There is a Providence which guides human affairs, though its workings are mysterious to us.

The goodness of human nature

Since human nature is bestowed by Heaven, it is not inherently evil or sinful. Rather, it is essentially good. Because of this, we have a natural ability to discover what is good and to do it, and thus to overcome evil.

This view, assumed by Confucius, was developed explicitly especially by his follower Mencius. For Mencius the inherent goodness of human nature is demonstrated by the universal sense of kinship that human beings feel for one another, by their instinctive sympathy and compassion for others in distress. However, this natural goodness must be nurtured and cultivated. If it is not, it can lose its force and become submerged in evil.

Evil arises in society because men do not cultivate their own humanity, because they allow their feelings and their actions to fall out of harmony with

131

their own natures as human beings, and do not treat others with the respect and fellow-feeling that is their due.

The Way, Tao (*Pinyin*, Dao)

The word *Tao* means a path or road. There is a Path of Heaven and a Path of Man. The Path of Heaven, the *T'ien Tao*, is the will of Heaven for human beings, Heaven's way of dealing with us. This is often inscrutable, for example, in the suffering it allows.

For the most part, when Confucius speaks about the *Tao* he means the Path of Man, the *Ren Tao*. This is the path that man ought to travel, because it has been ordained by Heaven. Heaven has given us a certain nature, and that nature requires us to live and behave in a certain way. The Path of Man is above all a moral path, and following it means above all carrying out our moral duty, living as we ought to live. To follow the Path fully is too difficult a goal, too high an ideal for ordinary mortals to attain. Only the ancient sages and kings understood it and trod it properly. Thus the Path becomes a synonym for the teachings of Confucius.

The Path not only points out to us how we should act in our private lives, but also indicates what should be done in public life, the life of society. The Path is the way the ruler must follow in governing the state and in carrying out the sacrifices.

The princely or noble man, Chün-tzu (*Pinyin*, Junzi)

This is the man who embodies the *Tao* in his own life. Originally meaning a member of the royal family, the term came to mean any person whose habitual conduct was noble. It can sometimes be translated as "gentleman." It is the Confucian ideal. The truly noble man embodies all the virtues.

> The Master said, A gentleman takes as much trouble to discover what is right as lesser men take to discover what will pay.
>
> (*Analects*, IV, 16)

> The Master said, The gentleman calls attention to the good points in others; he does not call attention to their defects. The small man does just the reverse of this.
>
> (*Analects*, XII, 16)

Human-heartedness, Ren

This is the greatest of virtues, and properly understood it includes all the others. It means, initially, to have a sense of kinship with other men, to have a strong feeling of belonging to the same species and even being of one body with them. At its most developed, it means to be truly and fully human. It is the highest perfection of goodness, a sublime moral ideal beyond the reach of ordinary mortals. Often it can be translated simply as goodness. Its most fundamental element is compassion, a profound sense of fellow-feeling with those in distress. If a child falls into a well, says Mencius, there is no one so lacking in *ren* that he will not try to pull him out. The person who is truly and fully human practices every virtue to the highest extent: he loves and respects those who are good; within the family he is a true father, son, and brother; in public life he does what is right even at cost to himself; he is loyal to his superiors, and concerned for the welfare of the people.

In the Confucian view, although human-heartedness should be evident in our relationships with all people, it should not be evident equally. It should be exercised first and chiefly towards one's own family and blood relatives, who should always have precedence in our concerns. It is within the family that a person learns how to be human-hearted, and once it has been learned and practiced there, it will naturally extend itself to all men in due degree.

Mencius said, "Humanity attains its finest flower in the service of parents."

Justice, righteousness, I (*Pinyin*, Yi)

This is the virtue that consists in doing what is right in our dealings with others. It means above all not causing harm. The just man does not seek his own gain at the expense of others, is not prejudiced, and has the courage to do his duty even at the cost of his own life. "Righteousness is the principle of setting things right and proper, and the greatest application of it is in honoring the worthy" (*Mean*, 20).

Filial piety and brotherly love, Hsiao *and* T'i

The family is the foundation on which civil society rests. If civil society is to be in a healthy condition, its family life must first be healthy. As we have just pointed out, in the Confucian view relationships between family members have a paramount importance. This is carried so far that loyalty to one's family should supersede even loyalty to the state. Once Confucius was asked what a man should do if he discovered that his father had committed a crime. He replied: Put him on your back and carry him to the nearest border!

Of all relationships in society the cardinal one is that between father and son. It is the hinge of civilization. The father must love his son and care for him; he is responsible for his son's welfare. The son must respect and obey his father, and see to his welfare. A father who neglects his son may perhaps achieve great things but cannot claim to be truly human; similarly, a son who does not respect and obey his father may become renowned in society but is not truly human.

The relationship between elder brother and younger brother mirrors that between father and son: the elder brother is responsible for the welfare of the younger, and the younger owes respect to the elder.

Proper behavior towards parents and elder brothers is the trunk* of goodness.

(*Analects*, I, 1)

The Master said, In serving his father and mother a man may gently remonstrate with them. But if he sees that he has failed to change their opinion, he should resume an attitude of deference and not thwart them; may feel discouraged, but not resentful.

(*Analects*, IV, 18)

The Master said, While father and mother are alive, a good son does not wander far afield . . .

(*Analects*, IV, 19)

The Master said, While a man's father is alive, you can only see his intentions; it is when his father dies that you discover whether or not he is capable of carrying them out. If for the whole three years of mourning he manages to carry on the household exactly as in his father's day, then he is a good son indeed.

(*Analects*, I, 11)

Later Confucianists expanded this into the doctrine of the Five Relationships:

1   Father and son: the father must love and care for the son, and the son must respect and obey the father.
2   Husband and wife: the husband must treat his wife fairly, and the wife must respect and obey her husband.
3   Elder brother and younger brother: the elder brother must care for the younger, and the younger must respect the elder.
4   Ruler and minister: the ruler must be concerned for his subjects' well-being; and the minister must obey and be loyal to the ruler.
5   Older and younger in general: those who are older must show humane consideration towards those younger than them, and those who are younger must respect those older than them.

These relationships are not understood as between equals, but between superior and inferior. They are paternalistic. The latter four are modeled on the first, which is the pattern for society.

Since the relationship between children and parents is so central, there is an obligation to marry and have children. The Confucian tradition does not encourage the monastic or celibate life. This was a bone of contention with Taoism and especially with Buddhism. Mencius said, "There are three contraventions of the rules of filial piety, and of these the greatest is to have no progeny."

---

*   The foundation, as opposed to the leaves and branches.

The rules of good behavior, Li

Just as the inner life of the noble man is governed by *ren*, so his outer life is directed by *li*. This is a broad concept, covering all conduct that is fitting or appropriate under the circumstances one finds oneself in. On the one hand it means politeness and consideration, what we would term good manners. Different people should be treated differently: we ought not to treat our close relatives in the same way as we treat strangers, for example. *Li* includes such things as the way we dress, our demeanor, and our general manner toward others. It also includes much that we would consider ethics, such as the duties of an employee towards his employer. In addition it includes formal rituals and ceremonies, both those customary in daily life, such as the way we greet others or say goodbye, and those that are specifically part of religion and the public life of the state, such as the state sacrifices. At all times one should ask oneself what sort of behavior the circumstances require.

> The relative degree of affection we ought to feel for our relatives and the relative grades in the honoring of the worthy give rise to the rules of propriety.
>
> (*Mean*, 20)

Confucians recognized the danger that an insistence on correct external behavior can lead to insincerity, and responded by emphasizing the importance of sincerity. The formal ceremony should be carried out because it is the fitting thing to do under the circumstances, and one should try to feel the emotions represented in the ceremony, on the assumption that if we do externally what is appropriate, eventually we will come to have the corresponding inner feelings and attitudes.

Evil arises in society not because human nature is sinful, but because, perhaps initially from mere oversight, people fail to treat others with the respect that is their due. Harmony will be created in society by the deliberate practice of the formalities of polite behavior.

People interact with one another not only through words and actions, but also through music, which has great power to move people's feelings. This led Confucius to include it together with *li*. The music used on an occasion must be fitting and appropriate. Some music is beautiful and noble, and inspires the mind with virtue, while other music panders to low and shameful feelings.

> The Master said, A man who is not Good [*ren*], what can he have to do with ritual? A man who is not Good, what can he have to do with music?
>
> (*Analects*, III, 3)

Concern for others, altruism, Shu

Whereas *ren* is an interior attitude implying concern for the welfare of others, *shu* is the external manifestation of that in public life, putting oneself in the place of others. Confucius expressed it in the rule: "Do not do to others what you would not want done to yourself." The gentleman does not cause pain to others.

Conscientiousness, Chung (*Pinyin*, Zhong)

The subordinate must place his superior's interests before his own personal benefit. The noble man will never seek his own gain at his master's expense, but rather will promote his master's welfare even at the cost of his own.

On the other hand, if his superior's policies force the subordinate to choose between doing wrong or losing his position, he will sacrifice his position. One must put ethical principle and one's own integrity above the demands of one's superior.

The Power of Virtue, Te (*Pinyin*, De)

The chief power of government in Confucius' view is not so much its power to enforce its will by law, but its moral power, that is, its power to influence the inner character, the heart and soul, of the people by its own moral example. If the ruler follows the Path selflessly, the people will follow the Path. If he is a man of *ren*, a man who embodies compassion and fellow-feeling for others in his life, the people will become a people of *ren*. If he exemplifies justice in his own life, the people will obey the law.

> The Master said, He who rules by moral force (*te*) is like the polestar, which remains in its place while all the lesser stars do homage to it.
>
> (*Analects*, II, 1)

Harmony, Ho (*Pinyin*, He)

The Confucian seeks a twofold harmony, individual and social.

1   The aim of the individual must be to attain harmony with his own nature as a human being, that is, to become fully human. To the extent that he accomplishes this he will achieve harmony with Heaven, which has conferred his nature on him, and with the rest of the universe.
2   If individuals attain this harmony with Heaven, the result will be a harmonious social order, in which superiors carry out their duties to their subordinates, and subordinates fulfill their obligations to their superiors, for the welfare of society as a whole.

The mean

Harmony is a balance between extremes. To be truly virtuous, that is, truly human, it is important not to go to excess in either one direction or the other.

Concern for others must be balanced by a proper respect for oneself; respect for oneself must be balanced by concern for others. It is necessary to have the right inner attitudes; it is also necessary to speak and act toward others in the right external manner.

The rectification of names

The names by which we call things should correspond to their reality, and conversely we must see to it that the reality lives up to the name. This is important in the Confucian tradition, not only for the sake of truthfulness in a narrow sense, but as part of the larger view that human beings should be in harmony with their natures. The father should be a true father, and the son should be a true son. This means that a father should act in the way that is fitting and appropriate for fathers to act, and a son should act in the way that is fitting and appropriate for sons to act. If a man does not act like a father, we should avoid speaking of him as a father; and if a man does not act like a son, we should find some other way of speaking about him than by calling him a son. Similarly, the husband should be a true husband, and the wife a true wife; the ruler should be a true ruler, and the minister a true minister. And so on for every rank and station in life.

Worldly goods

The Confucian tradition does not despise the goods of this world, but welcomes them, and desires that mankind should prosper materially. On the other hand, neither does it believe in making a fetish of them. If it is important to have a certain minimum of material goods, it is even more important not to care too much about them, and especially never to do anything low or mean in order to obtain them. However, Confucians have typically despised trade and commerce.

Government

As we have seen, Confucian teaching points out not only how we should act in our private lives, but also how the state should be governed. In this it emphasizes above all the personal character of the ruler, rather than, for example, the rule of objective law, as has developed in the West. In the Confucian view, if the personal character of the ruler is what it should be, the state will necessarily be governed well, and if the personal character of the ruler is deficient, the state will inevitably be governed badly.

> The Master said, If the ruler himself is upright, all will go well even though he does not give orders. But if he himself is not upright, even though he gives orders, they will not be obeyed.
>
> (*Analects*, XIII, 6)

> Tzu-kung asked about government. The Master said, Sufficient food, sufficient weapons, and the confidence of the common people. Tzu-kung said, Suppose you had no choice but to dispense with one of these three, which would you forgo? The Master said, Weapons. Tzu-kung said, Suppose you were forced to dispense with one of the two that were left, which would you forgo? The Master said, Food. For from of old death has been the lot of all men; but a people that no longer trusts its rulers is lost indeed.
>
> (*Analects*, XII, 7)

Human destiny

The Confucian tradition does not speculate about life after death. Our destiny, as far as we can know it, is to lead a life on this earth that will embody the Will of Heaven. What lies beyond the grave is hidden from us, and we must leave it in the hands of Heaven. Confucians do not rule out the possibility of life after death. They simply refrain from discussing it, since anything we may say about it can only be guesswork. The Confucian faith is that "There is a divine order which works for love and righteousness, and in obedience to that divine order man will find his highest good." (Howard Smith)

> Tzu-lu ventured a question about the dead. The Master said, Till you know about the living, how are you to know about the dead?
>
> (*Analects*, XI, 11)

Yang *and* Yin

During the fourth century BC the doctrine of *yang* and *yin* was formulated. This is the view that everything in nature is composed of two different but complementary cosmic forces.

Yang is male, bright, warm, active, positive; it is embodied in the sky, summer, the sun, day. *Yin* is female, shady or misty, cool, passive, negative; it is embodied in the earth, winter, the moon, night. *Yang* is born at the winter solstice, and waxes until it reaches its apogee at the summer solstice. *Yin* is born at the summer solstice, and waxes until it reaches its apogee at the winter solstice. The Chinese character for *yang* probably represents a hillside illuminated by the sun, the character for *yin* a hillside in the shade.

It is not that one of these is good and the other bad, or that one is better than the other (at least as the doctrine was originally formulated; later it was developed in a variety of ways). Both forces are necessary. This is depicted in the *yin–yang* symbol by the fact that each one interpenetrates the other. All objects in the universe, including male and female human beings, are made up of both. Evil results from an imbalance between them.

The doctrine of *yang* and *yin* was quickly adopted into the Confucian tradition, helping to illuminate the idea of harmony with and in nature. It also came to play a role of fundamental significance in Taoism, as we shall see in the next chapter.

P'an Ku holding the *yin* and *yang* symbol (Circa Photo Library)

Modern Developments

In 1912 the Chinese empire, which had been the official sponsor of Confucianism for some two thousand years, came to an end, after a long period of decline. A revolution overthrew the Manchu dynasty which had governed for several centuries, and a republic was set up. The Confucian tradition was widely blamed for the nation's decline and regarded as obsolete. The government of the republic proved too weak, however, to control the forces of discord, and chaos ensued. Two main political parties emerged, the Nationalists (*Kuomintang*), who were still relatively Confucian in sympathy, and the Communists, each with an army of their own. In the aftermath of World War II war broke out again between these two groups. In 1949 the Communists under Mao Tse-tung defeated the Nationalists, who took refuge on the island of Taiwan.

On the mainland Confucius was execrated, and his place as the supreme teacher of the Chinese people was taken in effect by Mao Tse-tung. Thus a whole generation of Chinese have now grown up who are unacquainted with the thought of the man who, more than any other individual, has shaped their culture. In the last few years, however, as the Communist Party has embraced the free market, the attack on Confucius has been relaxed. Indeed, there are signs that in the current movement to develop "socialism with Chinese characteristics," Confucius may be returning to favor as China's most characteristic sage.

139

In the other Chinese territories, such as Taiwan and Singapore, the teachings of Confucius continued to receive the support of the government. However, there is a widespread feeling that Confucianism is no longer adequate to the demands of the modern era, and in practice few people study it with zeal. It remains to be seen whether, now that it is no longer the official philosophy of an empire, Confucianism can regain intellectual vigor and the allegiance of the Chinese people.

This question arises in two particular forms. One is whether the Confucian tradition can be reconciled with democracy, and even provide an ethical foundation for it. For Confucianism in its traditional form has been considered strongly aristocratic in its values. The other is whether it can be reconciled with capitalism and the free market. For, as we remarked above, traditionally the followers of Confucius have looked down on commerce, though today many overseas Chinese entrepreneurs venerate Confucius fervently. At the same time, some observers have noted a spiritual emptiness at the heart of modern secular Chinese culture, which, to the extent that it has become economically successful, has tended to be markedly materialistic. Yet there are also a growing number of scholars who see in the Confucian tradition a wealth of resources for coping with these contemporary problems. In the meantime it remains true that the fundamental values of East Asian society are still in many ways Confucian, whether this is recognized or not, as for example in the primary role of the family.

Summary of Ancient Chinese Religion and the Confucian Tradition

1   The Shang:

    (a)   Man will prosper if he is in harmony with Heaven and Earth, that is, with nature.

    (b)   Ancestors must be venerated.

    (c)   The cosmos is ruled over by the Supreme Ancestor, Shang Ti.

2   The Chou:

    (a)   Shang Ti is Heaven, *T'ien*.

    (b)   Heaven is the supreme moral power, which gives all things their natures, and sets moral standards for human behavior in virtue of human nature.

    (c)   Only a just government has the mandate of Heaven, the *T'ien Ming*, and so the right to rule.

3   Confucius:

    (a)   Man must follow the Will of Heaven, inscribed in human nature.

    (b)   The Will of Heaven is that we be truly and fully human: the all-encompassing virtue of human-heartedness or love and concern for others, *ren*.

(c)   The Five Relationships are the basis of society, showing concern on the one side, and respect on the other.

(d)   It is important always to follow the rules of good external conduct, *li*.

Questions for discussion

1   Does Confucius have anything of interest to say to us today?

2   Could a modern Westerner be a Confucian?

3   Chinese society in Confucius' day had an aristocracy and a peasantry, but little or no middle class. The values of the Confucian philosophy are therefore aristocratic values. Modern Western societies, by contrast, are middle-class societies. Would this have any implications for modern Westerners interested in Confucianism?

4   What value do the concepts of *yang* and *yin* have?

Test questions

1   Explain the importance of ritual, *li*, in early China.

2   Explain the Chou belief in the mandate of Heaven, *T'ien Ming*.

3   What are the Five Classics?

4   What are the Four Books?

5   Explain the following Confucian ideas:

(a)   *T'ien*, Heaven
(b)   *Tao*, the Way
(c)   *Chun-tzu*, the Noble Man
(d)   *Ren*, human-heartedness
(e)   *I*, justice
(f)   The Five Relationships
(g)   *Yang* and *yin*

Additional reading

Eber, Irene (ed.), *Confucianism: The Dynamics of Tradition*, New York, Macmillan, 1986.

Fingarette, Herbert, *Confucius – The Secular as Sacred*, New York, Harper & Row, 1972.

Fung Yu-lan, *A Short History of Chinese Philosophy*, ed. Derk Bodde, New York, Free Press, 1948. China's most noted modern philosopher.

Smith, D. Howard, *Chinese Religions from 1000 BC to the Present Day*, New York, Holt, Rinehart & Winston, 1968. A fine historical survey with a sure touch.

Smith, D. Howard, *Confucius*, Frogmore, St Albans, UK, Paladin Press, 1973. An excellent work.

Taylor, Rodney L., *The Religious Dimensions of Confucianism*, Albany, State University of New York Press, 1990.

Thompson, Laurence G., *Chinese Religion*, Belmont, CA, Wadsworth, 1989. Conveys the rich diversity of religious expression in China.

Tu Wei-ming, *Confucian Thought: Selfhood as Creative Transformation*, Albany, State University of New York Press, 1985.

Confucianism: Texts

The Doctrine of the Mean

The Chinese title of this book is *Chung Yung*. *Chung* means standing in the middle, without leaning to one side or the other; *yung* means undeviating, unchanging. The American poet Ezra Pound translated it as "The Unwobbling Pivot."

The sentences of this text, like those of many Chinese classics, are extremely compressed, and within a certain range very different interpretations are often possible.

1 What Heaven imparts to man is called human nature. To follow our nature is called the Way. Cultivating the Way is called education.

The Way cannot be separated from us for a moment. What can be separated from us is not the Way.

Therefore the superior man is cautious over what he does not see and apprehensive over what he does not hear. There is nothing more visible than what is hidden and nothing more manifest than what is subtle. Therefore the superior man is watchful over himself when he is alone.

Before the feelings of pleasure, anger, sorrow, and joy are aroused it is called equilibrium [*chung*, centrality, mean]. When these feelings are aroused and each and all attain due measure and degree, it is called harmony. Equilibrium is the great foundation of the world, and harmony its universal path. When equilibrium and harmony are realized to the highest degree, heaven and earth will attain their proper order and all things will flourish.

The principles that should govern our conduct are rooted in our nature as human beings, a nature given us by God. To acquire a fuller understanding of those principles, we should turn to the instruction given by the sages.

Since the Way is given to us by our nature, we do not have to look far afield to find out how to live; all we have to do is search within our own hearts. See # 13.

Human nature as such is something abstract, it cannot be seen with one's physical eyes, yet nothing is more obvious to us: we can usually tell easily whether a being is a member of the human race, and whether a human being is behaving in a humane fashion.

The superior man is watchful over himself when he is alone because his nature is still with him then, and he must still constantly decide whether he will act in accordance with it. If he betrays his own nature when he is alone, he is very likely to betray it when in the company of others.

Before we encounter some situation which arouses our feelings, we are by nature in a state of emotional balance. Once our emotions are aroused, however, it becomes difficult to preserve that balance. The person who can maintain his emotional balance even in difficult situations is the person who is truly in harmony with his nature. If all human beings could keep their emotional balance in trying situations, human society would have few problems.

This first chapter summarizes the main message of the book. The remaining chapters give statements of Confucius which develop these ideas in more detail.

2   Confucius said, "The Noble Man [exemplifies] the Mean (*chung-yung*). The inferior man acts contrary to the Mean. The Noble Man [exemplifies] the Mean because, as a Noble Man, he can maintain the Mean at any time. The inferior man [acts contrary to] the Mean because, as an inferior man, he has no caution."

Only the man of true nobility can follow the Mean, because he is cautious and circumspect. The inferior man is reckless, and so constantly contravenes it.

3   Confucius said, "Perfect is the Mean. For a long time few people have been able to follow it."

4   Confucius said, "I know why the Way is not pursued. The intelligent go beyond it and the stupid do not come up to it. I know why the Way is not

understood. The worthy go beyond it and the unworthy do not come up to it. There is no one who does not eat and drink, but there are few who can really know flavor."

5 Confucius said, "Alas! How is the Way not being pursued!"

6 Confucius said, "Shun was indeed a man of great wisdom! He loved to question others and to examine their words, however ordinary. He concealed what was bad in them and displayed what was good. He took hold of their two extremes, took the mean between them, and applied it in his dealing with the people. This was how he became Shun (the sage-emperor)."

7 Confucius said, "Men all say, 'I am wise'; but when driven forward and taken in a net, a trap, or a pitfall, none knows how to escape. Men all say, 'I am wise'; but should they choose the course of the Mean, they are not able to keep it for a round month."

8 Confucius said, "Hui was a man who chose the course of the Mean, and when he got hold of one thing that was good, he clasped it firmly as if wearing it on his breast and never lost it."

9 Confucius said, "The empire, the states, and the families can be put in order. Ranks and emolument can be declined. A bare, naked weapon can be tramped upon. But the Mean cannot [easily] be attained."

Confucius gives a list of difficult things – governing the empire, declining high office, trampling on a naked sword – and then says that all these things are easier than following the Mean.

10 Tzu-lu asked about strength. Confucius said, "Do you mean the strength of the South, the strength of the North, or the strength you should cultivate yourself? To be genial and gentle in teaching others and not to revenge unreasonable conduct – this is the strength of the people of the South. The superior man lives by it. To lie under arms and meet death without regret – this is the strength of the people of the North. The strong man lives by it. Therefore the superior man maintains harmony [in his nature and conduct] and does not waver. How unflinching is his strength! He stands in the middle position and does not lean to one side. How unflinching is his strength! When the Way prevails in the state, [if he enters public life] he does not change from what he was in private life. How unflinching is his strength! When the Way does not prevail in the state, he does not change even unto death. How unflinching is his strength!"

11 "There are men who seek for the abstruse, and practice wonders. Future generations may mention them. But that is what I will not do. There are superior men who act in accordance with the Way, but give up when they have gone half way. But I can never give up. There are superior men who

are in accord with the Mean, retire from the world and are unknown to their age, but do not regret. It is only a sage who can do this."

12 "The Way of the superior man functions everywhere and yet is hidden. Men and women of simple intelligence can share its knowledge; and yet in its utmost reaches, there is something which even the sage does not know.

"Men and women of simple intelligence can put it into practice; and yet in its utmost reaches there is something which even the sage is not able to put into practice. Great as heaven and earth are, men still find something in them with which to be dissatisfied.

"Thus with [the Way of] the superior man, if one speaks of its greatness, nothing in the world can contain it, and if one speaks of its smallness, nothing in the world can split it.

"The Book of Odes says, 'The hawk flies up to heaven; the fishes leap in the deep.' This means that [the Way] is clearly seen above and below. The Way of the superior man has its simple beginnings in the relation between man and woman, but in its utmost reaches, it is clearly seen in heaven and on earth."

No matter how ordinary a person may be, the Law of Nature always retains some foothold within him. On the other hand, no matter how wise and enlightened a person may be, there is always some way in which he falls short.

13 Confucius said, "The Way is not far from man. When a man pursues the Way and yet remains away from man, his course cannot be considered the Way. The Book of Odes says, 'In hewing an axe handle, the pattern is not far off.' [Yet] if we take an axe handle to hew another axe handle and look askance from the one to the other, we may still think the pattern is far away.

"Therefore the superior man governs men as men, in accordance with human nature, and as soon as they change [what is wrong], he stops. Conscientiousness (*chung*) and altruism (*shu*) are not far from the Way. What you do not wish others to do to you, do not do to them.

"There are four things in the Way of the superior man, none of which I have been able to do:

- To serve my father as I would expect my son to serve me: that I have not been able to do.
- To serve my ruler as I would expect my ministers to serve me: that I have not been able to do.
- To serve my elder brothers as I would expect my younger brothers to serve me: that I have not been able to do.

- To be the first to treat friends as I would expect them to treat me: that I have not been able to do.

"In practicing the ordinary virtues and in the exercise of care in ordinary conversation, when there is deficiency, the superior man never fails to make further effort, and when there is excess, never dares to go to the limit. His words correspond to his actions and his actions correspond to his words. Isn't the superior man earnest and genuine?"

14 The superior man does what is proper to his position and does not want to go beyond this.

If he is in a noble station, he does what is proper to a position of wealth and honorable station. If he is in a humble station, he does what is proper to a position of poverty and humble station.

If he is in the midst of barbarian tribes, he does what is proper in the midst of barbarian tribes. In a position of difficulty and danger, he does what is proper to a position of difficulty and danger. He can find himself in no situation in which he is not at ease with himself.

In a high position he does not treat his inferiors with contempt. In a low position he does not court the favor of his superiors.

He rectifies himself and seeks nothing from others, hence he has no complaint to make. He does not complain against Heaven above or blame men below.

Thus it is that the superior man lives peacefully and at ease and waits for his destiny (*ming*, Mandate of Heaven, fate), while the inferior man takes to dangerous courses and hopes for good luck.

Confucius said, "In archery we have something resembling the Way of the superior man. When the archer misses the center of the target, he turns around and seeks for the cause of failure within himself."

15 The Way of the superior man may be compared to traveling to a distant place: one must start from the nearest point. It may be compared to ascending a height: one must start from below.

The Book of Odes says, "Happy union with wife and children is like the music of lutes and harps. When brothers live in concord and at peace, the harmony is sweet and delightful. Let your family live in concord, and enjoy your wife and children."

Confucius said, "How happy will parents be!"

16 Confucius said, "How abundant is the display of power of spiritual beings! We look for them but do not see them. We listen to them but do not hear them. They form the substance of all things and nothing can be without them. They cause all people in the world to fast and purify themselves and put on the richest dresses to perform sacrifices to them. Like the spread of overflowing water they seem to be above and to be on the left and the right.

"The Book of Odes says, 'The coming of spiritual beings cannot be surmised. How much less can we get tired of them?' Such is the manifestation of the subtle. Such is the impossibility of hiding the real (*ch'eng*)."

The interpretation of this passage is disputed. Confucius may be saying that the spirits are genuinely powerful even though they are invisible, thus continuing the earlier point that the most important things are evident even though not manifest to the senses; or he may be saying, on the contrary, that people attribute more power to the spirits than they actually possess. This would perhaps be more in line with his usual policy of not discussing them.

17 Confucius said, "Shun was indeed greatly filial! In virtue he was a sage; in honor he was the Son of Heaven (emperor); and in wealth he owned all within the four seas (China). Temple sacrifices were made to him, and his descendants preserved the sacrifices to him. Thus it is that he who possesses great virtue will certainly attain to corresponding position, to corresponding wealth, to corresponding fame, and to corresponding long life.

"For Heaven, in the production of things, is sure to be bountiful to them, according to their natural capacity. Hence the tree that is well taken care of is nourished and that which is about to fall is overthrown. The Book of Odes says, 'The admirable, amiable prince displayed conspicuously his excellent virtue. He put his people and his officers in concord. And he received his emolument from Heaven. It protected him, assisted him, and appointed him king. And Heaven's blessing came again and again.'

"Therefore he who possesses great virtue will surely receive the appointment of Heaven."

18 Confucius said, "King Wen was indeed the only one without sorrow! He had King Chi for father and King Wu for son. His father laid the foundation of [the great work of the Chou dynasty] and his son carried it on. King Wu continued the enterprise of King T'ai, King Chi, and King Wen. Once he buckled on his armor [and revolted against wicked King Chou of Shang], the world came into his possession, and he did not personally lose his great reputation throughout the empire. In honor he was the Son of Heaven, and in wealth he owned all within the four seas. Temple sacrifices were made to him, and his descendants preserved the sacrifices to him.*

"King Wu received Heaven's Mandate to rule in his old age. Duke Chou carried to completion the virtue of King Wen and King Wu. He honored T'ai and Chi with the posthumous title of king. He sacrificed to the past reigning dukes of the house with imperial rites. These rites were extended to the feudal lords, great officers, officers, and the common people.

"If the father was a great officer, and the son a minor officer, when the father died, he was buried with the rite of a great officer but afterward sacrificed to with the rite of a minor officer. If the father was a minor officer

* King Wen (reigned 1171–1122 BC) was the founder of the Chou dynasty. King Wu (reigned 1121–1116 BC) was his successor. King T'ai was King Ch'i's father. Duke Chou was King Wu's brother (d. 1094 BC).

and the son was a great officer, then the father was buried with the rite of a minor officer but afterward sacrificed to with the rite of a great officer.

"The rule for one year of mourning for relatives was extended upward to include great officers, but the rule for three years of mourning was extended upward to include the Son of Heaven. In mourning for parents, there was no difference for the noble or the commoner. The practice was the same."

19 Confucius said, "King Wu and Duke Chou were indeed eminently filial. Men of filial piety are those who skillfully carry out the wishes of their forefathers and skillfully carry forward their undertakings.

"In spring and autumn they repaired their ancestral temple, displayed their ancestral vessels and exhibited the ancestral robes, and presented the appropriate offerings of the season. The ritual of the ancestral temple is in order to place the kindred on the left or on the right according to the order of descent. This order in rank meant to distinguish the more honorable or humbler stations. Services in the temple are arranged in order so as to give distinction to the worthy [according to their ability for those services]. In the pledging rite the inferiors present their cups to their superiors, so that people of humble stations may have something to do. In the concluding feast, honored places were given people with white hair, so as to follow the order of seniority.

"To occupy places of their forefathers, to practice their rites, to perform their music, to reverence those whom they honored, to love those who were dear to them, to serve the dead as they were served while alive, and to serve the departed as they were served while still with us: this is the height of filial piety.

"The ceremonies of sacrifices to Heaven and Earth are meant for the service of the Lord on High, and the ceremonies performed in the ancestral temple are meant for the service of ancestors. If one understands the ceremonies of the sacrifices to Heaven and Earth and the meaning of the grand sacrifice and the autumn sacrifice to ancestors, it would be as easy to govern a kingdom as to look at one's palm."

20 Duke Ai asked about government. Confucius said, "The governmental measures of King Wen and King Wu are spread out in the records. With their kind of men, government will flourish. When their kind of men are gone, their government will come to an end.

"When the right principles of man operate, the growth of good government is rapid, and when the right principles of soil operate, the growth of vegetables is rapid. Indeed, government is comparable to a fast-growing plant. Therefore the conduct of government depends upon the men.

"The right men are obtained by the ruler's personal character. The cultivation of the person is to be done through the Way, and the cultivation of the Way is to be done through humanity.

"Humanity (*ren*) is [the distinguishing characteristic of] man, and the greatest application of it is in being affectionate toward relatives.

Ren is *ren*: "humanity is man." A famous aphorism, which sums up the core of the Confucian teaching. In Chinese, the pronunciation of the term for "humanity" is the same as that for "man," although the characters are different.

It is characteristic of the Confucian ethic to emphasize first the importance of the family, and only secondly our relationships with the rest of mankind. We show our humane character first and foremost by showing affection to our blood relatives.

"Righteousness (*i*) is the principle of setting things right and proper, and the greatest application of it is in honoring the worthy.

Righteousness or justice means making things right, that is, doing what is right. We carry it out by treating people as they deserve, which means in the first place honoring those who deserve honor.

"The relative degree of affection we ought to feel for our relatives and the relative grades in the honoring of the worthy give rise to the rules of propriety (*li*).

The idea of appropriate or fitting behavior arises because people are not all the same. There are important differences between them, especially between our relatives, some of whom are closer to us by blood than others, and between the good and the bad, the worthy and the unworthy, and our behavior should reflect that fact.

"Therefore the ruler must not fail to cultivate his personal life.

"Wishing to cultivate his personal life, he must not fail to serve his parents.

"Wishing to serve his parents, he must not fail to know man.

"Wishing to know man, he must not fail to know Heaven.

"There are five universal ways [in human relations], and the way by which they are practiced is three. The five are those governing the relationship between ruler and minister, between father and son, between husband and wife, between elder and younger brothers, and those in the intercourse between friends. These five are universal paths in the world.

"Wisdom, humanity, and courage, these three are the universal virtues. The way by which they are practiced is one.

"Some are born with the knowledge [of these virtues]. Some learn it through study. Some learn it through hard work. But when the knowledge is acquired, it comes to the same thing.

"Some practice them naturally and easily. Some practice them for their advantage. Some practice them with effort and difficulty. But when the achievement is made, it comes to the same thing."

Confucius said, "Love of learning is akin to wisdom. To practice with vigor is akin to humanity. To know to be shameful is akin to courage. He who knows these three things knows how to cultivate his personal life.

"Knowing how to cultivate his personal life, he knows how to govern other men. And knowing how to govern other men, he knows how to govern the empire, its states, and the families.

"There are nine standards by which to administer the empire, its states, and the families. They are:

cultivating the personal life,
honoring the worthy,
being affectionate to relatives,
being respectful toward the great ministers,
identifying oneself with the welfare of the whole body of officers,
treating the common people as one's own children,
attracting the various artisans,
showing tenderness to strangers from far countries,
and extending kindly and awesome influence on the feudal lords.

"If the ruler cultivates his personal life, the Way will be established.

If he honors the worthy, he will not be perplexed.

If he is affectionate to his relatives, there will be no grumbling among his uncles and brothers.

If he respects the great ministers, he will not be deceived.

If he identifies himself with the welfare of the whole body of officers, then the officers will repay him heavily for his courtesies.

If he treats the common people as his own children, then the masses will exhort one another [to do good].

If he attracts the various artisans, there will be sufficiency of wealth and resources in the country.

If he shows tenderness to strangers from far countries, people from all quarters of the world will flock to him.

And if he extends kindly and awesome influence over the feudal lords, then the world will stand in awe of him.

"To fast, to purify, and to be correct in dress [at the time of solemn sacrifice], and not to make any movement contrary to the rules of propriety – this is the way to cultivate the personal life.

"To avoid slanderers, keep away seductive beauties, regard wealth lightly, and honor virtue – this is the way to encourage the worthy.

"To give them honorable position, to bestow on them ample emoluments, and to share their likes and dislikes – this is the way to encourage affection for relatives.

"To allow them many officers to carry out their functions – this is the way to encourage the great ministers.

"To deal with them loyally and faithfully and to give them ample emoluments – this is the way to encourage the body of officers.

"To require them for service only at the proper time [without interfering with their farm work] and to tax them lightly – this is the way to encourage the common masses.

"To inspect them daily and examine them monthly and to reward them according to the degree of their workmanship – this is the way to encourage the various artisans.

"To welcome them when they come and send them off when they go and to commend the good among them and show compassion to the incompetent – this is the way to show tenderness to strangers from far countries.

"To restore lines of broken succession, to revive states that have been extinguished, to bring order to chaotic states, to support those states that are in danger, to have fixed times for their attendance at court, and to present them with generous gifts while expecting little when they come – this is the way to extend kindly and awesome influence on the feudal lords.

"There are nine standards by which to govern the empire, its states, and the families, but the way by which they are followed is one. In all matters if there is preparation they will succeed; if there is no preparation, they will fail. If what is to be said is determined beforehand, there will be no stumbling. If the business to be done is determined beforehand, there will be no difficulty. If action to be taken is determined beforehand, there will be no trouble. And if the way to be pursued is determined beforehand, there will be no difficulties.

"If those in inferior positions do not have the confidence of their superiors, they will not be able to govern the people.

There is a way to have the confidence of the superiors: If one is not trusted by his friends, he will not have the confidence of his superiors.

There is a way to be trusted by one's friends: If one is not obedient to his parents, he will not be trusted by his friends.

There is a way to obey one's parents: If one examines himself and finds himself to be insincere, he will not be obedient to his parents.

There is a way to be sincere with oneself: If one does not understand what is good, he will not be sincere with himself.

"Sincerity is the Way of Heaven. To think how to be sincere is the way of man. He who is sincere is one who hits upon what is right without effort and apprehends without thinking. He is naturally and easily in harmony with the Way. Such a man is a sage. He who tries to be sincere is one who chooses the good and holds fast to it.

"Study it (the way to be sincere) extensively, inquire into it accurately, think over it carefully, sift it clearly, and practice it earnestly.

When there is anything not yet studied, or studied but not yet understood, do not give up.

When there is any question not yet asked, or asked but its answer not yet known, do not give up.

When there is anything not yet thought over, or thought over but not yet apprehended, do not give up.

When there is anything not yet sifted, or sifted but not yet clear, do not give up.

When there is anything not yet practiced, or practiced but not yet earnestly, do not give up.

"If another man succeed by one effort, you will use a hundred efforts. If another man succeed by ten efforts, you will use a thousand efforts. If one really follows this course, though stupid, he will surely become intelligent, and though weak, will surely become strong."

21 It is due to our nature that enlightenment results from sincerity.

It is due to education that sincerity results from enlightenment.

Given sincerity, there will be enlightenment, and given enlightenment, there will be sincerity.

22 Only those who are absolutely sincere can fully develop their nature.

If they can fully develop their nature, they can then fully develop the nature of others.

If they can fully develop the nature of others, they can then fully develop the nature of things.

If they can fully develop the nature of things, they can then assist in the transforming and nourishing process of Heaven and Earth.

If they can assist in the transforming and nourishing process of Heaven and Earth, they can thus form a trinity with Heaven and Earth.

23 The next in order are those who cultivate to the utmost a particular goodness. Having done this, they can attain to the possession of sincerity. As there is sincerity, there will be its expression. As it is expressed, it will become conspicuous. As it becomes conspicuous, it will become clear. As it becomes clear, it will move others. As it moves others, it changes them. As it changes them, it transforms them. Only those who are absolutely sincere can transform others.

24 It is characteristic of absolute sincerity to be able to foreknow. When a nation or family is about to flourish, there are sure to be lucky omens. When a nation or family is about to perish, there are sure to be unlucky omens. These omens are revealed in divination and in the movements of the four limbs. When calamity or blessing is about to come, it can surely know beforehand if it is good, and it can also surely know beforehand if it is evil. Therefore he who has absolute sincerity is like a spirit.

25 Sincerity means the completion of the self, and the Way is self-directing. Sincerity is the beginning and end of things. Without sincerity there would be nothing. Therefore the superior man values sincerity. Sincerity is not only the completion of one's own self, it is that by which all things are completed.

The completion of the self means humanity. The completion of all things means wisdom. These are the character of the nature, and they are the Way in which the internal and the external are united. Therefore whenever it is employed, everything done is right.

26   Therefore absolute sincerity is ceaseless. Being ceaseless, it is lasting. Being lasting, it is evident. Being evident, it is infinite. Being infinite, it is extensive and deep. Being extensive and deep, it is high and brilliant. It is because it is extensive and deep that it contains all things. It is because it is high and brilliant that it overshadows all things. It is because it is infinite and lasting that it can complete all things.

In being extensive and deep, it is a counterpart of Earth. In being high and brilliant, it is a counterpart of Heaven. In being infinite and lasting, it is unlimited. Such being its nature, it becomes prominent without any display, produces changes without motion, and accomplishes its ends without action.

The Way of Heaven and Earth may be completely described in one sentence: They are without any doubleness and so they produce things in an unfathomable way.

The Way of Heaven and Earth is extensive, deep, high, brilliant, infinite, and lasting. The heaven now before us is only this bright, shining mass; but when viewed in its unlimited extent, the sun, moon, stars, and constellations are suspended in it and all things are covered by it.

The earth before us is but a handful of soil; but in its breadth and depth, it sustains mountains like Hua and Yueh without feeling their weight, contains the rivers and seas without letting them leak away, and sustains all things.

The mountain before us is only a fistful of straw; but in all the vastness of its size, grass and trees grow upon it, birds and beasts dwell on it, and stores of precious things (minerals) are discovered in it.

The water before us is but a spoonful of liquid, but in all its unfathomable depth, the monsters, dragons, fishes, and turtles are produced in them, and wealth becomes abundant because of it.

The Book of Odes says, "The Mandate of Heaven, how beautiful and unceasing." This is to say, this is what makes Heaven to be Heaven.

Again, it says, "How shining is it, the purity of King Wen's virtue!" This is to say, this is what makes King Wen what he was. Purity likewise is unceasing.

(Wing-tsit Chan (ed.), *A Sourcebook in Chinese Philosophy*,
Princeton, Princeton University Press, 1963)

Questions for discussion

1   What is meant by saying that "There is nothing more visible than what is hidden and nothing more manifest than what is subtle" (# 1)? What is being referred to?

2   What is meant by saying "In hewing an axe handle, the pattern is not far off" (# 13)?

3   What is the point of the last paragraph in section 14?

4   What does it mean, to be filial? (See # 19.)

5   How would you contrast the Confucian theory of government with that of the modern Western democracies? (See # 20.)

Mencius

Mencius said, "He who exerts his mind to the utmost knows his nature. He who knows his nature knows Heaven. To preserve one's mind and to nourish one's nature is the way to serve Heaven." (7A: 1, Chan)

Mencius said, "It is a feeling common to all mankind that they cannot bear to see others suffer. The Former Kings had such feelings, and it was this that dictated their policies. One could govern the entire world with policies dictated by such feelings, as easily as though one turned it in the palm of the hand.

"I say that all men have such feelings because, on seeing a child about to fall into a well, everyone has a feeling of horror and distress. They do not have this feeling out of sympathy for the parents, or to be thought well of by friends and neighbours, or from a sense of dislike at not being thought a feeling person. Not to feel distress would be contrary to all human feeling. Just as not to feel shame and disgrace and not to defer to others and not to have a sense of right and wrong are contrary to all human feeling. This feeling of distress is the first sign of Humanity. This feeling of shame and disgrace is the first sign of Justice. This feeling of deference to others is the first sign of Propriety. This sense of right and wrong is the first sign of wisdom. Men have these four innate feelings just as they have four limbs. To possess these four things, and to protest that one is incapable of fulfilling them, is to deprive oneself. To protest that the ruler is incapable of doing so is to deprive him. Since all have these four capacities within themselves, they should know how to develop and to fulfill them. They are like a fire about to burst into flame, or a spring about to gush forth from the ground. If, in fact, a ruler can fully realize them, he has all that is needed to protect the entire world. But if he does not realize them fully, he lacks what is needed to serve even his own parents"

(2A: 6, W. A. C. H. Dobson, *Mencius*, Toronto, University of Toronto Press, 1963).

Question for discussion

1   Is it true, in your opinion, that everyone has a feeling of horror and distress on seeing a child about to fall into a well?

5

Taoism

The Spirit of Taoism

Once upon a time there was a peasant who saved up his money for many years until eventually he had enough to buy a horse. When he returned home from the market leading his new horse his next-door neighbor came in to congratulate him. But the peasant, being a good Taoist, replied, "Who knows what's good and what's bad!"

During the night his new horse escaped, and all his savings were lost. His next-door neighbor came in to commiserate with him. But the peasant, being a good Taoist, replied, "Who knows what's good and what's bad!"

The following day the horse returned, bringing with him a wild horse. Quickly the peasant sent his sons out to catch both of them. Now he had two horses. His next-door neighbor came in to congratulate him. But the peasant replied, "Who knows what's good and what's bad!"

The next day his eldest son was out breaking in the wild horse, when he fell off and broke his leg. The next-door neighbor came in to commiserate with him. But the peasant replied, "Who knows what's good and what's bad!"

Shortly after that the Emperor's army came around seeking conscripts for the war then taking place, and they would have taken the peasant's eldest son, but since he now had a broken leg, he could go free. The next-door neighbor came in to congratulate him. But the peasant replied, "Who knows what's good and what's bad!"

Thus good fortune changes into bad fortune, and bad fortune into good.

(A version of the story told in the *Huai Nan Tzu*, ch. 18)

Question for discussion

1 Why is it so difficult to know for certain what is good and what is bad?

The Taoist View of Life

The Taoist approach to life has been profoundly shaped by two remarkable books: the *Classic of the Way and its Power*, the *Tao Te Ching*, possibly written in its present form around the fourth century BC, which contains teachings attributed to the sage Lao Tzu; and the *Chuang Tzu*, written somewhat later, which contains the teachings of the sage Chuang Chou. While there are some differences between the two books, they are one in their basic teaching: harmony with Nature.

Like the Confucian tradition, Taoism, at least in the form discussed here, is better described as a religious philosophy than as a religion. While the Confucian tradition focuses on human nature, and its expression in the family and in civilized society, Taoists are concerned instead with Cosmic Nature. Man has the wellsprings of his being in the deep, unfathomable force that has given rise to the mountains and the rivers, the earth and the sky, trees and fish and birds, the cycle of summer and winter, the splendor of life and the finality of death. Man is part of Nature, and will find wisdom and well-being only in harmony with its mysterious powers. With the poet Wordsworth, the Taoist is

> . . . well pleased to recognize
> In Nature and the language of the sense
> The anchor of my purest thoughts, the nurse,
> The guide, the guardian of my heart, and soul
> Of all my moral being.
> (*Tintern Abbey*)

Elsewhere Wordsworth sings, in words that a Taoist would strongly agree with:

> Come forth into the light of things,
> Let Nature be your Teacher.
> She has a world of ready wealth,
> Our minds and hearts to bless –
> Spontaneous wisdom breathed by health,
> Truth breathed by cheerfulness.
> One impulse from the vernal wood
> May teach you more of man,
> Of moral evil and of good,
> Than all the sages can.
> (*The Tables Turned*)

The roots of the Taoist teachings lie in the ancient Shang view of the unity of man with Heaven and Earth, that is, with Nature. As we saw, the Shang had a highly developed sense of beauty, though they do not seem to have been strongly influenced by considerations of morality. Morality was emphasized by the Chou, and Confucius responded to the difficulties of his age by advocating a return to

157

the moral philosophy of the Chou. The Taoist sages, however, reject this, advocating instead a return to Nature.

In opposition to Confucianism, which emphasizes the need for social responsibility, Taoism proclaims a spontaneous life without concern for respectability. Nature is not moral in the human sense: it is neither just nor compassionate. It brings us life, but it also brings us death. Its values are very different from human values. The Taoist call to return to Nature thus involves the abandonment of conventional standards. Whereas the Confucian writings are earnest and literal, the Taoist literature is witty and poetic, mystical and imaginative, delighting in paradox and contradiction. Taoism has stimulated and inspired the arts in China immensely. It was also destined to make a big contribution to the development of Buddhism in China and Japan. It has been said that there is scarcely any idea in Ch'an Buddhism that is not to be found in some form already in Taoism.

It has often been remarked that these two approaches, of Confucianism and Taoism, correspond to two sides of the cultivated Chinese character, the Confucian answering to the side employed during the day, when the duties of one's public office must be carried out, and the Taoist that of the evening, when the scholar can relax in the privacy of his own rooms and the company of his friends, with a glass – even quite a few glasses – of rice wine. Like yang and yin, Confucianism and Taoism complement one another and need one another.

Lao Tzu and Chuang Tzu (Pinyin, Laozi and Zhuangzi)

Tradition ascribes the *Tao Te Ching* to a sage called Lao Tzu, who is supposed to have lived around the time of Confucius, and to have spent his life as an obscure government official. The Grand Historian of China, Ssu-ma Chien, tells us that at an advanced age he gave up his post and headed westwards on a donkey, intending to spend his remaining years in the regions to the west. When he came to the Hankao Pass, the gatekeeper, recognizing him as a wise man, asked him before he departed to leave mankind some statement of his philosophy. At this Lao Tzu went off and in a short time wrote this little treatise, which consists of less than 6,000 words, gave it to the gatekeeper, and resumed his journey, never to be seen again.

Almost from the beginning scholars have been puzzled by the identity of Lao Tzu. Chinese historians mention several other men that he might or might not be identical with. The *Tao Te Ching* in its present form bears the marks of having been written around the fourth century BC, well after the time of Confucius, though it may contain earlier passages. Some have concluded that there was no such person as Lao Tzu, and that the work is a compilation of the work of several authors. "Lao Tzu" could even be simply a title, "The Old Master," rather than a personal name. On the other hand the book preserves the same unique spirit from beginning to end.

An image of Lao Tzu (Circa Photo Library)

The *Tao Te Ching* is written in a most unusual style, terse, vigorous, and profound, with striking images and memorable paradoxes. From the viewpoint of grammar much of its phrasing can be read in different senses. It compresses a great amount of thought into a very small space, its very vagueness serving to enhance its message.

Chuang Chou is a more definite character, who probably lived from about 369 to 286 BC, around the same time as Mencius. According to tradition, he came from a place called Meng, which probably means that he was a descendant of the earlier Shang people, and he once served as "an official in the lacquer garden." The book bearing his name is charming and delightful by any standards. It is written with great gusto and has the distinction of being the only religious classic in any major tradition with a sense of humor. The first seven chapters are the core of the work.

Like Confucianism, Taoism (usually pronounced "Dowism" in English, as the t in *Tao* is unaspirated, like the t in "stop") is initially a philosophy and a way of life for the scholarly and governing class, and acquires religious significance because of this, as well as because of its doctrines. The chief of these are described in the following pages.

159

The Tao, *the Way* (*Pinyin,* Dao)

This is the fundamental concept of Taoism. It is the transcendent source of all things, the inexhaustible spring out of which all life and movement flow. It is the origin of Heaven and Earth. It does not change in itself, but it produces all the change in the universe. It is a fountain of constant renewal. It does not have a definite form that could be grasped by the human mind, but it pervades the world. It fosters all things: it "produces them, makes them grow, nourishes them, shelters them, brings them up and protects them." Only by being in harmony with the *Tao* can human beings prosper and flourish.

> There is a thing formless yet complete.
> It existed before Heaven and Earth.
> Motionless and fathomless,
> It stands alone and never changes.
> It pervades everywhere and never becomes exhausted.
> It may be regarded as the Mother of all beneath Heaven.
> We do not know its name, but we call it *Tao.*

Wu, *non-being*

The *Tao* is empty. This means it is empty of itself, not self-important or full of itself. It does not have a "big ego." The same thing is stated by saying that the *Tao* is "non-existent." For a wheel to be able to function as a wheel, there must be an empty space at its center where the axle can fit; for a cup to be able to function as a cup it must have an empty, hollowed space within it which can contain liquid. For a window to be able to function as a window, or a door as a door, there must be a place where there is no wall. For a painting to be effective, sometimes there must be a space without color. For a speech to be effective, the speaker must sometimes pause, there must be silence. Things can achieve success, not in spite of their limits, but because of them. Similarly in regard to man: for a man to be able to function as a man he must be empty of self.

This indicates the nature of the *Tao.* Since it is empty of itself, it can foster all things. It is not possessive, does not dominate over things, or try to impose some artificial form on them which does not accord with their natures.

The *Tao* is like water. Water does not try to impose its own form on what it encounters but on the contrary is gentle and yielding, fitting into the nooks and crannies of whatever contains it, yet nothing is more powerful.

Spontaneity

The *Tao* acts spontaneously, it is ever fresh and new. It is not a mere mechanism, acting out of some iron necessity, but it originates activity out of its own depths; it takes the initiative, as living things are wont to do. It does not follow a prearranged pattern, but is unpredictable. It is never exhausted, but always able to bring forth new things.

The Taoist would agree enthusiastically with the English poet Gerard Manley Hopkins, who wrote:

> . . . nature is never spent;
> There lives the deepest freshness deep down things;
> And though the last lights off the black West went,
> Oh, morning at the brown brink eastwards springs –
> Because the Holy Ghost over the bent
> World broods with warm breast and with ah! bright wings.
> (*God's Grandeur*)

The Tao *is impartial, not humane*

As we saw, the Confucians had asserted that Heaven was humane, that it was concerned for human welfare, and that the moral standards of justice and compassion appropriate to human nature were written into the basic framework of the universe. The Taoists reject this view. The *Tao* does indeed provide for human welfare in a certain sense, because it gives us life and everything that goes with it, but that kind of goodness transcends conventional human ideas of what is good and bad, beautiful and ugly. Heaven and Earth are ruthless, says Lao Tzu, and treat all creatures like straw dogs. The straw dogs were used in sacrifice, but then discarded and trampled upon afterwards. Similarly, he says, the sage is ruthless, and treats the people like straw dogs.

The relativity of values

This idea is closely connected with the preceding one. Conventional values are relative to one another. A thing is beautiful in comparison to what is ugly, and good by comparison to what is bad. This means that each conventional value suggests its opposite. To have a concept of beauty, I must at the same time have a concept of ugliness, and to attribute goodness to someone, I must implicitly think of evil. If I view life as good in the conventional sense, that immediately leads me to view death as bad. If happiness is good, then pain and sorrow are evil. Yet the *Tao* which gave me life also gives me death, and pain and sorrow are part of life. To respond properly to Nature we must give up all conventional value judgements, abandon all our usual likes and dislikes, and simply accept what Nature gives us.

This is what the *Tao Te Ching* means when it says:

> When all in the world understand beauty to be beautiful,
> Then ugliness exists.
> When all understand goodness to be good,
> Then evil exists.

> Thus existence suggests non-existence;
> Easy gives rise to difficult;
> Short is derived from long by comparison;
> Low is distinguished from high by position;
> Resonance harmonizes sound;
> After follows before.
> Therefore, the Sage carries on his business without action, and
> gives his teaching without words.

Chuang Tzu puts the same idea in this way:

> Everything has its "that," everything has its "this". . . So I say, "that" comes out of "this" and "this" depends on "that" – which is to say that "this" and "that" give birth to each other. But where there is birth there must be death; where there is death there must be birth. Where there is acceptability there must be unaccep-tability; where there is unacceptability there must be acceptability. Where there is recognition of right there must be recognition of wrong; where there is recogni-tion of wrong there must be recognition of right. Therefore the sage does not proceed in such a way, but illuminates all in the light of Heaven.

The wise man makes room in his mind for both the acceptable and the un-acceptable, for what the generality of people consider right and also what they consider wrong.

> He too recognizes a "this," but a "this" which is also "that," a "that" which is also "this." His "that" has both a right and a wrong in it; his "this" too has both a right and a wrong in it. So, in fact, does he still have a "this" and "that"? Or does he in fact no longer have a "this" and "that"?

> A state in which "this" and "that" no longer find their opposites is called the hinge of the Tao. When the hinge is fitted into the socket, it can respond endlessly. Its right then is a single endlessness and its wrong too is a single endlessness. So, I say, the best thing to use is clarity.

Our ordinary value judgements, says Chuang Tzu, are merely derived from convention:

> What is acceptable we call acceptable; what is unacceptable we call unacceptable. A road is made by people walking on it; things are so because they are called so. What makes them so? Making them so makes them so. What makes them not so? Making them not so makes them not so. Things all must have that which is so; things all must have that which is acceptable. There is nothing that is not so, nothing that is not acceptable. For this reason, whether you point to a little stalk or a great pillar, a leper or the beautiful Hsi-shih [the Chinese equivalent of Cleopatra], things ribald and shady or things grotesque and strange, the Tao makes them all into one.

It is not that we have to make things one. Things are already one in the *Tao*, and all we have to do is realize it. We get emotionally involved in trying to have an impact on things without realizing that in the end it makes no difference.

> To wear out your brain trying to make things into one without realizing that they are all the same – this is called "three in the morning." What do I mean by "three in the morning"? When the monkey trainer was handing out acorns, he said, "You get three in the morning and four at night." This made all the monkeys furious. "Well, then," he said, "you get four in the morning and three at night." The monkeys were all delighted. There was no change in the reality behind the words, and yet the monkeys responded with joy and anger.

The Taoist attitude towards death is illustrated strikingly in Chuang Tzu's reaction to the death of his wife. When his friend Hui Tzu went to convey his condolences, he found Chuang Tzu sitting with his legs sprawled out, pounding on a tub and singing.

> "You lived with her, she brought up your children and grew old," said Hui Tzu. "It should be enough simply not to weep at her death. But pounding on a tub and singing – this is going too far, isn't it?"
>
> Chuang Tzu replied, "You're wrong. When she first died, do you think I didn't grieve like anyone else? But I looked back to her beginning and the time before she was born. Not only the time before she was born, but the time before she had a body. Not only the time before she had a body, but the time before she had a spirit.
>
> "In the midst of the jumble of wonder and mystery a change took place and she had a spirit. Another change and she had a body. Another change and she was born. Now there's been another change and she's dead. It's just like the progression of the four seasons, spring, summer, fall, winter.
>
> "Now she's going to lie down peacefully in a vast room. If I were to follow after her bawling and sobbing, it would show that I don't understand anything about fate. So I stopped." (ch. 2)

To insist on conventional human values is a sign that harmony with the *Tao* has been lost. People hope for good luck, but good luck changes into bad luck, and bad luck changes into good luck. Whether an event constitutes good fortune or bad depends on its ultimate consequences, and often we never know what those are. Hence, no one really knows what is truly good luck and what is bad. This is the point of the story from the *Huai Nan Tzu* quoted at the beginning of the chapter.

Because every value suggests its opposite, too much of an emphasis on one value has the effect of highlighting its opposite too. Thus in human affairs, if the pendulum swings too far in one direction, it will eventually reverse and go in the opposite direction. This is a version of what some later thinkers have called the Law of Unintended Consequences, that our actions very often have the opposite effect to what we intend. The Taoists employed this argument

163

especially against the Confucians. The Confucians insisted on positive virtue, on goodness, filial piety, justice, fitting behavior, concern for others, conscientiousness, and so on. In the Taoist view all this zeal was likely to have precisely the opposite effect. The Taoist therefore allows nature to take its course. Instead of being laboriously conscientious, his life is relaxed and carefree. Instead of interfering in other people's lives, he leaves them alone.

> Do away with learning, and grief will not be known.
> Do away with sageness and eject wisdom, and the people will be more benefited a hundred times.
> Do away with benevolence and eject righteousness, and the people will return to filial duty and parental love.
>
> (*Tao Te Ching*, 19)

To achieve a true understanding of human life and the world our fundamental perspective has to undergo a revolution. Our normal perspective on life is so narrow that it is inescapably caught up in delusion. We can see things as they truly are only by attaining a transcendent viewpoint, the Great Understanding.

According to Chuang Tzu, the perspective of the Man of Tao is like that of the legendary bird, the p'eng, compared to a cicada or a quail. The wings of the p'eng are thousands of miles across and cover the whole sky; it rises 90,000 miles into the air, and roils the waters for 3,000 miles. The cicada and the quail are totally unable to grasp the perspective of the p'eng, and laugh at it, "Where does he think *he's* going? I give a great leap and fly up, but I never get more than ten or twelve yards before I come down fluttering among the weeds and brambles" (*Chuang Tzu*, 1).

The difference between our conventional perspective and the Great Understanding is like the difference of outlook between the morning mushroom, which lives for only a few hours and never sees the evening, or the summer cicada, which never experiences the spring or autumn, and the legendary rose of Sharon which lived for 16,000 years.

Chuang Tzu's fantastic imagination, together with his emphasis on the relativity of our ordinary perspective, lead him to the brink of a radical skepticism about our ordinary knowledge. He asks if it is even possible for us to come to know the truth. Once, he says, he dreamt he was a butterfly, "flitting and fluttering around, happy with himself and doing as he pleased. He didn't know he was Chuang Chou. Suddenly he woke up and there he was, solid and unmistakable Chuang Chou. But he didn't know if he was Chuang Chou who had dreamt he was a butterfly, or a butterfly dreaming he was Chuang Chou."

Chuang Tzu recounts with approval the remarks of the sage Wang Ni to a friend who asked him "Do you know what all things agree in calling right?"

> "How would I know that?" said Wang Ni.
> "Do you know that you don't know it?"
> "How would I know that?"
> "Then do things know nothing?"

"How would I know that? However, suppose I try saying something. What way do I have of knowing that if I say I know something I don't really not know it? Or what way do I have of knowing that if I say I don't know something I don't really in fact know it? Now let me ask you some questions. If a man sleeps in a damp place, his back aches and he ends up half paralyzed, but is this true of a loach? If he lives in a tree, he is terrified and shakes with fright, but is this true of a monkey? Of these three creatures, then, which one knows the proper place to live? Men eat the flesh of grass-fed and grain-fed animals, deer eat grass, centipedes find snakes tasty, and hawks and falcons relish mice. Of these four, which knows how food ought to taste? Monkeys pair with monkeys, deer go out with deer, and fish play around with fish. Men claim that Mao-ch'iang and Lady Li were beautiful, but if fish saw them they would dive to the bottom of the stream, if birds saw them they would fly away, and if deer saw them they would break into a run. Of these four, which knows how to fix the standard of beauty for the world? The way I see it, the rules of benevolence and righteousness and the paths of right and wrong are all hopelessly snarled and jumbled. How could I know anything about such discriminations?"

Wu wei, *inactive action, laissez-faire, non-interference*

This follows from the relativity of values. The *Tao* is not self-important, but empty of self, and so it does not try to impose an artificial, external order on things; it does not interfere or meddle, but allows each thing to develop and flourish according to its own natural inclination. Things do not have to be told what they need: each thing already knows what it needs, from its own nature. The Man of Tao does not interfere officiously in other people's lives, as if he knew better than they what was good for them, but simply lets them be.

Literally, *wu* means "not," and *wei* means "action," so that *wu wei* means "inaction." But the Taoist concept does not mean simply doing nothing, out of laziness as it were. It means that there are times when it is better to do nothing, when action, however well intended, will do more harm than good, when the mere attempt to "do good" can be destructive. There are times when a deliberate neglect can be beneficial. To take action under such circumstances is an indication more of an exaggerated sense of one's own importance than of a genuine desire for the welfare of others.

If we want a tree to grow, for example, we do not have to command it to grow, or give it instructions how to do that: it already knows how to grow, and wants to grow. All we have to do is let it be, and avoid harming it. If, instead, we insist on forcing it into some preconceived pattern according to our desire, we may only kill it.

The Tao *is ever inactive, and yet there is nothing that it does not do*

Wu wei goes further, however, than just letting things be themselves. It also includes the idea of acting in such a way as to respect the nature of things.

Chuang Tzu tells of a cook who used the same knife for 19 years without having to sharpen it.

> Cook Ting was cutting up an ox for Lord Wen-hui. At every touch of his hand, every heave of his shoulder, every move of his feet, every thrust of his knee – zip! zoop! He slithered the knife along with a zing, and all was in perfect rhythm, as though he were performing the dance of the Mulberry Grove or keeping time to the Ching-shou music.
>
> "Ah, this is marvelous!" said Lord Wen-hui. "Imagine skill reaching such heights!"
>
> Cook Ting laid down his knife and replied, "What I care about is the Tao, which goes beyond skill. When I first began cutting up oxen, all I could see was the ox itself. After three years I no longer saw the whole ox. And now – now I go at it by spirit and don't look with my eyes. Perception and understanding have come to a stop and spirit moves where it wants. I go along with the natural makeup, strike in the big hollows, guide the knife through the big openings, and follow things as they are. So I never touch the smallest ligament or tendon, much less a main joint.
>
> "A good cook changes his knife once a year – because he cuts. A mediocre cook changes his knife once a month – because he hacks. I've had this knife of mine for nineteen years and I've cut up thousands of oxen with it, and yet the blade is as good as though it had just come from the grindstone. There are spaces between the joints, and the blade of the knife has really no thickness. If you insert what has no thickness into such spaces, then there's plenty of room – more than enough for the blade to play about it. That's why after nineteen years the blade of my knife is still as good as when it first came from the grindstone.
>
> "However, whenever I come to a complicated place, I size up the difficulties, tell myself to watch out and be careful, keep my eyes on what I'm doing, work very slowly, and move the knife with the greatest subtlety, until – flop! the whole thing comes apart like a clod of earth crumbling to the ground. I stand there holding the knife and look all around me, completely satisfied and reluctant to move on, and then I wipe off the knife and put it away."
>
> "Excellent!" said Lord Wen-hui. "I have heard the words of Cook Ting and learned how to care for life!"

The **Tao** *is paradoxical, and cannot be put into words*

The *Tao* far surpasses the power of the human mind to grasp it. If we could understand it, it would not be the *Tao*. By its nature the *Tao* transcends all human concepts and forms of thought. This is a thought we have already encountered in connection with Brahman and the Buddha nature. Taoism, however, carries it further in holding that the rational, reflective mind is more of an obstacle than a help in comprehending the *Tao*. Deeper than our human conventions, the *Tao* brings into question the most fundamental human conceptions. The *Tao Te Ching* expresses this by saying that the *Tao* is "nameless." Consequently, the only language appropriate to the *Tao* is that of paradox and contradiction. "The Tao that can be expressed is not the eternal Tao" (*Tao Te Ching*, ch. 1).

Paradox is the natural Taoist language not only for the *Tao*, but also for human activity. Typical statements of the *Tao Te Ching* are that the the best soldier is not soldierly; the best fighter is not ferocious; the best conqueror does not take part in war; the best employer of men keeps himself below them; the best ruler is not noticed; the good traveler leaves no track; the weakest things in the world can overmatch the strongest things in the world; the greatest perfection seems imperfect; the loudest sound can scarcely be heard; be bent, and you will remain straight; he who speaks, does not know; he who knows, does not speak.

The Man of Tao

The Man of *Tao* is very different from other men. He judges things by altogether different standards. He looks at every event from the perspective of eternity. He loves and fosters all things:

> To the good I act with goodness;
> To the bad I also act with goodness:
> Thus goodness is attained.
>
> The sage is always a good savior of men,
> And no man is rejected.

The Man of *Tao* does not push himself forward, but is sensitive to the demands of nature:

> He is cautious, like one who crosses a stream in winter;
> He is hesitating, like one who fears his neighbors;
> He is modest, like one who is a guest;
> He is yielding, like ice that is going to melt;
> He is simple, like wood that is not yet wrought."

The Man of *Tao* clings to the yin rather than the yang.

> He who knows the masculine and yet keeps to the feminine
> Will become a channel drawing all the world towards it.

The *Chuang Tzu* sometimes speaks as if the Man of *Tao* possessed superhuman abilities and could not be injured.

The Perfect Man is godlike. Though the great swamps blaze, they cannot burn him; though the great rivers freeze, they cannot chill him; though swift lightning splits the hills and howling gales shake the sea, they cannot frighten him. A man like this rides the clouds and mist, straddles the sun and moon, and wanders beyond the four seas. Even life and death have no effect on him, much less the rules of profit and loss!

(Chuang Tzu, 2)

167

Probably such statements were originally intended only as rhetorical exaggeration, but some later Taoists took them literally.

Government

All this implies a philosophy of government. This is not merely an appendix to Taoism, but a central concern of it. The *Tao Te Ching* was written to provide the governing class – which as we saw had a religious function and was the nearest thing to a priesthood in China – with a philosophy.

Government should be like the *Tao*. It must seek the people's good, not its own. The best government will be the one that governs least. A good government will not try to impose any preconceived pattern on people's lives. It will not meddle in people's affairs or interfere with their activities. It will seek only to prevent harm from being done. For the rest, it will respect people's natures, and allow each to prosper and flourish in his own way.

> Govern a great state as you would cook a small fish. (That is, do it gently.)
> In ruling men and in serving Heaven, the sage uses only moderation.
> When the government is blunt and inactive, the people will be happy and prosperous.
> The more laws and regulations are given, the more robbers and thieves there are.
> The people starve.
> Because their officials take heavy taxes from them, therefore they starve.
> The people are hard to rule.
> Because their officials meddle with affairs, therefore they are hard to rule.

The *Chuang Tzu* carries distrust of government even further, suggesting that the wise man will avoid taking office, or at least view with detachment the chance to exercise power.

> Yao wanted to cede the empire to Hsü Yu. "When the sun and moon have already come out," he said, "it's a waste of light to go on burning the torches, isn't it? When the seasonal rains are falling, it's a waste of water to go on irrigating the fields. If you took the throne, the world would be well ordered. I go on occupying it, but all I can see are my failings. I beg to turn over the world to you."
>
> Hsü Yu said "You govern the world and the world is already well governed. Now if I take your place, will I be doing it for a name? But name is only the guest of reality! Will I be doing it so I can play the part of a guest? When the tailor-bird builds her nest in the deep wood, she uses no more than one branch. When the mole drinks at the river, he takes no more than a bellyful. Go home and forget the matter, my lord. I have no use for the rulership of the world! Though the cook may not run his kitchen properly, the priest and the impersonator of the dead at the sacrifice do not leap over the wine casks and sacrificial stands and go take his place."
>
> Once, when Chuang Tzu was fishing in the P'u River, the king of Ch'u sent two officials to go and announce to him: "I would like to trouble you with the administration of my realm."

Ritual in a Taoist temple (Circa Photo Library)

Chuang Tzu held on to the fishing pole and, without turning his head, said, "I have heard that there is a sacred tortoise in Ch'u that has been dead for three thousand years. The king keeps it wrapped in cloth and boxed, and stores it in the ancestral temple. Now would this tortoise rather be dead and have its bones left behind and honored? Or would it rather be alive and dragging its tail in the mud?"

"It would rather be alive and dragging its tail in the mud," said the two officials.

Chuang Tzu said, "Go away! I'll drag my tail in the mud!"

Art and culture

Taoism has had a profound influence on Chinese culture. It has been a principal source of inspiration for China's poets and painters. Not only were its particular concepts, such as inactive action, its emphasis on spontaneity, and its rejection of conventional values attractive to them, but the whole carefree style of life that it stood for was congenial to them.

The role of Taoism in Chinese society does not stop with the poets and artists, but can be found in every aspect of Chinese life where taste is important, even in such mundane arts as cooking, where, largely because of Taoist principles, China has developed a subtle and sophisticated cuisine. The practice of T'ai Chi Chuan, or Chinese shadow-boxing as it used to be called, and the martial arts now so much in vogue in the West, are also indebted to Taoism.

Other Forms of Taoism

In addition to the Taoism outlined here, which in English is often called Philosophical Taoism, and which the Chinese call the School of Tao (*Tao Chia*), other forms of Taoism have developed:

- Esoteric Taoism is the name given to a movement which sought to avoid death and attain physical immortality by various special means, such as breathing exercises, vegetarianism, or sometimes simply not eating. Some of its techniques are still practiced.
- Popular Taoism, called Religious Taoism (*Tao Chiao*) in Chinese, is a form of popular Chinese religion which aims at longevity and prosperity through a variety of rituals, including the worship of gods and exorcisms. It is still very much alive, particularly in Chinese communities outside China, such as Taiwan and Singapore.

Some idea of the second form of Taoism may perhaps be gained from the exorcism ceremony. The Taoist priest first ascertains the person's animal sign from the year of his birth, and takes a paper image of that animal. For example, if he was born in the Year of the Dog, the priest will take a paper image of a dog. By means of prayers and incantations he then transfers into the paper image of the dog any illness or evil present in the person, and then burns the image.

Taoist Ethics

The question of our relationship to others is scarcely discussed in the *Chuang Tzu*, but the *Tao Te Ching* has several remarkable statements on the subject, of which the main ones are collected in the next chapter, under the heading "Love." The wise man is not full of himself, but empty of himself. This enables him to identify with others.

> The Sage has no self;
> He makes the self of the people his self.

Consequently he will act towards others with love. It is right to love those who are good, but the man who is empty of himself will also love those who are bad.

> To the good I act with goodness;
> To the bad I also act with goodness;
> Thus goodness is attained.

> Even if men be bad, why should they be rejected?
> Therefore the Sage is always a good savior of men,
> And no man is rejected.

We should love even those who hate us:

> Return love for great hatred.
> Otherwise, when a great hatred is reconciled, some of it will surely remain.

Even in battle, we should love those against whom we are fighting:

> He who fights with love will win the battle,
> He who defends with love will be secure.
> Heaven will save him, and protect him with love.

The wise man does not exact the last farthing, but is generous towards his partners in an agreement:

> The sage holds to the left half of an agreement, but does not exact what the other holder ought to do.
> The virtuous resort to agreement, the virtueless resort to exaction.

It should be acknowledged, however, that these statements are few in number, and a good deal hinges on the particular translation.

Summary of Taoism

1 The *Tao* is the fundamental principle of the universe, the inexhaustible spring of all life and movement.

2 It is empty of self.

3 It is spontaneous and natural.

4 It does not share conventional human values.

5 It governs the universe through "inactive action."

6 The Man of *Tao* loves all things, and acts by "inaction."

7 Government should rule as the *Tao* rules, by "inactive action."

Questions for discussion

1 To what extent is Taoism genuinely religious?

2 Would a Taoist viewpoint be compatible, in your opinion, with belief in a personal God?

3 Would it be compatible with belief in Brahman?

Test questions

1 Explain the concept of the *Tao*.

2 Explain the Taoist concept of emptiness.

3 Explain "inactive action."

4 Why does Taoism resist conventional value judgements?

5 How would you compare the Taoist philosophy of government with that of Confucius?

Additional reading

Kaltenmark, Max, *Lao Tzu and Taoism*, trans. from French by Roger Greaves, Stanford, CA, Stanford University Press, 1969.

Maspero, Henri, *Taoism and Chinese Religion*, Amherst, MA, University of Massachusetts Press, 1981.

Thompson, Laurence G., *Chinese Religion*, Belmont, CA, Wadsworth, 1989.

Waley, Arthur, *Three Ways of Thought in Ancient China*, London, George Allen & Unwin, 1939.

Welch, Holmes, *The Parting of the Way: Lao Tzu and the Taoist Movement*, London, Methuen, 1958.

Taoism: Texts

Tao Te Ching

Tradition ascribes this remarkable book to the sage Lao Tzu, a name which may be a personal name, "Master Lao," or a title, "The Old Master." Some of it may have been written in the sixth century BC, that is, about the same time as Confucius, as Chinese tradition asserts, or it may have been composed for the most part two or three centuries later, as many scholars think. Its spirit of naturalness and nonconformity has penetrated into almost every aspect of Chinese life, not only religion and philosophy, but also literature, art, medicine, and even cooking.

It has been commented on more than any other Chinese classic, and over 40 English translations have been published.

The Chinese text is terse and cryptic. Almost every sentence allows room for different interpretations, and no single translation is widely accepted. Furthermore, there is reason to think that portions of the text have been shifted around.

The translation used here is that by Ch'u Ta-Kao, *Tao Te Ching*, London, Allen & Unwin, 1937.

The Tao

1

The Tao that can be spoken of is not the eternal Tao;
The Name that can be named is not the unchanging Name.
The Nameless is the origin of Heaven and Earth.
The Named is the mother of the ten thousand things.

From non-being, therefore, we serenely observe the mysterious beginning of the
    Universe;

From being we clearly see the apparent distinctions.
These two are the same in source and become different when manifested.
This sameness is called profundity.
Infinite profundity is the gate whence comes the beginning of all wonders.

(Chapter 1)

Paragraph 1 The first two lines emphasize the transcendence of the *Tao*,
that it lies beyond the reach of our mortal minds.

"Heaven and Earth" is a classic phrase for the sum total of things, the
universe. The "ten thousand things" are the sum total of things viewed
from the aspect of their variety and multiplicity.

The Nameless, the *Tao*, is the realm of Non-being. The Named is the realm
of Being.

"Non-being" in the Taoist sense does not mean the complete absence of
being, as if first there was nothing at all and then inexplicably something
sprang into existence. Rather, what is meant is that fertile and creative
emptiness which, for example, makes a cup capable of holding water and
so functioning as a cup, or a window capable of letting light through
and so functioning as a window. If we look at a cup we see its being, the
porcelain or other material that makes it up. But if it were a solid block
of porcelain it could not hold any liquid. It can be used as a cup only
because its center is empty of being, because there is "non-being" at its
heart.

Paragraph 2 The original source of things lies in the primal oneness
and Non-being of the *Tao*. The distinctions of the universe, the differences
between one thing and another, come from their Being, the material that
makes them up. In the *Tao*, Being and Non-being are the same; the differences between the two emerge when the *Tao* gives rise to the manifest
universe, the world of varied and multiple things.

2

There is a thing inherent and natural,
Which existed before Heaven and Earth.
Motionless and fathomless,
It stands alone and never changes;
It pervades everywhere and never becomes exhausted.
It may be regarded as the Mother of the Universe.

I do not know its name.
If I am forced to give it a name, I call it Tao,

And I name it as supreme.
Supreme means functioning everywhere;
Functioning everywhere means far-reaching;
Far-reaching means returning.

Therefore Tao is supreme; heaven is supreme; earth is supreme; and man is also
   supreme.
There are in the universe four things supreme, and man is one of them.

Man models himself on Earth;
Earth models itself on Heaven;
Heaven models itself on Tao;
Tao follows what is spontaneously natural.

(Chapter 25)

"Far-reaching means returning." This is a typical statement of the *Tao Te Ching*. Chapter 40 remarks: "Reversal is the movement of the Tao." The Tao is like a pendulum: when it reaches one extreme, it naturally reverses itself and returns in the opposite direction.

The Man of Tao

10

In old times the perfect man of Tao was subtle, penetrating and so profound
   that he can hardly be understood.
Because he cannot be understood, I shall endeavour to picture him:

He is cautious, like one who crosses a stream in winter;
He is hesitating, like one who fears his neighbours;
He is modest, like one who is a guest;
He is yielding, like ice that is going to melt;
He is simple, like wood that is not yet wrought;
He is vacant, like valleys that are hollow;
He is dim, like water that is turbid.

Who is able to purify the dark till it becomes slowly light?
Who is able to calm the turbid till it slowly clears?
Who is able to quicken the stagnant till it slowly makes progress?

He who follows these principles does not desire fullness.
Because he is not full, therefore when he becomes decayed he can renew.

(Chapter 15)

11

"Be humble, and you will remain entire."
Be bent, and you will remain straight.
Be vacant, and you will remain full.
Be worn, and you will remain new.

He who has little will receive.
He who has much will be embarrassed.

Therefore the Sage keeps to One
And becomes the standard for the world.
He does not display himself;
Therefore he shines.
He does not approve of himself;
Therefore he is noted.
He does not praise himself;
Therefore he has merit.
He does not glory in himself;
Therefore he excels.
And because he does not compete, therefore no one in the world can compete
    with him.

(Chapter 22)

"Be humble and you will remain entire" refers to the ancient practice of
punishment by mutilation. Criminals could be identified with relative ease
because they had typically lost a hand or a foot.

12

As Tao is to the world so are streams and valleys to rivers and seas.
Rivers and seas can be kings to all valleys because the former can well lower
    themselves to the latter.
Thus they become kings to all valleys.
Therefore the Sage, in order to be above the people, must in words keep below
    them;
In order to be ahead of the people, he must in person keep behind them.
Thus when he is above, the people do not feel his burden;
When he is ahead, the people do not feel his hindrance.
Therefore all the world is pleased to hold him in high esteem and never get tired
    of him.

Because he does not compete; therefore no one competes with him.

(Chapter 66)

13

Attain to the goal of absolute emptiness;
Keep to the state of perfect peace.
All things come into existence,
And thence we see them return.

Look at the things that have been flourishing;
Each goes back to its origin.

Going back to the origin is called peace;
It means reversion to destiny.
Reversion to destiny is called eternity.
He who knows eternity is called enlightened.
He who does not know eternity is running blindly into miseries.

Knowing eternity he is all-embracing.
Being all-embracing he can attain magnanimity.
Being magnanimous he can attain omnipresence.
Being omnipresent he can attain supremacy.
Being supreme he can attain Tao.

He who attains Tao is everlasting.
Though his body may decay he never perishes.

(Chapter 16)

Non-being, emptiness

14

Thirty spokes unite in one nave,
And because of the part where nothing exists we have the use of a carriage
  wheel.

Clay is moulded into vessels,
And because of the space where nothing exists we are able to use them as
  vessels.

Doors and windows are cut out in the walls of a house,
And because they are empty spaces, we are able to use them.

Therefore, on the one hand we have the benefit of existence,
And on the other, we make use of non-existence.

(Chapter 11)

15

The weakest things in the world can overmatch the strongest things in the
   world.

Nothing in the world can be compared to water for its weak and yielding
   nature;
Yet in attacking the hard and the strong nothing proves better than it.
For there is no other alternative to it.

The weak can overcome the strong and the yielding can overcome the hard:
This all the world knows but does not practice.

Therefore the Sage says:
He who sustains all the reproaches of the country can be the master of the land;
He who sustains all the calamities of the country can be the king of the world.

These are words of truth,
Though they seem paradoxical.

(Chapter 78)

16

Man when living is soft and tender;
When dead he is hard and tough.
All animals and plants when living are tender and fragile;
When dead they become withered and dry.

Therefore it is said: the hard and tough are parts of death;
The soft and tender are parts of life.
This is the reason why the soldiers when they are too tough cannot carry the
   day;
The tree when it is too tough will break.

The position of the strong and great is low,
And the position of the weak and tender is high.

(Chapter 76)

Inactive action

17

Act non-action;
Undertake no undertaking;
Taste the tasteless.

The Sage desires the desireless, and prizes no articles that are difficult to get.
He learns no learning, but reviews what others have passed through.
Thus he lets all things develop in their natural way, and does not venture to act.

Regard the small as great; regard the few as many.
Manage the difficult while they are easy;
Manage the great while they are small.

All difficult things in the world start from the easy;
All great things in the world start from the small.
The tree that fills a man's arms arises from a tender shoot;
The nine-storeyed tower is raised from a heap of earth;
A thousand miles' journey begins from the spot under one's feet.

Therefore the Sage never attempts great things, and thus he can achieve what is
   great.

He who makes easy promises will seldom keep his word;
He who regards many things as easy will find many difficulties.
Therefore the Sage regards things as difficult, and consequently never has
   difficulties.

(Chapter 63)

18

He who knows does not speak,
He who speaks does not know.

He who is truthful is not showy,
He who is showy is not truthful.

He who is virtuous does not dispute,
He who disputes is not virtuous.

He who is learned is not wise,
He who is wise is not learned.

Therefore the Sage does not display his own merits.

(Chapter 81)

19

He who pursues learning will increase every day;
He who pursues Tao will decrease every day.
He will decrease and continue to decrease,
Till he comes to non-action;
By non-action everything can be done.

(Chapter 48)

20

In dwelling, think it a good place to live;
In feeling, make the heart deep;
In friendship, keep on good terms with men,
In words, have confidence;
In ruling, abide by good order;
In business, take things easy;
In motion, make use of the opportunity.
Since there is no contention, there is no blame.

(Chapter 8)

Love

Just as the *Tao* fosters and nourishes all things, so also should we.

22

I have three treasures, which I hold and keep safe:
The first is called love;
The second is called moderation;
The third is called not venturing to go ahead of the world.

Being loving, one can be brave;
Being moderate, one can be ample;
Not venturing to go ahead of the world, one can be the chief of all officials.

Instead of love, one has only bravery;
Instead of moderation, one has only amplitude;
Instead of keeping behind, one goes ahead:
These lead to nothing but death.

For he who fights with love will win the battle;
He who defends with love will be secure.
Heaven will save him, and protect him with love.

(Chapter 67)

23

Return love for great hatred.
Otherwise, when a great hatred is reconciled, some of it will surely remain.
How can this end in goodness?

Therefore the Sage holds to the left half of an agreement but does not exact
  what the other holder ought to do.
The virtuous resort to agreement;
The virtueless resort to exaction.

"The Tao of heaven shows no partiality;
It abides always with good men."

(Chapter 79)

24

The Sage has no self (to call his own);
He makes the self of the people his self.

To the good I act with goodness;
To the bad I also act with goodness;
Thus goodness is attained.

To the faithful I act with faith;
To the faithless I also act with faith:
Thus faith is attained.

The Sage lives in the world in concord, and rules over the world in simplicity.
Yet what all the people turn their ears and eyes to,
The Sage looks after as a mother does her children.

(Chapter 49)

25

Even if men be bad, why should they be rejected?
Therefore the Sage is always a good saviour of men,
And no man is rejected;

He is a good saviour of things,
And nothing is rejected:
This is called double enlightenment.

Therefore good men are bad men's instructors,
And bad men are good men's materials.
Those who do not esteem their instructors,
And those who do not love their materials,
Though expedient, are in fact greatly confused.
This is essential subtlety.

(Chapter 27)

Government

26

Albeit one governs the country by rectitude,
And carries on wars by stratagems,
Yet one must rule the empire by meddling with no business.

The empire can always be ruled by meddling with no business.
Otherwise, it can never be done.
How do I know it is so?
By this:
The more restrictions and avoidances are in the empire,
The poorer become the people;

The sharper the implements the people keep,
The more confusions are in the country;

The more arts and crafts men have,
The more are fantastic things produced;

The more laws and regulations are given,
The more robbers and thieves there are.

Therefore the Sage says;
Inasmuch as I betake myself to non-action, the people of themselves become
    developed.
Inasmuch as I love quietude, the people of themselves become righteous.
Inasmuch as I make no fuss, the people of themselves become wealthy.
Inasmuch as I am free from desire, the people of themselves remain simple.

(Chapter 57)

27

Govern a great state as you would cook a small fish. (i.e. do it gently).

(Chapter 60)

28

When the government is blunt and inactive the people will be happy and
    prosperous;
When the government is discriminative, the people will be dissatisfied and rest-
    less.
It is upon misery that happiness rests;
It is under happiness that misery lies.
Who then can know the supremacy (good government)?
Only when the government does no rectifying.

Otherwise, rectitude will again become stratagem,
And good become evil.
Men have been ignorant of this, since long ago.

Therefore the Sage is square but does not cut others;
He is angled but does not chip others;
He is straight but does not stretch others;
He is bright but does not dazzle others.

(Chapter 58)

29

The people starve.
Because their officials take heavy taxes from them, therefore they starve.

The people are hard to rule.
Because their officials meddle with affairs, therefore they are hard to rule.

The people pay no heed to death.
Because they endeavour to seek life; therefore they pay no heed to death.

(Chapter 75)

30

He who assists a ruler of men with Tao does not force the world with arms.
He aims only at carrying out relief, and does not venture to force his power
  upon others.

When relief is done, he will not be assuming,
He will not be boastful; he will not be proud;
And he will think that he was obliged to do it.
So it comes that relief is done without resorting to force.

When things come to the summit of their vigour, they begin to grow old.
This is against Tao.
What is against Tao will soon come to an end.

(Chapter 30)

Fighting battles

31

An ancient tactician has said: "I dare not act as a host but would rather act as a
  guest;
I dare not advance an inch but would rather retreat a foot."

This implies that he does not marshal the ranks as if there were no ranks;
He does not roll up his sleeves as if he had no arms;
He does not seize as if he had no weapons;
He does not fight as if there were no enemies.

No calamity is greater than underestimating the enemy;
To underestimate the enemy is to be on the point of losing our treasure.

Therefore when opposing armies meet in the field the truthful will win.

(Chapter 69)

Questions for discussion

1   What is meant by saying, in # 11, "Be bent, and you will remain straight.
Be vacant, and you will remain full"? Is it true, in your opinion?

2   What is meant by saying, in # 20, "In dwelling, think it a good place to
live"?

Chuang Tzu

The Book of "Master Chuang" is one of the most delightful books in any
language. Its viewpoint is always fresh and unconventional. Chuang Tzu
sees Nature as constantly changing and in flux, and as constantly imposing
change on us. These changes are not arbitrary or absurd, however, but
are the expression of a profound principle of naturalness which resides
within the world and energizes it, the *Tao*. The *Tao* gives us both life and
death, both wealth and poverty, both health and sickness, both old age and
new birth. To be in harmony with Nature means accepting the changes
that it brings about in our lives no matter how contrary to our conventional desires.

Chuang Tzu, whose personal name was Chuang Chou, lived from about
399 to 295 BC. Only the first seven chapters of the book are ascribed to
him with certainty by scholars. The translation used here is that by Burton
Watson, *The Complete Works of Chuang Tzu*, New York, Columbia University Press, 1968.

From Chapter 6: The Great and Venerable Teacher

He who knows what it is that Heaven does, and knows what it is that man does,
has reached the peak. Knowing what it is that Heaven does, he lives with

Heaven. Knowing what it is that man does, he uses the knowledge of what he knows to help out the knowledge of what he doesn't know, and lives out the years that Heaven gave him without being cut off midway – this is the perfection of knowledge.

However, there is a difficulty. Knowledge must wait for something before it can be applicable, and that which it waits for is never certain. How, then, can I know that what I call Heaven is not really man, and what I call man is not really Heaven? There must first be a True Man before there can be true knowledge.

What do I mean by a True Man? The True Man of ancient times did not rebel against want, did not grow proud in plenty, and did not plan his affairs. A man like this could commit an error and not regret it, could meet with success and not make a show. A man like this could climb the high places and not be frightened, could enter the water and not get wet, could enter the fire and not get burned. His knowledge was able to climb all the way up to the Way like this.

The True Man of ancient times slept without dreaming and woke without care; he ate without savoring and his breath came from deep inside. The True Man breathes with his heels; the mass of men breathe with their throats. Crushed and bound down, they gasp out their words as though they were retching. Deep in their passions and desires, they are shallow in the workings of Heaven.

The True Man of ancient times knew nothing of loving life, knew nothing of hating death. He emerged without delight; he went back in without a fuss. He came briskly, he went briskly, and that was all. He didn't forget where he began; he didn't try to find out where he would end. He received something and took pleasure in it; he forgot about it and handed it back again. This is what I call not using the mind to repel the Way, not using man to help out Heaven. This is what I call the True Man.

Since he is like this, his mind forgets; his face is calm; his forehead is broad. He is chilly like autumn, balmy like spring, and his joy and anger prevail through the four seasons. He goes along with what is right for things and no one knows his limit. Therefore, when the sage calls out the troops, he may overthrow nations but he will not lose the hearts of the people. His bounty enriches 10,000 ages but he has no love for men. Therefore he who delights in bringing success to things is not a sage; he who has affections is not benevolent; he who looks for the right time is not a worthy man; he who cannot encompass both profit and loss is not a gentleman; he who thinks of conduct and fame and misleads himself is not a man of breeding; and he who destroys himself and is without truth is not a user of men . . .

This was the True Man of old: his bearing was lofty and did not crumble; he appeared to lack but accepted nothing; he was dignified in his correctness but not insistent; he was vast in his emptiness but not ostentatious. Mild and cheerful, he seemed to be happy; reluctant, he could not help doing certain things; annoyed, he let it show in his face; relaxed, he rested in his virtue. Tolerant, he seemed to be part of the world; towering alone, he could be checked by nothing; withdrawn, he seemed to prefer to cut himself off; bemused, he forgot what he was going to say.

He regarded penalties as the body, rites as the wings, wisdom as what is timely, virtue as what is reasonable. Because he regarded penalties as the body, he was benign in his killing. Because he regarded rites as the wings, he got along in the world. Because he regarded wisdom as what is timely, there were things that he could not keep from doing. Because he regarded virtue as what is reasonable, he was like a man with two feet who gets to the top of the hill. And yet people really believed that he worked hard to get there. Therefore his liking was one and his not liking was one. His being one was one and his not being one was one. In being one, he was acting as a companion of Heaven. In not being one, he was acting as a companion of man. When man and Heaven do not defeat each other, then we may be said to have the True Man.

Life and death are fated – constant as the succession of dark and dawn, a matter of Heaven. There are some things which man can do nothing about – all are a matter of the nature of creatures. If a man is willing to regard Heaven as a father and to love it, then how much more should he be willing to do for that which is even greater! If he is willing to regard the ruler as superior to himself and to die for him, then how much more should he be willing to do for the Truth!

When the springs dry up and the fish are left stranded on the ground, they spew each other with moisture and wet each other down with spit – but it would be much better if they could forget each other in the rivers and lakes. Instead of praising Yao (an ancient emperor, considered the model of virtue), and condemning Chieh, it would be better to forget both of them and transform yourself with the Tao.

The Great Clod burdens me with form, labors me with life, eases me in old age, and rests me in death. So if I think well of my life, for the same reason I must think well of my death.

You hide your boat in the ravine and your fish-net in the swamp and tell yourself that they will be safe. But in the middle of the night a strong man shoulders them and carries them off, and in your stupidity you don't know why it happened. You think you do right to hide little things in big ones, and yet they get away from you. But if you were to hide the world in the world, so that nothing could get away, this would be the final reality of the constancy of things.

You have the audacity to take on human form and you are delighted. But the human form has 10,000 changes that never come to an end. Your joys, then, must be uncountable. Therefore, the sage wanders in the realm where things cannot get away from him, and all are preserved. He delights in early death; he delights in old age; he delights in the beginning; he delights in the end. If he can serve as a model for men, how much more so that which the 10,000 things (that is, the whole world) are tied to and all changes alike wait upon!

The Tao has its reality and its signs but is without action or form. You can hand it down but you cannot receive it; you can get it but you cannot see it. It is its own source, its own root. Before Heaven and Earth existed it was there, firm from ancient times. It gave spirituality to the spirits and to God; it gave birth to Heaven and to earth. It exists beyond the highest point, and yet you cannot call it lofty; it exists beneath the limit of the six directions, and yet you cannot call it deep. It was born before Heaven and Earth, and yet you cannot say it has been there for long; it is earlier than the earliest time, and yet you cannot call it old . . .

Master Ssu, Master Yu, Master Li, and Master Lai were all four talking together. "Who can look upon non-being as his head, on life as his back, and on death as his rump?" they said. "Who knows that life and death, existence and annihilation, are all a single body? I will be his friend!"

The four men looked at each other and smiled. There was no disagreement in their hearts and so the four of them became friends.

All at once Master Yu fell ill. Master Ssu went to ask how he was. "Amazing!" said Master Yu. "The Creator is making me all crookedy like this! My back sticks up like a hunchback and my vital organs are on top of me. My chin is hidden in my navel, my shoulders are up above my head, and my pig-tail points at the sky. It must be some dislocation of the yin and yang!"

Yet he seemed calm at heart and unconcerned. Dragging himself haltingly to the well, he looked at his reflection and said, "My, my! So the Creator is making me all crookedy like this!"

"Do you resent it?" asked Master Ssu.

"Why no, what would I resent? If the process continues, perhaps in time he'll transform my left arm into a rooster. In that case I'll keep watch on the night. Or perhaps in time he'll transform my right arm into a crossbow pellet and I'll shoot down an owl for roasting. Or perhaps in time he'll transform my buttocks into cartwheels. Then, with my spirit for a horse, I'll climb up and go for a ride. What need will I ever have for a carriage again?

"I received life because the time had come; I will lose it because the order of things passes on. Be content with this time and dwell in this order and then neither sorrow nor joy can touch you. In ancient times this was called the "freeing of the bound." There are those who cannot free themselves, because they are bound by things. But nothing can ever win against Heaven – that's the way it's always been. What would I have to resent?"

Suddenly Master Lai grew ill. Gasping and wheezing, he lay at the point of death. His wife and children gathered round in a circle and began to cry.

Master Li, who had come to ask how he was, said, "Shoo! Get back! Don't disturb the process of change!" Then he leaned against the doorway and talked to Master Lai. "How marvelous the Creator is! What is he going to make of you next? Where is he going to send you? Will he make you into a rat's liver? Will he make you into a bug's arm?"

Master Lai said, "A child, obeying his father and mother, goes wherever he is told, east or west, south or north. And the yin and yang – how much more are they to a man than father or mother! Now that they have brought me to the verge of death, if I should refuse to obey them, how perverse I would be! What fault is it of theirs?

"The Great Clod burdens me with form, labors me with life, eases me in old age, and rests me in death. So if I think well of my life, for the same reason I must think well of my death.

"When a skilled smith is casting metal, if the metal should leap up and say, 'I insist upon being made into a Mo-yeh!' [a famous sword] he would surely regard it as very inauspicious metal indeed. Now, having had the audacity to take on human form once, if I should say, 'I don't want to be anything but a man! Nothing but a man!' the Creator would surely regard me as a most inauspicious sort of person. So now I think of Heaven and Earth as a great furnace, and the Creator as a skilled smith. Where could he send me that would not be all right? I will go off to sleep peacefully, and then with a start I will wake up."

From Chapter 17: Autumn Floods

Chuang Tzu and Hui Tzu were strolling along the dam of the Hao River when Chuang Tzu said, "See how the minnows come out and dart around where they please! That's what fish really enjoy!"

Hui Tzu said, "You're not a fish – how do you know what fish enjoy?"

Chuang Tzu said, "You're not I, so how do you know I don't know what fish enjoy?"

Hui Tzu said, "I'm not you, so I certainly don't know what you know. On the other hand, you're certainly not a fish – so that still proves you don't know what fish enjoy!"

Chuang Tzu said, "Let's go back to your original question, please. You asked me how I know what fish enjoy – so you already knew I knew it when you asked the question. I know it by standing here beside the Hao."

Question for discussion

1 If we should accept and not reject pain and death because they are part of nature, does the same hold for what we would normally call moral evil, such as causing harm to the innocent? Give a reason for your answer.

6

Chinese Buddhism

The Spirit of Chinese Buddhism

Master, what is the First Principle?
If I told you, it would become the Second Principle.

Once a monk asked Tung-shan, "What is the Buddha?"
Tung-shan replied, "Three pounds of flax."

How wondrously supernatural! How miraculous! I draw water, I carry fuel!

When you say "Yes," you get thirty blows of my stick; when you say "No," you get
thirty blows of my stick just the same."

Question for discussion

1   Why must the First Principle be beyond formulation? (The meaning of
these enigmatic statements is discussed on p. 195.)

The Chinese Buddhist View of Life

The form of Buddhism that was introduced into China was predominantly
Mahayana. Confucianism and Taoism were philosophies for the governing class.
Mahayana Buddhism, by contrast, was for everyone. It introduced *personal*
religion into China; this was found to fill a need, and has been adopted by the
Chinese as a necessary complement to their own indigenous traditions.

The introduction of Buddhism into China was not accomplished without
effort, however. Some aspects of Buddhism were abhorrent to the Chinese. In

the Confucian tradition the family occupies a central place, as we have seen, and Buddhism ran counter to this through its dedication to celibacy. The Buddhist clergy were required to shave their heads, which greatly offended the Confucian belief that one's body is sacred to one's parents and should not be mutilated. A special difficulty was that Buddhism was imported from another country: no mention of the Buddha could be found in the Chinese classics. Despite these obstacles, however, Buddhism succeeded in the task of adapting itself to its new circumstances, becoming almost universally adopted by the Chinese people.

An important element in this was its affinity with Taoism, which seemed preordained to fit Buddhist ideas. "Buddhism could not have appealed to the Chinese mind," says the poet and historian Laurence Binyon, "if China had not already developed ideas of a kindred order: I mean the ideas associated with Lao Tzu and his followers" (*The Spirit of Man in Asian Art*, Lecture III, New York, Dover, 1965). In becoming Chinese and Taoist, Buddhism became more practical and down-to-earth, more focused on the here and now, more appreciative of the natural world and its beauty, and more devoted to direct action. In return it gradually gave up its Indian heritage of abstract philosophical thought.

As we saw in Chapter 2, two main versions of Mahayana had developed in India, one meditational, the other devotional, and these continued in China. We shall focus here primarily on the meditational.

Meditational Chinese Buddhism is a conflation of Indian Buddhism with Taoism, fusing into one the Indian concern with the liberation of the self and the Chinese focus on nature. The result is a unique view of life which preserves both the profundity of the Buddha and the intellectual vigor and love of paradox of the Taoist sages.

Chinese Buddhism keeps everything of significance that is most characteristic of Taoism, except that the place of the *Tao* is in many respects occupied instead by the Buddha nature. The Buddha nature is the true nature of all beings; and in addition it has qualities usually ascribed to the *Tao*. Our liberation lies in realizing our identity with it.

Ch'an Buddhism (Pinyin, Chan)

Ch'an is the Chinese form of the Sanskrit *dhyana*, meaning "meditation." Meditation, of course, was not peculiar to Ch'an: all forms of Buddhism have practiced it, whether Indian or Chinese. Yet in Ch'an meditation has an importance that it has for no other form of Buddhism: it is in effect the sole means to the attainment of Enlightenment – so far as it makes sense to speak of a "means" at all in this regard. In its single-minded dedication to meditation, Ch'an Buddhism ruthlessly downgrades every other prop of the spiritual life.

The aim of Ch'an Buddhism is to experience the Enlightenment that the Buddha experienced. Nothing else can substitute for this. It is something that must take place within the individual, out of the resources that are present within the individual – resources which include, however, the fullness of the Buddha nature. Each person's Enlightenment must be authentically his. Even the teachings of the historical Buddha are not to be followed blindly, for they are external to the individual. On similar grounds Ch'an does not rely on argument or philosophical reasoning. The experience of Enlightenment is not the conclusion of a syllogism, but a direct intuition of the mind. It is not a theory, but an action. It is not something that can be obtained from books or from any source outside oneself.

This is not to say that Ch'an makes no use whatever of externals. It does study the teachings of the Buddha and recite the Scriptures, and it naturally expresses itself in certain ways, especially in special crafts and arts, some of which are mentioned below (pp. 197–8). But it does not rely upon these or expect them to *produce* Enlightenment.

Legend has it that Ch'an Buddhism owes its origin to the historical Buddha himself. The story is told that one day the Buddha announced that he was going to preach a sermon. When the time came he stood up, but said nothing, and merely held up a lotus flower. At this one of his disciples, Kasyapa, smiled. The Buddha thereupon announced that Kasyapa alone had understood his point, and declared him to be his chosen successor.

According to Ch'an tradition, this unique form of Buddhism was brought from India to China around AD 520 by an Indian monk, Bodhi-Dharma. The story is told of his encounter with the Emperor Wu, who said to him, "Since my enthronement I have built many monasteries, had many scriptures copied and had many monks and nuns invested. How great is the merit thus achieved?"

Bodhi-Dharma replied, "No merit at all."

The Emperor then asked, "What is the Noble Truth in its highest sense?"

"It is empty, no nobility whatever."

"Who then is it that is facing me?"

"I do not know, Sire."

Baffled, the Emperor ended the conversation.

Bodhi-Dharma went off and sat in meditation in front of a wall for nine years before making his first disciple. This was Hui K'o, who, according to Ch'an tradition, approached Bodhi-Dharma and asked for instruction, but received no reply. To show his determination to achieve the truth at any cost, Hui K'o, standing in the snow, cut off his left arm. At that, Bodhi-Dharma accepted him as a disciple and made him his spiritual heir. Although historians are strongly inclined to doubt these stories, and believe that Ch'an Buddhism was a later and purely Chinese development, the stories express the nature of the movement well.

Traditionally the distinctive features of Ch'an are summed up in four points:

1 A special transmission outside the scriptures.
2 No dependence on words or letters.
3 Direct pointing at the mind.
4 Seeing into one's nature and the attainment of Buddhahood.

Japanese rock garden at Ryoanji Temple, Kyoto (Photo © David H. Wells/CORBIS)

Ch'an Buddhism fuses into one the Indian Mahayana Buddhist concern with overcoming the individual self and the mind through the intuition of the Buddha nature, and the Taoist emphasis on non-being, spontaneity, inactive action, and paradox. Since Ch'an Buddhism is better known to many Westerners in its Japanese form, Zen, we shall include some references to this.

A special transmission outside the scriptures

Unlike other forms of Buddhism, Ch'an is transmitted not by the study of the Buddhist scriptures, but through the living interaction of master and disciple. It is not possible to practice Ch'an alone; one must have a master. The scriptures are dead words which, left to themselves, only encourage the mind to follow its usual conventional analytical and conceptual ways of thinking. It is in the encounter with the living force of the master that the disciple comes up against the hard and vivifying edge of concrete reality. For this reason Ch'an insists that the disciple give absolute obedience to the master. Meditation is not carried on independently, but under the master's direct guidance and oversight. The master may use words, but he may also use any other method that will bring about the desired result. This has sometimes led to charges that Ch'an is authoritarian. In Japan during the Middle Ages Zen was employed as a method of training the samurai, and more recently during World War II it was used to train the military, because of its insistence on discipline and on the rigorous control of the emotions.

Even today it is not uncommon for business corporations to send executives for a time to Zen monasteries.

No dependence on words or letters

Reality is concrete, not abstract. The Buddha nature is not an abstraction, but the most definite and concrete actuality. Words, however, are merely pale imitations of reality. As the Taoist master Chuang Tzu said, "Name is only the guest of Reality." The name of a thing is no substitute for the thing itself. Reality is encountered in action, not in words. Among other things, this means that the reality of Ch'an cannot be grasped by reading this textbook.

This distrust of words applies even to the highest words. Ch'an Buddhism does not talk about the high topics that religion in general talks about: the divine, salvation, good and evil, and so on. It does not even like to talk about Nirvana or the Buddha. When it talks, it talks the language of pots and pans, of cultivating the ground, walking in the snow – concrete things.

> Without a jot of ambition left
> I let my nature flow where it will.
> There are ten days of rice in my bag
> And, by the hearth, a bundle of firewood.
> Who prattles of illusion or nirvana?
> Forgetting the equal dusts of name and fortune,
> Listening to the night rain on the roof of my hut,
> I sit at ease, both legs stretched out.
>
> (Ryokan)

In this spirit the Ch'an master I-hsuan said: "Kill everything that stands in your way. If you should meet the Buddha, kill the Buddha. If you should meet the Patriarchs, kill the Patriarchs. If you should meet the arhats on your way, kill them too" (Ch'en, p. 358). This means, on the one hand, that the Buddha you have in your mind, the conventional concept of the Buddha, is not the true Buddha, but only an obstacle to Enlightenment. In addition, it also means that too much talk about the Buddha is a distraction from accomplishing what the Buddha accomplished.

The master Hsuan-chien told his disciples to do just the ordinary things, to drink when thirsty, to eat when hungry, to rest when tired.

There are neither Buddhas nor Patriarchs; Bodhi-Dharma was only an old bearded barbarian. Sakyamuni and Kasyapa, Manjusri and Samantabhadra (Bodhisattvas, the one the patron of scholars, the other the protector of those who preach the Dharma) are only dungheap coolies . . . Nirvana and bodhi are dead stumps to tie your donkeys.

Seeking the Buddha in one's own heart

The Ch'an or Zen Buddhist seeks the Buddha not externally, as a divine figure to be worshipped by prayers and ceremonies, but in the depth of his own heart. The true nature of each individual person is nothing less than the Buddha nature of infinite wisdom and compassion, except that, in our normal existence we are prevented from realizing this by the operation of our minds. The Buddha nature is spontaneous, but our minds tend to be routine and mechanical. The Buddha nature is active, but our minds tend to be theoretical. The Buddha nature is paradoxical, but our minds want to be logical and literal. The Buddha nature is dynamic, but our minds are conventional. The Buddha nature is empty, but our minds are full of desire. The Buddha nature is boundless, but our minds are narrow. Our task, then, is to overcome our ordinary mind so that our true nature, our Buddha nature, can appear.

Wu, *Enlightenment*

When this happens, we attain Enlightenment, called *Wu* in Chinese, and *satori* in Japanese. It is not a permanent state, but a momentary illumination, which can be lost and regained. When it is attained, everything is transformed – and yet, at the same time, we can say that nothing has changed. Everything is still what it was, except that we see it in a new perspective.

> The moon's the same old moon,
> The flowers exactly as they were,
> Yet I've become the thingness
> Of all the things I see!
>
> (Bunan)

The Buddha nature is not only the true nature of human beings, but also of all beings in the universe. Therefore to attain to a realization of one's own Buddha nature brings with it a realization of one's inner affinity with the world around.

The Ch'an Master Ch'ing Yuan said:

> Before you study Ch'an, mountains are mountains and rivers are rivers.
> While you study Ch'an, mountains are no longer mountains and rivers are no longer rivers.
> When you have attained enlightenment, mountains are again mountains and rivers again rivers.

This means: When you first start to practice meditation, you begin to focus on the Buddha nature of the mountain rather than the mountain, and so the mountain is no longer a mountain. But when you have attained Enlightenment, you see that the mountain is the Buddha nature just by being a mountain, and all you need to do is focus on the mountain. In an important sense, you can forget about the Buddha nature. It is just this sense of the marvelous and transcendent character of ordinary life and ordinary things that perhaps most distinguishes Ch'an Buddhism.

> Earth, mountains, rivers – hidden in this nothingness,
> In this nothingness – earth, mountains, rivers revealed.
> Spring flowers, winter snows;
> There's no being nor non-being, nor denial itself.
>
> (Saisho)

In the light of this knowledge, let us return to the sayings quoted at the beginning of this chapter. In Ch'an practice these could provide material for long meditation, and our explanations here are necessarily brief and superficial. The first one is probably sufficiently self-explanatory for our purposes. It echoes the statements of the *Tao Te Ching*, that the *Tao* that can be uttered is not the real *Tao*, and that he who speaks does not know. Chuang Tzu said, "If the Tao is made clear, it is not the Tao."

The second saying expresses the fact that the true nature of three pounds of flax, as of everything else in the world, is just precisely the Buddha nature. Conversely then, the master says that the Buddha nature is three pounds of flax.

The third one expresses the splendor of the everyday, the ordinary. Drawing water from a well and carrying firewood are viewed by the world as mundane and humdrum activities, but to the eye attuned to the Buddha nature they are supernatural and miraculous, like all the other natural things in the universe. The Buddha dwells hidden in the inconspicuous things of daily life. To take them just as they come, that is all that Enlightenment amounts to.

The fourth saying expresses the shock therapy methods of the Lin Chi school, which are meant to shatter our usual way of looking at things, in order to make way for a radically fresh way of seeing.

Meditation

Since the first aim of Ch'an Buddhism is a transformation of the mind, the chief activity of the Ch'an monk is meditation. It aims at overcoming and eliminating our ordinary mental activity, replacing it with a direct intuition of our nature as the Buddha nature. This is the "still point" of the mind where all the barriers that separate the individual mind from the rest of reality are broken down, and the sense of ego and self-identity are overcome. It is a perspective at once transcendent and immanent. It is not easily achieved, and yet, say the masters of Ch'an, it is what is most natural to us.

The celebrated Zen teacher D. T. Suzuki quotes the medieval Catholic writer Meister Eckhardt as expressing also the Zen point of view: "Simple people conceive that we are to see God as if He stood on that side and we on this. It is not so; God and I are one in the act of my perceiving Him".

Meditation is typically practiced following a certain procedure, called in Japanese *zazen*, "sitting in meditation." It may be carried on for as long as 10 or 12 hours in a day.

Sudden versus gradual Enlightment

Ch'an Buddhism developed into two different schools, one, the Northern School, which held that Enlightenment was a gradual process, the culmination of many efforts over a long period, the other, the Southern School, which saw it as a sudden and unpredictable event. In the view of the latter school, Enlightenment either takes place or it does not; there is no half-way state; if it takes place, it does so completely. The Northern School has long ago ceased to exist, but the Southern School continues in existence to this day, especially in Japan.

Lin Chi

Lin Chi and Tsao Tung are the two main branches of the Southern School. The Lin Chi (Pinyin, Linji; Japanese, Rinzai) branch developed what may be called shock therapy, the purpose of which is to jolt the mind out of its routine analytical and conceptual way of thinking and lead it back to its natural and spontaneous activity. The master may shout at the student, or hit him physically: Lin Chi Buddhism does not stop short of violence.

The following story comes from Japan:

> Date-Jitoku . . . wanted to master Zen, and with this in mind made an appointment to see Ekkei, abbot of Shokokuji in Kyoto and one widely known for his rigorous training methods. Jitoku was ambitious and went to the master full of hopes for the interview. As soon as he entered Ekkei's room, however, even before being able to utter a word, he received a blow.
>
> He was, of course, astonished, but as it is a strict rule of Zen to do or say nothing unless asked by the master, he withdrew silently. He had never been so mortified. No one had ever dared strike him before, not even his lord. He went at once to Dokuon, who was to succeed Ekkei as abbot, and told him that he planned to challenge the rude and daring master to a duel.
>
> "Can't you see that the master was being kind to you?" said Dokuon. "Exert yourself in zazen, and you'll discover for yourself what his treatment of you means."
>
> For three days and nights Jitoku engaged in desperate contemplation, then, suddenly, he experienced an ecstatic awakening. This, his satori, was approved by Ekkei.
>
> Jitoku called on Dokuon again and after thanking him for the advice said, "If it hadn't been for your wisdom, I would never have had so transfiguring an experience. As for the master, well, his blow was far from hard enough."

The Lin Chi school is also famous for having developed the *kung an* (Pinyin, *gong an*; Japanese, *koan*), literally, a public case or problem, a riddle to which there is no logical answer, designed to jolt the mind out of its conventional habits. Left to itself the mind insists on making a distinction between the subject and object of a sentence. But for Ch'an this distinction is a mistake, and the *kung an* is designed to eliminate it.

> A monk asked Chao-chou, "What is the meaning of the First Patriarch's visit to China?" "The cypress tree in the front courtyard."
>   A monk asked, "All things are said to be reducible to the One; but where is the One to be reduced?" Chao-chou answered, "When I was in the district of Ch'ing I had a robe made that weighed seven chin."

Tsao Tung (Japanese, Soto)

Instead of the shock tactics of Lin Chi, Tsao Tung cultivates the more peaceful method of silent meditation under the direction of a master. The master teaches each student individually and confidentially, and may even make use of reason and argument in their proper place. The Japanese reformer Dogen said, "Just to pass the time sitting straight, without any thought of acquisition, without any sense of achieving enlightenment – this is the way of the Founder . . . Truly the merit lies in the sitting." This is not meant in the sense of inactivity, but of being fully present in the present moment. The poems of Ryokan are a good expression of the spirit of Soto (see above, p. 169).

Enlightenment not our doing

It should not be imagined, however, that these techniques, such as meditation, or the use of the *kung an*, are means by which the individual achieves Enlightenment. Properly speaking, there are no means to achieve Enlightenment. Enlightenment is not an effect brought about by causes. It is simply the seeing of something, namely the Buddha nature, that had been there all the time. The noted writer Edward Conze explains, "[Enlightenment] is an act of the Absolute itself, not our own doing. One cannot do anything at all to become enlightened. To expect austerities or meditation to bring forth salvation is like 'rubbing a brick to make it into a mirror'" (*Buddhism: Its Essence and Development*, New York, Harper, 1959).

Spontaneity and the arts

The Buddha nature is the source of all creativity; it is active, alive, and spontaneous. Correspondingly, the enlightened mind and heart will act with perfect naturalness and spontaneity, rather than simply in mechanical accordance with the rules of logic, or as the result of planning and calculation.

  This shows itself in a special way in the arts and crafts. Just as Taoism has had a vast influence on the arts in China, Ch'an Buddhism gives a special place to them, and has exercised a profound influence on them in China and especially in

Japan. The Zen sense of beauty is spare, and its style is characterized by great economy in the use of materials.

Some arts are especially associated with Zen: the haiku in poetry; sumi-e in painting; fencing; landscape gardening; and the Tea Ceremony. Following Chinese models, Japanese poetry often describes a scene from nature, and then, without any transition, an emotion symbolized in some way by the scene; sometimes the emotion is merely implied. The haiku is a poem of 17 syllables which frequently follows this form, and is especially apt for expressing feelings with Zen terseness. Zen poetry is typically marked by a sense of aloneness. Here are three classic examples by Basho (1644–94):

> The ancient pond
> A frog leaps in –
> > The sound of water.

> > On the withered branch
> A crow has alighted –
> > The end of autumn.

> > Such stillness –
> The cries of the cicadas
> > Sink into the rocks.

Sumi-e is a form of painting which must be done rapidly because of the materials, and there is no opportunity for retouching or altering in any way what has once been done. As a result the painting must be carried out with the utmost spontaneity, in one act, as it were. Sumi-e painting is usually not realistic but symbolic.

Fencing became a Zen art because the samurai needed training to overcome fear in the face of death, which they were liable to encounter every day. As a Zen art, fencing focuses not on technique but on the mental attitude of the swordsman, which must be one of absolute detachment from his own personal fate, a total indifference to whether he lives or dies.

Tea was originally used by Zen monks to keep themselves alert during meditation. In the course of time the ceremony of tea-drinking came to assume some of the characteristics of a religious rite, though in its fully developed form it is a secular performance. Its purpose is to provide a haven of quiet from the stresses of daily life. It is carried out in a special hut entered through a very low door – so that the samurai had to take off both their swords. The inside is of natural wood, sparsely decorated, with a vase containing a single stem of flowers. The full ceremony takes about four hours.

Devotional Chinese Buddhism

Devotional Chinese Buddhism has vastly more adherents than Ch'an Buddhism. Ch'an has been influential because it has appealed to intellectuals, artists, and rulers, but devotional Buddhism appeals to the masses. A form of Mahayana like Ch'an, devotional Buddhism worships the Buddhas and Bodhisattvas as divine saviors for the next life and helpers with the problems of this life. Whereas meditational Buddhism can be practiced only by a few since it is a full-time undertaking, devotional Buddhism can be practiced by all and is a popular religion. The worship of the Buddhas and Bodhisattvas is carried out in temples administered by priests. A temple will typically contain a central statue of the divine figure to whom it is chiefly dedicated, together with surrounding statues of other popular divinities. One pays one's respects to a Buddha or Bodhisattva by a ceremony of bowing to the statue, usually while holding incense sticks in the hands.

This form of Chinese Buddhism is derived from a form of Indian Buddhism known as Pure Land Buddhism, which is based on the Indian scripture, the *Sukhavati-vyuha Sutra*. We have already seen some of the main features of this above (see p. 80). In its Chinese version it centers on the Buddha A Mi T'o (Amitabha in Indian Buddhism), who by the power of his love, compassion, and grace saves those who have faith in him. They are reborn in paradise, the Pure Land of the West. The Pure Land is not Nirvana, but the attainment of Nirvana from the Pure Land will be effortless.

The Bodhisattva Kuan Yin (a female figure derived from the male Indian Bodhisattva Avalokiteshvara) plays a role in East Asian Buddhism as significant as that of the Virgin Mary in Catholicism and Orthodox Christianity. In East Asia she is the most popular and important Bodhisattva, for many people the main focus of their spiritual lives.

On the surface devotional Buddhism appears to be very different from meditational Buddhism. In truth, however, the two complement rather than oppose one another, since their fundamental beliefs concerning the Buddha nature are essentially the same. It is not uncommon, especially in Japan, for a layman who usually practices devotional Buddhism to spend some time in a monastery learning the skills and mental discipline of meditation, and conversely a monk will regularly bow before a statue of the Buddha or a Bodhisattva.

Chinese Buddhist Ethics

We have seen in Chapter 2 that Theravada Buddhism has no room, properly speaking, for the concept of justice, but only for an ethics of love and compassion. In discussing Mahayana Buddhism, and especially Ch'an, we must go further.

Ethics, since it deals with relationships between people, presupposes individuality. It assumes that you and I are distinct beings, that I am not you and you are not me. Otherwise there can be no question of my treating you either well or badly. If you and I are a single being, and there are no other beings distinct from us, ethics is eliminated. If you and I are a single being at bottom or in our essence, but on the phenomenal level, the level of appearances, we appear as two distinct beings, then ethics will belong solely to the realm of the phenomenal, not to the level of reality. This is the situation in Ch'an Buddhism, and in Mahayana Buddhism generally. Ethics belongs to the world of appearance, not to the world of reality. The Buddha nature transcends all conceptions of ethics, of moral or immoral behavior.

From the perspective of ethics, that is, of our social existence, this can be a dangerous situation. Everything will depend on how the theory is translated into practice. At different times the practice has been different. Taoist sages of the T'ang dynasty sometimes reveled in improper behavior. Tantric Buddhism (which we do not discuss in this book) professed to look upon immoral behavior under certain circumstances as an exercise in detachment.

Modern Developments

The problem of the relationship of Ch'an Buddhism to ethics came into the spotlight in 1997 with the publication of *Zen at War* by Brian Victoria, a Zen priest, which revealed the enthusiastic, not to say fanatical, support of Japanese Zen Buddhist leaders for Japan's attack on Pearl Harbor in 1941 and the war it launched between Japan and the United States. The close relationships that have sometimes existed between Zen Buddhism and the military in Japan have been pointed out above.

In September 2001, however, moved by Brian Victoria's revelations and by the terrorist attacks of September 11, the leaders of Myoshin-ji, the chief temple of a large Zen sect, offered a public apology for the wartime behavior of their fellow-religionists. Other Zen Buddhist leaders have subsequently made similar apologies. It seems fair to say that a genuine transformation may perhaps be taking place in the relationship of Zen Buddhism to ethics.

Many forms of Buddhism flourish in Taiwan, Hong Kong, and Singapore, as well as among the Chinese in other countries. Even in mainland China itself, with the decline of Communist zeal, the practice of Buddhism is gradually regaining its former popularity.

Summary of Chinese Buddhism

1   Chinese Buddhism is a synthesis of elements from Indian Buddhism and Taoism.

2   Meditational Buddhism involves seeking the Buddha in one's own heart.

3   Meditational Buddhism is characterized by concreteness, spontaneity, love of paradox, and aversion to theory, which also mark out Taoism.

4   Devotional Buddhism seeks rebirth in the Pure Land of the Buddha A Mi T'o.

Question for discussion

1   Does Ch'an Buddhism have a place for the concept of justice?

Test questions

1   What are the chief differences between Chinese and Indian Buddhism?

2   What is the Pure Land?

3   What is meant by the Buddha nature in Ch'an Buddhism?

4   What is the attitude of Ch'an Buddhism towards speculative philosophy?

5   Why does Ch'an Buddhism believe in transmission outside the scripture?

6   Why in Ch'an Buddhism is it necessary to have a master?

Additional reading

Blofeld, John, *Gateway to Wisdom*, Boulder, CO, Shambala, 1980. Based on the author's personal experiences.

Ch'en, Kenneth, *Buddhism in China: A Historical Survey*, Princeton, Princeton University Press, 1964. Thorough coverage of the history of Buddhism in China.

Suzuki, D. T., *Zen Buddhism*, ed. William Barrett, Garden City, NY, Doubleday, 1956.

Waley, Arthur, *Three Ways of Thought in Ancient China*, London, George Allen & Unwin, 1939. A classic.

Chinese Buddhism: Texts

The Platform Scripture of the Sixth Patriarch

The Sixth Patriarch of Ch'an Buddhism was Hui-neng (638–713), who founded the School of Sudden Enlightenment, which exists to this day. The School of Gradual Enlightenment, once its competitor, founded by Shen-hsiu, no longer exists. The Platform Scripture was probably composed by a disciple of Hui-neng. "Thusness" is a term for the Buddha nature or Emptiness.

Monk Hung-jen [the Fifth Patriarch, 601–75] asked Hui-neng: "Whence have you come to pay homage to me? What do you want from me?"

Hui-neng answered: "Your disciple is from Lingnan. A citizen of Hsin Chou, I have come a great distance to pay homage, without seeking anything except the Law of the Buddha."

The Great Master reproved him, saying: "You are from Lingnan and, furthermore, you are a barbarian. How can you become a Buddha?"

Hui-neng answered: "Although people are distinguished as northerners and southerners, there is neither north nor south in Buddha nature. In physical body, the barbarian and the monk are different. But what is the difference in their Buddha nature?"

The Great Master intended to argue with him further, but, seeing people around, said nothing. Hui-neng was ordered to attend to duties among the rest. It happened that one monk went away to travel. Thereupon Hui-neng was ordered to pound rice, which he did for eight months.

One day the Fifth Patriarch called all his pupils to come to him. As they assembled, he said: "Let me say this to you. Birth and death are serious matters.

You people are engaged all day in making offerings [to the Buddha], going after blessings and rewards only, and you make no effort to achieve freedom from the bitter sea of life and death. Your self-nature seems to be obscured. How can blessings save you? Go to your rooms and examine yourselves. He who is enlightened, use his perfect vision of self-nature and write me a verse. When I look at his verse, if it reveals deep understanding, I shall give him the robe and the Law and make him the Sixth Patriarch. Hurry, hurry!"

At midnight Shen-hsiu, holding a candle, wrote a verse on the wall of the south corridor, without anyone knowing about it, which said:

> Our body is the tree of Perfect Wisdom,
> And our mind is a bright mirror.
> At all times diligently wipe them,
> So that they will be free from dust.

The Fifth Patriarch said: "The verse you wrote shows some but not all understanding. You have arrived at the front of the door but you have not yet entered it. Ordinary people, by practicing in accordance with your verse, will not degenerate. But it will be futile to seek the Supreme Perfect Wisdom while holding to such a view. One must enter the door and see his self-nature. Go away and come back after one or two days of thought. If you have entered the door and seen your self-nature, I shall give you the robe and the Law."

Shen-hsiu went away and for several days could not produce another verse.

Hui-neng also wrote a verse . . . which says:

> The tree of Perfect Wisdom is originally no tree.
> Nor has the bright mirror any frame.
> Buddha-nature is forever clear and pure.
> Where is there any dust?

Another verse:

> The mind is the tree of Perfect Wisdom.
> The body is the clear mirror.
> The clear mirror is originally clear and pure.
> Where has it been affected by any dust?

Monks in the hall were all surprised at these verses. Hui-neng, however, went back to the rice-pounding room. The Fifth Patriarch suddenly realized that Hui-neng was the one of good knowledge but was afraid lest the rest learn it. He therefore told them: "This will not do." The Fifth Patriarch waited till midnight, called Hui-neng to come to the hall, and expounded the Diamond Sutra. As soon as Hui-neng heard this, he understood. That night the Law was imparted to him without anyone knowing it, and thus the Law and the robe [emblematic] of Sudden Enlightenment were transmitted to him.

"You are now the Sixth Patriarch," said the Fifth Patriarch to Hui-neng, "The robe is the testimony of transmission from generation to generation. As to the Law, it is to be transmitted from mind to mind. Let people achieve understanding through their own effort."

The Fifth Patriarch told Hui-neng: "From the very beginning, the transmission of the Law has been as delicate as a hanging thread of silk. If you remain here, some one might harm you. You had better leave quickly."

[Hui-neng, having returned south, said]: I came and stayed in this place [Canton] and have not been free from persecution by government officials, Taoists, and common folk. The doctrine has been transmitted down from past sages; it is not my own idea. Those who wish to hear the teachings of the past sages should purify their hearts. Having heard them, they should first free themselves from their delusions and then attain enlightenment."

Great Master Hui-neng declared: "Good friends, perfection is inherent in all people. It is only because of the delusions of the mind that they cannot attain enlightenment by themselves. They must ask the help of the enlightened and be shown the way to see their own nature. Good friends, as soon as one is enlightened, he will achieve Perfect Wisdom.

"Good friends, in my system, meditation and wisdom are the bases. First of all, do not be deceived that the two are different. They are one reality and not two. Meditation is the substance (t'i) of wisdom and wisdom is the function (yung) of meditation. As soon as wisdom is achieved, meditation is included in it, and as soon as meditation is attained, wisdom is included in it. Good friends, the meaning here is that meditation and wisdom are identified. A follower after the Way should not think wisdom follows meditation or vice versa or that the two are different. To hold such a view would imply that the dharmas possess two different characters. To those whose words are good but whose hearts are not good, meditation and wisdom are not identified. But to those whose hearts and words are both good and for whom the internal and external are one, meditation and wisdom are identified.

"Self-enlightenment and practice do not consist in argument. If one concerns himself about whether [meditation or wisdom] comes first, he is deluded. Unless one is freed from the consideration of victory or defeat, he will produce the [imagining of] dharmas and the self, and cannot be free from the characters [of birth, stagnation, deterioration, and extinction].

"Good friends, there is no distinction between sudden enlightenment and gradual enlightenment in the Law, except that some people are intelligent and others stupid. Those who are ignorant realize the truth gradually, while the enlightened ones attain it suddenly. But if they know their own minds and see their own nature, then there will be no difference in their enlightenment. Without enlightenment, they will be forever bound in transmigration.

"Good friends, in my system, from the very beginning, whether in the sudden enlightenment or gradual enlightenment tradition, absence of thought has been instituted as the main doctrine, absence of phenomena as the substance, and nonattachment as the foundation. What is meant by absence of phenomena?

Absence of phenomena means to be free from phenomena when in contact with them. Absence of thought means not to be carried away by thought in the process of thought. Nonattachment is man's original nature. [In its ordinary process] thought moves forward without a halt; past, present, and future thoughts continue as an unbroken stream. But if we can cut off this stream by an instant of thought, the Dharma-Body will be separated from the physical body, and at no time will a single thought be attached to any dharma. If one single instant of thought is attached to anything, then every thought will be attached. That will be bondage. But if in regard to all dharmas, no thought is attached to anything, that means freedom. This is the reason why nonattachment is taken as the foundation.

"Good friends, to be free from all phenomena means absence of phenomena. Only if we can be free from phenomena will the reality of nature be pure. This is the reason why absence of phenomena is taken as the substance.

"Absence of thought means not to be defiled by external objects. It is to free our thoughts from external objects and not to allow dharmas to cause our thoughts to rise. If one stops thinking about things and wipes out all thought, then as thought is terminated once and for all, there will be no more rebirth. Take this seriously, followers of the Path. It is bad enough for a man to be deceived himself through not knowing the meaning of the Law. How much worse is it to encourage others to be deceived! Not only does he fail to realize that he is deceived, but he also blasphemes against the scripture and the Law. This is the reason why absence of thought is instituted as the doctrine.

"All this is because people who are deceived have thoughts about sense-objects. With such thoughts, pervasive views arise, and all sorts of defilements and erroneous thoughts are produced from them.

"However, the school instituted absence of thought as the doctrine. When people are free from views, no thought will arise. If there are no thoughts, there will not even be 'absence of thought.' Absence means absence of what? Thought means thought of what? Absence means freedom from duality and all defilements. Thought means thought of Thusness and self-nature. True Thusness is the substance of thought and thought is the function of True Thusness. It is the self-nature that gives rise to thought. [Therefore] in spite of the functioning of seeing, hearing, sensing, and knowing, the self-nature is not defiled by the many sense-objects and always remains as it truly is. As the Vimalakirti Scripture says: 'Externally it skillfully differentiates the various dharma-characters and internally it abides firmly in the First Principle.'

"Good friends, in this system sitting in meditation is at bottom neither attached to the mind nor attached to purity, and there is neither speech nor motion. Suppose it should be attached to the mind. The mind is at bottom an imagination. Since imagination is the same as illusion, there is nothing to be attached to. Suppose it were attached to purity, man's nature is originally pure. It is only because of erroneous thought that True Thusness is obscured. Our original nature is pure as long as it is free from erroneous thought. If one does not realize that his own nature is originally pure and makes up his mind to attach himself to purity, he is creating an imaginary purity. Such purity does not exist. Hence we know that what is to be attached to is imaginary.

"This being the case, in this system, what is meant by sitting in meditation? To sit means to obtain absolute freedom and not to allow any thought to be caused by external objects. To meditate means to realize the imperturbability of one's original nature. What is meant by meditation and calmness? Meditation means to be free from all phenomena and calmness means to be internally unperturbed. If one is externally attached to phenomena, the inner mind will at once be disturbed, but if one is externally free from phenomena, the inner nature will not be perturbed. The original nature is by itself pure and calm. It is only because of causal conditions that it comes into contact with external objects, and the contact leads to perturbation. There will be calmness when one is free from external objects and is not perturbed. Meditation is achieved when one is externally free from phenomena and calmness is achieved when one is internally unperturbed. Meditation and calmness mean that externally meditation is attained and internally calmness is achieved.

"All scriptures and writings of the Mahayana and Hinayana schools as well as the twelve sections of the Canon were provided for man. It is because man possesses the nature of wisdom that these were instituted. If there were no man, there would not have been any dharmas. We know, therefore, that dharmas exist because of man and there are all these scriptures because there are people to preach them.

"Among men some are wise and others stupid. The stupid are inferior people, whereas the wise ones are superior. The ignorant consult the wise and the wise explain the Law to them and enable them to understand. When the ignorant understand, they will no longer be different from the wise. Hence we know that without enlightenment, a Buddha is no different from all living beings, and with enlightenment, all living beings are the same as a Buddha. Hence we know that all dharmas are immanent in one's person. Why not seek in one's own mind the sudden realization of the original nature of True Thusness?"

The Great Master said to Chi-ch'eng [pupil of Shen-hsiu]: "I hear that your teacher in his teaching transmits only the doctrine of discipline, calmness, and wisdom. Please tell me his explanation of these teachings."

Chi-ch'eng said: "The Reverend Shen-hsiu said that discipline is to refrain from all evil actions, wisdom is to practice all good deeds, and calmness is to purify one's own mind. These are called discipline, calmness, and wisdom. This is his explanation. I wonder what your views are."

Patriarch Hui-neng answered: "His theory is wonderful, but my views are different."

Chi-ch'eng asked: "How different?"

Hui-neng answered: "Some people realize [the Law] more quickly and others more slowly."

Chi-ch'eng then asked the Patriarch to explain his views on discipline, calmness, and wisdom.

The Great Master said: "Please listen to me. In my view, freeing the mind from all wrong is the discipline of our original nature. Freeing the mind from all disturbances is the calmness of our original nature. And freeing the mind from all delusions is the wisdom of our original nature."

Master Hui-neng continued: "Your teacher's teaching of discipline, calmness, and wisdom is to help wise men of the inferior type but mine is to help superior people. When one realizes his original nature, then discipline, calmness, and wisdom need not be instituted."

Chi-ch'eng said: "Great Master, please explain why they need not be instituted."

The Great Master said: "The original nature has no wrong, no disturbance, no delusion. If in every instant of thought we introspect our minds with Perfect Wisdom, and if it is always free from dharmas and their appearances, what is the need of instituting these things? The original nature is realized suddenly, not gradually step by step. Therefore there is no need of instituting them."

Chi-ch'eng bowed, decided not to leave Ts'ao-li Mountain, but immediately became a pupil and always stayed close by the Master.

(From Liu-tsu t'an-ching, in *Taisho daizokyo*, in William Theodore De Bary, Wing-tsit Chan, and Burton Watson, *Sources of Chinese Tradition*, vol. 1, New York, Columbia University Press, 1964)

Question for discussion

1 What is the difference between the verse composed by Shen-hsiu and those of Hui-neng?

I-hsuan: A Sermon

I-hsuan (d. 867) was Ch'an Master Hui-chao of the Lin Chi school. This sermon brings out especially the doctrine of seeing one's own nature.

The important thing in the study of Buddhism is to achieve a true understanding. If true understanding is achieved, one will not be defiled by birth and death and wherever he may be he will be free. It is not necessary to achieve anything of particular excellence, but this will come by itself.

Followers of the Path, from days of yore, worthy masters had their ways of helping people. As to my way, it is intended merely to help people from being deceived. If you need to use it, do so and don't hesitate any more.

Why are students today not successful? What is the trouble? The trouble lies in their lack of self-confidence. If you do not have enough self-confidence, you will busily submit yourself to all kinds of external conditions and their transformations, and be enslaved and turned around by them and lose your freedom. But if you can stop the mind that seeks [those external conditions] in every instant of thought, you will then be no different from the old masters.

Do you wish to know the old masters? They are none other than you who stand before me listening to my sermon. You students lack self-confidence and therefore seek outside yourselves. Even if what you have found is all literary excellence, you will not get the real ideas of the old masters.

Make no mistake! If you miss it in this life, you will have to go through the three worlds [the world of sensuous desire, the world of form, and the formless world of pure spirit] for many, many long periods. If you are carried away by the external world to which you have thrown yourselves, you will be reborn in the womb of an ass or a cow.

Followers of the Path, my views are no different from those of Shakyamuni [the Buddha]. They are being applied in many ways; what is wanting in them? The light emanating from our six senses is never interrupted or stopped. If you realize this, you will enjoy peace throughout life.

Reverend Sirs, there is no peace in the three worlds, which are like a house on fire. They are not places for you to dwell in for long. The devil of impermanence may visit any of us at any time without regard to rank or age. If you do not want to be different from the old masters, don't seek outside yourself. The light of purity which shines out of every thought of yours is the Dharma-Body within you. The light of non-discrimination that shines out of every thought of yours is the Body of Bliss within you. The light of non-differentiation that shines out of every thought of yours is the Transformation-Body within you. These Three Bodies are you who are now listening to my talk on the Law. It is only by not seeking or pursuing outside that this can have its effect.

According to scholars of the scriptures, these Three Bodies are to be taken as the Ultimate Principle. But my view is different. They are but names and words and they all depend on something. As the ancients said, the body is dependent on its meaning and the ground is described in terms of its substance. It is clear that the body of Dharma-Nature and its ground are but reflections of light. Reverend Sirs, know and get hold of this person who handles this light, for he is the original source of all the Buddhas and the final abode of truth-seekers everywhere.

Your bodily make-up of the four elements [of earth, water, air, and fire] does not understand how to talk or listen. Nor does the liver, the stomach, the kidneys, or the bladder. Nor does vacuity of space. Then who understands how to talk or listen? It is the single light which is formless but very clear before your eyes. It is this that understands how to talk and listen. If you realize this, you will be no different from the old masters.

But don't let this realization be interrupted at any time. You will find it everywhere. It is only because wrong imagination is produced, insight is obstructed, thoughts are changed, and essence becomes different that we transmigrate in the three worlds and suffer all kinds of pain. As I view it, you all have a profound realization of this and none will fail to be emancipated.

Followers of the Path, the Mind has no form and penetrates the ten directions. In the eye it sees, in the ear it hears, in the nose it smells, in the mouth it speaks, in the hand it grasps, and in the leg it runs. Originally it is but clear intelligence which divides itself into six natural functions. Let the mind be free from all external searching. You will be emancipated wherever you are.

Why do I say so? What is the idea? It is only because Followers of the Path cannot cut off the thought of seeking outside that old masters play tricks on you.

Followers of the Path, if you view things as I do, you will be able to sit on and break the heads of the Bliss- and Transformation-Buddhas. The bodhisattvas who have successfully gone through the ten stages [toward Buddhahood] will look like hirelings. Those who have attained the stage of full enlightenment will be like prisoners. Arhats [saints in the Hinayana] and pratyeka-buddhas [who have attained Enlightenment through self-exertion] will be like outhouses. And Perfect Wisdom and Nirvana will be like a stake to which donkeys are fastened.

Why so? It is only because followers of the Path do not understand that all periods of time are empty that there are such hindrances. This is not the case with the one who has truly attained the Path. He follows all conditions and works out all past karmas. He freely wears any garment. He walks wherever he wants to walk and sits wherever he wants to sit. He does not for a single instant think of seeking Buddhahood.

Why so? An ancient saying says: "If one seeks after Buddhahood, the Buddha will become the cause of transmigration."

Reverend Sirs, time is precious. Don't make the mistake of following others in desperately studying meditation or the Path, learning words or phrases, seeking after the Buddha or patriarchs or good friends. Followers of the Path, you have only one father and one mother. What else do you want? Look into yourselves. An ancient sage said that Yajnadatta thought he had lost his head [and sought after it], but when his seeking mind was stopped he realized that he had never lost it.

Reverend Sirs, be yourselves and don't pretend anything. There are some old bald-headed fools who cannot tell good from bad and therefore see all kinds of spirits and ghosts, point to the east or to the west, and prefer rain or shine. People like this are sure some day to pay up their debts and swallow burning iron-balls before Old Yama [Lord of Hades]. Sons and daughters of good families become possessed of such fox-spirits and go astray. Poor blind fellows. The day will come when they will have to pay up their board.

(From Lin-chi Hui-chao ch'an-shih yu-lu, in *Taisho daizokyo*,
XLVII, 497, in De Bary, Chan, and Watson,
Sources of Chinese Tradition, vol. 1)

Question for discussion

1 I-hsuan says that his way is intended merely to help people not to be deceived. How are people deceived, in his view?

Pen-chi: Questions and Answers

Pen-chi (840–901) was a Ch'an Master of Ts'ao-shan. These questions and answers are examples of the "public case," or *kung an* (Japanese, *koan*), typically employed in the School of Sudden Enlightenment to jolt the mind out of its normal thought forms. They are taken from his *Recorded Sayings*.

1 Yun-men asked: "If a person who is difficult to change should come to you, would you receive him?"
The Master answered: "Ts'ao-shan has no such leisure."

2 Monk Ch'ing-jui asked: "I am lonely and poor. Please help me, Master."
"Teacher Jui, please come near."
As Jui went near, the Master said: "Someone drank three cups of wine brewed by the House of Pai in Ch'uan-chou, and still said that his lips were not wet."

3 Ching-ch'ing asked: "What is the Principle of Pure Vacuity like, since after all it has no body?"
The Master said: "The Principle is originally like that. Where did facts [the external world, body] arise?"
Ching-ch'ing said: "Principle is the same as facts and facts are the same as Principle."
The Master said: "It is all right to insult Ts'ao-shan himself, but what are you going to do with all the divine eyes [that is, how can you cheat all wise men]?"

4 A monk said: "Your disciple is sick all over. Please cure me."
The Master said: "I shall not cure you."
The monk said: "Why don't you cure me?"
The Master said: "So that you neither live nor die."

5 A monk asked: "Aren't monks persons of great compassion?"
The Master said: "Yes."
The monk said: "Suppose the six bandits [sensuous desires] come at them. What should they do?"
The Master answered: "Also be compassionate."

The monk asked: "How is one to be compassionate?"

The Master said: "Wipe them out with one sweep of the sword."

The monk asked: "What then?"

"The Master said: "Then they will be harmonized."

6   A monk asked: "Master, are the eye and the eyebrow acquainted with each other?"

The Master answered: "Not acquainted."

The monk asked: "Why not acquainted?"

The Master said: "They are in the same place."

The monk said: "Why are they not separated?"

The Master said: "The eyebrow is not the eye and the eye is not the eyebrow."

The monk said: "What is the eye?"

The Master answered: "To the point!"

The monk asked: "What is the eyebrow?"

The Master said: "I have my doubts."

The monk asked: "Why do you doubt?"

The Master said: "If I don't doubt, it would mean to the point."

7   A monk asked: "What kind of people are those who avoid the company of all dharmas?"

The Master said: "There are so many people in the city of Hung-chou. Where would you say they have gone?"

8   A monk asked: "In admitting phenomenon, what is true?"

The Master said: "Phenomenon is truth and truth is phenomenon."

The monk asked: "How is that revealed?"

The Master lifted the tea tray.

9   A monk asked: "How is illusion true?"

The Master answered: "Illusion is originally true."

The monk asked: "How is illusion manifested?"

The Master answered: "Illusion is manifestation and manifestation is illusion."

10 Question: "What kind of people are those who are always present?"

The Master said: "It happens that Ts'ao-shan has gone out for a while."

Question: "What kind of people are those who are always absent?"

The Master said: "Difficult to find such."

11 A monk asked; "What did Patriarch Lu indicate by facing the cliff?"

The Master covered his ears with his hands.

12 A monk asked: "An ancient wise man said, 'There has never been a person who, having fallen to the ground, does not rise from the ground.' What is falling?"

The Master said: "The fact is recognized."

The monk said: "What is rising?"

The Master said: "Rising."

13 Question: "In the teachings we have received, it is said, 'The great sea does not harbor a corpse.' What is the great sea?"

The Master said: "It embraces all things."

The monk asked: "Why not harbor a corpse?"

The Master said: "He whose breath has stopped clings to nothing."

The Master continued: "Things are not its accomplishments, and the breathless has its own character."

The monk asked: "With regard to progress toward the highest truth, is there anything else?"

The Master said: "It is all right to say yes or no, but what are you going to do with the Dragon King who holds the sword?"

14 A monk asked: "How can silence be expressed?"

The Master answered: "I will not express it here."

The monk said: "Where will you express it?"

The Master said: "Last night at midnight I lost three pennies by my bed."

15 The Master asked the monk: "What are you doing?"

The monk answered: "Sweeping the floor."

The Master said: "In front of the Buddha figure or behind it?"

The monk answered: "Both at the same time."

The Master said: "Give your sandals to Ts'ao-shan."

16 A monk asked: "What kind of companions in the Path should one associate with so that one may always learn from what one has not learned?"

The Master said: "Sleep in the same bed."

The monk said: "This is still what the monks have learned. How can one always learn from what one has not learned?"

The Master said: "Different from trees and rocks."

The monk asked: "Which is first and which is afterward?"

The Master said: "Not seeing the Path, one can always learn from what one has not learned."

17 A monk asked: "Who is the one who holds the sword in the state?"

The Master said: "Ts'ao-shan."

The monk said: "Whom do you intend to kill?"

The Master said: "I shall kill all."

The monk said: "Suppose you suddenly meet your parents. What will you do?"

The Master said: "Why discriminate?"

The monk said: "But there is yourself!"

The Master said: "Who can do anything about me?"

The monk said: "Why not kill yourself?"

The Master said: "No place to start."

18 A monk asked: "What kind of people are always sinking into the sea of life and death?"

The Master answered: "The second month."

The monk said: "Don't they try to free themselves?"

The Master said: "Yes, they do but there is no way out."

The monk said: "If they are free, what kind of people will accept them?"

The Master said: "Prisoners."

19 A monk raised a case [*koan*], saying: "Yo-shan asked me how old I was. I said seventy-two. Yo-shan asked, 'Is it seventy-two?' When I said 'yes,' he struck me. What is the meaning of that?"

The Master said: "The first arrow is bad enough. The second one will penetrate even deeper."

The monk asked: "How can the beating be avoided?"

The Master said: "When the imperial edict is in force, all the feudal lords yield the way."

20 A monk asked Hsiang-yen: "What is the Path?"

Hsiang-yen answered: "There is music from [the wind blowing at] the dried wood."

The monk asked: "Who are those in the Path?"

Hsiang-yen answered: "There is an eye-pupil in the skull."

The monk did not understand and went to ask Shih-shuang what is meant by music from the dried wood.

Shih-shuang said: "There is still joy there."

The monk said: "What about the eye-pupil in the skull?"

Shih-shuang said: "There is still consciousness there."

The monk did not understand either. He presented the case to the Master, who said: "Shih-shuang is a Shravaka [who attains Enlightenment on hearing the teachings of the Buddha] and therefore takes such a view." Thereupon he showed the monk the following verse:

> When there is music from dried wood, the Path is truly seen.
> The skull has no consciousness; the eye begins to be clear.
> When joy and consciousness [seem to be] at an end, they are not so.
> Who discriminates what is clear amidst what is turbid?

Thereupon the monk again asked the Master: "What does it mean by music from the dried wood?"

The Master said: "Life is not cut off."

Question. "What does it mean by an eye-pupil in the skull?"

The Master answered: "It is not dried up."

Question: "Is there anything more?"

The Master said: "Throughout the world not a single person has not heard."

Question: "From what poem is 'There is music from the dried wood'?"

The Master said: "I don't know what poem."

All of those who heard him were disappointed.

21 Question: "What is the basic meaning of the law of the Buddha?"

The Master said: "Filling all streams and valleys."

22 Question: "Whenever there is any question, one's mind is confused. What is the matter?"
The Master said: "Kill, kill!"

  (From Ts'ao-shan Pen-chi ch'an-shih yu-lu, in *Taisho daizokyo*, XLVII, in De Bary, Chan, and Watson, *Sources of Chinese Tradition*, vol. 1)

Question for discussion

1 Explain the meaning of nos. 2, 8, and 22.

Part *III*

The Religions of Semitic Origin

Judaism, Islam, and Christianity

These three religions share several fundamental conceptions:

1 *God* They believe in a single divine being, who is personal, that is, possessing mind and will; eternal, that is, not subject to the limits of time or change, all-powerful, all-knowing, and all-good. That is, all three religions are examples of what is called ethical monotheism.
2 *Creation* God creates a world distinct from himself (none of these religions are monistic in their mainstream forms); a world which is real, not illusory, though totally dependent on God; a world which is good.
3 *Revelation* In a unique historical event God reveals his will, requiring obedience, disobedience being sin. The revelation in each case is given in writing.
4 *Immortality and judgement* There is a life after death. At death God will judge each individual, for reward or punishment.

These religions emphasize the significance of:

- persons as superior to nature;
- the individual human person, who must answer for his thoughts and deeds;
- the moral value of justice;
- law;
- history, which moves not in an everlasting cycle, but in a straight line, from a beginning to an end.

By contrast with most of the other religions we have discussed, the places of worship of the religions of Semitic origin – synagogue, church, and mosque – are communal, being designed for the gathering of an assembly.

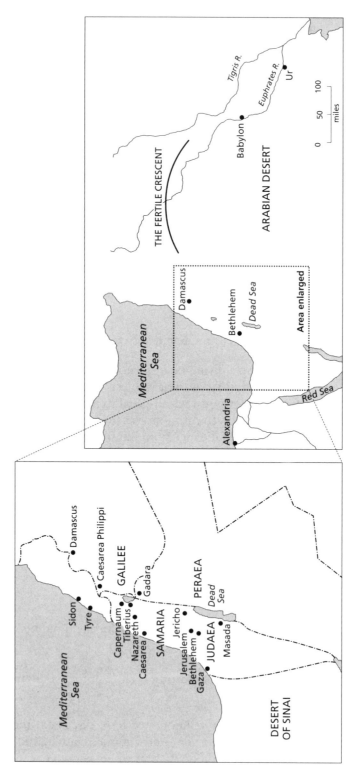

Palestine

Palestine and Babylon

7

Judaism

Although the religion we call Judaism today has its roots in the ancient past, it is very different from the biblical religion out of which it grew. We must make a distinction between Israelite (or Hebrew) religion and Rabbinic Judaism.

Israelite Religion

By this is meant the religion described in the Hebrew scriptures or Hebrew Bible (which Christians call the Old Testament).

These books were composed over several hundred years, from about 900 BC to about 100 BC, the earliest being certain portions of the first five books, the Pentateuch, and the latest being the book of Esther. Not all of them had a directly religious origin, but they were subsequently given religious significance by being collected together into a single authoritative compilation.

The spirit of Israelite religion

It happened, late one afternoon, when David arose from his couch and was walking upon the roof of the king's house, that he saw from the roof a woman bathing; and the woman was very beautiful. And David sent and inquired about the woman. And one said, "Is not this Bathsheba, the daughter of Eliam, the wife of Uriah the Hittite?" So David sent messengers, and took her; and she came to him, and he lay with her . . . Then she returned to her house. And the woman conceived; and she sent and told David, "I am with child."

So David sent word to Joab, "Send me Uriah the Hittite." And Joab sent Uriah to David. When Uriah came to him, David asked how Joab was doing, and how the people fared, and how the war prospered. Then David said to Uriah, "Go down to your house, and wash your feet." And Uriah went out of the king's house, and there followed him a present from the king. But Uriah slept at the door of the king's house with all the servants of his lord, and did not go down to his house. When they told David, "Uriah did not go down to his house," David said to Uriah, "Have you not come from a journey? Why did you not go down to your house?" Uriah said to David, "The ark and Israel and Judah dwell in booths; and my lord Joab and the servants of my lord are camping in the open field; shall I then go to my house, to eat and drink, and to lie with my wife? As you live, and as your soul lives, I will not do this thing."

Then David said to Uriah, "Remain here today also, and tomorrow I will let you depart." So Uriah remained in Jerusalem that day, and the next. And David invited him, and he ate in his presence and drank, so that he made him drunk; and in the evening he went out to lie on his couch with the servants of his lord, but he did not go down to his house.

In the morning David wrote a letter to Joab, and sent it by the hand of Uriah. In the letter he wrote, "Set Uriah in the forefront of the hardest fighting, and then draw back from him, that he may be struck down, and die." And as Joab was besieging the city, he assigned Uriah to the place where he knew there were valiant men. And the men of the city came out and fought with Joab; and some of the servants of David among the people fell. Uriah the Hittite was slain also.

Then Joab sent and told David all the news about the fighting; and he instructed the messenger, "When you have finished telling all the news about the fighting to the king, then, if the king's anger rises, and if he says to you, 'why did you go so near the city to fight? Did you not know that they would shoot from the wall? Who killed Abimelech the son of Jerubbesheth? Did not a woman cast an upper millstone upon him from the wall, so that he died at Thebez? Why did you go so near the wall?' then you shall say, 'Your servant Uriah the Hittite is dead also.'"

So the messenger went, and came and told David all that Joab had sent him to tell. The messenger said to David, "The men gained an advantage over us, and came out against us in the field; but we drove them back to the entrance of the gate. Then the archers shot at your servants from the wall; some of the king's servants are dead; and your servant Uriah the Hittite is dead also." David said to the messenger, "Thus shall you say to Joab, 'Do not let this matter trouble you, for the sword devours now one and now another; strengthen your attack upon the city, and overthrow it.' And encourage him."

When the wife of Uriah heard that Uriah her husband was dead, she made lamentation for her husband. And when the mourning was over, David sent and brought her to his house, and she became his wife, and bore him a son. But the thing that David had done displeased the Lord.

And the Lord sent Nathan to David. He came to him, and said to him, "There were two men in a certain city, the one rich and the other poor. The rich man had very many flocks and herds; but the poor man had nothing but one little ewe lamb, which he had bought. And he brought it up, and it grew up with him and with his children; it used to eat of his morsel, and drink from his cup, and lie in his bosom, and it was like a daughter to him. Now there came a traveller to the rich man, and he was unwilling to take one of his own flock or herd to prepare for the wayfarer who had come to him, but he took the poor man's lamb, and prepared it for the man who had come to him."

Then David's anger was greatly kindled against the man; and he said to Nathan, "As the Lord lives, the man who has done this deserves to die; and he shall restore the lamb fourfold, because he did this thing, and because he had no pity."

218

Nathan said to David, "You are the man. Thus says the Lord, the God of Israel, 'I anointed you king over Israel, and I delivered you out of the hand of Saul; and I gave you your master's house, and your master's wives into your bosom, and gave you the house of Israel and of Judah; and if this were too little, I would add to you as much more. Why have you despised the word of the Lord, to do what is evil in his sight? You have smitten Uriah the Hittite with the sword, and have taken his wife to be your wife, and have slain him with the sword of the Ammonites. Now therefore the sword shall never depart from your house, because you have despised me, and have taken the wife of Uriah the Hittite to be your wife. Thus says the Lord, 'Behold, I will raise up evil against you out of your own house; and I will take your wives before your eyes, and give them to your neighbor, and he shall lie with your wives in the sight of the sun. For you did it secretly; but I will do this thing before all Israel, and before the sun.'"

David said to Nathan, "I have sinned against the Lord." And Nathan said to David, "The Lord also has put away your sin; you shall not die. Nevertheless, because by this deed you have utterly scorned the Lord, the child that is born to you shall die." And Nathan went to his house.

(2 Samuel 11: 2–12: 15; Revised Authorized Version)

Questions for discussion

1 What terms would you normally use to describe David's deeds against Uriah?

2 What does Nathan mean by referring to them as "sin"?

The Origins of the Israelite People and their Religion

The historical facts appear to be that a number of tribes of diverse origin, mostly Canaanite and speaking Aramaic, lived in the hill country of Palestine around 1200 BC, some of them worshipping the god Yahweh among others. In the course of repeated wars against the "Sea Peoples" or Philistines living on the coast, the hill tribes developed a sense of national unity and eventually founded a united kingdom. Their religion gradually became monotheistic, centering on the figure of Yahweh, and was enshrined in a series of sacred writings. These writings recounted legends of earlier figures such as Adam, Noah, Abraham, Isaac, and Jacob, considered as the fathers of the united people, and stories of a period of slavery in Egypt and of redemption from it by the power of Yahweh – stories which, it must be conceded, modern scholars have largely been unable to verify – as well as the laws promulgated by Yahweh. The worship of a single God probably developed at about the same time as the nation was unified under a single king. According to the Bible the nation reached its widest boundaries during the reigns of David and Solomon, and was subsequently divided into a northern and a southern half. The northern, termed Israel, was destroyed by the Assyrians in the eighth century BC, and the southern, named Judah, was destroyed in the sixth century BC by the Babylonians, who carried the educated and administrative classes off into captivity in Babylon. There some of these writings were brought together and edited in the authoritative collection known as the Pentateuch, Torah, or Books of Moses, the first five books of the Bible. Over the following centuries further compilations of these and similar materials were made, until the Hebrew Bible came to take the form it now has, around AD 100.

The Israelite View of Life

Israelite religion was the first to develop the concept of a single personal God who created and governs the entire world. The historic achievement of the Israelites lay not only in their monotheism, however, but above all in the moral character they ascribed to this God. While the gods of other peoples are often immoral and given to the whole range of human crimes, the God of the Hebrew people is just and holy, and demands justice and holiness of men, as the story of David and Nathan testifies. Hebrew religion was the first to embrace *ethical monotheism*. An offense against morality is by that fact an offense against God's command, and therefore against God himself. This is the concept of sin.

This God, who bears the name Yahweh, showed especial love for the Israelite people over the other peoples of the world by revealing himself to their fathers, redeeming them from slavery in Egypt, and giving them political power over the land of Palestine. In return he requires them to obey his commands. These commands are both ritual and moral, and carry heavy punishments in this life for transgressions. Sin can be unwitting as well as deliberate, but it can be atoned for by offering sacrifice. If they obey his commands, God promises them well-being in this life. Thus Israelite religion in its traditional form is concerned with the achievement of well-being in this life through obedience to the commands of God.

After death, the soul of man descends into a shadowy existence in Sheol, where it enjoys neither much sorrow nor much bliss.

Israelite religion is a religion animated by the fear of God, but also by trust in God. On the one hand, "it is a terrible thing to fall into the hands of the Living God." But on the other, he has shown that he loves his people, and if they carry out his commands, he will be faithful to them.

> The Lord is my shepherd,
> I shall not want . . .
> Even though I walk through the valley of the shadow of death,
> I fear no evil;
> For thou art with me.
>
> (Psalm 23)

220

God and creation

Yahweh appears to have been at first associated with a shrine on Mount Sinai, before being adopted as the sole God of the Hebrews. During the earliest period of the religion, the Hebrew people accepted that the gods of other peoples existed, such as Baal or Astarte, but the Hebrews for the most part worshipped only their own God. This state of affairs has been called henotheism. In the course of time, however, the religion became genuinely monotheistic: Yahweh came to be considered as the only true God, the creator of heaven and earth.

The concept of creation which characterizes Judaism and its daughter religions, Christianity and Islam, interprets the relationship between the world and the divine differently from the Upanishads and Buddhism. According to the Upanishads and Mahayana Buddhism, the divine is the sole genuine reality, and the world is essentially an illusion which our minds impose on that divine reality, in a sense revealing it, but also in an important and obvious sense concealing it. Both forms of religion are monistic. According to the Hebrew concept of creation, by contrast, the world is real, and distinct from God. Creation is not monistic, but, perhaps we might say, pluralistic. Although the world is dependent on God for its existence, and continues to be dependent on him throughout its history, God is not the world, and the world is not God. The relationship between God and the world is more like that between a carpenter and a chair that he makes, or an artist and his painting, whereas for the Upanishads and Mahayana Buddhism the relationship is more like that between, say, ourselves as we are in reality, and as we appear in a concave or convex mirror which distorts our image, or between the magician's stage assistant who is not actually sawn in half, and the illusion the magician creates that she is sawn in half. (The main biblical account of creation is given on pp. 243–5.)

Salvation history

A distinctive feature of Israelite religion is its sanctification of the history of the Hebrew people, as salvation history. Yahweh not only created heaven and earth, but he also brought about certain definite events which were believed to have happened in the history of the Hebrew people. He appeared to Moses in a burning bush, rescued the people from slavery in Egypt, fed them in the desert, revealed his Law to them through Moses on Mount Sinai, led them back into Palestine, and appointed Saul and David as kings.

> A wandering Aramean was my father; and he went down into Egypt and sojourned there, few in number; and there he became a nation, great, mighty, and populous. And the Egyptians treated us harshly, and afflicted us, and laid upon us hard bondage. Then we cried out to the Lord the God of our fathers, and the Lord heard our voice, and saw our affliction, our toil, and our oppression; and the Lord brought us out of Egypt with a mighty hand and an outstretched arm, with

great terror, with signs and wonders; and he brought us into this place and gave us this land, a land flowing with milk and honey."

(Deuteronomy 26: 5–9; Revised Authorized Version)

When the nation was all but destroyed by the Babylonians, this event was seen as a punishment inflicted by God for the sins of the people. Eventually, the people hoped, God would send his chosen servant, the Messiah, who would restore Israel to its rightful place among the nations, ushering in an era of lasting peace and prosperity.

Just as the Israelite concept of creation is different from that of the Indian religions mentioned, so also is their concept of history. In the Upanishads and Buddhism, the course of the world is cyclical. Samsara is an everlasting cycle of birth, death, and rebirth, and the same holds true for the world as a whole: eon succeeds eon, and in each eon the illusory world arises and eventually declines back into nothingness before arising again in the next eon. In the Hebrew concept, by contrast, history is a straight line, beginning with creation, and continuing on to its final consummation. It is more like a drama, with a beginning, a middle, and an end.

The covenant

The combined emphasis on justice and on history which marks Israelite religion shows itself especially in the fact that the relationship between the Hebrew people and their God Yahweh was described in terms of a legal contract, a solemn agreement which binds both parties in justice. According to this contract, the Hebrew people had the obligation to observe the Law which Yahweh would give them. Yahweh, in his turn, obligated himself to increase their number, and to give them possession of the land of Canaan or Palestine. The covenant was not a contract between equals, but of the sort which a ruler might impose on his subjects or a conqueror on the conquered.

The terms of the contract were set forth initially by Yahweh to Abraham, the legendary father of the Hebrew people:

Behold, my covenant is with you, and you shall be the father of a multitude of nations. No longer shall your name be Abram, but your name shall be Abraham; for I have made you the father of a multitude of nations. I will make you exceedingly fruitful; and I will make nations of you, and kings shall come forth from you. And I will establish my covenant between me and you and your descendants after you throughout their generations for an everlasting covenant, to be God to you and to your descendants after you. And I will give to you, and to your descendants after you, the land of your sojournings, all the land of Canaan, for an everlasting possession; and I will be their God.

(Genesis 17: 5–8)

This contract was renewed and enlarged by God with Moses. After rescuing the people from the Egyptians, God had Moses lead them to Mount Sinai (the location of which has proved impossible to identify), where amid thunder and lightning he gave them his complete Law.

The Law of Moses

The most celebrated part of the Law given by God to Moses is the Ten Commandments, the classic summary of man's duties towards God and his neighbor:

> And God spoke all these words, saying,
> "I am the Lord your God, who brought you out of the land of Egypt, out of the house of bondage. You shall have no other gods before me.
> You shall not make for yourself a graven image . . . you shall not bow down to them or serve them . . .
> You shall not take the name of the Lord your God in vain . . .
> Remember the sabbath day, to keep it holy. Six days you shall labor; and do all your work; but the seventh day is a sabbath to the Lord your God . . .
> Honor your father and your mother . . .
> You shall not kill.
> You shall not commit adultery.
> You shall not steal.
> You shall not bear false witness against your neighbor.
> You shall not covet your neighbor's house; you shall not covet your neighbor's wife, or his manservant, or his maidservant, or his ox, or his ass, or anything that is your neighbor's.
>
> (Exodus 20: 1–17)

In addition to these ten commandments (which are recorded in the Bible in two slightly different versions, in Exodus 20 and Deuteronomy 5), God gave many other laws to Moses for the Hebrew people (the traditional count is 613), which cover a wide variety of subjects, including the sacrifices to be carried out, the feast days to be observed, the penalties to be inflicted for various crimes such as murder and robbery, sexual conduct, the obligations of ritual purity, the forgiveness of debts, and so on. These laws are not restricted to the purely religious sphere, but also include many that regulate the civil life of the community. In effect, the Mosaic Law provides a sacred constitution for the nation of Israel.

The central activity of the religion was the offering of animals, grain, and fruits in sacrifice to Yahweh. The Law prescribes rituals for carrying out several different kinds of sacrifice, including the sacrifice of praise, the peace offering, the sin offering, the guilt offering, and the sacrifices to be offered on the various holy days and holy occasions. The text laying down the procedure for carrying out the sacrifice of praise, the burnt offering or holocaust, is given on pages 248–9. The feast days prescribed by the Law are described in the section on Rabbinic Judaism (see pp. 232–3).

A rabbi removing the Torah from the Ark of the Covenant (Circa Photo Library)

The Torah

The Law of Moses can be found in five books written in Hebrew: Genesis, Exodus, Leviticus, Numbers, and Deuteronomy. Together these books make up the Pentateuch (the "Five Scrolls") or Torah. Genesis contains the story of the creation of the world, and the histories of the fathers of the Hebrew people, including the first covenant with Abraham. Exodus tells the story of the rescue of the people out of Egypt. Leviticus contains the main provisions of the Law. Numbers gives a variety of further ordinances and stories, and Deuteronomy is a summary of the material in the preceding books.

Scholars have found that these books are largely composed of earlier documents that have been rearranged and edited. The book of Genesis, for example, is compiled from sections taken from three main sources, a document scholars call J, which refers to God by the name Yahweh, one called E, which refers to him by the name El or Elohim, and one called P, representing the traditions of the priestly caste. The task of collecting these documents together in their present form was probably carried out in Babylon during the exile in the sixth century BC.

These books, the Torah, make up the core or foundation of the Hebrew Bible and have traditionally been considered its most sacred part. In addition, the Bible contains two other collections: the Prophets and the Writings.

The prophets

While the basic features of Hebrew religion as described in the Torah were probably created by the priestly caste, another group also played a large role: the prophets. The word "prophet" from its etymology means "one who speaks on behalf of another," and in its religious sense it means one who speaks on behalf of God. The prophets gave the Hebrew people instructions in the name of God concerning the various courses of action they should take as a people. Above all, the prophets called on the Hebrew people to repent of their sins.

The major prophetical books in the Bible are: Isaiah, Jeremiah, Lamentations, and Ezekiel. In addition there are thirteen smaller or "minor" ones (Daniel, Hosea, Joel, Amos, Obadiah, Jonah, Micah, Nahum, Habakkuk, Zephaniah, Haggai, Zechariah, and Malachi).

The earlier prophets addressed themselves to the Hebrew people as a whole, because it was the people as a whole who were committed to observing the covenant with Yahweh. According to the message of these prophets it was permissible to punish the whole people because of the transgressions of some. But with the prophet Jeremiah a stronger sense of the individual emerged. According to Jeremiah a person's fate depended on his own actions. From that time on Hebrew religion addressed itself more and more to the individual conscience rather than simply to the people as such.

The synagogue system

In 587 BC Israel was conquered by the Babylonians, who destroyed the Temple in Jerusalem and sent much of the population into exile in Babylon. As we have remarked, it was probably here that the Torah was compiled. In 538 BC the Persian emperor Cyrus conquered Babylon and ended the Jewish captivity. For the next 200 years Israel was part of the Persian Empire. After the return from the Exile work began on rebuilding the Temple, but at the same time a novel religious system was set up: the synagogue system. A synagogue is a hall for meeting, prayer, and study. Although the center of the religion continued to be the sacrifices in the Temple in Jerusalem, synagogues were constructed in towns and villages throughout the land, and the study of the written Law or Torah became a matter of paramount importance. Alongside the priests a second religious class developed, the rabbis, or teachers of the divine law.

However, not all the Jews wished to return to Palestine; some had prospered in Babylon and stayed on there. Subsequently other Jewish communities developed in the Persian Empire, and then in the Greek and Roman Empires, till by the year AD 70 there were probably more Jews living outside Palestine than in it.

This is called the Diaspora or Dispersion. The religion of these communities also came to center on the synagogue.

The rabbinical schools came to develop the view that, alongside the Written Torah, God had communicated to Moses an Unwritten or Oral Torah, which was handed down from generation to generation by word of mouth. This unwritten Law contained many precepts and legal regulations not found in the written Law. It provided the basis for the subsequent development of Rabbinic Judaism.

By the time of Jesus, Hebrew religion had become markedly diverse in comparison to the Rabbinic Judaism of later times. On the one hand, the traditional beliefs and sacrifices, which were concerned solely with obtaining well-being in this world, were preserved by the priestly caste, the Sadducees, whose God was still essentially the national God of the Jewish people. But other groups had emerged with different beliefs and practices. As the result of Persian or other influences, belief had developed in a future life, and a judgement beyond the grave leading to Paradise or to Hell. The Pharisees, a group dedicated to keeping the Law of Moses in their personal life, emerged and came to accept this view, and with it a view of God which tended to emphasize his universal character as the God of all mankind. Both the Sadducees and the Pharisees had their rabbis or scribes, men who specialized in the knowledge of the Law, interpreting it in the light of their respective principles. A form of Jewish monasticism had developed, known as the Essene movement, which regarded the Sadducees as corrupt. In addition, the belief had become widespread that the messianic age would soon arrive, bringing with it the end of the world, and various messianic communities had developed. Some expected the Messiah to be a human being, while in other writings he is described as a pre-existent heavenly being. In Galilee, in the north, bands of religious guerrillas formed, the Zealots, with the intent of overthrowing Roman rule. Outside of Palestine, the Jewish community was assimilating Graeco-Roman culture and philosophy, a trend embodied in the Greek translation of the Hebrew Bible, the Septuagint, made about 200 BC, and in the figure of Philo of Alexandria, a contemporary of Jesus.

In AD 70, after a Jewish revolt, the Romans destroyed Jerusalem and the Temple and would not allow it to be rebuilt. After a further revolt was put down in AD 135 Jews were forbidden to enter Jerusalem. This left only the synagogue system and the rabbinate, which were to provide the foundation for the emergence of Rabbinic Judaism.

Rabbinic Judaism

The spirit of Judaism

Rabbi Bunam used to tell young men who came to him for the first time the story of Rabbi Eisik, son of Rabbi Yekel in Cracow. After many years of great poverty which had never shaken his faith in God, he dreamed someone bade him look for a treasure in Prague, under the bridge which leads to the king's palace. When the dream recurred a third time, Rabbi Eisik prepared for the journey and set out for Prague. But the bridge was guarded day and night and he did not dare to start digging. Nevertheless he went to the bridge every morning and kept walking around it until evening.

Finally the captain of the guards, who had been watching him, asked in a kindly way whether he was looking for something or waiting for somebody. Rabbi Eisik told him of the dream which had brought him here from a faraway country. The captain laughed: "And so to please the dream, you poor fellow wore out your shoes to come here! As for having faith in dreams, if I had had it, I should have had to get going when a dream once told me to go to Cracow and dig for treasure under the stove in the room of a Jew – Eisik, son of Yekel, that was the name! Eisik, son of Yekel! I can just imagine what it would be like, how I should have to try every house over there, where one half of the Jews are named Eisik, and the other Yekel!" And he laughed again. Rabbi Eisik bowed, traveled home, dug up the treasure from under the stove, and built the House of Prayer which is called "Reb Eisik's Shul."

"Take this story to heart," Rabbi Bunam used to add, "and make what it says your own: There is something you cannot find anywhere in the world, not even at the zaddik's, and there is, nevertheless, a place where you can find it."

(Martin Buber, *Tales of the Hasidim*, trans. Olga Marx, New York, Schocken Books, 1947)

Questions for discussion

1 What is this thing that cannot be found anywhere in the world?

2 If it cannot be found in the "world," where can it be found?

The Emergence of Judaism

The religion called Judaism today was developed during the centuries which followed the destruction of Jerusalem and the Temple, as a result of the new political circumstances in which the Jewish community found itself. Thus Judaism properly so called developed not before Christianity, but contemporaneously with it, and as an alternative to it. While the ethical monotheism which characterized Hebrew religion was preserved, the conception of the divine law was transformed.

The Law of Moses had been given to the Jewish people as the law, both religious and civil, of an independent political state, the Jewish nation. After AD 135, however, this no longer existed. In Palestine only a remnant of the people remained. The center of the Jewish population moved first northwards, to Galilee, and then eastwards, to Mesopotamia, the land of Babylon between the two rivers, the Tigris and the Euphrates, then part of the Persian Empire. A Jewish population also existed in the cities of the Roman Empire, and in AD 212 they were made Roman citizens, but in the fourth century the empire became officially Christian, and Jewish religion, previously held in honor, came under condemnation. The Jewish community retreated into itself, and the absorption of Graeco-Roman culture came to an end.

Under these circumstances much of the Law could not be carried out. The temple sacrifices could no longer be offered. The powers of government could no longer be used to enforce the often severe punishments attached to infractions of the Law. The festivals could no longer be the national events they were intended to be. The synagogue, however, could and did survive, and with it the study of the Law. With the synagogue survived the Pharisees, who possessed the only form of Jewish religion that appeared to be still viable.

The Talmud

The basis for a readjustment and reinterpretation of Jewish religion was provided by the tradition of the Oral Law. This was law which, it was believed, had been revealed by God to Moses, but not written down, and which had been transmitted from generation to generation by word of mouth. This contained, for example, the "fences of the Law," various prescriptions regarding the washing of hands, tithings, fasts, and so on, which served to "protect" the Torah, and which had been condemned so strongly by Jesus. The concept of an oral law provided the flexibility needed in order to adapt the Torah to the new circumstances.

The discussions of this Oral Law by the rabbis of the period, who were called the Tannaim, were collected and codified by Rabbi Judah (135–217) in a document called the Mishnah, or "Repetition." The discussions of the Mishnah by a later group of rabbis, the Amoraim, were collected in a further document, the Gemara, or "Completion." The Mishnah and the Gemara together make up the Talmud, a word which means "teaching" or "learning." It is the Talmud, rather than the Bible directly, which provides the foundation of Rabbinic Judaism.

The legal material in the Talmud, indicating how a Jew must act, is termed "Halakhah"; in addition there is material representing the sermons of the rabbis, termed "Haggadah." Other material related to the Mishnah has been preserved in the Tosephta ("addition") and in the Targums, Aramaic translations of the Hebrew Bible.

Much of the Talmudic interpretation of scripture follows the method known as Midrash, in which each word and even letter of the scripture is taken as having a definite meaning, indeed many meanings latent or implicit, all complementing one another. Thus each generation can find new lessons in the text. The term *Midrash* is also used for the class of writings employing this method.

Following the arrangement of the Mishnah, the Talmud is organized in six "orders," each containing a number of "tractates." These are further subdivided into chapters, and these again into paragraphs or sentences.

The Talmud is a multi-volume work, rather like an encyclopedia of Jewish lore. It exists in two versions, the Babylonian and the Palestinian. The Palestinian Talmud, the smaller of the two, and a more irregular collection, was completed around the fourth century AD, while the Babylonian Talmud, much larger and more authoritative, was completed in the sixth century. References to the Talmud without qualification are usually to the Babylonian version.

"It is the Talmud which inspires those virtues associated with the Jew, sobriety, benevolence, sense of social justice, strong affection for family ties and desire for knowledge and social education" (I. Epstein).

Enlargement of the Torah

Correspondingly, the concept of Torah has been enlarged. Originally it meant the first five books of the Hebrew scriptures, and the divine law which they contain. Now the concept of Torah is widened to include the Talmud. Furthermore, the study of Torah is considered a form of worship, and is also called Torah. Indeed the whole of Jewish religious life is now often described as "doing Torah."

The transformation of Jewish religion

Although Rabbinic Judaism is continuous in many ways with the earlier Israelite religion, it also differs from it in important respects. Some of these differences have already been touched upon. The most notable is the abandonment of the ritual sacrifices of animals, grain, and fruits which had been carried out in the Temple in Jerusalem. These had been the centerpiece of Israelite religion. Even before the destruction of Jerusalem the Pharisees had already largely lost interest in them, and, although it might have been possible to resurrect them after the destruction of the Temple by the Romans in AD 70, no attempt was made to do so. In Rabbinic Judaism they are replaced by the rituals of the synagogue.

A further alteration was in the enforcement of the Law. Under Israelite religion, many provisions of the Law were enforced by heavy penalties, including the death penalty (see especially Leviticus 20 – although these penalties were probably lighter than the traditional Semitic ones). Adultery, incest, homosexual intercourse, witchcraft, blasphemy, and cursing one's parents, for example, were punishable by death. In Rabbinic Judaism these provisions are superseded by the laws of the larger societies in which Jews live. The law of "an eye for an eye, and a tooth for a tooth" (*lex talionis*) was transformed into monetary compensation, for example.

Under Israelite religion the festivals had been national and agricultural. Now their religious aspect was emphasized. Previously the Passover and the Feast of Unleavened Bread were two distinct festivals, the one succeeding the other; now the name of Passover was extended to include both. The Feast of Weeks became the Feast of Revelation.

The Temple was replaced by the synagogue. But it was also replaced in some respects by the family. Since Judaism is an ethnic religion, the religion of a particular people, the preservation of the religion depends upon the biological preservation of the people, and that in turn depends upon the family. Rabbinic

Judaism centers in significant ways on the home. One becomes a member of the religion by being born of a Jewish mother, not by means of a ceremony of initiation, not even circumcision. Many important ceremonies are carried out in the home, such as the Passover Seder. Overall the religious life of the home is as important as the life of the synagogue.

A further difference between Israelite religion, at least in its later forms, and Rabbinic Judaism relates to the question of diversity. As we saw earlier, during the century or so before the destruction of Jerusalem the religion of the Jewish people flourished in a great variety of forms and movements, all of which had some claim to be considered authentically Jewish, including monastic movements and various forms of messianism. With the fall of Jerusalem this diversity was brought to an end. The Talmud created a single paradigm, a single authoritative tradition, for what could be considered genuinely Jewish, and this tradition has been preserved faithfully down to the present day. The best reflection of this mainstream tradition is by general consent the *Shulchan Aruch* of Joseph Caro, published in 1565, a compendium of Jewish law which takes account of the differences between Sephardic and Ashkenazic laws and practices (see below, p. 238).

Continuities

If Rabbinic Judaism is different in many ways from the earlier Israelite religion, it is also continuous with it in fundamental respects. Above all, it has preserved the Pharisaic conception of God, as the one universal God of all men, the heavenly Father, in whose image man is made. During the Middle Ages this conception was further developed by Jewish philosophers and theologians such as Maimonides, as a being all-good, all-powerful (omnipotent), and all-wise (omniscient). The tendency of Jewish thought has been to be more reserved about God than Christian thinkers have been about our ability to know God. For Maimonides we can know what God is not, but we cannot in any proper sense know what he is.

The traditional faith of Judaism

Although the Jewish faith has never been enshrined in an official creed, its main outlines are sufficiently clear.

- The world is not the product of mere chance, but the deliberate creation of a supreme being, God.
- There is only one God. This fundamental conviction is expressed strongly in the Shema, a proclamation of faith: "Hear, O Israel, the Lord our God, the Lord is one."
- God not only brought the universe into being, but also sustains it in existence at each moment.
- God is not a material being, but spirit, that is, mind and will.

- God is supremely wise, good, and powerful.
- There is a natural moral law which is the expression of his will. To act contrary to God's will is sin (*het, aberah*).
- God has revealed his will additionally in the Torah.
- God acts constantly in human history, to guide and direct it according to his purposes, and to provide spiritual and material blessings to man.
- Because God is so far above men, however, there are severe limitations on the extent to which men can comprehend him.
- In the end the Jewish people will somehow be vindicated and liberated by God, in the Messianic Age, when a descendant of David will establish a perfect society.
- After death the individual will be judged by God, and rewarded or punished.

An ethnic religion

Although Judaism is a monotheistic religion, and considers that its God is the one true God of all men, it is also an ethnic or national religion, not a universal one. In the ancient world, it is true, Judaism for some centuries had universalistic aspirations, for to the polytheistic culture of the Roman Empire it took the message of a single God, coupled with high ethical ideals. But from the time the empire converted to Christianity, Judaism has been content to be the religion of the Jewish people, and no longer aspires to be a religion for all mankind. It is focused on the unique identity of the Jewish people as the people dedicated to preserving the worship of the one true God. Thus Judaism maintains the concept of the "Chosen People"; this is understood, however, to imply more of obligation than of privilege, namely the obligation to carry out the divine will, and to be a light to the Gentiles, those who are not Jewish (*kiddush ha shem*, "sanctify the Name").

The holy days

Judaism sanctifies everyday life, by means of many devices designed to provide reminders of the individual's relationship with God. It accomplishes this especially through the celebration of holy days, rites of passage, dietary laws, and the use of symbols in prayer.

A prominent part in Jewish life is played by the holy days, days of special significance governed by special regulations, and marked by special customs and ceremonies. In general the holy days are derived from divine commands contained in the scriptures, but now understood without the animal sacrifices originally commanded. (Many of the holy days were originally secular agricultural observances, predating the biblical religion.)

In conjunction with this section the reader is recommended to read also the passages from the Talmud referring to each holy day, beginning on page 260. The chief holy days are:

The Sabbath   In the Law, God singles this day out for special enforcement: "Thou shalt keep holy the Sabbath day." It is a day of rest, on which no work may be performed, and is in many respects the chief Jewish day of observance. It is celebrated from sunset on Friday to sunset on Saturday, and was probably derived originally from the phases of the moon.

Sabbath observance begins in the home, with a ritual lighting of candles shortly before sunset. A synagogue service takes place after this, on the Friday evening, and is followed by a ceremonial meal in the home. The principal service is traditionally conducted in the synagogue on the Saturday morning, followed by a further one in the afternoon.

Synagogue services cannot begin until a quorum, called a *minyan*, is reached. This may sometimes result in the service starting later than the published time. The traditional minyan consists of ten men.

The institution of the Sabbath, and with it of the week as the unit of work, has been adopted throughout the world, and has had a far-reaching influence on human life. Prior to it, holidays from work, though sometimes frequent, were irregular.

Rosh Hashanah   This is the Jewish New Year. Usually falling in September, it commemorates God's act of creation, and inaugurates a period of repentance. Work is prohibited, though not as stringently as on the Sabbath. The regular synagogue service is conducted in the evening, and the main ceremonies are held the following morning, marked by the blowing of the ram's horn, the *Shofar*.

Yom Kippur   The Day of Atonement, celebrated on the eighth day after Rosh Hashanah. This is the most solemn day of the Jewish year, the prayers and readings emphasizing the necessity of repentance for sin, and the seeking of forgiveness from those one has injured. After a preliminary ceremony in the evening, during which the haunting melody of the *Kol Nidrei* is sung, the main synagogue service, which includes a commemoration of the cleansing of the Temple, is held the following afternoon, closing with a final blowing of the Shofar.

Rosh Hashanah and Yom Kippur together are referred to as the High Holy Days, or Days of Awe.

Sukkot   The Feast of Tabernacles or Huts, celebrated for eight days after Yom Kippur. Originally commanded in the book of Leviticus as an autumn harvest festival, it commemorates the shelter and protection God gave the Jewish people during their years of wandering in the desert. Temporary huts are erected, where meals are taken. On the first and last days work is prohibited, and various synagogue services are conducted during the week.

Simhat Torah, the "Joy of Torah," the last day of Sukkot, marks the end and the beginning of the annual cycle of readings from the Torah.

Hanukah This festival commemorates the victory of a Jewish army over an oppressive ruler in the second century BC. Although traditionally a minor holiday, the only one not derived from scripture, in the United States Hanukah has become in effect a major one by popular demand, since it falls during the season of Christmas.

Purim The Festival of Lots, a Jewish carnival, occasioned by the story told in the book of Esther, of the triumph of Queen Esther and the Jewish community over Haman, viceroy of the Persian Empire, their enemy. The Talmud not only permits but even commands Jews on this day to become drunk. The feast falls in February or March.

Pesach, Passover Originally a spring festival, this was adapted to commemorate the Exodus, the deliverance of the Jewish people from slavery in Egypt. The biblical Pesach had lasted for only one day, followed immediately by the Feast of Unleavened Bread. The Talmud, however, extends the term *Passover* to include both, and it now lasts for seven days, during which no leaven or yeast (*hametz*) may be eaten, but only unleavened bread (*matzah*). The feast is celebrated primarily not in the synagogue but in the home, with a ritual meal, the Seder, during which the story of the Exodus is recounted.

Shavuot, Pentecost Originally a spring harvest festival, Shavuot is celebrated 40 days after Passover. As a religious feast, it commemorates the giving of the Law to Moses on Mount Sinai.

Rites of passage

Circumcision, B'rit Milah The book of Genesis narrates that when God entered into the covenant with Abraham, he commanded that all male descendants of Abraham were henceforth to be circumcised, that is, to have the foreskin of the male sexual organ surgically removed. "This is my covenant, which you shall keep, between me and you and your descendants after you: Every male among you shall be circumcised. You shall be circumcised in the flesh of your foreskins, and it shall be a sign of the covenant between me and you" (Genesis 17: 10–11). Nowadays circumcision is commonly practiced in many societies by non-Jews too, for reasons of health and hygiene.

For a Jew circumcision is the physical testimony that he is a member of the Jewish people. It is performed on the eighth day after birth by a specially trained practitioner, the *mohel*, who is now usually also a physician, and it may be performed in his office, in a hospital, or in the home. It is at this time that the child receives a name.

Circumcision does not make the person a Jew, which happens automatically, according to rabbinic law, by the simple fact of being born of a Jewish mother.

Baby girls traditionally receive their names also in the synagogue on the first Sabbath after their birth; today the ceremony is widely held in the home.

A boy before the Torah: Bar Mitzvah celebration (Barrie Searle/Circa Photo Library)

Bar Mitzvah   Traditionally the obligations of the Jewish Law apply chiefly to males, from their thirteenth year. The Bar Mitzvah ceremony marks a boy's passage from childhood to full adult responsibility in the Jewish community. He becomes, for example, capable of being one of the 10 men required for the traditional minyan. *Mitzvah* is "a commandment," and *Bar Mitzvah* means "son of the commandment." The focal point of the ceremony, usually held in the synagogue on a Sabbath morning, is the reading by the youth of passages from the Torah in Hebrew.

In the American Jewish community, in non-Orthodox synagogues, a similar ceremony has been created for girls, the Bat Mitzvah.

Mourning for the dead, Shiva   This is a ceremony of prayer and readings from scripture performed in the home of the deceased for seven days after the funeral. For close relatives it is followed by a longer period of mourning, the *Sheloshim.*

Other features of Judaism

Kashrut, the dietary laws   Many peoples have developed the concept of ritual purity: in order to take part in a sacrifice or other solemn ceremony, one must be clean. This typically includes a prohibition on certain foods viewed as unclean. Hinduism and Islam, among the religions studied in this book, have regulations concerned with food and eating. The Law of Moses similarly desig-

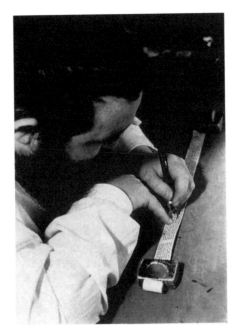

A scribe preparing the inscriptions to be placed in tefillin (Barrie Searle/Circa Photo Library)

nates some foods as clean, or kosher, and other foods as unclean, and Rabbinic Judaism has preserved these dietary restrictions, while interpreting them in its own way. Clean or permitted foods are:

- all vegetables and plants,
- all four-footed animals that chew the cud and have parted hooves,
- all fish having both fins and scales,
- all birds or fowl accepted by tradition.

Unclean or prohibited foods include:

- all animals and fish that do not meet the above requirements,
- any animal that has died of natural causes,
- blood,
- birds or fowl not accepted by tradition,
- any mixture of meat and milk, but not of fish and milk.

These requirements exclude among other foods the pig and all meat from it, such as ham and bacon; rabbit; horse; all beasts and birds of prey; and all eels and shellfish.

Animals and fowl must be slaughtered in a prescribed ritual way which ensures a rapid death and drains the blood from the animal.

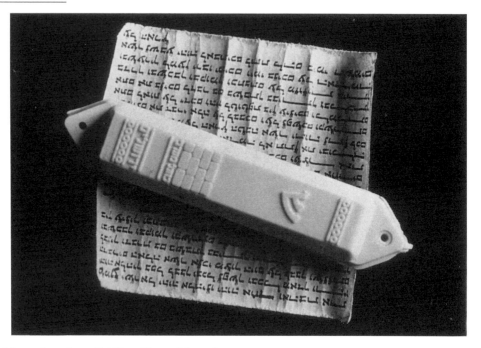

Mezuzah and scroll (Circa Photo Library)

Symbols used in prayer: tallit, tefillin, mezuzah, kippah The tallit is a prayer shawl with four corners, with a symbolic tassel, or tzitzit, on each corner. It is worn by male worshippers during prayer, especially in the synagogue.

Tefillin (plural) are straps attached to small cubical boxes which contain pieces of parchment with portions of the Torah written on them. The straps are wound around the left arm and the head during prayer. Their purpose is to fulfill the divine command to keep God's word always before one's eyes.

The mezuzah is a small parchment scroll containing biblical texts, attached to the doorposts of the home.

The kippah (Yiddish, *yarmulka*) is a skull cap worn by men during prayer. Orthodox Jews wear it at all times as a sign of the presence of God.

The use of the Divine Name: Yahweh and Adonai The true name of God is Yahweh, "I Who Am." Out of reverence, however, Orthodox Jews never utter this name, but substitute for it wherever it may be found one of the other names of God. The commonest substitute is *Adonai*: Lord.

Kabbalah

This is an esoteric movement, mystical and highly speculative, which grew up within Judaism especially during the Middle Ages, though its roots may go back into the ancient past. It claims to present the hidden truth of divine revelation (the name *Kabbalah* means "traditional teachings"). The Kabbalah aims to overcome the gap between the infinite God, often referred to as "the boundless," *en sof*, who is pure goodness, and the finite world, which contains evil. Instead of viewing the world as the creation of God, and so as fundamentally distinct from him, the Kabbalah tends to see the world as an emanation from God, still remaining in an essential identity with him, only now broken and needing to be restored to its original harmony. The Kabbalah emphasizes God's immanence in the world, and has affinities with the Upanishads and with Mahayana Buddhism, as well as with Sufi mysticism in Islam. The most important Kabbalistic work is the *Zohar*, or "Book of Splendor," published by Moses de Leon in the thirteenth century.

Hasidism

A movement founded by the Rabbi Israel Baal Shem (1700–60), and owing much to the Kabbalah, Hasidism views human life and action as cooperation with God in the work of deliverance, and emphasizes prayer rather than the study of Torah in a narrow sense. By contrast with the traditional messianic hopes, which viewed redemption as coming simply by the sovereign act of God, Baal Shem taught that God himself suffers from the sinfulness of the world, and needs human help to overcome it. Every human activity, if performed in the spirit of joyful service of God, contributes to the coming of the Messiah and the world's redemption.

The Hasidic movement continues a lively existence at the present time, with large congregations, especially in New York. Hasids typically follow distinctive conventions in dress.

Branches of modern Judaism

Like the other major religions, Judaism emerged in a world which has now gone. Many beliefs and regulations of the Torah and the Talmud do not fit easily into the changed conditions of modern Western life. On the one hand, Judaism must live in the modern world and cannot totally divorce itself from it; on the other, it may lose its identity if it accommodates itself to that world too completely. The stresses and strains of this situation have led to the emergence of several different branches of Judaism, each representing a different attempt to respond to the problem. Each branch possesses its own organization of rabbis and its own system of synagogues.

Orthodox This is the most ancient and traditional, and the one that has made the fewest concessions to the modern world. Orthodox Jews observe as far as possible the full letter of the Jewish Law as laid down in the Talmud. They keep the dietary rules strictly, for example, follow the Talmudic rules for the observance of the Sabbath, carry out the synagogue services in Hebrew, maintain the ancient separation of the sexes in the synagogue, and do not ordain women as rabbis. They do not recognize other forms of Judaism.

The German rabbi, Samson Raphael Hirsch (1808–88) established Neo-Orthodox Judaism, which makes some slight concessions to modernity, as a way of allowing Orthodox Jews to participate more fully in the life of the non-Jewish societies in which they lived.

Reform Originating in Germany during the nineteenth century, Reform Judaism is a liberal adaptation to modern conditions, emphasizing the spirit rather than the letter of the Jewish Law. In place of the authoritative revelation on Mount Sinai, Reform Judaism views revelation as taking place through nature and the human spirit. It largely omits the rituals in the home, though preserving them in the synagogue. Reform Jews do not typically follow the traditional dietary rules. They conduct their synagogue services in the vernacular, perhaps with some Hebrew. They have ordained women as rabbis, and do not separate the sexes in the synagogue. For Reform Jews the main significance of Judaism lies in its ethics, though it also has room for mysticism.

Conservative This form of Judaism, also developed in Germany, stands midway between Orthodox and Reform, preserving some aspects of traditional Judaism but altering others to adjust to modern conditions. Conservative Jews typically use both Hebrew and vernacular translations in the synagogue, respect the dietary rules but do not necessarily feel bound to follow them strictly, have ordained women as rabbis, though more reluctantly than the Reform, and do not separate the sexes in the synagogue. Conservative Judaism is the most widespread form of Judaism in the United States, but does not exist to anything like the same extent elsewhere.

Reconstructionist Founded in the United States in the twentieth century by Rabbi Mordecai Kaplan, Reconstructionist Judaism focuses especially on the Jewish people. It views Judaism as "an evolving religious civilization," the expression of Jewish life and culture. Kaplan understands God as an impersonal "transnatural power." Reconstructionist Judaism is committed to the principle that the religious dimension of Jewish life must reflect the advances in knowledge and ethical insight that each age achieves. Reconstructionist Jews typically follow the dietary rules, at least to some extent, as a sign of Jewish identity, but ordain women as rabbis, and do not separate the sexes in the synagogue.

Ashkenazim and Sephardim

Ashkenazim are Jews who live or previously lived in northern and eastern Europe, or their descendants, while Sephardim are those who lived in Spain or Muslim countries. These are two distinct cultures within Judaism, having sometimes widely different customs, including different pronunciations of Hebrew. In Israel the Sephardic pronunciation has been officially adopted.

The Holocaust

During the Second World War the Nazis, viewing the Jewish people as an international conspiracy against Germany, killed several million entirely innocent Jews using methods of mass extermination. This event, which has come to be known as the Holocaust, the biblical name for a burnt sacrifice, has left a profound wound on the Jewish mind. How could God allow such a thing? How could such an event possibly have a meaning? Many Jewish thinkers and writers have attempted to grapple with this terrible event, but the dismay it has caused continues unabated.

The Land of Israel

One consequence of the Second World War and the Holocaust, however, has been of epochal significance for Judaism: the foundation of the state of Israel. After 2,000 years, the Jewish people again have a homeland in Palestine, the land they believe was promised by God to Abraham. If the Holocaust has shaken the Jewish world to its foundations, the successful launching of the state of Israel has brought about a tremendous increase in Jewish self-confidence.

On the other hand, the existence of the state of Israel is violently opposed by the Arab population, the Palestinians, who were dispossessed by it, and by many throughout the Muslim world. This question is discussed more fully below (see p. 284).

Jewish Ethics

There is a considerable difference between Orthodox Judaism and the other branches, Conservative, Reformed, and Reconstructionist. For the Orthodox, life is to be lived strictly according to the rules of *Halakhah* in the Talmud, understood in its direct and literal sense (see above, p. 228). This material of course was compiled some 1,500 years ago in the Middle East under conditions of life very different from those that prevail in modern Western societies today. It is extremely difficult to live strictly according to *Halakhah* and still be integrated into the life of a modern society. Some idea of *Halakhah* can be gained from the selections given in the next chapter (see pp. 243–9).

For the other forms of Judaism, while *Halakhah* is to be respected and taken into account as part of the tradition, it is only one source of ethics. There are many questions that *Halakhah* does not answer. For example, it has little to say about the political realm. The Hebrew Bible is also a source, especially the prophetic books, but the Bible is often open to a variety of interpretations and practical applications.

The general spirit of Jewish ethics has historically been against any rigid application of principles. Principles tend to be considered rather as ideals to be aimed for depending on the circumstances rather than as fixed and invariable rules.

One of the most important sources of ethical considerations for a Jew is the survival and prosperity of the Jewish community. During the twentieth century this led most Jews to support social and governmental policies which were socialistic, or at least "liberal" in the American sense of the term, rather than nationalistic or conservative, since on the one hand conservative nationalism has often tended to become anti-Semitic, and on the other, the Hebrew prophets could be interpreted as supporting socialistic goals.

(In the United States the term "liberal" suggests fairness and equality, while elsewhere it generally suggests freedom, something quite different. European "liberals" believe typically in completely free markets, for example, while American "liberals" in general tend to believe in the regulation of markets to secure societal goals, such as the greater protection of the disadvantaged.)

In place of the traditional conception of ethics, which emphasizes individual responsibility, socialistic or American liberal ethics generally emphasizes collective or societal responsibility for the solution of social problems.

The policies favored by most Jews include such things as the regulation of working hours and wages, and in general the regulation of economic activity to favor equality, the creation of the welfare state, the separation of church and state, the prohibition of discrimination, and the legalization of abortion on demand. Although the Jewish community has benefited from the capitalist economy, it has also been among that system's severest critics.

Two developments have served to mitigate this inclination, however: the creation of the state of Israel and the collapse of communism. The creation of the state of Israel required a new Jewish nationalism, especially in view of the threats to Israel's existence, and therefore a new Jewish conservatism. This has included a more positive view of the concept of a just war.

The collapse of the communist regimes has raised doubts about the viability of socialism in general. The economic system of the state of Israel, for example, was initially set up in a socialistic mode, of which the collective farms known as kibbutzim were an expression, but this has proved to be economically no longer viable. Some Jewish intellectuals have been among those who once considered themselves "liberal" but who have now embraced a more conservative philosophy, and who are widely termed "neo-conservative." This is a position that once again, more in line with traditional Western thought, emphasizes individual rather than collective responsibility.

If we compare Judaism, or the Hebrew religion which preceded it, with the religions of Indian or Chinese origin, certain features of it stand out. It emphasizes the superiority of human beings over nature, as beings with a mind and will, capable of exercising personal responsibility, of taking moral factors into account, and subject to moral obligation. Lacking a belief in rebirth or the transmigration of souls, it draws a clear line between human beings and animals. By the same token it emphasizes the significance of the individual. The category of what we might call personhood is of paramount importance in Judaism. (This may be reflected in the widespread modern use of the German and Yiddish term *mensch*, meaning "a genuinely human being," as a term of strong approbation.) It is also reflected in the fact that mainstream Judaism has traditionally interpreted the supreme reality in personal terms: the transcendent reality is not an impersonal force, but knows, speaks, and wills.*

Correspondingly, Judaism is a historical religion. It emphasizes the significance of human history, the uniqueness of every human action and every historical event. There is no ever-recurring cycle of birth, death, and rebirth. With this it focuses more on moral relationships between human beings, on justice and charity, than on harmony with nature or the liberation of the ego. All of these characteristics were inherited by its daughter religions, Christianity and Islam.

Summary of Hebrew Religion and Judaism

Hebrew Religion

1   Ethical monotheism.

2   God makes a covenant with the Hebrew people.

3   He requires observance of his Law, the Torah.

4   The Torah focuses especially on the Temple and ritual sacrifice.

5   It also focuses on justice.

Judaism

1   Judaism continues the Israelite conception of God.

2   It transforms the conception of the Law to make allowance for the changed political circumstances following the destruction of the Temple in AD 70.

3   Ritual sacrifices are eliminated.

4   The synagogue system and rabbinate replace the Temple and priesthood.

5   Its immediate basis is the Talmud rather than the Bible.

6   Enlargement of the concept of Torah to include the Talmud.

7   A religion of the individual and the family, and of everyday life, expressed in holy days, rites of passage, dietary laws, and the use of symbols in prayer.

---

*   Exceptions must be made for the Kabbalah, which, like other mystical movements, has tended to regard the concept of personhood as too limited to apply to the divine reality, and to Recon-structionism, which has tended not to believe in a transcendent reality. Maimonides, the eminent medieval Jewish thinker, emphasized that we can know only what God is not, not what he is. It could perhaps be argued that it is just this discomfort with the personal conception of God that has made it difficult for these movements and thinkers to achieve full acceptance in the Jewish community.

241

Questions for discussion

1 What reasons might incline you to believe in the existence of a personal God?

2 What reasons might incline you not to so believe?

3 To what extent can the idea of human rights be traced back to ancient Hebrew religion?

4 How would you compare and contrast Judaism with Confucianism?

Test questions

1 Explain what is meant by "ethical monotheism."

2 Explain the concept of revelation.

3 Explain the idea of the covenant.

4 Explain the concept of Torah.

5 What is the Talmud?

6 What was the role of ritual sacrifice in Hebrew religion and Judaism?

7 Describe the worldview of Judaism, comparing and contrasting it to that of Theravada Buddhism.

Additional reading

Borowitz, Eugene B., *Liberal Judaism*, New York, Union of American Hebrew Congregations, 1984.

De Lange, Nicholas, *Judaism*, Oxford, Oxford University Press, 1986.

Dorff, Elliot N. and Newman, Louis E., *Contemporary Jewish Ethics and Morality: A Reader*, Oxford, Oxford University Press, 1995.

Fackenheim, Emil, *What is Judaism?* New York, Summit Books, 1987.

Gaster, Theodor H., *Festivals of the Jewish Year*, New York, Morrow, 1978 (1st pub. 1952).

Neusner, Jacob, *The Way of Torah: An Introduction to Judaism*, Belmont, CA, Wadsworth, 1988.

Steinberg, Milton, *Basic Judaism*, New York, Harcourt Brace Jovanovich, 1975.

Trepp, Leo, *The Complete Book of Jewish Observance*, New York, Behrman House/Summit Books, 1980.

Wouk, Herman, *This is My God*, New York, Doubleday, 1959.

Judaism: Texts

Israelite Religion

The Hebrew Bible is traditionally divided into the Law, the Prophets, and the Writings.

The Law

The Pentateuch or Torah, the first five books of the Hebrew Bible, make up the section of it known as the Law.

God the creator

In the beginning God created the heavens and the earth. The earth was without form and void, and darkness was upon the face of the deep; and the Spirit of God was moving over the face of the waters. And God said, "Let there be light"; and there was light. And God saw that the light was good; and God separated the light from the darkness. God called the light Day, and the darkness he called Night. And there was evening and there was morning, one day.

And God said, "Let there be a firmament in the midst of the waters, and let it separate the waters from the waters." And God made the firmament and separated the waters which were under the firmament from the waters which were above the firmament. And it was so. And God called the firmament Heaven. And there was evening and there was morning, a second day.

And God said, "Let the waters under the heavens be gathered together into one place, and let dry land appear." And it was so. God called the dry land Earth, and the waters that were gathered together he called Seas. And God saw that it was good. And God said, "Let the earth put forth vegetation, plants yielding seed, and fruit trees bearing fruit in which there is seed, each according to their own kind, upon the earth." And it was so. The earth brought forth vegetation, plants yielding seed according to their own kinds, and trees bearing fruit in which is their seed, each according to its kind. And God saw that it was good. And there was evening and there was morning, a third day.

And God said, "Let there be lights in the firmament of the heavens to separate the day from the night; and let them be for signs and for seasons and for days and years, and let them be lights in the firmament of the heavens to give light upon the earth." And it was so. And God made the two great lights, the greater light to rule the day, and the lesser light to rule the night; he made the stars also. And God set them in the firmament of the heavens to give light upon the earth, to rule over the day and over the night, and to separate the light from the darkness. And God saw that it was good. And there was evening and there was morning, a fourth day.

And God said, "Let the waters bring forth swarms of living creatures, and let birds fly above the earth across the firmament of the heavens." So God created the great sea monsters and every living creature that moves, with which the waters swarm, according to their kinds, and every winged bird according to its kind. And God saw that it was good. And God blessed them, saying, "Be fruitful and multiply and fill the waters in the seas, and let the birds multiply on the earth." And there was evening and there was morning, a fifth day.

And God said, "Let the earth bring forth living creatures according to their kinds: cattle and creeping things and beasts of the earth according to their kinds." And it was so. And God made the beasts of the earth according to their kinds and the cattle according to their kinds, and everything that creeps upon the ground according to its kind. And God saw that it was good.

Then God said, "Let us make man in our image, after our likeness; and let them have dominion over the fish of the sea, and over the birds of the air, and over the cattle, and over all the earth, and over every creeping thing that creeps upon the earth." So God created man in his own image, in the image of God he created him; male and female he created them.

And God blessed them, and God said to them, "Be fruitful and multiply, and fill the earth and subdue it; and have dominion over the fish of the sea and over the birds of the air and over every living thing that moves upon the earth." And God said, "Behold, I have given you every plant yielding seed which is upon the face of all the earth, and every tree with seed in its fruit; you shall have them for food. And to every beast of the earth, and to every bird of the air, and to everything that creeps on the earth, everything that has the breath of life, I have given every green plant for food." And it was so. And God saw everything that he had made, and behold it was very good. And there was evening and there was morning, a sixth day.

Thus the heavens and the earth were finished, and all the host of them. And on the seventh day God finished his work which he had done, and he rested on the seventh day from all his work which he had done. So God blessed the seventh day and hallowed it, because on it God rested from all his work which he had done in creation.

(Genesis 1: 1–2: 3)

Revelation

The covenant

The selection of Abraham

Now the Lord said to Abram, "Go from your country and your kindred and your father's house to the land that I will show you. And I will make of you a great nation, and I will bless you, and make your name great, so that you will be a blessing. I will bless those who bless you, and him who curses you I will curse; and by you all the families of the earth shall bless themselves."

(Genesis 12: 1–3)

When Abram was ninety-nine years old the Lord appeared to Abram, and said to him, "I am God Almighty; walk before me, and be blameless. And I will make my covenant between me and you, and will multiply you exceedingly."

Then Abram fell on his face; and God said to him, "Behold, my covenant is with you, and you shall be the father of a multitude of nations. No longer shall your name be Abram, but your name shall be Abraham; for I have made you the father of a multitude of nations. I will make you exceedingly fruitful; and I will make nations of you, and kings shall come forth from you. And I will establish my covenant between me and you and your descendants after you throughout their generations for an everlasting covenant, to be God to you and to your descendants after you."

(Genesis 17: 1–7)

The land

And I will give to you, and to your descendants after you, the land of your sojournings, all the land of Canaan, for an everlasting possession; and I will be their God.

(Genesis 17: 8)

The command of circumcision

And God said to Abraham, "As for you, you shall keep my covenant, you and your descendants after you throughout their generations. This is my covenant, which you shall keep, between me and you and your descendants after you: Every male among you shall be circumcised. You shall be circumcised in the flesh of your foreskins, and it shall be a sign of the covenant between me and you. He that is eight days old among you shall be circumcised; every male throughout your generations, whether born in your house, or bought with your money from any foreigner who is not of your offspring, both he that is born in your house and he that is bought with your money, shall be circumcised. So shall my covenant be in your flesh an everlasting covenant. Any uncircumcised male who is not circumcised in the flesh of his foreskin shall be cut off from his people; he has broken my covenant."

(Genesis 17: 9–14)

The revelation to Moses

Now Moses was keeping the flock of his father-in-law, Jethro, the priest of Midian; and he led his flock to the west side of the wilderness, and came to Horeb, the mountain of God.

And the angel of the Lord appeared to him in a flame of fire out of the midst of a bush; and he looked, and lo, the bush was burning, yet it was not consumed. And Moses said, "I will turn aside and see this great sight, why the bush is not burnt."

When the Lord saw that he turned aside to see, God called to him out of the bush, "Moses, Moses!"

And he said, "Here am I."

Then he said, "Do not come near; put off your shoes from your feet, for the place on which you are standing is holy ground."

And he said, "I am the God of your fathers, the God of Abraham, the God of Isaac, the God of Jacob." And Moses hid his face, for he was afraid to look at God.

Then the Lord said, "I have seen the affliction of my people who are in Egypt, and have heard their cry because of their taskmasters; I know their suffering, and I have come down to deliver them out of the hand of the Egyptians, and to bring them up out of that land to a good and broad land, a land flowing with milk and honey, to the place of the Canaanites, the Hittites, the Amorites, the Perizzites, the Hivites, and the Jebusites . . .

"Come, I will send you to Pharaoh that you may bring forth my people, the sons of Israel, out of Egypt."

But Moses said to God, "Who am I that I should go to Pharaoh, and bring the sons of Israel out of Egypt?"

He said, "But I will be with you; and this shall be the sign for you, that I have sent you: when you have brought forth the people out of Egypt, you shall serve God upon this mountain."

Then Moses said to God, "If I come to the people of Israel and say to them, 'The God of your fathers has sent me to you,' and they ask me, 'What is his name?' what shall I say to them?"

God said to Moses, "I AM WHO I AM." And he said, "Say this to the people of Israel, 'I AM has sent me to you.'"

(Exodus 3: 1–14)

Sinai

On the third new moon after the people of Israel had gone forth out of the land of Egypt, on that day they came into the wilderness of Sinai . . .

And Moses went up to God, and the Lord called to him out of the mountain, saying, "Thus you shall say to the house of Jacob, and tell the people of Israel: You have seen what I did to the Egyptians, and how I bore you on eagles' wings and brought you to myself. Now therefore, if you will obey my voice and keep my covenant, you shall be my own possession among all peoples; for all the earth is mine, and you shall be to me a kingdom of priests and a holy nation. These are the words which you shall speak to the children of Israel."

So Moses came and called the elders of the people, and set before them all these words which the Lord had commanded him.

And all the people answered together and said, "All that the Lord has spoken we will do."

And Moses reported the words of the people to the Lord. And the Lord said to Moses, "Lo, I am coming to you in a thick cloud, that the people may hear when I speak with you, and may also believe you for ever."

Then Moses told the words of the people to the Lord. And the Lord said to Moses, "Go to the people and consecrate them today and tomorow, and let them wash their garments, and be ready by the third day; for on the third day the Lord will come down upon Mount Sinai in the sight of all the people. And you shall set bounds for the people round about, saying, 'Take heed that you do not go up into the mountain or touch the border of it; whoever touches the mountain shall be put to death; no hand shall touch him, but he shall be stoned or shot; whether beast or man, he shall not live.' When the trumpet sounds a long blast, they shall come up to the mountain."

So Moses went down from the mountain to the people, and consecrated the people; and they washed their garments. And he said to the people, "Be ready by the third day; do not go near a woman."

On the morning of the third day there were thunders and lightnings, and a thick cloud upon the mountain, and a very loud trumpet blast, so that all the people who were in the camp trembled.

Then Moses brought the people out of the camp to meet God; and they took their stand at the foot of the mountain. And Mount Sinai was wrapped in smoke, because the Lord descended upon it in fire; and the smoke of it went up like the smoke of a kiln, and the whole mountain quaked greatly. And as the sound of the trumpet grew louder and louder, Moses spoke, and God answered him in thunder. And the Lord came down upon Mount Sinai, to the top of the mountain; and the Lord called Moses to the top of the mountain, and Moses went up.

And the Lord said to Moses, "Go down and warn the people, lest they break through to the Lord to gaze and many of them perish. And also let the priests who come near to the Lord consecrate themselves, lest the Lord break out upon them."

And Moses said to the Lord, "The people cannot come up to Mount Sinai, for thou thyself didst charge us, saying, 'Set bounds about the mountain, and consecrate it.'"

And the Lord said to him, "Go down, and come up bringing Aaron with you; but do not let the priests and the people break through to come up to the Lord, lest he break out against them." So Moses went down to the people and told them.

(Exodus 19)

The laws given to Moses

The Ten Commandments

And God spoke all these words, saying, "I am the Lord your God, who brought you out of the land of Egypt, out of the house of bondage.

"You shall have no other gods before me.

"You shall not make for yourself a graven image, or any likeness of anything that is in heaven above, or that is in the earth beneath, or that is in the water under the earth; you shall not bow down to them or serve them; for I the Lord your God am a jealous God, visiting the iniquity of the fathers upon the children to the third and the fourth generation of those who hate me, but showing steadfast love to thousands of those who love me and keep my commandments.

"You shall not take the name of the Lord your God in vain; for the Lord will not hold him guiltless who takes his name in vain.

"Remember the sabbath day, to keep it holy. Six days you shall labor, and do all your work; but the seventh day is a sabbath to the Lord your God; in it you shall not do any work, you, or your son, or your daughter, your manservant, or your maidservant, or your cattle, or the sojourner who is within your gates; for in six days the Lord made heaven and earth, the sea, and all that is in them, and rested the seventh day; therefore the Lord blessed the sabbath day and hallowed it.

"Honor your father and your mother, that your days may be long in the land which the Lord your God gives you.

"You shall not kill.

"You shall not commit adultery.

"You shall not steal.

"You shall not bear false witness against your neighbor.

"You shall not covet your neighbor's house; you shall not covet your neighbor's wife, or his manservant, or his maidservant, or his ox, or his ass, or anything that is your neighbor's.

(Exodus 20: 1–17)

The sacrifice of praise: the burnt offering or holocaust

The Lord called Moses, and spoke to him from the tent of meeting, saying, "Speak to the people of Israel, and say to them, When any man of you brings an offering to the Lord, you shall bring an offering of cattle from the herd or from the flock.

If his offering is a burnt offering from the herd, he shall offer a male without blemish; he shall offer it at the door of the tent of meeting, that he may be accepted before the Lord; he shall lay his hand upon the head of the burnt offering, and it shall be accepted for him to make atonement for him. Then he shall kill the bull before the Lord; and Aaron's sons the priests shall present the blood, and throw the blood round about against the altar that is at the door of the tent of meeting. And he shall flay the burnt offering and cut it into pieces; and the sons of Aaron the priest shall put fire on the altar, and lay wood in order upon the fire; and Aaron's sons the priests shall lay the pieces, the head, and the fat, in order upon the wood that is on the fire upon the altar; but its entrails and its legs he shall wash with water. And the priest shall burn the whole on the altar, as a burnt offering, an offering by fire, a pleasing odor to the Lord.

(Leviticus 1: 1–9)

Devotion to the one true God

Hear, O Israel: The Lord our God is one Lord; and you shall love the Lord your God with all your heart, and with all your soul, and with all your might.

And these words which I command you this day shall be upon your heart; and you shall teach them diligently to your children, and shall talk of them when you sit in your house, and when you walk by the way, and when you lie down, and when you rise. And you shall bind them as a sign upon your hand, and they shall be as frontlets between your eyes. And you shall write them on the doorposts of your house and on your gates.

(Deuteronomy 6: 4–9)

Questions for discussion

1   In order to believe that the universe was created by a personal God, is it necessary to take literally the details of the account in Genesis?

2   What is meant by the term "sin"?

The Prophets

The aim of the prophets was to purify Jewish religion, preventing it from lapsing into an empty ceremonialism.

249

Justice

1

What to me is the multitude of your sacrifices? says the Lord;
I have had enough of burnt offerings of rams, and the fat of fed beasts;
I do not delight in the blood of bulls, or of lambs, or of he-goats . . .

Bring no more vain offerings;
Incense is an abomination to me.
New moon and sabbath and the calling of assemblies –
I cannot endure iniquity and solemn assembly.

Your new moons and your appointed feasts my soul hates;
They have become a burden to me,
I am weary of bearing them.
When you spread forth your hands,
I will hide my eyes from you;
Even though you make many prayers,
I will not listen;
Your hands are full of blood.

Wash yourselves;
Make yourselves clean;
Remove the evil of your doings from before my eyes;
Cease to do evil,
Learn to do good;
Seek justice,
Correct oppression;
Defend the fatherless,
Plead for the widow.

Come now, let us reason together, says the Lord:
Though your sins are like scarlet, they shall be as white as snow;
Though they are red like crimson, they shall become like wool.

(Isaiah 1: 11–18)

2

[Yahweh:]

Cry aloud, spare not,
Lift up your voice like a trumpet;
Declare to my people their transgression,
To the house of Jacob their sins.

Yet they seek me daily,
And delight to know my ways,

As if they were a nation that did righteousness
And did not forsake the ordinance of their God;
They ask of me righteous judgements,
They delight to draw near to God.

[The people:]

Why have we fasted, and thou seest it not?
Why have we humbled ourselves,
And thou takest no knowledge of it?

[Yahweh:]

Behold, in the day of your fast you seek your own pleasure,
And oppress all your workers.
Behold, you fast only to quarrel and to fight,
And to hit with wicked fist.
Fasting like yours this day
Will not make your voice to be heard on high.

Is such the fast that I choose,
A day for a man to humble himself?
Is it to bow down his head like a rush,
And to spread sackcloth and ashes under him?
Will you call this a fast,
And a day acceptable to the Lord?

Is not this the fast that I choose:
To loose the bonds of wickedness,
To undo the thongs of the yoke,
To let the oppressed go free,
And to break every yoke?

Is it not to share your bread with the hungry,
And bring the homeless poor into your house;
When you see the naked, to cover him,
And not to hide yourself from your own flesh?

Then shall your light break forth like the dawn,
And your healing shall spring up speedily;
Your righteousness shall go before you,
The glory of the Lord shall be your rear guard.
Then you shall call, and the Lord will answer;
You shall cry, and he will say: Here I am.

(Isaiah 58: 1–9)

The messianic king

There shall come forth a shoot from the stump of Jesse,
And a branch shall grow out of his roots.
And the Spirit of the Lord shall rest upon him,
The spirit of wisdom and understanding,
The spirit of counsel and might,
The spirit of knowledge and the fear of the Lord.
And his delight shall be in the fear of the Lord.

He shall not judge by what his eyes see,
Or decide by what his ears hear;
But with righteousness he shall judge the poor,
And decide with equity for the meek of the earth;
And he shall smite the earth with the rod of his mouth,
And with the breath of his lips he shall slay the wicked.
Righteousness shall be the girdle of his waist,
And faithfulness the girdle of his loins.

The wolf shall dwell with the lamb,
And the leopard shall lie down with the kid,
And the calf and the lion and the fatling together,
And a little child shall lead them.
The cow and the bear shall feed;
Their young shall lie down together;
And the lion shall eat straw like the ox.
The suckling child shall play over the hole of the asp,
And the weaned child shall put his hand on the adder's den.
They shall not hurt or destroy in all my holy mountain;
For the earth shall be full of the knowledge of the Lord,
As the waters cover the sea.

(Isaiah 11: 1–9)

Questions for discussion

1 What does it mean, for a person to "oppress" another?

2 What is stated about the Messiah in this passage from Isaiah?

The Psalms

The Psalms, the first and most important of the Writings, are a collection of religious poetry compiled for use in the worship of the Temple after the

Babylonian exile. There are many puzzles associated with them, especially concerning the frequent use of the first person singular in psalms that appear to have been used in communal or collective ceremonies. Nonetheless they remain in many ways the most moving expression of the spirituality of the Hebrew people.

1

Have mercy on me, O God,
According to your steadfast love;
According to your abundant mercy
Blot out my transgressions.
Wash me thoroughly from my iniquity,
And cleanse me from my sin!

For I know my transgressions,
And my sin is ever before me.
Against you, you only, have I sinned,
And done that which is evil in your sight,
So that you are justified in your sentence
And blameless in your judgement.
Behold, I was brought forth in iniquity,
And in sin did my mother conceive me.

Behold, you desire truth in the inward being;
Therefore teach me wisdom in my secret heart.
Purge me with hyssop, and I shall be clean;
Wash me, and I shall be whiter than snow.
Fill me with joy and gladness;
Let the bones which you have broken rejoice.
Hide your face from my sins,
And blot out all my iniquities.

Create in me a clean heart, O God,
And put a new and right spirit within me.
Cast me not away from your presence,
And take not your holy Spirit from me.
Restore to me the joy of your salvation,
And uphold me with a willing spirit.
Then I will teach transgressors your ways,
And sinners will return to you.
Deliver me from blood guiltiness, O God,
God of my salvation,
And my tongue will sing aloud of your deliverance.

O Lord, open my lips,
And my mouth shall show forth your praise.
For you take no delight in sacrifice;
Were I to give a burnt offering,
You would not be pleased.
The sacrifice acceptable to God
Is a broken spirit.
A broken and contrite heart, O God,
You will not despise.

(Psalm 51: 1–17)

2

The Lord is my shepherd,
I shall not want.
He makes me to lie down in green pastures.
He leads me beside still waters;
He restores my soul.
He leads me in paths of righteousness
For his name's sake.

Even though I walk through the valley of the shadow of death,
I fear no evil;
For thou art with me;
Thy rod and thy staff,
They comfort me.

Thou preparest a table before me
In the presence of my enemies.
Thou anointest my head with oil,
My cup overflows.
Surely goodness and mercy shall follow me
All the days of my life;
And I shall dwell in the house of the Lord
Forever.

(Psalm 23)

3

O Lord, you have searched me and known me!
You know when I sit down and when I rise up;
You discern my thoughts from afar.
You search out my path and my lying down,
You are acquainted with all my ways.
Even before a word is on my tongue,
Lo, O Lord, you know it altogether.

You beset me behind and before,
And lay your hand upon me.
Such knowledge is too wonderful for me;
It is high, I cannot attain it.

Whither shall I go from your Spirit?
Or whither shall I flee from your presence?
If I ascend to heaven, you are there!
If I make my bed in Sheol, you are there!
If I take the wings of the morning
And dwell in the uttermost parts of the sea,
Even there your hand shall lead me,
And your right hand shall hold me.
If I say, "Let only darkness cover me,
And the light about me be night,"
The night is bright as the day,
For darkness is as light with you.

(Psalm 139: 1–12)

Questions for discussion

1   What is meant by the term "prayer"?

2   Put in your own words the main ideas of Psalm 51.

3   Put in your own words the main ideas of Psalm 23.

Rabbinic Judaism: The Talmud

The Talmud is rather like an encyclopedia of Jewish law. It consists of a basic text, the Mishnah, and an extended commentary, the Gemara. The Mishnah is a codification of the Oral Law divided into six orders, each consisting of a number of tractates. The whole Talmud can be understood as a response to the changed conditions of life in which the Jewish community found itself from about the beginning of the Christian era.

God

1

How do we know that the Holy One, praised be He, prays? It is written, "I will bring them to My holy mountain and make them rejoice in My house of prayer"

255

[Isaiah 56: 7]. This verse states not "their house of prayer" but "My house of prayer," from which we infer that the Holy One, praised be He, prays. What is His prayer? Rav Tuviah bar Zutra, quoting Rav, said, "May it be My will that My compassion overcomes My wrath, and that it prevail over My attribute of strict justice. May I deal with My children according to the attribute of compassion; may I not deal with them according to the strict line of justice."

(*Berakhot 7a*)

> This passage reflects the method of interpreting scripture called Midrash, and with it the poetic and sometimes whimsical character of the Talmud. According to the canons of strict logic it would scarcely make sense to say that God prays, but the authors of the Talmud nonetheless find a way to say it, thus emphasizing the importance of prayer.

2

Rabbi Judah said, quoting Rav: The day consists of twelve hours. During the first three hours, the Holy One, praised be He, is engaged in the study of Torah. During the second three He sits in judgment over His entire world. When He realizes that the world is deserving of destruction, He rises from the Throne of Justice, to sit in the Throne of Mercy. During the third group of three hours, He provides sustenance for the entire world, from huge beasts to lice. During the fourth, He sports with the Leviathan, as it is written, "Leviathan, which You did form to sport with" [Psalm 104: 26] . . . During the fourth group of three hours (according to others) He teaches schoolchildren.

(*Avodah Zarah 3b*)

> Similarly, it does not make literal sense that God, who exists outside of time, should divide his "day" up into periods, but the effect of this poetical device is to humanize God.

3

Rabbi Nehemiah said: When the Israelites did that wicked deed [i.e. when they constructed and worshipped the golden calf] Moses sought to appease God, who was angry with them. He said, "Lord of the universe! They have made an assistant for You. Why should You be angry with them? This calf will assist You: You will cause the sun to shine and the calf will cause the moon to shine; You will take care of the stars and the calf will take care of the planets; You will cause the dew to fall and the calf will make the winds to blow; You will cause the rain to fall and the calf will cause vegetation to sprout."

The Holy One, praised be He, said to Moses, "You are making the same mistake that the people are making. This calf is not real!"

Moses then replied, "If that is so, why should You be angry with Your children?"

(Exodus Rabbah 43: 6)

Here again God is humanized, since it is possible to argue with him and show him that he is wrong.

4

Rabbi Joshua said "Wherever you find a description of the greatness of the Holy One, praised be He, you find a description of His consideration for the lowly. This is written in the Torah, repeated in the Prophets, and stated for the third time in the Writings. In the Torah it is written: "For the Lord your God is God of gods and Lord of lords . . ." [Deuteronomy 10: 17], and in the verse following it is written, "He executes justice for the fatherless and the widow."

It is repeated in the Prophets: "For thus says the high and lofty One who inhabits eternity, whose name is holy, 'I dwell in the high and holy place'" [Isaiah 57: 15]. And the verse continues "and also with him who is of a contrite and humble spirit." It is stated for the third time in the Writings: "Extol Him who rides upon the skies, whose name is the Lord" [Psalm 68: 5], and in the verse following it is written "Father of the fatherless and protector of widows."

(Megillah 31*a*)

Torah

5

Rabbi Simlai expounded: Six hundred and thirteen commandments were transmitted to Moses on Mount Sinai. Three hundred sixty five of them are negative commandments [i.e. prohibitions], corresponding to the number of days in the solar year. The remaining two hundred forty eight are positive commandments [i.e. injunctions], corresponding to the number of limbs in the human body.

After Moses, David came and reduced the six hundred and thirteen commandments to eleven, as it is written: "Lord, who shall sojourn in Your tabernacle? Who shall dwell on Your holy mountain? He who walks blamelessly, and does what is right, and speaks truth in his heart, who does not slander with his tongue, and does no evil to his friend, nor takes up a reproach against his neighbor, in whose eyes a reprobate is despised, but honors those who fear the Lord, who swears to his own hurt and does not change, who does not put out his money at interest, and does not take a bribe against the innocent" [Psalm 15: 1–5].

Then Isaiah came and reduced the commandments to six, as it is written, "He who walks righteously and speaks uprightly, he who despises the gain of oppressions, who shakes his hands lest they hold a bribe, who stops his ears from hearing of bloodshed, and shuts his eyes from looking upon evil" [Isaiah 33: 15] . . .

Then Micah came and reduced them to three, as it is written, "It has been told you, O man, what is good, and what the Lord requires of you: To do justice, to love mercy, and to walk humbly with your God" [Micah 6: 8] . . .

Then Isaiah came again and reduced them to two. "Thus says the Lord: Keep justice and do righteousness" [Isaiah 56: 1].

Amos came and reduced them to one, as it is written, "Thus says the Lord to the house of Israel: Seek Me and live" [Amos 5: 4] . . .

Habakkuk came and also reduced them to one, as it is written, "The righteous shall live by his faith" [Habakkuk 2: 4].

(*Makkot* 24a)

6

Rabbi Huna and Rabbi Jeremiah said in the name of Rabbi Hiyya bar Abba: It is written, "They have forsaken Me and have not kept My law" [Jeremiah 16: 11]. This is to say: "If only they had forsaken Me but kept My law! Since they then would have been occupied with it, the light which is in it would have restored them to the right path."

(*Lamentations Rabbah*, proem II)

Circumcision

7

Rabbi Ishmael says: Great is circumcision, whereby the covenant was made thirteen times [the word "covenant" is repeated 13 times in the seventeenth chapter of Genesis, where the commandment is given].

Rabbi Jose says: Great is circumcision, for it overrides even the stringency of the Sabbath [circumcision may be performed on the Sabbath if it is the eighth day after birth].

Rabbi Joshua ben Korha says: Great is circumcision, for it was not suspended so much as an hour even for the sake of Moses [See Exodus 4: 24–5] . . .

Rabbi Judah says: Great is circumcision, for despite all the religious duties which Abraham fulfilled, he was not called "perfect" until he was cirumcised, as it is written, "Walk before Me and be perfect, and I will make My covenant [i.e. circumcision] between Me and you" [Genesis 17: 1–2].

Great is circumcision, for the Holy One, praised be He, had not created the world but for it, as it is written "Thus says the Lord: But for My covenant [i.e. circumcision] day and night, I had not set forth the ordinances of heaven and earth" [Jeremiah 33: 25].

(Mishnah *Nedarim* 3: 11)

Marriage and the family

8

A wife must do the following for her husband: grind flour, bake bread, wash clothes, cook food, give suck to her child, make ready his bed and work in wool. If she brought him one maidservant [from her father's house], she need not grind or bake or wash. If she brought two maidservants she need not cook or give her child suck. If she brought three maidservants, she need not make ready his bed or work in wool. If four, she may sit all day and do nothing. Rabbi Eliezer says: Even if she brought one hundred maidservants he should force her to work in wool, for idleness leads to unchastity.

(Mishnah *Ketubot* 5: 5)

9

No man may abstain from fulfilling the commandment "Be fruitful and multiply" [Genesis 1: 28], unless he already has children. According to the School of Shamai, "children" here means two sons, while the School of Hillel states that it means a son and a daughter, for it is written, "Male and female He created them" [Genesis 5: 2]. If he married a woman and lived with her for ten years and she bore no child, he is not permitted to abstain from fulfilling the commandment. If he divorced her she may marry another, and the second husband may live with her for ten years. If she had a miscarriage, the period of ten years is reckoned from the time of the miscarriage. The duty to be fruitful and multiply is incumbent upon the man but not upon the woman. Rabbi Johanan ben Baroka says: Concerning them both it is written: "God blessed them and God said to them: Be fruitful and multiply" [Genesis 1: 28].

(Mishnah *Yebamot* 6: 6)

Parents and children

10

They asked Rav Ulla: To what point must one honor his parents? He told them: Go and see how a non-Jew named Dama ben Netinah treated his father in Ashkelon. The sages once sought to conclude a business transaction with him, through which he would gain 600,000 gold denarii. But the key to his vault was under the pillow of his sleeping father, and he refused to disturb him.

(*Kiddushin* 31a)

11

The disciples of Rabbi Eliezer the Great asked him to give an example of honoring one's parents. He said: Go and see what Dama ben Netinah did in Ashkelon. His mother was feeble-minded and she used to strike him with a shoe in the presence of the council over which he presided, but he never said more than "It is enough, mother." When the shoe fell from her hand he would pick it up for her, so that she would not be troubled.

(Jerusalem Peah 1: 1)

Love your neighbor

12

A heathen once came to Shammai and said, "I will become a convert on the condition that you teach me the entire Torah while I stand on one foot." Shammai chased him away with a builder's measuring stick. When he appeared before Hillel with the same request, Hillel said, "Whatever is hateful to you, do not do to your neighbor. That is the entire Torah. The rest is commentary; go and learn it."

(Mishnah *Shabbat* 31*a*)

The Sabbath

13

The principal categories of work [forbidden on the Sabbath] are forty less one: sowing, plowing, reaping, binding sheaves, threshing, winnowing, cleansing crops, grinding, sifting, kneading, baking, shearing, washing, beating or dyeing wool, spinning, weaving, making two loops, weaving two threads, separating two threads, tying a knot, loosening a knot, sewing two stitches, ripping in order to sew two stitches, hunting a gazelle, slaughtering or flaying or salting it or curing its hide, scraping it or cutting it up, writing two letters, erasing in order to write two letters, building, pulling down, putting out a fire, lighting a fire, striking with a hammer and taking anything from one domain to another [e.g. from a private domain to a public domain or vice versa]. These are the principal categories of work: forty less one.

(Mishnah *Shabbat* 7: 2)

14

Whenever there is doubt as to whether a life may be in danger, the laws of the Sabbath may be suspended.

(Mishnah *Yoma* 8: 6)

15

One may warm water for a sick person on the Sabbath . . . We do not wait until the Sabbath is over, on the assumption that he will get better, but we warm the water for him right away, because whenever there is doubt as to whether or not a life may be in danger, the laws of the Sabbath may be suspended . . . And this [violation of the Sabbath laws, whatever it might have to be] is not to be done by Gentiles or by minors [who are not obligated to observe the Sabbath law anyway] but by Jewish adults.

(Mishnah *Yoma* 84*b*)

Passover

16

On the night preceding the fourteenth of Nisan [Passover begins on the fifteenth] the *hametz* must be searched out by the light of a candle. Any place into which hametz is never brought need not be searched. [Hametz is any food containing a fermented substance.]

(Mishnah *Pesahim* 1: 1)

17

Rabbi Meir says: Hametz may be eaten through the fifth hour [i.e. 11 a.m.] on the fourteenth of Nisan, but at the start of the sixth hour it must be burned. Rabbi Judah says: It may be eaten through the fourth hour, held [neither eaten nor burned] during the fifth hour, and it must be burned at the start of the sixth hour.

(Mishnah *Pesahim* 1: 4)

18

So long as hametz may be eaten, a man may give it as fodder to cattle, wild animals and birds, or sell it to a non-Jew, and he is permitted to derive benefit from it in any fashion. But when the time is past [and hametz may no longer be eaten] it is forbidden to derive benefit from it, nor may one light an oven or stove with it. Rabbi Judah says: Removal of the hametz [Exodus 12: 15] may be accomplished by burning. But the sages say: Hametz may be crumbled and scattered to the wind or thrown into the sea.

(Mishnah *Pesahim* 2: 1)

19

If [on the fourteenth of Nisan] a man was on his way to slaughter his Passover offering or to circumcise his son or to participate in the wedding banquet at the home of his father-in-law and he remembered that he had left hametz in his house, he may return and remove it if he has time to do so and yet fulfill his religious obligation; otherwise, he may annul the hametz in his heart [thus decreeing that it be considered as dirt, and as not in his possession]. If he was on his way to help those endangered by soldiers, a flood, thieves, a fire, or a falling building, he should annul the hametz in his heart [and not try to return by any means, since his action may save a life]. However, if he was on his way to celebrate Passover at a place of his own choosing, he must return home at once to remove the hametz.

(Mishnah *Pesahim* 3: 7)

20

Where it is the custom to do work until noon on the day before Passover, people may do so. Where it is the custom not to do work, people may not work. If a man went from a place where they do to a place where they do not, or from a place where they do not to a place where they do, we apply the more stringent custom of both the place which he has left [in case he should return] and the place to which he has gone. Let no man act in a manner different from local custom, lest it lead to conflict.

(Mishnah *Pesahim* 4: 1)

21

They mix him the second cup [of the four cups of wine which are drunk at the Passover table]. Then the son asks his father – and if the son does not understand the procedure, his father teaches him how to ask – "Why is this night different from other nights? On all other nights we may eat either leavened or unleavened bread, but on this night we eat only unleavened bread. On all other nights we may eat all types of herbs, but on this night we eat only bitter herbs. On all other nights we eat meat roasted, stewed or cooked, but on this night we eat only roasted meat. On all other nights we dip but once, but on this night we dip twice." The father instructs the son according to the understanding of the son. He begins with the disgrace and ends with the glory. And he expounds, beginning with "A wandering Aramean was my father..." [Deuteronomy 26: 5] and continuing until he finishes the entire section.

(Mishnah *Pesahim* 10: 4)

Rosh Hashanah

22

Rabbi Abbahu said: Why is the horn of a ram sounded on Rosh Hashanah? The Holy One, praised be He, said, "Sound before Me the horn of a ram, that I might be reminded of the binding of Isaac, the son of Abraham, and thus consider your fulfillment of this commandment [of sounding a horn] as though you had bound yourself upon an altar before Me. [See the story of Abraham and Isaac on p. 199 above, where at God's command Abraham sacrifices a ram in place of Isaac.]

(*Rosh Hashanah* 16a)

23

Rabbi Kruspedal said, quoting Rabbi Johanan: On Rosh Hashanah [when the world is judged], three books are opened in the heavenly court: one for the wicked, one for the righteous, and one for those in between. The fate of the righteous is inscribed and sealed then and there: Life. The fate of the wicked is inscribed and sealed then and there: Death. The fate of those in between lies in doubt from Rosh Hashanah until Yom Kippur. If, during those days, they show their worth through their deeds, they are inscribed and sealed for Life; and if not, they are inscribed and sealed for death.

(*Rosh Hashanah* 16*b*)

Yom Kippur

24

On Yom Kippur, eating, drinking, washing, anointing with oil, wearing of sandals and sexual intercourse are forbidden. A king or bride may wash their faces, and a woman after childbirth may wear sandals, according to Rabbi Eliezer. But the sages forbid it.

(Mishnah *Yoma* 8: 1)

25

Young children are not to fast on Yom Kippur. But one or two years before they come of age they should be trained [by fasting part of the day], that they may become well versed in the commandments.

(Mishnah *Yoma* 8: 4)

26

If a pregnant woman smells food and craves it on Yom Kippur, she may be fed until she recovers. One who is ill may be fed at the word of experts [i.e. medical advisers]. If no experts are readily available, he may be fed at his own wish, until he says "Enough."

(Mishnah *Yoma* 8: 5)

(Arthur Hertzberg, *Judaism*, New York, Washington Square Press, 1970)

Questions for discussion

1   Discuss passages 1 and 2. Does God actually pray? Does he actually have a day of 12 hours? Do you see any value in speaking of God in this fashion?

2   Compare passage 5 with passage 12.

Muslims in percent of the
total population, 2001

0.0–25.0%
25.1–50.0%
50.1–75.0%
75.1–100.0%

The Muslim world

8

Islam

The Spirit of Islam

The following excerpt is taken from an autobiographical novel *Heirs to the Past* by the Muslim writer Driss Chraïbi. The occasion is the funeral of the old father of the family, for which the émigré son, Driss Ferdi, has returned from the secular rationalism of Paris, where he has spent the last 16 years in a steady erosion of his Muslim convictions and identity.

Then a man stood up . . . and began to chant. What he chanted was of no importance. It was not the words, nor the meaning, nor even the symbolism, which moved our hearts, the men, women and children who were there. We forgot why we were there the moment he began to chant. It was the incantation, and the end of our woes and miserable little problems, the aching and yet serene longing for that other life which is ours and to which we are all destined to return, the victors and the defeated, the fully developed and those who are still at the larva state, the faithful and the atheists, through God's great compassion. There was all of that in the voice of the man who stood chanting in the sun, and we were in his voice, I was in his voice despite the vast legacy of incredulity that I had received from the West. When he reached the end of a verse, he paused, and so it came about – an outburst of fervour. And while he chanted it was like a man in the wilderness chanting his faith. And the voice rose and swelled, changed in tone, became tragic, soared and then floated down on our heads like a seagull gliding gently and softly, little more than a whisper. And so – never again will I go in search of intellectuals, of written truths, synthetic truths, of collections of hybrid ideas which are nothing but ideas. Never again will I travel the world in search of a shadow of justice, fairness, progress, or schemes calculated to change mankind. I was weary and I was returning to my clan. The man who was not even aware of his voice or of his faith was alive and held the secret of life – a man who could not even have been a dustman in this world of founts of knowledge and of civilization. Peace and everlasting truth were in him and in his voice, while all was crumbling around him and on the continents.

(Driss Chaïbi, *Heirs to the Past*, trans. Len Ortzen, London, Heinemann Educational Books, 1971)

Question for discussion

1 The speaker is here described as being led by the chanter's voice to experience some larger perspective than the merely intellectual. What could account for this experience?

The Muslim View of Life

The Muslim view of life shares a great deal with the Jewish and Christian views to which it is related. The world has been created by a personal God, who has revealed his will to man. At death God judges each soul accordingly, either for heaven or for hell.

In the Muslim view, the most important thing is to acknowledge the absolute supremacy of God. Since God is our Creator and our Judge, he deserves our complete and total submission, and that submission in turn will bring us eternal salvation.

The Emergence of Islam

The Arab peoples before Mohammed worshipped numerous gods and spirits. Sacred stones, trees, and springs were venerated, and spirits were believed to inhabit the desert. The inhabitants of Mohammed's native city, Mecca, worshipped a high god named Allah together with other divinities, including three goddesses known as the "Daughters of Allah." The name *Allah* is a combination of *al*, which is the definite article "the," and *ilah*, the usual word for "God," and thus means "*the* God." An important center of this worship was a cubical structure called the Ka'bah, containing a sacred Black Stone, which remains a center of pilgrimage in Islam.

There were also Jews and Christians in Arabia. Furthermore, according to Islamic tradition, there were native Arab monotheists called *hanifs*, neither Jews nor Christians, whose belief in the one and only God had descended in an independent tradition from Abraham (whom the Koran views as a Muslim).

Mohammed (Arabic, Muhammad)

Mohammed was born in Mecca, a member of the dominant tribe there known as the Koraish (Arabic, *Quraish*), probably around AD 570. His father, whose name was Abdullah, or "slave of Allah," died before he was born, and his mother Aminah died when he was six. He was brought up first by his grandfather, who made a modest living by providing pilgrims with water from a well sacred to Allah, so the boy was associated with the religious life from an early age. When, after only two years, his grandfather died, Mohammed was transferred to the care of his uncle, Abu Talib, also a religious man, and later one of his strongest personal supporters (though Abu Talib never embraced Islam).

In his twenties Mohammed came to be employed by a wealthy widow, Khadija, as overseer of her camel caravans, and journeyed with them to Syria. When he was 25, and she 40, they married, and she bore him six children.

In time Mohammed became more and more contemplative. He associated with the hanifs, and would go off into the hills for several days at a time in order to pray and meditate.

Revelation

During these excursions Mohammed began to have a series of extraordinary experiences. One night while he was asleep a spiritual being of great power appeared to him, identifying himself as the Angel Gabriel, and announcing that Mohammed was to be the messenger of God. On subsequent occasions and throughout the rest of his life, Gabriel made many revelations to him, which Mohammed was able afterwards to remember exactly. These revelations were couched in an exalted poetic language, which speakers of Arabic consider to be of unsurpassed beauty. They were committed to memory by his followers and eventually written down. Collected after Mohammed's death, they make up the Koran, the sacred scripture of Islam.

The Koran (Arabic, Qur'an)

The chief message of the Koran is the absolute supremacy of God. There exists only one God, and his power is unlimited. He is in complete control of the universe, and human beings owe him total submission. The Arabic word for submission is *islam*.

The word *Koran* (or *Qur'an*), meaning "recitation," comes from the command of the Angel Gabriel to Mohammed. The Koran is organized in chapters, called suras, of various lengths, some very short, some quite long. Predominantly, the statements of the Koran are placed on the lips of God.

To Muslims the Koran is a miracle of beauty and inspiration. It is often described as the only miracle to which Islam lays claim.

The Hegira (Arabic, Hijra)

In his native city, Mecca, Mohammed made little headway. His revelations aroused violent opposition from the merchants, who feared for their trade, which depended on the traditional religion. He made few converts. In the city of Medina, some

300 miles to the north, however, he was regarded much more favorably. The city was torn by strife, and leading citizens of Medina secretly invited Mohammed to move there and serve as religious leader and arbitrator, promising to become Muslims and obey him. This he did. In the year 622 of the Christian era, under cover of darkness, he left Mecca and travelled to Medina. This event is called the Hegira (or Hijra), the "emigration." It is considered the founding event of Islam as a religion. The year in which it took place was adopted as the first year of the Islamic calendar.

Mohammed in Medina (Arabic, Madina)

Gradually Mohammed became the sole ruler of Medina, and transformed it into an Islamic society. The worship of all other gods but Allah was eliminated, the forms of public prayer were established, with Friday as the weekly day of prayer, the fast of Ramadan was established and the mosque was created as the place of prayer. The brotherhood of all Muslims was stressed, and an official system of almsgiving was organized to help the poor.

In addition, Mohammed organized armed raids on the Meccan caravans traversing the desert because the Meccans had confiscated the Muslims' property. The Meccans replied by sending guards to defend them. The armed forces on both sides grew, leading to a series of battles from which Mohammed's forces emerged the victors. He became the chief political power in Arabia.

The return to Mecca (Arabic, Makka)

In AD 630 Mohammed resolved to capture Mecca. He gathered together a large army and proceeded to the city, which surrendered to him. He transformed Mecca into an Islamic city on the model of Medina, smashing the images of the gods, and setting the Ka'bah up as the central shrine of Islam. Two years later he died.

The expansion of Islam

After Mohammed's death many Arab tribes began to withdraw their allegiance to Islam. His successors, the Caliphs, declared them apostates, sent armies out against them, and quickly overcame them. Finding they were so easily victorious, the Muslim armies continued to advance into more remote territories subject to the Persian and Roman Empires. Both empires were unpopular, and the Muslim armies were welcomed. Within a few short years they were masters of an enormous empire stretching from present-day Afghanistan to Egypt and as far west as Spain.

The status of Mohammed

Muslims do not regard Mohammed as divine, or as a savior, but as a mere man. Although a mere man, however, he is the Prophet, the man through whom

Al Haram Mosque, Mecca (Photo © Sipa Press/Rex Features)

God has made his final revelation to mankind. This is expressed by his title "The Seal of the Prophets," that is, the last and decisive prophet. There are no more prophets after him, for there are no revelations from God after the Koran.

Although Islamic tradition does not regard Mohammed as divine, it does consider him sinless, and regards him as the highest model of behavior. The strongest argument for any belief or action is that it follows Mohammed's example.

Sunna and hadith

Because of Mohammed's immense prestige, the Koran is not the only authority in Islam. Everything that Mohammed said or did is authoritative, and constitutes a *Sunna*, an approved custom or tradition. As a result, a large body of literature has developed tracing various actions and sayings to him and his companions. A report attributing some saying or action to Mohammed or his companions is called a *hadith*, and in practice they play as large a role in Muslim life as the Koran itself. The hadith is a special Muslim literary form. Typically it begins by giving the chain of witnesses, called an *isnad*, who have handed the report on to one another: A told B, who told C, who told D, and so on, that Mohammed did or said such and such. (The proper plural of hadith in Arabic is

269

ahadith; however, hadith seems to be widely used in English for both singular and plural.)

The Doctrines of Islam

The main doctrines of Islam are usually summed up under five headings.

One God

The most basic belief of Islam is that there exists a single personal God. This is a belief it shares with Judaism and Christianity. Perhaps even more strongly than those religions, if possible, Islam emphasizes that there is only one God. It rejects polytheism with the utmost intensity.

This emphatic monotheism is expressed in the Witness, or *Shahada*, uttered daily by devout Muslims:

> There is no God but Allah, and Mohammed is his prophet.
> *La ilaha illa Allah; Muhammad rasul Allah.*

The force of this belief is, first, to assert that all the other divinities that mankind has worshipped in the course of its history are mere myths, empty figments of the imagination.

Second, the belief provides the true God with a definite historical identity. God is not a mere abstract idea. One of the gods men have worshipped is actually the true God, namely Allah, the god worshipped specifically in Mecca by Mohammed's tribesmen even before he was born. It was he, and no other, who revealed the Koran to Mohammed. (The Arabic language has no capital letters, and so no way of distinguishing between "god" and "God.")

Third, the belief implies the absolute supremacy of Allah. He is in complete control of the universe. Whatever happens, happens only by his will. He is unique. Nothing can be compared to him or put in the same category with him. The Muslim theologian Al-Ghazali says:

> He in His essence is one without any partner, single without any similar, eternal without any opposite, separate without any like. He is One: prior with nothing before Him, from eternity, without any beginning, abiding in existence with none after Him, to eternity without an end, subsisting without ending, abiding without termination . . . Measure does not bind him and boundaries do not contain Him.
> (Quoted in Duncan B. Macdonald, *Development of Muslim Theology,*
> *Jurisprudence and Constitution Theory*, New York, 1903, p. 303;
> see also Cragg, *House of Islam*, p. 14.)

To place any created thing on the same level as God is to commit the sin of *shirk*, tantamount to blasphemy. This is why polytheism is so strongly detested:

it is felt to insult the unique dignity of God by associating imaginary beings with him. In the Muslim view, Christians also commit this sin by believing in Jesus as the Son of God, for God cannot have a son, that is, another being of the same nature as himself.

Angels

The Koran was revealed to Mohammed not directly by God, but by the Angel Gabriel speaking on behalf of God. It is therefore a doctrine of Islam that there exist spiritual beings in addition to man. The highest of these are the angels, the messengers and servants of God who carry out his will in the world. The Koran mentions Michael in addition to Gabriel.

Besides the angels, there is another kind of invisible being called the *jinn* (plural; the singular is *jinni*, the origin of the "genie" in the story of Aladdin's lamp). The jinn were created by God out of fire and, unlike the angels, they eventually die. They are of both sexes and can be good or evil. Iblis, or Satan, is a jinni.

Prophets and scriptures

Although non-Muslims view Islam as the youngest of the major religions, Islam does not regard itself in the same way. It sees itself as identical with the first revelation God gave to mankind. The Koran mentions some 25 individuals to whom God gave the essentials of the Koranic message in earlier times. These are the prophets. A prophet in this sense is not necessarily a person who predicts the future, but one who speaks on behalf of God. They include Adam, Noah, Abraham (Ibrahim), Joseph (Yusuf), Moses (Musa), Aaron (Harun), David (Dawud), John the Baptist (Yahya), and Jesus (Isa). All of these were Muslims.

To each one God entrusted a scripture, containing essentially the same message as the Koran: of submisssion of God: to Moses, for example, he gave the Torah; to David the Psalms; to Jesus the Gospel. But in each case the scriptures were corrupted or misinterpreted. As a result these texts have no authority for Muslims. It was to correct these distortions that God sent Mohammed, revealing to him again the true Koran. It alone is now the pure scripture, possessing the original form given it by God, and so it supersedes all the earlier ones.

Islam, then, is simply the true form of what Judaism and Christianity ought to be and would be if they had remained faithful to their original inspiration.

Resurrection and the Last Judgement

As mentioned above, the Koran describes itself as a book of warning. What it warns mankind about is the Last Judgement. Almost every page of the Koran contains an urgent reminder that at the end of time, in an earth-shaking cataclysm in which he will raise all the dead to life, God will pass an eternal sentence on every human being. Those who believe the revelation given through Mohammed and who do good works will be rewarded with the delights of heaven. Those who did not believe will be consigned to the torments of hell.

However, like the earlier forms of Christianity (see below, p. 328), Islam has a doctrine of purgatory. After death the souls of those who do not deserve hell but are not yet ready to enter heaven will undergo a period of temporary suffering which will prepare them for entrance into heaven.

The divine decree and predestination

Since the Koran lays so much emphasis on the judgement of God, it plainly believes that human beings have free will. Those who are condemned to hell receive that punishment because they deserve it, since God is just. But this must not be understood to mean that human actions lie outside the scope of God's control. Nothing lies outside God's control, and that includes the free actions of men. It can be said, then, that God predestines some to heaven and some to hell. Yet this does not abolish man's responsibility for his own deeds and misdeeds.

This doctrine is more controversial than the other four, since it seems to imply a contradiction. In general Muslim thinkers have been content to admit that it is a profound mystery, and leave it at that (the principle of *Bila Kayf*), emphasizing that what counts in Islam is not theory but practice.

> His beauty if it thrill thy heart,
> If thou a man of passion art,
> Of time and of eternity,
> Of being and non-entity,
>   Ask not.

> When thou has passed the basses four,
> Behold the sanctuary door,
> And having satisfied thine eyes,
> What in the sanctuary lies,
>   Ask not.

('Attar)

The Law: Shariah and Fiqh

The Koran reveals the will of God for mankind. This constitutes a Law, which all are bound to obey on penalty of eternal condemnation. This Islamic law in its totality is termed the *Shariah*, meaning "the path." The shariah includes laws concerning not only strictly religious matters, but also many other aspects of life, such as marriage and the family, inheritance, divorce, and government. Like the Jewish "Torah" Shariah is a broad term, including not only law but also faith and the entire Muslim way of life.

The Shariah cannot be questioned since it is divine. However, the practical application of the Shariah to the conditions of life is a matter of human

The Dome of the Rock, Jerusalem (Barrie Searle/Circa Photo Library)

interpretation and about this there can be different opinions. There is a science of the law, which is called *Fiqh*.

The five pillars of Islam

There are five religious practices that Islam enjoins on its followers as a minimum: the shahada; worship (salat); legal almsgiving (zakat); fasting (sawm); and pilgrimage to Mecca (hajj).

The Shahada

This is the Witness or profession of faith mentioned above: "There is no God but Allah, and Mohammed is his prophet." The statement itself made in the Witness bears the title of the *Kalimah*. It is this statement that makes a person a Muslim. Anyone who utters it during the course of his life, even if only once, is accounted a Muslim. It also forms part of the formal daily prayer, described next.

Worship: salat

All Muslims, both men and women, are required to perform ritual or formal prayer, called *Salat*. This prayer is not so much a request for favors or blessings as a public recognition of the sovereignty of God. It includes various bodily postures such as bowing, sitting, standing, and prostration with the forehead touching the floor, while reciting such phrases as *Allahu akbar* ("God is most great") and the Shahada. This public prayer is not the same as private prayer (*du'a*), for which no special formula is prescribed.

The ritual must be performed five times a day: at dawn, midday, mid-afternoon, sunset, and in the evening before going to bed. The form of this prayer is given in the next chapter (see pp. 309–11). The prayer is to be recited facing Mecca. The direction toward Mecca from wherever one may happen to be is called the *Kibla*. In the mosque it is marked by a niche in the wall, called the *mihrab*. Ideally the prayer should be performed in a mosque, but if that is not feasible any clean place will do, indoors or outdoors. Muslims often use a prayer mat for this purpose. At a mosque, shortly before the time for prayer, the muezzin (*mu'adhdhin*) chants the call to prayer (the *adhan*) from the minaret.

The sacred day of the week for Muslims is Friday. It is not a day of rest, unlike the Sabbath in Judaism and Sunday in Christianity. However, all men (but not women) are required to take part in the Friday noon prayer at a mosque, if one is available. The Friday service follows a special form, including a sermon by the leader (the *imam*).

The word mosque comes from *masjid*, meaning a place of prostration. Strictly speaking, it does not have to be a building but can be simply a piece of open ground dedicated to prayer. The mosque can legitimately be used for many purposes related to religion: as a school, meeting place, or even for eating and sleeping, if necessary.

Legal almsgiving: zakat

Muslims are strongly encouraged to provide help to those in need. In addition to private charity, Islamic law requires the payment of a special tax for this purpose, called the *Zakat*. It is to be paid at the end of each year, in proportion to one's possessions.

As originally formulated, it is paid only on certain classes of goods above a minimum, such as animals, agricultural products, precious metals, and objects intended for sale. The modern times it includes paper money and the money held in bank accounts.

Today the zakat is not administered by the state in any Muslim country; it is voluntary, and often collected by mosque.

Fasting: sawm

For a month each year Muslims are required to fast. The fast occurs during the ninth month, Ramadan, and consists in abstaining from all food and drink from sunrise to sunset.

The fast of Ramadan is not exactly like the Christian Lent. There is no limit-ation on eating or drinking during the night, and this is usually a party time, when families and friends get together and celebrate. There is an especially

274

Praying on 'Id al-Fitr note the signs of zakat in the foreground (John Smith/Circa Photo Library)

joyous celebration (the *'Id al-Fitr*) at the end of the month, one of the two chief feast days of Islam.

The official Islamic year is lunar, consisting of twelve months each of four weeks exactly, and is therefore shorter than our regular, solar year. As a result the month of Ramadan cycles backwards throughout the regular year, and occurs in different seasons. Consequently the length of the fast from sunrise to sunset varies greatly, from the middle of summer to the middle of winter. Ramadan is relatively easy to keep when it occurs in winter, but in midsummer it is more difficult.

Pilgrimage to Mecca: the hajj

As far as circumstances permit, every Muslim should go on pilgrimage to the sacred city of Mecca at least once in his lifetime. The city of Mecca is sacred because it was the site of the original, pre-Islamic worship of Allah. In that capacity it had been a center of pilgrimage long before the time of Mohammed. Only Muslims are allowed to enter the city. The proper time for the pilgrimage is a period of four days during the twelfth month of the Islamic year, and so, like Ramadan, it cycles backwards through the seasons.

Men must wear a distinctive white two-piece garment in place of their usual clothes. Those who have taken part in the pilgrimage agree that this uniform clothing, submerging all outward differences such as race, age, and wealth, conveys a profound experience of the unity and brotherhood of Muslims. Women may wear the costumes of their regions, but now usually wear white too.

The high point of the pilgrimage is the commemoration of the sacrifice carried out by Abraham. (As we have seen, Muslims view Abraham as a Muslim.) God had commanded Abraham to kill his only son Isma'il in sacrifice, as a test of faith, and Abraham made preparations to do so, but at the last moment God instructed him to kill a ram instead, which he did. (In the Hebrew Bible the son in the story was Isaac.) To commemorate this, the pilgrims perform animal sacrifices, and thousands of animals are killed in the space of an hour, creating a considerable problem in the disposal of the carcasses.

The day on which this is done, the tenth of the month, is celebrated not only in Mecca but throughout the Muslim world as the Feast of Sacrifice (*'Id al Adha*), and is the second of the two great Muslim feast days.

Jihad

This term, often translated as "holy war," literally has the broader meaning of "struggle, exertion." It signifies the general effort to advance the cause of Islam, a duty sometimes ranked as a sixth Pillar. Mohammed spoke of a twofold jihad: one internal or spiritual and the harder, the struggle against oneself, against the unbeliever within one's own heart; the other external and easier, against the enemies of Islam.

Islam prohibits wars fought purely for territorial gain, but allows war not only for self-defense, but also for the purpose of extending the domain of Islam:

> Make war on the unbelievers and hypocrites and deal rigorously with them. (Koran 9: 73)
>
> Make war on them until idolatry is no more and Allah's religion reigns supreme. (Koran 8)
>
> Fight for the sake of God those that fight against you, but do not attack them first. God does not love the aggressors [or, transgressors]. Kill them wherever you find them. Drive them out of the places from which they drove you. Idolatry is worse than carnage. (Koran 2: 190–1; see below, p. 293)
>
> Fighting is obligatory for you. (see below, p. 294)

The Koran also states: "There shall be no compulsion in religion" (2: 256). However, at the present time this is usually interpreted to mean only that force should not be used to convert an adult to Islam.

Islam has never developed an explicit theory of the just war. The Hadith, however, gives certain rules for the *conduct* of war, forbidding, for example, wanton killing, and in general the killing of children, women, elderly men, monks, farmers, and hired employees.

The People of the Book

The People of the Book are those who possess sacred books, chiefly Jews and Christians. Although Islam condemns Judaism and Christianity as distortions of the true religion, it accords them a special tolerance not shown to other religions. The Koran appears to teach that polytheists must be given the choice of conversion or death, though later opinion interpreted that as applying only to the era of the Koran. The People of the Book, however, must be allowed to continue to practice their faith. On the other hand, they are prohibited from making converts, and they must pay a special tax and wear distinctive clothing. In practice, the enforcement of these rules under Muslim governments has varied greatly from place to place.

In time this classification was extended to the Zoroastrians, in Persia, and to Hindus, Buddhists and Jains, since they also possess sacred books.

Clean and unclean

In order to take part in the ritual prayer and many other observances, a person must be ritually clean. Ritual uncleanliness is caused by various events considered as polluting. It is not the same thing as sin, for it does not necessarily imply any moral guilt, but if it has been contracted it must be removed before prayer. The concept is similar to that of kashrut in Judaism.

Pollution may:

1 be acquired from external sources (this is called *najasa*), such as contact with a wet discharge from an animal or human being (blood, urine, pus, feces); or
2 be the result of an action (this is called *hadath*). Hadath may be major or minor.

Major hadath result from seminal emission in the male or orgasm in the female. Minor hadath occur from any loss of consciousness, such as sleep, fainting, drunkenness, from urinating, or from touching the skin of the opposite sex. Purification is obtained by washing, in the case of minor hadath, or by taking a complete bath, with major hadath. For this reason every mosque has facilities for washing.

The left hand is always regarded as unclean. It is never used to greet, to give gifts, or to touch another, but is used for toilet activities. Similarly the left foot is considered to be inauspicious, and is not to be used to make the first step into the mosque or on a journey.

Circumcision

Circumcision is considered a form of purification (it is often called simply *tahara*, which means purification) and is obligatory for all Muslim boys, although the age at which it is done varies from region to region; in some areas it is performed in infancy, in others as late as at the age of 10 or 12. The operation is carried out privately, but is traditionally accompanied by some kind of festivity, including music and feasting. Although it is not mentioned in the Koran, it is recommended in the Hadith.

"Circumcision" is also widely practiced on girls, in the form of cutting away all or part of the clitoris, although this is not so much an Islamic obligation as a folk custom, which is also practiced in some non-Islamic societies. It is done in private, without any celebration. The reasons given for it are varied, and the practice is usually enforced by women.

The Organization of Islam

Ideally Islam has no priesthood or clergy. The prayer service in the mosque can in principle be led by any believer. There is, however, a recognized class of those who are knowledgeable about the religious law comparable to the Jewish Rabbinate. This class is called the *Ulama*. One becomes a member of it, a *Mawla*, by studying with recognized older scholars who themselves have studied with recognized olders scholars back in an unbroken chain to the Prophet. The question as to what belongs officially to Islam and what does not is settled authoritatively by the agreement (*ijma'*) of the ulama. Mohammed is reported in a hadith to have said, "My people will never agree together on an error."

The title *mufti* is sometimes given to an expert outstanding for his knowledge of the law, frequently one who occupies an official position. When an authority is consulted on a particular question involving the interpretation of the law, the response he gives is called a *fatwa*. This is directly binding only on the questioner. Some fatwas, however, have attained a wider force.

Official decisions on matters of the religious law in particular cases, such as property, marriage and divorce, and inheritance, are made by a judge called a *qadi*, who is appointed by the civil ruler from among the members of the Ulama. At the present time, however, most Muslim countries have instead adopted modern Western legal systems. Calls to implement the Shari'ah usually mean, not to replace the modern system of administering the law with the ancient one, but to insert more content from the Shari'ah into the modern system.

Islam and Society

Islam is not only a private or individual religion. Many of its laws can be carried out only in a Muslim society, where the civil law follows Islamic principles. For example, Muslim law requires that property be inherited according to certain rules, with sons typically receiving twice as much as daughters. Muslim law regarding marriage and divorce has many provisions that can operate only if supported by the civil law (or at least not prohibited by it. Muslim law can also function effectively in the absence of a state or civil government.) For example, a man can divorce his wife without any judicial process, by simply repeating to her three times (usually with an interval between them) "I divorce you." A woman cannot sign a marriage contract, but it must be signed for her by her male guardian, and so on.

Muslims of the most traditional sort cannot be content to live in a secular society in the Western sense, which provides freedom of religion to all. In their view Islam requires a society in which the government is Islamic and Islam is the official religion. Ideally the whole world should be a single Islamic empire.

Further than this, the most traditional form of Islam requires not only political dominance but also economic and cultural superiority. The Islamic society ought to be the most advanced, the most prosperous. For many Muslims the combined political, economic, and cultural predominance of the West in modern times is a cause of dismay. This is especially true because of the sexual freedom widely permitted in the West, which is offensive to traditional Muslims. Some Muslims consider that the chief reason for their nations' decline in power is that they have not implemented the Shari'ah strictly and fully. The Ayatollah Khomeini's rule in Iran from 1979 to 1989 was inspired largely by this view.

At the present time, however, the general question of the relationship of Islam to society is the subject of much debate, and a growing number of Muslims, especially those living in the Western democracies, have adopted a more liberal viewpoint.

Sunni and Shiite Islam

The division between Sunni and Shiite Islam is a question of the form of authority in Islam. On Mohammed's death, a majority of his followers recognized his kinsman Abu Bakr as his successor or *Caliph*. Abu Bakr in turn was followed by three successors, all four being known as "the rightly guided Caliphs." Muslims who recognize their authority are termed Sunni, meaning followers of the tradition stemming from the Prophet. In Sunni Islam the ultimate source of authority is considered to be the Muslim community. This is the most widespread form of Islam.

Some of Mohammed's followers, however, maintained that Mohammed during his lifetime had designated his son-in-law Ali as his successor, and they refused to recognize the authority of Abu Bakr. These were the Party of Ali, or *Shi'at Ali*. In the view of Shiite Islam, authority resides not in the community but in the divinely appointed leader, the successor of Ali, called the Imam. God provides an Imam in every age, even though sometimes he may be hidden. Shiite Islam predominates in Iran, and has large communities in several other countries such as Iraq and Lebanon. There are several different Shiite sects, who recognize different Imams. Many expect the return to the twelfth and last Imam, who went into "occultation" during the Middle Ages.

While Sunni and Shiite agree on the broad principles of Islam, Shiite Islam has distinctive practices of its own. One of these is the celebration of the Tenth Day of (the month of) Muharram, commemorating the death of Ali's son Husayn in battle against other Muslims. Husayn's suffering quickly came to be interpreted as voluntary self-sacrifice. It is regarded by the Shia as redemptive, and celebrated in a dramatic "passion play" in which the participants flagellate themselves with chains and smear themselves with blood, ritually sharing in Husayn's fate.

Sufism

A Sufi aims to attain spiritual union with God through love. Conscious of God's love, the Sufi makes it the central goal of his existence to love God in return. The high point of this life of spiritual love is sometimes described as a mystical marriage with God. The Sufi emphasis on love for God and union with him tends to relegate the details of the law to a matter of secondary concern. For the Sufi, it is often the spiritual significance of the law that is important, rather than its literal fulfillment. For similar reasons Sufism is relatively indifferent to political concerns.

Sufism exists both in Sunni and in Shiite Islam. It is organized in brotherhoods or orders which each typically owe allegiance to a particular spiritual master.

Orthodox Sufism maintains the distinction between the individual and God, viewing them as two separate realities. This is important if the individual is to be said to love God and obey him. Some Sufis have gone further, however, seeing the individual as essentially only an appearance of God, like a reflection in a mirror. This is the conception of monism, that there exists only a single reality. As we saw earlier, monism also occurs in Hinduism, for example, in the doctrine of some of the Upanishads, that Brahman alone is real; as well as in Mahayana Buddhism, in the view that the Buddha nature is the true identity of all that is. Consequently there are some fundamental similarities between these otherwise very diverse viewpoints. Some Sufis have expressed this monistic outlook by saying that they are identical with God, a statement which has called down savage persecution on them from orthodox Muslims, for whom it is blasphemy. On the other hand, some Sufis such as Ibn Arabi have been generally accepted and their book widely studied.

Sufis have produced some of the finest poetry in Islam, and among all Islamic literature some of the most accessible to non-Muslims. For a non-Muslim who wishes to understand the spiritual life of Islam, Sufi poetry provides perhaps the best introduction. The lines quoted above p. 272, are from a longer poem by the Sufi poet 'Attar.

At the present time Sufism is the object of heated dispute. While many view it as the highest and noblest achievement of Islam, others are bitterly opposed to it as too liberal, and some see it as largely responsible for the decline of Islam as a political force.

Muslim Ethics

For the traditional Muslim, the Koran is the only source of absolutely certain knowledge in this world, since it is the word of God. Ethics, then, is a question of what the Koran says about any action – together with the reliable guide to it, the Hadith.

Ethics is concerned with the good. But what is the good? Is it something objective, which can be discovered by reason, or is it simply decided by the will of God? Does God command an action because it is just by its very nature, or is it just for the sole reason that God commands it? The traditional Muslim opinion is that actions are just because God commands them. It is considered that this view is necessary to maintain the absolute supremacy of God, for otherwise, it is argued, God would be subject to something outside of himself. It follows that the good or the just cannot be discovered by reason. Although in earlier centuries a group known as the Mu'tazilites did allow for an ethics based directly on reason, they did not long survive. Ethics must be based only on revelation, that is, Koran and Hadith. Consequently, Islamic ethics, like Orthodox Jewish ethics, is more a matter of the group, the collective, rather than of the individual conscience.

Koran and Hadith, however, do not address every question directly, and often leave room for different interpretations. The general term for this interpretation is *ijtihad*. In the early years of Islam a great deal of ijtihad was carried out by scholars, based largely on reasoning by analogy (*qiyas*), until by about the tenth century there was general agreement that everything that needed to be done in elaborating the divine law as a blueprint for Muslim life and society had been accomplished. This view is referred to as "the closing of the door of ijtihad." Since then no further interpretation is admitted, but only application to particular circumstances.

Qiyas, or reasoning by analogy, means using a statement in the Koran about one action to make a decision about a similar action not mentioned there explicitly.

On this basis, Muslims recognize a universal moral law which prohibits harmful actions such as murder, robbery, adultery, and bearing false witness, because they are condemned in various places in the Koran. In addition, there is the specific Islamic law, which is binding only on Muslims. We have already seen the provisions of this regarding jihad and war in general (above, p. 276).

The interpretations of the revealed law by scholars are organized into a number of schools, named after their founders, which each tend to emphasize different principles, and to prevail in different territories. The most prominent schools are those founded by:

- al-Shafi'i, of Cairo, which tends to rely on reasoning by analogy;
- Malik, of the Hijaz (the province of Arabia which includes Mecca and Medina), which tends to raise the question of the general usefulness of an action;

- Abu Hanifa, of Baghdad, which prevails in many non-Arab areas such as Turkey and India, and tends to allow more room for individual judgement;
- Ibn Hanbal, which is strictly traditionalist and largely restricted to Saudi Arabia.

These are Sunni schools. The Shiite community has its own schools.

The overall effect of this ethical system in the past has been to consign moral judgements into the hands of the interpreters of divine revelation, the Ulama. With the advance of education in the Muslim community, however, more individuals are taking it on themselves to make such judgements, and here the tendency has been to refer rather more to the Koran than to the Hadith.

Modern Developments

Since the seventeenth century, with the rise of science, the emergence of democracy, and the development of the capitalist economy, Western society, which once lagged behind the Muslim world, has leaped dramatically ahead of it, becoming more knowledgeable, more technologically advanced, wealthier, more powerful, and, at least in its own view, more humane. The Islamic world, by contrast, sank into a general state of poverty and powerlessness during this period. As a result, during the eighteenth and nineteenth centuries, many Muslim lands were colonized by Western nations. Although colonization brought benefits, such as modern methods of communication, transport, medicine, and economic and political organization, the superiority of the West has been experienced by many Muslims as an extreme humiliation.

In general, there have been two kinds of response to this. On the one hand, some Muslims, especially those who have been educated or live in Western societies, have argued that Islam can and should expand its intellectual horizons to include worthwhile features of the modern world such as science, democracy, capitalism, and the recognition of human rights. This would suggest a further development in the process of interpretation, ijtihad, which is sometimes referred to as "opening the door of ijtihad."

On the other hand, there are many Muslims who believe the opposite, that the decline of the Muslim world has been caused by failure to implement the original Koranic law. According to this view, there must be a return to original Islam, the full, true, authentic Islam of the early Muslims, setting aside the accretions of later centuries. It is believed that if this were done it would lead to economic development and political power, and the restoration of the Muslim world to its former supremacy. The whole world would ultimately become a single Muslim empire. This message has found a wide audience around the world.

An important reform movement has been Wahhabism, founded by Muhammad al-Wahhab in Saudi Arabia. It represents an attempt to purify and strengthen Islam by returning to the rules developed during the early Muslim centuries, rejecting the developments of later times. It is hostile to everything that can be considered in any way to amount to shirk, idolatry, such as the popular veneration of saints. This has led it to attack both Sufism and Shiism as idolatrous because they have fostered the veneration of saints. It is opposed to ornamentation in architecture, demanding simplicity. It requires the strict practice of the traditional Islamic law, and in some respects is even stricter than the original. To enforce its version of Islam it has routinely relied upon coercion.

The battle to restore the Islam of the original Muslims (who are known by the name *salaf*, whence the movement itself is called the *salafiyya*) therefore includes two further battles: against the occupying forces of the Western colonial powers, which now include especially the state of Israel, and against those Muslim rulers who are secularized and who reject the salafiyya. In English this movement is sometimes called Radical or Fundamentalist Islam.

Radical Islam and Islamic terrorism

Following the revelation of the horrors of the Nazi death camps and the attempted genocide of the Jewish people, in 1947 the United Nations General Assembly recommended the establishment of two states in the territory of Palestine: a Jewish state and an Arab state. The Jewish state was to provide a national home for the Jewish people, and the Arab state was to provide a home for the Arabs displaced by the creation of the Jewish state.

Palestine at this time was governed by Great Britain, who did not favor the plan, fearing it would result in injustice to the Arabs. The United States initially supported the plan, but then turned against it. Illegal Jewish immigration into Palestine had already been going on for many years, and two Jewish organizations, the Irgun and the Stern Gang, had long engaged in terrorist activity to support the Jewish settlers against opposition from both Arabs and British.

The Arab nations rejected the United Nations plan, arguing that the United Nations had no authority to dispose of Arab land and its people, and armed conflict broke out between Arabs and Jews. The Jewish community declared its independence, as the state of Israel. Surrounding Arab states thereupon declared war on the new state, a war which was decisively won by Israel. The displaced Palestinians were housed in camps, which were intended to be temporary but which, in the absence of a political settlement, became permanent. Once the state of Israel had come into existence, the United States provided it with considerable financial support.

In September 1972, at the Olympic Games in Munich, the Israeli team was attacked by a band of Palestinian terrorists. In the ensuing battle 11 Israelis and five Palestinians were killed. Since then a long series of terrorist attacks, often suicidal, have been perpetrated by Muslims against non-Muslims, especially Israelis and Americans, culminating in the attacks on the World Trade Center in New York and the Pentagon in September 2001. In Israel Palestinian suicide-terrorist attacks against Israelis continue at the time of writing on an almost daily basis, arguably with the connivance of the Palestinian Authority. Many terrorist attacks appear to have been not merely the work of private individuals or groups but supported by Islamic governments such as those of Libya, Iran, Syria, and Iraq.

At the same time radical Muslim groups have carried out armed rebellions against established governments in several nations such as the Philippines, Algeria, and India. Muslim regimes in Iran, Afghanistan, and Nigeria have implemented the most extreme provisions of the Koranic law. Writers considered to have insulted the Prophet or Islam have been made the subject of death fatwas (a declaration by a religious authority that a certain person may lawfully be killed by anyone). All this has led to questions about the nature of Islam, especially its relationship to violence. Is Islam capable of living in peace with other peoples and religions?

It cannot be denied that the Koranic approval of armed warfare against non-Muslims is troubling. Yet today the vast majority of Muslims live in peace with their neighbors. Every religion is capable of being interpreted and practiced in a variety of ways. Similar provisions can be found in the Jewish Torah, which even the most orthodox Jews today would scarcely think of carrying out. It would seem then that the answer to this question must be that peaceful coexistence with Islam is possible.

In the train of events leading to the Muslim violence of recent decades, there can be little doubt that by far the principal factor is the existence of the state of Israel. Muslim opinion views the establishment of Israel as a straightforward case of robbery: their land was taken and their people expelled by force. The Muslim population of Palestine were never given the chance to approve or disapprove of the scheme, and have never been compensated for their losses. This historic robbery was carried out and has been maintained with the support of the West, especially of the United States. In the view of Radical Muslims, the state of Israel must be eliminated. With regard to America and the West, the goal of Radical Islam and of Muslim terrorism is to persuade them to give up their support of Israel and withdraw entirely from the Middle East.

In the Jewish view, on the other hand, the Arab population lost its right to its land by refusing to accept the decision of the United Nations to partition Palestine into a Jewish state and a Palestinian one. This refusal left the matter to a contest of armed force, which Israel won.

In some respects, perhaps the principal contest at the present time lies within the Muslim community, between those who are willing to agree to a peaceful settlement with Israel and those who are not.

Summary of Islam

1   The chief message of the Koran is the absolute supremacy of God.

2   The main doctrines of Islam concern:

   the existence of a single God;
   angels;
   prophets and scriptures;
   resurrection and the Last Judgement;
   The divine decree and predestination.

3   The principal duties incumbent on a Muslim are the Five Pillars of Islam:

recital of the shahada;
formal prayer, salat;
legal almsgiving, zakat;
fasting, sawm;
pilgrimage to Mecca, hajj.

4   Islam is not only a private or personal religion, but a social one.

Question for discussion

1   Several of the founding fathers of the United States, for example, George Washington, Thomas Jefferson, and Benjamin Franklin, were Deists, that is, they believed in the existence of God, a divine Providence, and a life after death. How does this differ from Islam?

Test questions

1   Explain the Muslim doctrine of God.

2   Explain what is meant by saying that Mohammed is "The Seal of the Prophets." What is the significance of this for the Muslim view of Judaism and Christianity?

3   Explain why Islam is not merely a private religion for individuals, but a social religion requiring adoption by the civil society.

Additional reading

Cragg, Kenneth, *The House of Islam*, Encino, CA, Dickenson, 1975.
    Thoughtful, sympathetic, knowledgeable, with an extensive bibliography.
Cragg, Kenneth, *The Call of the Minaret*, Maryknoll, NY, Orbis, 1985.
Denny, Frederick M., *An Introduction to Islam*, New York, Macmillan, 1985.
    An excellent introduction, with a comprehensive bibliography.
De Pasquier, Roger, *Unveiling Islam*, Cambridge, UK, Islamic Texts Society, 1992.
Esposito, John, *Islam: The Straight Path*, New York, Oxford University Press, 1991.
Gibb, H. A. R., *Mohammedanism: An Historical Survey*, New York, Oxford University Press, 1962.
Hourani, George F., *Reason and Tradition in Islamic Ethics*, Cambridge, UK, Cambridge University Press, 1985.
Renard, John, *In the Footsteps of Mohammed: Understanding the Islamic Experience*, Mahwah, NJ, Paulist Press, 1992.

Islam: Texts

The Koran (Arabic, Qur'an)

With the exception of the first Sura and a few other passages, the Koran has the form of a collection of instructions and sermons addressed to Muhammad by Allah. Muhammad himself could neither read nor write, but his utterances, made over many years, were committed to memory by his followers and were probably all written down, separately, before his death. They were not collected together, however, till after his death. The first caliph, Abu Bakr, is said to have commanded Muhammad's secretary, Zayd ibn Thabit, to collect the scattered sayings into a single volume. However, disagreements arose about the true text, and the Caliph Uthman commissioned a committee, including Zayd, to produce an official version, which was distributed throughout the Muslim Empire. All earlier texts were then burned.

Sura 1: The Exordium (the Fatiha)

In the name of Allah, the Compassionate, the Merciful.

Praise be to Allah, Lord of Creation,
The Compassionate, the Merciful,
King of the Last Judgement!

You alone we worship
And to You alone we pray for help.
Guide us in the straight path,
The path of those whom You have favored,

Not of those who have incurred Your wrath,
Nor of those who have gone astray.

Sura 93: Daylight

In the Name of Allah, the Compassionate, the Merciful
By the light of day,
and by the fall of night,
your Lord has not forsaken you,
nor does he abhor you.

The life to come holds a richer prize for you than this present life.
You shall be gratified with what your Lord will give you.

Did He not find you an orphan and give you shelter?
Did He not find you in error and guide you?
Did He not find you poor and enrich you?

Therefore do not wrong the orphan,
nor chide away the beggar.
But proclaim the goodness of your Lord.

Sura 92: Night

In the Name of Allah, the Compassionate, the Merciful

By the night,
when she lets fall her darkness,
and by the radiant day!
By Him that created the male and the female,
your endeavours have different ends!

For him that gives in charity
and guards himself against evil
and believes in goodness,
We shall smooth the path of salvation;
but for him that neither gives nor takes
and disbelieves in goodness,
We shall smooth the path of affliction.
When he breathes his last,
his riches shall not avail him.

It is for Us to give guidance,
Ours is the life of this world,
Ours the life to come.

I warn you, then, of the blazing fire,
in which none shall burn save the hardened sinner,
who denies the truth and gives no heed.
But the good man who purifies himself by almsgiving
shall keep away from it;
and so shall he that does good works for the sake of the Most High only,
seeking no recompense.
Such men shall be content.

Sura 107: Alms

In the Name of Allah, the Compassionate, the Merciful

Have you thought of him that denies the Last Judgement?
It is he who turns away the orphan
and does not urge others to feed the poor.

Woe to those who pray
but are heedless in their prayer;
who make a show of piety
and give to alms to the destitute.

Sura 75: The Resurrection

In the Name of Allah, the Compassionate, the Merciful

I swear by the Day of Resurrection,
and by the self-reproaching soul!
Does man think We shall never put his bones together again?
Indeed, We can remould his very fingers!

Yet man would ever deny what is to come.
"When will this be," he asks, "this Day of Resurrection?"

But when the sight of mortals is confounded
and the moon eclipsed;
when sun and moon are brought together –
on that day man will ask:
"Whither shall I flee?"

No, there shall be no escape.
For on that day all shall return to Allah.

On that day man shall be informed of all that he has done
and all that he has failed to do.
He shall become his own witness;

his pleas shall go unheeded . . .
Yet you love this fleeting life
and are heedless of the life to come.

On that day there shall be joyous faces,
looking towards their Lord.
On that day there shall be mournful faces,
dreading some great affliction.

But when a man's soul is about to leave him
and those around him cry:
Will no one save him?
when he knows it is the final parting
and the pangs of death shall assail him –
on that day to your Lord he shall be driven.
For in this life he neither believed nor prayed;
he denied the truth,
and, turning his back,
went to his kinsfolk elated with pride.

Well have you deserved this doom;
well have you deserved it.
Well have you deserved this doom:
too well have you deserved it!

Does man think that he lives in vain?
Was he not a drop of ejected semen?
He became a clot of blood;
then Allah formed and moulded him
and gave him his male and female parts.
Is He then not able to raise the dead to life?

Sura 2: The Cow*

In the Name of Allah, the Compassionate, the Merciful

This book is not to be doubted.
It is a guide to the righteous,
Who have faith in the unseen
And are steadfast in prayer;
Who bestow in charity a part of what We give them;
Who trust what has been revealed to you

---

* The name of this Sura is derived from the story included in it about God's command to the Israelite people to sacrifice a cow and their attempts to evade the sacrifice.

And to others before you,
And firmly believe in the life to come.

These are rightly guided by their Lord;
These shall surely triumph . . .

Righteousness

Those that suppress any part of the Scriptures
which Allah has revealed
in order to gain some paltry end
shall swallow nothing but fire into their bellies.
On the Day of Resurrection Allah will neither speak to them
nor purify them.
Theirs shall be a woeful punishment.

Such are those that barter guidance for error
and forgiveness for punishment.
How steadfastly they seek the fire of Hell!
That is because Allah has revealed the Book with the truth;
those that disagree about it are in schism.

Righteousness does not consist in whether you face
towards the east or the west.
The righteous man is he
who believes in Allah
and the Last Day,
in the angels
and the Scriptures
and the prophets;

who for the love of Allah
gives his wealth to his kinsfolk,
to the orphans, to the needy,
to the wayfarers
and to the beggars,
and for the redemption of captives;

who attends to his prayers
and pays the alms-tax;
who is true to his promises
and steadfast in trial and adversity
and in times of war.
Such are the true believers;
such are the God-fearing.

Retaliation

Believers, retaliation is decreed for you in bloodshed:
a free man for a free man,
a slave for a slave,
and a female for a female.

He who is pardoned by his aggrieved brother
shall be prosecuted according to usage
and shall pay him a liberal fine.

This is a merciful dispensation from your Lord.
He that transgresses thereafter shall be sternly punished.

Men of understanding!
In retaliation you have a safeguard for your lives;
perchance you will guard yourselves against evil.

Wills

It is decreed that when death approaches,
those of you that leave property
shall bequeath it equitably to parents and kindred.
This is a duty incumbent on the righteous.

He that alters a will after hearing it
shall be accountable for his crime.
Allah hears all and knows all.

He that suspects an error or an injustice
on the part of a testator
and brings about a settlement among the parties
incurs no guilt.
Allah is forgiving and merciful.

The fast

Believers, fasting is decreed for you
as it was decreed for those before you;
perchance you will guard yourselves against evil.
Fast a certain number of days,
but if any one of you is ill or on a journey
let him fast a similar number of days later on;
and for those that can afford it there is a ransom:
the feeding of a poor man.

He that does good of his own accord
shall be well rewarded;
but to fast is better for you,
if you but knew it.

In the month of Ramadhan the Koran was revealed,
a book of guidance with proofs of guidance
distinguishing right from wrong.
Therefore whoever of you is present in that month
let him fast.
But he who is ill or on a journey
shall fast a similar number of days later on.
Allah desires your well-being, not your discomfort.
He desires you to fast the whole month
so that you may magnify Him
and render thanks to Him for giving you His guidance.

When My servants question you about Me,
tell them that I am near.
I answer the prayer of the suppliant
when he calls to Me;
therefore let them answer My call
and put their trust in Me,
that they may be rightly guided.

It is now lawful for you to lie with your wives
on the night of the fast;
they are a comfort to you
as you are to them.

Allah knew that you were deceiving yourselves.
He has relented towards you and pardoned you.

Therefore you may now lie with them
and seek what Allah has ordained for you.

Eat and drink until you can tell a white thread from a black one
in the light of the coming dawn.
Then resume the fast till nightfall
and do not approach them,
but stay at your prayers in the mosques.

These are the bounds set by Allah:
do not come near them.
Thus He makes known His revelations to mankind
that they may guard themselves against evil.

Do not usurp one another's property by unjust means,
nor bribe with it the judges
in order that you may knowingly and wrongfully deprive others of their possessions.
They question you about the phases of the moon.
Say: "They are seasons fixed for mankind and for the pilgrimage."

Righteousness does not consist
in entering your dwellings from the back.
The righteous man is he
that fears Allah.
Enter your dwellings by their doors
and fear Allah,
so that you may prosper.

It was the custom of pagan Arabs, on returning from pilgrimage, to enter their homes from the back.

Fighting

Fight for the sake of Allah
Those that fight against you,
But do not attack them first.

Allah does not love the aggressors.
Kill them wherever you find them.
Drive them out of the places
From which they drove you.

Idolatry is worse than carnage.

But do not fight them
Within the precincts of the Holy Mosque
Unless they attack you there;
If they attack you put them to the sword.

Thus shall the unbelievers be rewarded:
But if they mend their ways,
Know that Allah is forgiving and merciful.

Fight against them
Until idolatry is no more
And Allah's religion reigns supreme.

But if they mend their ways,
Fight none except the evil-doers.

A sacred month for a sacred month:
Sacred things too are subject to retaliation.

If any one attacks you,
attack him as he attacked you.
Have fear of Allah,
and know that Allah is with the righteous.

Generosity

Give generously for the cause of Allah
and do not with your own hands cast yourselves into destruction.

Be charitable;
Allah loves the charitable.

Fighting II

Fighting is obligatory for you,
much as you dislike it.
But you may hate a thing although it is good for you,
and love it although it is bad for you.
Allah knows, but you do not.

They ask you about fighting in the sacred month.
Say: "To fight in this month is a grave offence,
but to debar others from the path of Allah,
to deny Him, and to expel His worshippers from the Holy Mosque,
is far more grave in His sight.
Idolatry is worse than carnage."

They will not cease to fight against you
until they force you to renounce your faith –
if they are able.
But whoever of you recants and dies an unbeliever,
his works shall come to nothing
in this world and in the world to come.

Such men shall be the tenants of Hell,
and there they shall abide for ever.

Those that have embraced the faith
and those that have fled their land

and fought for the cause of Allah,
may hope for Allah's mercy.
Allah is forgiving and merciful.

Drinking and gambling

They ask you about drinking and gambling.
Say: "There is great harm in both,
although they have some benefit for men;
but their harm is far greater than their benefit."

Alms II

They ask you what they should give in alms.
Say: "What you can spare."
Thus Allah makes plain to you His revelations,
so that you may reflect upon this world
and the hereafter.

Orphans

They question you concerning orphans.
Say: "To deal justly with them is best.
If you mix their affairs with yours,
remember they are your brothers.
Allah knows the just from the unjust.

If Allah pleased, He could afflict you.
He is mighty and wise."

Marriage

You shall not wed pagan women,
unless they embrace the faith.
A believing slave-girl is better than an idolatress,
although she may please you.

And do not marry idolaters,
unless they embrace the faith.
A believing slave is better than an idolater,
although he may please you.

These call you to Hell-fire;
but Allah calls you, by His will,
to Paradise and to forgiveness.

He makes plain His revelations to mankind,
so that they may take heed.

They ask you about menstruation.
Say: "It is an indisposition.
Keep aloof from women during their menstrual periods
and do not touch them until they are clean again.
Then have intercourse with them as Allah enjoined you.
Allah loves those that turn to Him in repentance
and strive to keep themselves clean."

Women are your fields:
go, then, into your fields as you please.

Do good works and fear Allah.
Bear in mind that you shall meet Him.

Give good news to the believers.
Do not make Allah the subject of your oaths
when you swear that you will deal justly
and keep from evil
and make peace among men.
Allah knows all and hears all.
He will not call you to account
for that which is inadvertent in your oaths.
But He will take you to task
for that which is intended in your hearts.
Allah is forgiving and lenient.

Those that renounce their wives on oath must wait four months.
If they change their mind, Allah is forgiving and merciful;
but if they decide to divorce them,
know that He hears all and knows all.

Divorced women must wait,
keeping themselves from men,
three menstrual courses.

It is unlawful for them,
if they believe in Allah and the Last Day,
to hide what He has created in their wombs:
in which case their husbands would do well to take them back,
should they desire reconciliation.

Women shall with justice have rights
similar to those exercised against them,
although men have a status above women.

Allah is mighty and wise.

Divorce may be pronounced twice,
and then a woman must be retained in honour
or allowed to go with kindness.

It is unlawful for husbands to take from them
anything they have given them,
unless both fear that they may not be able
to keep within the bounds set by Allah;
in which case it shall be no offence for either of them
if the wife ransom herself.

These are the bounds set by Allah;
do not transgress them.
Those that transgress the bounds of Allah are wrongdoers.

If a man divorce his wife, he cannot remarry her
until she has wedded another man
and been divorced by him;
in which case it shall be no offence for either of them
to return to the other,
if they think that they can keep within the limits set by Allah.

Such are the bounds of Allah.
He makes them plain to men of understanding.
When you have renounced your wives
and they have reached the end of their waiting period,
either retain them in honour
or let them go with kindness.

But you shall not retain them in order to harm them
or to wrong them.
Whoever does this wrongs his own soul.

Do not make game of Allah's revelations.
Remember the favours He has bestowed upon you,
and the Book and the wisdom which He has revealed for your instruction.

Fear Allah and know that He has knowledge of all things.

If a man has renounced his wife
and she has reached the end of her waiting period,
do not prevent her from remarrying her husband
if they have come to an honourable agreement.

This is enjoined on every one of you who believes in Allah and the Last Day;
it is more honourable for you and more chaste.
Allah knows, but you do not.

Mothers shall give suck to their children
for two whole years
if the father wishes the suckling to be completed.
They must be maintained and clothed in a reasonable manner
by the father of the child.
None shall be charged with more than he can bear.

A mother should not be allowed to suffer on account of her child,
nor should a father on account of his child.

The same duties devolve upon the father's heir.
But if, after consultation, they choose by mutual consent to wean the child,
they shall incur no guilt.
Nor shall it be any offence for you
if you prefer to have a nurse for your children,
provided that you pay her what you promise,
according to usage.

Have fear of Allah
and know that He is cognizant of all your actions.
Widows shall wait,
keeping themselves apart from men,
for four months and ten days after their husbands' death.

When they have reached the end of their waiting period,
it shall be no offence for you
to let them do whatever they choose for themselves,
provided that it is decent.
Allah is cognizant of all your actions.

It shall be no offence for you openly to propose marriage to such women
or to cherish them in your hearts.
Allah knows that you will remember them.
Do not arrange to meet them in secret,
and if you do, speak to them honourably.

But you shall not consummate the marriage
before the end of their waiting period.
Know that Allah has knowledge of all your thoughts.

Therefore take heed and bear in mind
that Allah is forgiving and lenient.

It shall be no offence for you
to divorce your wives before the marriage is consummated
or the dowry settled.

Provide for them with fairness;
the rich man according to his means
and the poor man according to his.
This is binding on righteous men.

If you divorce them before the marriage is consummated,
but after their dowry has been settled,
give them the half of their dowry,
unless they or the husband agree to forgo it.
But it is more proper that the husband should forgo it.

Do not forget to show kindness to each other.
Allah observes your actions.

Attend regularly to your prayers,
including the middle prayer,
and stand up with all devotion before Allah.
When you are exposed to danger
pray while riding or on foot;
and when you are restored to safety
remember Allah,
as He has taught you what you did not know.

You shall bequeath your widows a year's maintenance
without causing them to leave their homes;
but if they leave of their own accord,
no blame shall be attached to you
for any course they may deem fit to pursue.
Allah is mighty and wise.

Reasonable provision should also be made for divorced women.
That is incumbent on righteous men.
Thus Allah makes known to you His revelations
that you may grow in understanding.

Consider those that fled their country in their thousands
for fear of death.
Allah said to them: "You shall perish,"
and then He brought them back to life.
Surely Allah is bountiful to mankind,
but most men do not give thanks.

Fight for the cause of Allah
and bear in mind that He hears all and knows all.

Who will grant Allah a generous loan?
He will repay him many times over.
It is Allah who enriches and makes poor.
To Him you shall all return.

> (*The Koran*, trans. N. J. Dawood, Harmondsworth, Penguin, 1956)

Question for discussion

1   What similarities and what dissimilarities do you see between the Koran and the Torah?

Hadith

The first revelation of the Koran

Wahb b. Kaysan told me that Ubayd said to him: The Apostle would pray in seclusion on Mount Hira each year for a month to practice religious exercises, as was the custom of the Quraysh* in heathen days. When he completed the month and returned from his seclusion, first of all he would go to the Ka'ba and walk around it seven times, or as often as pleased God; then he would go to his house until in the year when God sent him, in the month of Ramadan, he set forth to Hira as was his wont, and his family with him.

When it was the night on which God honored him with his mission, and showed mercy on His servants thereby, Gabriel brought him the command of God.

"He came to me," said the Apostle, "while I was asleep, with a piece of brocade whereon was writing, and said "Recite!" and I said "What shall I recite?"

He pressed me with it so tightly that I thought it was death; then he let me go and said "Recite!"

I said, "What shall I recite?"

He pressed me with it again so that I thought it was death, then he let me go and said "Recite!"

I said "But what shall I read?"

And this I said only to deliver myself from him lest he should do the same to me again, but he said:

---

*   Muhammad's tribe.

> "Recite: In the Name of thy Lord who created,
>   Created man from blood clotted,
> Recite: Thy Lord is the most beneficent,
>   who taught by the Pen,
>   Taught that which they knew not unto men."

So I recited it, and he departed from me. And I awoke from my sleep, and it was as though these words were written on my heart.

Now none of God's creatures was more hateful to me than an (ecstatic) poet or a man possessed; I could not even bear to look at them. I thought, "Woe is me – poet or possessed! Never shall Quraysh say that of me! I will go to the top of the mountain and throw myself down that I may kill myself and gain rest!"

When I was midway on the mountain, I heard a voice from heaven saying, "O Muhammad! Thou art the Apostle of God and I am Gabriel."

I raised my head towards heaven to see, and lo! Gabriel in the form of a man, with feet astride the horizon, saying, "O Muhammad! Thou art the Apostle of God, and I am Gabriel."

I stood gazing at him, moving neither forward nor backward; then I began to turn my face away from him, but towards whatever region of the sky I looked, I saw him as before.

I continued standing there, neither advancing nor turning back, until Khadija sent her messengers in search of me, and they gained the high ground above Mecca and returned to her while I was standing in the same place; then he parted from me, and I from him, returning to my family.

I went to Khadija* and sat by her thigh and drew close to her. She asked, "Why Abu al-Qasim (Father of al-Qasim), where hast thou been? By Allah, I have sent my messengers in search of thee, and they reached the high ground above Mecca and returned."

I said to her, "Woe is me – a poet, or a man possessed!"

She said, "I take refuge in Allah from that, O Abu al-Qasim! God would not treat you thus; He knows your truthfulness, your great trustworthiness, your fine character, and your kindness to your family. This cannot be, my dear [literally: son of my uncle]. Perhaps you have seen something."

"Yes, I have," I told her. Then I told her of what I had seen, and she said,

"Rejoice, O son of my uncle, and be of good heart! Verily by Him in whose hand is Khadija's soul, I have hope that thou wilt be the prophet of this people."

Then she rose and gathered her garments about her and set forth to her cousin Waraqa b. Naufal b. Asad b. Abd-al Uzza b. Qusayy, who had become a Christian and read the scriptures and learned from those who follow the Torah and the Gospel. And when she related to him what the Apostle of God told her he had seen and heard, Waraqa cried: "Holy! Holy! Verily, by Him in whose hand

---

* His wife.

is Waraqa's soul, if thou hast spoken to me the truth, O Khadija, there hath come unto him the greatest Namus [angel], who came to Moses, and lo, he will be the prophet of this people. Bid him to be of good heart."

So Khadija returned to the Apostle of God and told him what Waraqa had said, and that calmed his anxiety somewhat. And when the Apostle of God ... returned to Mecca ... Waraqa met him and said, "Son of my brother, tell me what thou hast seen and heard."

The Apostle told him, and Waraqa said, "Surely by Him in whose hand is Waraqa's soul, thou art the prophet of these people. There has come to thee the greatest Namus, who came to Moses. Thou wilt be called a liar, and they will use thee despitefully and cast thee out and fight against thee. Should I live to see that day, I will help God in such wise as He knoweth."

Then he lowered his head and kissed Muhammad's forehead; and the Apostle went to his own house, encouraged by Waraqa's words, and with his anxiety relieved.

> (Ibn Ishaq, *Sirat Rasul Allah*, trans. by Alfred Guillaume, *The Life of Muhammad*, Oxford, Oxford University Press, 1955, pp. 105–7)

The first converts

Khadija ... was the first to believe in God and His Apostle, and the truth of the message. By her, God lightened the burden of the Prophet. He never met with contradiction and charges of falsehood, which saddened him, but God comforted him by her when he went home. She strengthened him, lightened his burden, proclaimed his truth, and belittled men's opposition. May God Almighty have mercy on her!

> (*The Life of Muhammad*, p. 111)

Ali, son of the Prophet's uncle Abu Talib, was the first male to believe in the Apostle of God, to pray with him, and to believe in his divine message, when he was a boy of ten. God favored him, in that he had been brought up in the care of the Prophet before Islam began.

A traditionist mentions that when the time of prayer began the Apostle used to go out to the glens of Mecca accompanied by Ali, who went unbeknown to his father ... there they would pray the ritual prayers. One day Abu Talib came upon them while they were praying, and said to the Apostle, "O nephew, what is this religion I see you practising?"

He replied, "O uncle, this is the religion of God, His angels, His Apostles, and the religion of our father Abraham. God has sent me as a messenger to mankind, and you, my uncle ... are the most worthy to respond and help me."

His uncle replied, "I cannot give up the religion which my fathers followed, but by God you shall never meet with any harm so long as I live". ... He said to Ali, "My son, what is this religion of yours?"

He answered, "I believe in God and in his Messenger and I declare what he brought is true, and pray with him."

They allege that Abu Talib said: "He would not call you to do anything but what is good, so cleave to him."

Zayd, the freedman of the Prophet, was the first male to accept Islam after Ali.

Then Abu Bakr b. Abi Quhafa . . . became a Muslim. He showed his faith openly and called others to God and His Apostle. He was a man whose society was desired, well liked, and of easy manners . . . a merchant of high character and kindliness. People used to come to him to discuss many matters . . . because of his wide knowledge, his experience of commerce, and his sociable nature. He began to call to God and to Islam all whom he trusted.

(*The Life of Muhammad*, pp. 114–15)

The night journey (isra') and ascension (mi'raj) of the Prophet

The following account reached me from Abdallah b. Mas'ud and Abu Sa'id al-Khudri, and A'isha the Prophet's wife, and Mu'awiyah b. Abi Sufyan, and al-Hasan al-Basri, and Ibn Shihab al-Zuhri and Qatada and other traditionists, and Umm Hani, daughter of Abu Talib. It is pieced together in the story that follows, each one contributing something of what he was told about what happened when he was taken on the night journey.

Al-Hasan said that the Apostle said: "While I was sleeping in the Hijr, Gabriel came and stirred me with his feet . . . he brought me out of the door . . . and there was a white animal, half mule, half donkey, with wings at its sides with which it propelled its feet . . ."

Qatada said that he was told the Apostle said: "When I came to mount him he shied. Gabriel placed his hand on its mane and said, "Are you not ashamed, O Buraq, to behave this way? By God, none more honourable before God than Muhammad has ever ridden you before." The animal was so ashamed that he broke out in a sweat and stood still so that I could mount him."

In his story al-Hasan said: "The Apostle and Gabriel went their way until they arrived at the temple in Jerusalem. There he found Abraham, Moses, and Jesus among a company of the Prophets. The Apostle acted as their leader in prayer. Then he was brought two vessels, one containing wine and the other milk. The Apostle took the milk and drank it, leaving the wine. Gabriel said: 'You have been rightly guided, and so will your people be, Muhammad. Wine is forbidden you.'"

One of Abu Bakr's family told me that A'isha, the Prophet's wife, used to say, "The Apostle's body remained where it was but God removed his spirit by night . . ."

I have heard that the Apostle used to say, "My eyes sleep while my heart is awake." Only God knows how the revelation came and what he saw. But whether he was asleep or awake, it was all true and actually happened.

One of whom I have no reason to doubt told me on the authority of Abu Sa'id al Khudri: I heard the Apostle say, "After the completion of my business in Jerusalem a ladder was brought to me finer than any I have ever seen. It was that to which the dying man looks when death approaches. My companion mounted it with me until we came to one of the gates of heaven called the Gate of the Watchers. An angel called Isma'il was in charge of it, and under his command were twelve thousand angels, each having twelve thousand under his command."

A traditionist who had got it from one who had heard it from the Apostle told me that the latter said, "All the angels who met me when I entered the lowest heaven smiled in welcome and wished me well except one, who said the same things but did not smile or show the joyful expression of the others. When I asked Gabriel the reason he told me that if he had ever smiled before or would smile hereafter he would have smiled at me, but he does not smile because he is Malik, the Keeper of Hell. I said to Gabriel, who holds the position with God which He has described to you, 'obeyed there, trustworthy' (Sura 74: 34). 'Will you not order him to show me Hell?' And he said 'Certainly! O Malik, show Muhammad Hell.' Thereupon he removed its covering and the flames blazed high into the air until I thought they would consume everything. So I asked Gabriel to order him to send them back to their place, and he did . . ."

In his tradition Abu Sa'id al-Khudri said that the Apostle said: "When I entered the lowest heaven I saw a man sitting there with the spirits of men passing before him. To one he would speak well and rejoice in him saying 'A good spirit from a good body' and of another he would say 'Faugh!' and frown . . . Gabriel told me this was our father Adam, reviewing the spirits of his offspring; the spirit of a believer excited his pleasure, and the spirit of a disbeliever excited his disgust.

"Then I saw men with lips like camels; in their hands were pieces of fire like stones which they used to thrust into their mouths and they would come out of their posteriors. I was told that these were those who sinfully devoured the wealth of orphans.

"Then I saw men like those of the family of Pharaoh with such bellies as I have never seen; there were passing over them as it were camels maddened by thirst when they were cast into Hell, treading them down, and they were unable to move out of the way. These were the usurers.

"Then I saw men with good fat meat before them side by side with lean stinking meat, eating the latter and leaving the former. These are those who forsake the women whom God has permitted them, and go after those He has forbidden.

"Then I saw women hanging by their breasts. These were those who had fathered bastards on their husbands . . .

"Then I was taken up to the second heaven and there were the two maternal cousins, Jesus Son of Mary and John son of Zakariah. Then to the third heaven and there was a man whose face was as the moon at the full. This was my brother Joseph son of Jacob. Then to the seventh heaven and there was a man sitting on a throne at the gate of the Immortal Mansion (al-bayt al-ma'mur).

Every day seventy thousand angels went in not to come back until the resurrection day. Never have I seen a man more like myself. This was my father Abraham. Then he took me into Paradise and there I saw a damsel with dark red lips and I asked her to whom she belonged, for she pleased me much when I saw her, and she told me 'Zayd ibn Haritha.'" The Apostle gave [his adopted son] Zayd the good news about her.

(*The Life of Muhammad*, pp. 181–6)

*The Hegira (Hijra) (AD 622)**

When God wished to display His religion openly and to glorify His prophet and fulfill His promise to him . . . while he was offering himself to the Arab tribes (at the fairs) as was his wont, he met at al-Aqaba a number of the Khazraj (of Medina), whom God intended to benefit.

Asim b. Umar b. Qatada told me on the authority of some of the shaykhs of his tribe that when the Apostle met them he learned by inquiry that they were of the Khazraj and allies of the Jews of Medina. He invited them to sit with him and expounded Islam and recited the Qur'an to them. Now God had prepared the way for Islam in that they lived side by side with the Jews who were people of the scriptures and knowledge, while they themselves were polytheists and idolators. They had often raided them, and whenever bad feeling arose the Jews would say to them, "A prophet will be sent soon! His day is at hand. We shall follow him and kill you by his aid as Ad and Iram perished."

So when they heard the Apostle's message they said one to another: "This is the very prophet of whom the Jews warned us. Don't let them get to him before us!" Thereupon they accepted his teaching and became Muslims, saying: "We have left our people, for no tribe is so divided by hatred and rancor as they. Perhaps God will unite them through you. So let us go and invite them to this religion of yours; and if God unites them in it, then no man will be mightier than you!" Thus saying they returned to Medina as believers.

(*The Life of Muhammad*, pp. 197–8)

The Apostle had not been given permission to fight or allowed to shed blood . . . he had simply been ordered to call men to God, endure insult, and forgive the ignorant. The Quraysh persecuted his followers, seducing some from their religion, and exiling others from their country. They had to choose whether to give up their religion, be maltreated at home, or to flee, some to Abyssinia, others to Medina.

When Quraysh became insolent toward God and rejected His gracious purpose, accused His prophet of lying, and ill-treated and exiled those who served Him and proclaimed His unity, believed in His prophet, and held fast to His religion, He gave permission to his Apostle to fight and to protect himself against those who wronged them and treated them badly . . .

---

*   See above, pp. 267–8.

When God had given permission to fight, and this clan of the Ansar had pledged their support to him in Islam, the Apostle commanded his companions . . . who were with him in Mecca to emigrate to Medina . . . So they went out in companies and the Apostle stayed in Mecca waiting for his Lord's permission to leave Mecca and migrate to Medina . . .

Except for Abu Bakr and Ali, none of his supporters were left but those under restraint and those who had been forced to apostasize . . .

When the Quraysh saw that the Apostle had a party and companions not of their tribe and outside their territory, and that his companions had migrated to join them, and knew that they had settled in a new home and had gained protectors, they feared that the Apostle might join them, since they knew that he had decided to fight them. So they assembled in their council chambers, the house of Qusayy b. Kilab where all their important business was conducted, to take counsel what they should do in regard to the Apostle, for now they feared him . . .

Thereupon Abu Jahl said that he had a plan which had not been suggested hitherto, namely that each clan should provide a young, powerful, well-born warrior . . . then each of these should strike a blow at him and kill him. Thus they would be relieved of him, and responsibility for his blood would lie on all of the clans. His clan could not fight them all and would have to accept the blood money, to which they would all contribute.

(*The Life of Muhammad*, pp. 212–22)

Among the verses of the Qur'an which God sent down about that day and what they had agreed on are: "And when the unbelievers plot to shut thee up or to kill thee or to drive thee out they plot, but God plots also, and God is the best of plotters" (Sura 8, 30).

Now Abu Bakr was a man of means and . . . he bought two camels and kept them tied up in his house supplying them with fodder in preparation for departure . . .

When the Apostle decided to go he came to Abu Bakr and the two of them left by a window in the back of the latter's house and made for a cave on Thaur, a mountain below Mecca. Having entered, Abu Bakr ordered his son Abdallah . . . to come to them by night with the day's news. He ordered Amir b. Fuhayra, his freedman, to feed his flock by day and to bring to them in the evening in the cave. Asma his daughter used to come by night with food to sustain them . . .

When three days had passed, and men's interest waned, the man they had hired came with their camels and one of his own. Asma came too with a bag of provisions, but finding she had forgotten a rope, she undid her girdle and used it to tie the bag to the saddle. Thus she got the name "She of the girdle.". . .

They rode off, and Abu Bakr carried his freedman Amir behind him to act as a servant on the journey . . .

(In Medina, each of the clans) came to him and asked him to enjoy their wealth and protection, but he said, "Let the camel go her way," for she was under

God's orders . . . Finally she came to the home of the Banu Malik b. al-Najjar where she knelt at (what later became the door of his mosque) which was used at that time as a drying floor for dates and belonged to two orphans of that clan. When it knelt, the Prophet did not alight, and it rose and went a short distance, then . . . returned to the place where it had knelt at first and knelt there again . . .

The Apostle alighted . . . when he asked to whom the date-store belonged, Mu'adh b. Afra told him the owners were orphans in his care . . . and he could take it for a mosque and he would pay the young men for it.

The Apostle ordered that a mosque (and lodgings for his family) be built, and he joined in the work to encourage the Muhajirin and the Ansar . . . (Emigrants and Medinans.)

(The Life of Muhammad, pp. 223–8)

When the Prophet was firmly established in Medina and his brethren the emigrants were gathered to him and the affairs of the helpers arranged, Islam became firmly established. Prayer was instituted, the alms-tax and fasting were prescribed, legal punishments were fixed, the forbidden and the permitted prescribed, and Islam took up its abode with them . . .

The people gathered to him at the appointed time of prayer . . . At first the Prophet thought of using a trumpet like that of the Jews who used it to summon to prayer. Afterwards he disliked the idea and ordered a clapper to be made . . . to be beaten when the Muslims should pray.

Meanwhile Abdallah b. Zayd b. Tha'laba b. Abdu Rabbihi, brother of Banu al-Harith, heard a voice in a dream, and came to the Apostle saying: "A phantom visited me in the night. There passed by me a man wearing two green garments carrying a clapper in his hand, and I asked him to sell it to me. When he asked me what I wanted it for I told him it was to summon people to prayer, where-upon he offered to show me a better way; it was to say thrice:

> 'Allahu Akbar! [God is most great] Allahu Akbar!
> I bear witness that there is no god but God!
> I bear witness that Muhammad is the Apostle of God!
> Come to prayer! Come to prayer!
> Come to salvation! Come to salvation!
> Allahu Akbar! Allahu Akbar!
> There is no god but God!'"

When the Apostle was told of this he said that it was a true vision if God so willed it, and that he should go with Bilal and communicate it to him so he might call to prayer thus, for Bilal had the most penetrating voice. When Bilal acted as the first muezzin Umar . . . came to the Apostle dragging his cloak on the ground and saying that he had seen precisely the same vision. The Apostle said, "God be praised for that!"

I was told this tradition . . . on the authority of Muhammad b. Abdallah b. Zayd b. Tha'laba himself. Muhammad b. Ja'far b. Zubayr told me on the authority of Urwa b. Zubayr of a woman of the Banu al-Najjar who said: "My house was the highest of those round the mosque, and Bilal used to give the call from the top of it every day. He would sit on the housetop waiting for the dawn; when he saw it, he would stretch out his arms and say, 'Oh God, I praise Thee and ask Thy help for Quraysh, that they may accept Thy religion.' I never knew him to omit those words for a single night."

(*The Life of Muhammad*, pp. 235–6)

The death of the Prophet

A'isha, the Prophet's wife, the daughter of Abu Bakr, said: "The Apostle returned from (prayers for the dead in) the cemetery to find me suffering from a severe headache, and I was saying, 'O, my head!'"

He said, "Nay, A'isha, O my head!"

Then he said, "Would it distress you if you should die before me so I might wrap you in your shroud and pray over you and bury you?"

I said, "Methinks I see you returning therefrom to my house and spending a bridal night in it with one of your wives!"

He smiled at that, and then his pain overtook him . . .

He called his wives and asked their permission to be nursed in my house, and they agreed . . ."

A'isha used to hear the Apostle say, "God never takes a prophet to Himself without giving him the choice."

"The last word I heard the Apostle saying was, "Nay, rather the Exalted Companion of paradise."

I said (to myself), "Then by God, he is not choosing us!" And I knew it was as he used to tell us, that a prophet does not die without being given the choice . . .

"The Apostle died in my bosom during my turn: I wronged none in regard to him. It was due to my ignorance and extreme youth that the Apostle died in my arms. Then I laid his head on a pillow, and got up beating my breast and slapping my face."

Sa'id b. al-Musayyib told me on the authority of Abu Hurayra: When the Apostle was dead, Umar got up and said, "Some of the disaffected will allege that the Apostle is dead, but by God he is not dead: he has gone to his Lord as Moses went and was hidden from his people for forty days, returning to them after it was said that he was dead. By God, the Apostle will return as Moses returned, and will cut off the hands and feet of those who allege that he is dead!"

When Abu Bakr heard this . . . he paid no attention but went into A'isha's house to the Apostle who was lying covered by a mantle of Yamani cloth. He uncovered his face and kissed him, saying, "Dearer than my father and my mother! You have tasted the death which God had decreed; a second death will never overtake you." Then he replaced the mantle and went out.

Umar was still speaking, and he said, "Gently, Umar, be quiet." But Umar went on talking. When Abu Bakr saw he would not be silent he went forward to the people, who came to him and left Umar. Giving thanks and praise to God, he said: "O men, if anyone worships Muhammad, Muhammad is dead. If anyone worships God, God is alive, immortal!"

Then he recited this verse: "Muhammad is nothing but an Apostle. Apostles have passed away before him. Can it be that if he were to die or be killed you would turn back on your heels? He who turns back does no harm to God, but God will reward the grateful" (Sura 3, 38).

Umar said, "By God, when I heard Abu Bakr recite these words, I was dumbfounded so that my legs would not bear me and I fell to the ground, knowing that the Apostle was indeed dead."

(*The Life of Muhammad*, pp. 105–7, 197–8, 212–22, 223–8, 235–6, 678–83)

Question for discussion

1   How would you compare the Hadith to the Talmud?

Prayer

Here is a description of Salat:

The saying of prayer (Salat) is obligatory upon every Muslim, male or female, five times a day, viz. early in the morning, a little after midday, in the afternoon, immediately after sunset and in the first part of the night before going to bed. The service consists of two parts – one part to be said alone, preferably in private, and the other in congregation, preferably in a mosque, but in case there is no congregation of Muslims both parts may be performed alone.

The morning or Fajr prayer consists of two Rak'ahs said alone, followed by two said in congregation. The midday or Zuhr prayer consists of four Raka'at said alone, followed by four said in congregation, and these again followed by two said alone. The afternoon or 'Asr prayer consists of four Raka'at said in congregation. The sunset or Maghrib prayer consists of three Raka'at said in congregation, followed by two said alone. The night or 'Isha prayer consists of four Raka'at said in congregation followed by two, and again by three, said alone. Besides these, there is the Tahajjud, or after midnight prayer, which is not obligatory, consisting of eight Raka'at said in twos.

Description of a Rak'ah

One Rak'ah is completed as follows:

1   Both hands are raised up to the ears in a standing position, with the face towards the Qiblah in Mecca, while the words Allahu Akbar (God is the greatest of all) are uttered. This is called the Takbir.

2   Then comes the Qiyam. The right hand is placed straight upon the forearm of the left, over the navel, while the standing position is maintained and the following prayer is recited (though there are other prayers too): "Glory to thee, O God, Thine is the praise and blessed is Thy Name and exalted is Thy majesty, and there is none to be served beside Thee . . . I betake me for refuge to God against the accursed satan."

   After this the Fatihah or opening Surah of the Qur'an is recited in the same position. At the close is said Amen, be it so, and then any portion of the Qur'an which the devotee wishes is recited by heart. Generally one of the shorter chapters at the close of the Holy Book is repeated and the Chapter termed Ikhlas is the one recommended.

3   Then, saying Allahu Akbar the worshipper lowers his head down, so that the palms of the hand reach the knees. In this position, which is called Ruku', phrases expressive of the divine glory and majesty are repeated at least three times. They are the following: "Glory to my Lord the great."

4   After this, the standing position is resumed, with the words: "God accepts him who gives praise to Him, O our Lord, Thine is the praise."

5   Then the worshipper prostrates himself, the toes of both feet, both knees, both hands, and the forehead touching the ground, and the following words expressing the divine greatness are uttered at least three times. This is the first Sijdah. "Glory to my Lord the most High."

6   Then the worshipper sits down in a reverential position (on his haunches). This is the Jalsah.

7   This is followed by a second prostration, or Sijdah, (as described under 5) with the repetition of the same words.

8   This finishes one Rak'ah. The worshipper rises and assumes a standing position for the second one, which is finished in the same manner as the first. But at the end of the second one, instead of assuming the standing position he sits down in a reverential position called the qada', and with the glorification of God he combines prayers for the holy prophets, for the faithful and for himself, called the Tahiyah, which runs as follows: "All prayers and worship rendered through words, actions and wealth, are due to God. Peace be upon you, O prophet and the mercy of God and His blessings. Peace be on us and the righteous servants of God. I bear witness that none is worthy to be worshipped save God and I bear witness that Muhammad is His servant and His Apostle."

9   If the worshipper intends more than two Raka'at he repeats also the following prayer of blessings upon the Prophet: "O God, magnify Muhammad

and the followers of Muhammad, as Thou didst magnify Abraham and the followers of Abraham. For surely Thou art praised and magnified. O God, bless Muhammad and the followers of Muhammad, as Thou didst bless etc."

The following prayer may also be added to this: "My Lord, make me, and my offspring also, to continue prayer. Our Lord, accept the prayer: grant Thy protection to me and to my parents and to the faithful on the day when the reckoning shall be made."

10   This closes the prayer, which ends at the Salam, or the greeting, being also the greeting of the Muslims to each other. The worshipper turns his head first to the right and then to the left, saying with each turn of the head: "Peace be upon you and the mercy of God."

(Sirdar Iqbal Ali Shah, Lights of Asia, London,
Arthur Barker, 1934, pp. 29–34)

Question for discussion

1   What do you find distinctive about the Islamic conception of public prayer?

9

Christianity

The Spirit of Christianity

An incident in the temple

And they went each to his home, and Jesus to the Mount of Olives. At daybreak he appeared again in the temple, and all the people gathered round him. He had taken his seat and was engaged in teaching them when the doctors of the law and the Pharisees brought in a woman detected in adultery. Making her stand out in the middle they said to him, "Master, this woman was caught in the very act of adultery. In the Law Moses has laid down that such women are to be stoned. What do you say about it?" They put the question as a test, hoping to frame a charge against him.

Jesus bent down and wrote with his finger on the ground. When they continued to press their question he sat up straight and said, "That one of you who is faultless shall throw the first stone." Then once again he bent down and wrote on the ground.

When they heard what he said, one by one they went away, the eldest first; and Jesus was left alone, with the woman still standing there. Jesus again sat up and said to the woman, "Where are they? Has no one condemned you?"

"No one, sir", she said.

Jesus replied, "No more do I. You may go; do not sin again."

(Gospel according to John 7: 53–8: 11; *New English Bible*)*

---

* Many scholars believe this story to be a later addition to the Gospel rather than part of the original text.

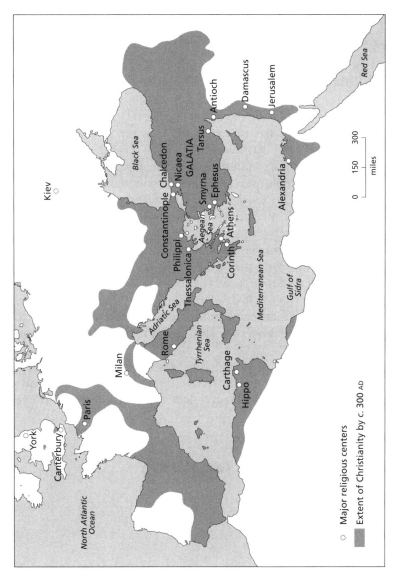

○ Major religious centers

▓ Extent of Christianity by c. 300 AD

North Atlantic Ocean

York
Canterbury
Paris
Milan
Rome
Adriatic Sea
Tyrrhenian Sea
Carthage
Hippo
Mediterranean Sea
Gulf of Sidra
Thessalonica
Philippi
Corinth
Athens
Aegean Sea
Constantinople
Chalcedon
Nicaea
GALATIA
Smyrna
Ephesus
Tarsus
Black Sea
Kiev
Antioch
Damascus
Jerusalem
Red Sea
Alexandria

0   150   300
miles

The world of early Christianity

Question for discussion

1 It is well-known that Jesus condemned adultery, following the traditional Jewish Law (see below, p. 292). How do you reconcile this with his action as depicted in this story? Could it have implications for the interpretation of Jesus' other statements supporting the Law?

The Christian View of Life

Although we have described Christianity as a religion of Semitic origin, this is only partly true. Christianity has two roots. One is the Jewish world of ethical monotheism; the other is the classical world of the Roman Empire.

Christianity began as a reform movement within Jewish religion, a movement aiming to call the Jewish people away from inessentials and back to what was most central in their faith. In the process it developed a message of universal significance, and one which found much more of a response outside the Jewish community, in the Graeco-Roman world.

The Christian view of life can perhaps be summed up in the phrase, the humanity of God. The God who made the heavens and the earth has become human, born as a child, growing to a man, teaching us the ways of God, and sharing our fate in suffering and death, for love of mankind. Although we are by nature sinful, he himself has made atonement for our sins, and has reconciled us to himself. "There is no greater love than this, that a man should lay down his life for his friends."

To understand the meaning of Christianity, it is helpful to understand both the condition of the Jewish community in Jesus' time, and also the state of religion in the Graeco-Roman world, which provided its larger context and eventually became its home.

The Jewish Community in Jesus' Time

As indicated in the chapter on Judaism, we know of some five groups which were prominent in Jewish life at this time.

The Pharisees

The Pharisees were a group dedicated to keeping the divine law in its fullness. The name probably derives from the Hebrew word for "separated," in the sense that their zeal for the law separated or distinguished them from the mass of the Jewish people. It was the Pharisees who had developed the doctrine of the Oral Law. They taught that, in addition to the commandments of the written Torah,

God had communicated to Moses further laws which were not written down, but were handed on by word of mouth from generation to generation, and which were also binding. These included the "fences of the Law," various prescriptions regarding the washing of hands, tithings, fasts, and so on, which served to "protect" the written Law. On the other hand, the Pharisees paid relatively little attention to the temple sacrifices.

In addition they accepted new beliefs, which had developed during the centuries while Palestine was under Persian and Hellenistic rule, in the immortality of the soul and the resurrection of the body. This brought about a fundamental change in Jewish religion, since its purpose was now no longer only to secure the well-being of the people in this life, but the eternal happiness of the individual in the life hereafter. The Pharisees enjoyed great prestige and support among the people.

The Sadducees

The Sadducees (probably from Zadok, an early priest) were a conservative and largely priestly party, intent on preserving the ancient traditions of the Jewish people, and opposed to the innovations of the Pharisees. They recognized only the Five Books of Moses as sacred scripture, viewing the Prophets and the Writings as merely human products, and rejecting the Pharisees' doctrine of the Unwritten Law. Correspondingly, they also rejected the new beliefs, accepted by the Pharisees, of the survival of the soul after death, and the resurrection of the body. They kept the ancient view that the purpose of Jewish religion was the survival and prosperity of the Jewish people in this life.

The Sadducees were concerned especially for the preservation of the Jewish nation. In their conception of God they emphasized his role as the God of the nation, rather than as the universal God of all men. In politics they were pragmatists, maintaining good relations with the Roman authorities as the best way to ensure the welfare of the nation. They constituted an upper class, somewhat remote from the ordinary people.

The Scribes

The Scribes, or Doctors of the Law (Greek, *grammateis*; Hebrew, *sopherim*), were a guild of professional scholars who studied and taught the divine Law in schools, not only in Jerusalem, but also in other cities with Jewish communities, such as Babylon. They had been a recognized class for several hundred years before the time of Jesus, arising with the development of the synagogue system. It was largely from their ranks that the judges and governmental administrators of the nation were drawn. Their modern descendants are the Rabbis.

Both Sadducees and Pharisees had their scribes, who followed their respective principles, but since the Pharisees were predominant among the people, it is the Pharisaical scribes who are meant in most of the Gospel references to them.

The Essenes

The Essenes were a somewhat monastic brotherhood, living in separate settlements, supporting themselves by manual labor, and holding their property in common, with some of their members practicing celibacy. However, they were not recluses, and often took an active part in political life. They were probably a branch of the Pharisees, and believed in the resurrection of the body. They were intensely patriotic, and their existence centered on the Torah. Although they accepted the temple sacrifices in principle, they refused to take part in them because they considered the Sadducees corrupt. It has been speculated that John the Baptist belonged to a branch of the Essenes.

The Zealots

The Zealots, centered in Galilee, were armed rebels devoted to the Torah and determined to overthrow Roman rule.

The Gentile Background

The Roman Empire

Palestine had been incorporated into the Roman Empire by Pompey in 63 BC. For the most part the Romans ruled their territories with a relatively light hand, allowing each people to continue to live by its own laws and customs. Palestine with its Jewish population was divided up into several territories, each with its own ruler. Galilee was ruled by Herod Antipas, who had to answer to Rome in important matters. Judaea was made into a Roman province and ruled directly by a Roman procurator, Pontius Pilatus; the day-to-day government, however, was left in the hands of the high priest in conjunction with the Sanhedrin, an assembly of the aristocracy. The Sanhedrin had the power to pronounce a Jew deserving of death, but needed Roman permission to carry out the execution.

Roman civic religion

The Roman state had an official religion, which was polytheistic, worshipping Jupiter, Mars, Juno, and numerous other gods. A rather impersonal religion, it aimed at securing the welfare of the state and the Roman people in this world. Rome was tolerant of other beliefs, but hostile to immoral rites and to secret societies. On his death in AD 14 the Emperor Augustus was deified, and subsequent emperors received divine honors even while alive, although educated Romans did not take this very literally. Ceremonial worship of the emperor was a test of fidelity to the state.

The mystery religions

The desire for a more personal religion was filled by imports from the East. Among them were the worship of Cybele, the Great Mother; of Attis, who died and rose again; of Isis, who resurrected her husband Osiris; and of Mithras, the Indian and Persian god mentioned in Chapter 1, whose birth was celebrated on December 25. These religions and others like them were known as "mystery" religions, from the Greek term *mysterion*, meaning an oath, in this case of secrecy.

In general these religions were characterized by several common features. Membership was obtained by a process of initiation, often long and complex. The god was friendly to man, and often suffered and died. By participating in the sacred rituals the devotee shared spiritually in the death and resurrected life of the god. The new spiritual existence had to be expressed in a life of moral purity.

An example of ritual employed in a mystery cult was the taurobolium. The individual stood in a cellar or pit, over which there was a grating, and a bull standing on the grating was ritually slaughtered, so that its blood ran down over the person below. The flowing of the blood, the principle of life, over the person was thought to unite him with the life of the divinity. This ceremony was used in the rites of Cybele.

The mystery religions aimed, not at material welfare in this world, but at spiritual salvation, including a future life. Their widespread acceptance paved the way for Christianity.

Jesus of Nazareth

Our knowledge of Jesus' life, so far as scholarship can establish it, is very limited. He was probably born in 4 BC and grew up in Nazareth. He spent perhaps three years teaching in public, was arrested as a subversive, and crucified. His disciples believed that he rose from the dead and ascended into heaven.

For the rest, we are dependent on the information provided by his followers. The Gospels, our chief sources of information, were not written as purely factual history in our modern sense, however. They include legends and differ on some important questions.

The Message of Jesus

The message of Jesus as we have it in the Gospels does not consist only of Jesus' own words, but contains much which was added later by the editors, expressing their particular concerns. The Gospel of Matthew, for example, was written for Christians from a Jewish background, and attempts to explain Jesus in terms of their assumptions. The Gospel of Luke, on the other hand, was written for Christians from a Gentile background, and explains Jesus in somewhat different terms, corresponding to their different assumptions. The first three Gospels

(Matthew, Mark, and Luke, called the Synoptic Gospels) have a great deal in common, and evidently make use of some of the same documents as sources. The Gospel of John was the last to be written, and is the most remote from the historical Jesus. Although scholars have worked on the text over many years, there is still much disagreement as to the original message of Jesus. Here we present it simply as it appears in the Gospels, as the early Christian community understood it.

Even so, we still face certain problems. Jesus speaks in dramatic terms; he tells vivid and arresting stories with striking images. As a result his words are in some ways usually entirely clear, yet in other respects they are often paradoxical and mysterious. It is not easy to summarize Jesus' teachings and reduce them to a systematic code.

The Law of Moses must be kept.   Jesus does not intend to found a new religion. He understands himself entirely as a Jew, not only ethnically but also religiously. He adopts wholeheartedly the standpoint of Jewish religion as his standpoint. He celebrates the Jewish festivals. His mission, he says, is to the Jewish people. He identifies the God of the Jewish people as his Father. Jesus does not distance himself from the Jewish Law, but reaffirms it. He has not come to abolish the Law, but to bring it to completion, he says. Even the most minute regulations of the Law must be observed.

> If any man therefore sets aside even the least of the Law's demands, and teaches others to do the same, he will have the lowest place in the kingdom of Heaven, whereas anyone who keeps the Law and teaches others so will stand high in the kingdom of Heaven.
>
> (Matthew 5: 17–19)

(Some scholars think this statement was added by the author of the Gospel of Matthew because of his Jewish audience.)

But the Law is not sufficient.   Jesus says that he has come to bring the Law to completion. This completion consists largely in what we might perhaps call an interiorization. The Law of Moses is mainly concerned with externals, whereas true religion is in the heart. To God, our inner attitudes are just as important as our visible actions. It is these inner attitudes that Jesus stresses as the decisive element in the religious life. It is not enough to refrain from the external action of committing murder, for example; we must also avoid the inner feeling of anger:

> You have learned that our forefathers were told, "Do not commit murder; anyone who commits murder must be brought to judgement." But what I tell you is this: Anyone who nurses anger against his brother must be brought to judgement. If he abuses his brother he must answer for it to the court; if he sneers at him he will have to answer for it in the fires of hell . . .

You have learned that they were told, "Do not commit adultery." But what I tell you is this: If a man looks on a woman with a lustful eye, he has already committed adultery with her in his heart.

(Matthew 5: 21–2, 27–8)

More than this, to those who injure us we must return the heroic response of love:

You have learned that they were told, "An eye for an eye, and a tooth for a tooth." But what I tell you is this: Do not set yourself against the man who wrongs you. If someone slaps you on the right cheek, turn and offer him your left. If a man wants to sue you for your shirt, let him have your coat as well"...
   You have learned that they were told, "Love your neighbor, hate your enemy." But what I tell you is this: Love your enemies and pray for your persecutors; only so can you be children of your heavenly Father, who makes his sun rise on good and bad alike, and sends the rain on the honest and the dishonest.

(Matthew 5: 38–40, 43–5)

Although some of the Pharisees, such as Hillel, had also stressed the primary importance of one's interior attitude, in Jesus' hands these statements take on a revolutionary force. He makes these additions to the Law on his own authority: "The Law says this . . . but I say . . . ," thereby implicitly setting himself up as an authority equal to the Law.

The Law exists for man, not man for the Law.   Human needs take precedence over the Law. Jesus is willing to bend the Law in order to help people in distress.

On one occasion Jesus and his disciples were walking through a field of wheat on the Sabbath, when some of his disciples, feeling hungry, began to pluck the ears of wheat and eat them. Some Pharisees who were accompanying them noticed this and said to him, "Look, your disciples are doing something which is forbidden on the Sabbath." Jesus defended them, however, pointing out that there was good precedent for what they were doing: King David once, when his men were hungry, went so far as to enter the Temple and seize the loaves of bread which had been consecrated to God, even though according to the letter of the Law they had no right to do so.

On another occasion Jesus entered a synagogue on the Sabbath and was asked by a man with a withered arm to heal him. The Pharisees raised the question whether it was permissible to heal someone on the Sabbath. Jesus responded that it undoubtedly was permissible.

"Suppose one among you has one sheep, which fell into a ditch on the Sabbath; is there one of you who would not catch hold of it and lift it out? And surely a man is worth far more than a sheep! It is therefore permitted to do good on the Sabbath." Turning to the man he said, "Stretch out your arm." He stretched it out, and it was made sound again like the other.

(Matthew 12:11–13)

Jesus condemns the "Unwritten Law" of the Scribes and Pharisees: it does not come from God, but is a purely human creation.

Approached once by a group of Pharisees who protested that his disciples neglected the sacred tradition of washing their hands before meals, Jesus responded that their objections were not in good faith, for they were willing to abandon the Written Law when it was to their own advantage to do so. For example, they allowed sons to give their wealth to the Temple instead of providing for their parents in need. "You have made God's law null and void out of respect for your tradition . . . A man is not defiled by what goes into his mouth, but by what comes out of it."

> Alas for you, lawyers and Pharisees, hypocrites! You pay tithes of mint and dill and cummin; but you have overlooked the weightier demands of the Law, justice, mercy, and good faith. It is these you should have practiced, without neglecting the others. Blind guides! You strain off a midge, yet gulp down a camel!
>
> (Matthew 23: 23–4)

Not only this, but he rejects the concept of unclean foods, Kashrut, which is part of the Law of Moses.

> On another occasion he called the people and said to them, "Listen to me, all of you, and understand this: nothing that goes into a man from outside can defile him; no, it is the things that come out of him that defile a man."
>
> When he had left the people and gone indoors, his disciples questioned him about the parable. He said to them, "Are you as dull as the rest? Do you not see that nothing that goes from outside into a man can defile him, because it does not enter into his heart but into his stomach, and so passes out into the drain?" Thus he declared all foods clean. He went on, "It is what comes out of a man that defiles him. For from inside, out of a man's heart, come evil thoughts, acts of fornication, of theft, murder, adultery, ruthless greed, and malice; fraud, indecency, envy, slander, arrogance, and folly; these evil things all come from inside, and they defile a man."
>
> (Mark 7: 14–23)

God is not only our Creator, Lord, and Judge, but our Father. Jesus constantly refers to God as his Father: "by calling God his own Father he claimed equality with God" (John 5: 18). But equally constantly he speaks of God as the Father of his audience:

> Is there a man among you who will offer his son a stone when he asks for bread, or a snake when he asks for fish? If you, then, bad as you are, know how to give your children what is good for them, how much more will your heavenly Father give good things to those who ask him! (Matthew 7: 9–11)

> This is how you should pray:
>
> "Our Father in heaven,
> thy name be hallowed;

thy kingdom come,
thy will be done,
on earth as in heaven.
Give us today our daily bread.
Forgive us the wrong we have done,
as we have forgiven those who have wronged us.
And do not bring us to the test,
but save us from evil."

(Matthew 6: 9–13)

Though the concept of God has otherwise notable similarities in the religions of Semitic origin, as Creator, Lord and Judge, this emphasis on the Fatherhood of God is a distinctive feature of Jesus' preaching and of Christianity.

The Law is kept fully by loving God and our fellow-men. In fact the only criterion by which men will ultimately be judged is the degree to which they have loved their fellow-men, since that automatically implies love for God, whether they are consciously aware of it or not. When the day of judgement comes, the good will be surprised to discover that they have passed the test, because they acted without any thought of God, and only out of concern for their fellow-men. Whatever is done for one's fellow-men is by that very fact done for God. Conversely, the wicked will be condemned even though they showed no explicit hatred towards God, because they failed to care for their fellow-man (Matthew 25: 31–46). "Always treat others as you would like them to treat you: that is the Law and the Prophets" (Matthew 7: 12).

Jesus' teachings inaugurate a new era: the Kingdom of God or Reign of God (or, as Matthew, reluctant to use the name of God because of the Jewish background of his audience, terms it, the Kingdom of Heaven). By this expression, which remains somewhat mysterious, Jesus apparently meant the realm in which God's will is obeyed, a realm which, while it reaches its acme in heaven, also extends to earth to embrace all those in this world who are obedient to God's will. Nothing is more important than to belong to this realm. It is not visible to the bodily eye, but is a spiritual reality. To enter it, men must repent of their sins, and forgive those who have sinned against them.

> The kingdom of Heaven is like treasure lying buried in a field. The man who found it, buried it again; and for sheer joy went and sold everything he had, and bought that field.
>
> (Matthew 13: 44)

Although Jesus opposes the religion of the Pharisees, that does not mean he is in the camp of their opponents, the Sadducees. Contrary to what the Sadducees believe, the soul lives on after death, and there will be a resurrection of the body.
A group of Sadducees presented him on one occasion with a conundrum intended to show that the idea of a bodily resurrection was ludicrous. There were

once seven brothers, of whom the first married and then died. Following the Law of Moses, the second brother married his widow, but then also died, but so on, the woman being married to each brother in turn when her previous husband died. If there were a resurrection of the body, the Sadducees pointed out, then in the resurrected world all seven of them would be her husbands at the same time, which would be absurd. Jesus' response was twofold: they did not sufficiently appreciate the power of God, who was fully able to raise the dead however impossible it might seem to us; and after the resurrection there will be no marriage.

In the same vein, on the cross Jesus tells one of the thieves crucified with him: "This day you shall be with me in Paradise," clearly implying the immortality of the soul.

One day Jesus will return, bringing the present age to an end in a universal cataclysm. Then the reign of God, now invisible to men, will be visible and triumphant.

> As soon as the distress of those days has passed, the sun will be darkened, the moon will not give her light, the stars will fall from the sky, the celestial powers will be shaken. Then will appear in heaven the sign that heralds the Son of Man. All the peoples of the world will make lamentation, and they will see the Son of Man coming on the clouds of heaven with great power and glory. With a trumpet blast he will send out his angels, and they will gather his chosen from the four winds, from the farthest bounds of heaven on every side.
>
> (Matthew 24: 29–31; NEB)

The Miracles of Jesus

According to the New Testament, Jesus worked many signs and wonders, feats impossible to an ordinary man. He cured many people instantaneously of illnesses normally incurable, and even brought the dead back to life. His own resurrection from the dead was only the greatest of many such deeds.

These miracles of Jesus were not merely an incidental aspect of his work. As narrated in the New Testament, they were the chief factor in winning the confidence of his disciples, for they provided a guarantee that his message was from God. As the man born blind states in the Gospel of John, "It is common knowledge that God does not listen to sinners; he listens to anyone who is devout and obeys his will. To open the eyes of a man born blind – it is unheard of since time began. If that man had not come from God he could have done nothing."

The Message of Paul about Jesus

Jesus preached only to the Jewish community; but for the most part his message found little echo. More than any other single individual, the person responsible for the spread of Christianity was Paul. On the one hand, he provided a most

A Greek Orthodox icon of the Resurrection (Circa Photo Library)

powerful interpretation of the significance of Jesus. On the other, he travelled far and wide across the Graeco-Roman world preaching the Christian message and organizing the infant church.

Paul never met Jesus personally or heard him speak, if we except the vision he experienced on the road to Damascus, which brought about his conversion. His knowledge of Jesus was derived from the Christians whom he first persecuted and then befriended. As a result, Paul makes little or no reference to Jesus' preaching as such. The focus in Paul's writings is not on what Jesus said, but on what he was, what he accomplished. His message can be summed up in the statement: Jesus is the Savior of mankind.

Just as Jesus did not present his teachings systematically, neither did Paul. We know his doctrines from the letters he wrote to various Christian communities, but these letters for the most part were written to deal with some particular practical problem that had arisen, and it is only within that framework that he discusses the Christian faith.

All men are sinners, and therefore need redemption. Paul states this most clearly in his letter to the Christian community in Rome, in which he makes three arguments, one applying to the Gentiles, the second to the Jews, and the third to the whole of mankind.

1   The Gentiles are sinners because they do not recognize the true God, even though it is obvious to the eye of reason that he exists, from the things he

323

The Easter procession, Granada, Spain (Ann & Bury Peerless)

has made. As a result of their idolatry God has given them up to every form of immorality.

> They are filled with every kind of injustice, mischief, rapacity, and malice; they are one mass of envy, murder, rivalry, treachery, and malevolence; whisperers and scandal-mongers, hateful to God, insolent, arrogant, and boastful; they invent new kinds of mischief, they show no loyalty to parents, no conscience, no fidelity to their plighted word; they are without natural affection and without pity.

(Romans 1: 29–31)

2 The Jews are sinners because, although they believe in God and acknowledge his Law, they do not keep it.

324

You, then, who teach your fellow-man, do you fail to teach yourself? You proclaim, "Do not steal"; but are you yourself a thief? You say, "Do not commit adultery"; but are you an adulterer? You abominate false Gods; but do you rob their shrines? While you take pride in the Law, you dishonour God by breaking it.

(Romans 2: 21–3)

3   All men are born in sin, as a result of Adam's sin. Adam as he came from the hand of God would have lived for ever. But when Adam sinned, God punished him by making him subject to death. This punishment was inflicted not only on Adam, however, but also on us his children, which shows that we too were included in his sin. The fact that we must all die is evidence that we are all sinners.

Jesus is the Savior of mankind by his death and resurrection.   His death was a sacrifice for men's sins, and his resurrection showed God's acceptance of that sacrifice.

But now, quite independently of Law, God's justice has been brought to light. The Law and the prophets both bear witness to it: it is God's way of righting wrong, effective through faith in Christ for all who have such faith – all, without distinction. For all alike have sinned, and are deprived of the divine splendour, and all are justified by God's free grace alone, through his act of liberation in the person of Christ Jesus. For God designed him to be the means of expiating sin by his sacrificial death, effective through faith.

(Romans 3: 21–5)

To become a Christian is to participate in Jesus' death, resurrection, and eternal life.   Through baptism in Christ we share in his life, which overcomes both the spiritual death of sin, and also the physical death of the body.

Shall we persist in sin . . . ? No, no! We died to sin: how can we live in it any longer? Have you forgotten that when we were baptized into union with Christ Jesus we were baptized into his death? By baptism we were buried with him, and lay dead, in order that, as Christ was raised from the dead in the splendour of the Father, so also we might set our feet upon the new path of life. For if we have become incorporate with him in a death like his, we shall also be one with him in a resurrection like his.

(Romans 6: 1–4)

It will be evident that there is some affinity between Paul's message about Jesus and the mystery religions. In both, the individual comes to share mystically in the eternal life of the deity, overcoming both spiritual and bodily death, through faith, a process of initiation, and participation in sacred rituals.

The Further Development of Christianity

The status of the Jewish Law: Jewish and Gentile Christianity

Jesus' disciples, who of course were all Jews, continued to obey the Jewish Law. There were some Gentiles living in Palestine who heard the message about Jesus and became interested in it. Many more Gentiles became followers of Jesus outside of Palestine through the preaching of Paul in the Diaspora. When this happened, the question immediately arose whether they also ought to be required to keep the Jewish Law.

Opinion on this was strongly divided. The original disciples of Jesus were inclined to favor their keeping the Law, at least some parts of it. Paul, on the other hand, drew the conclusion that if men were saved by the death and resurrection of Jesus, they were not saved by keeping the Law, and therefore the Gentile converts had no obligation to do so; the Law was only a temporary measure pending the advent of Christ (Galatians 3: 19).

By AD 70 there were in effect two Christian churches with two very different kinds of Christianity: the Jewish church, centered in Jerusalem, which retained its ties to the Jewish community and Jewish traditions and customs, and which understood Jesus and his preaching more in terms of his Jewish background; and the Gentile church, existing outside Palestine, which had no attachment to things Jewish at all, but believed in Jesus as the Savior of mankind preached by Paul.

In AD 70 the Romans destroyed Jerusalem, and with it the Jewish Christian church. This left the Gentile church as the only existing form of Christianity. What had begun as a reform movement within Jewish religion was now entirely separate from it.

Some Christian terms

It may be useful at this point to explain some Christian terms in common use. The language spoken by the early Gentile Christians was predominantly Greek, which is the language of the New Testament and other early Christian documents.

Christ   This is not a personal name, but a title, meaning in Greek "the Anointed One," that is, the Messiah. In classical Hebrew religion, anointing with olive oil was a ceremony of special importance, setting a person aside for a special purpose. Kings, priests, and prophets were anointed. The Hebrew word for "anointed" is *messiah*, the Greek translation of which is *christos*.

Church   The Greek term for the Christian community was *kyriake ekklesia*, *ekklesia* meaning "community," and *kyriake* coming from *kyrios*, a lord or master, and meaning "belonging to the Lord." *Kyriake ekklesia* thus means "the community of the Lord." The word "church" derives from *kyriake*, which can perhaps be seen more clearly in the Scottish word "kirk."

Christianity The early followers of Jesus called their religious faith simply "the Way." The word "Christian" came into use first in the city of Antioch, toward the end of the first century.

Catholic The Greek word *holos* means "the whole." *Kata* means "according to." The two words are combined into the adjectival form *katholikos*, meaning "universal."

The organization of the Christian Church

Paul, on arriving in a new town, would go along to the synagogue and introduce himself, would often be invited to speak at the Sabbath service. He would use the occasion to preach his message about Jesus, and this would be heard not only by Jews but also by Gentiles, for in the Diaspora numerous Gentiles were attracted to Judaism, because of its lofty conception of God and its high moral ideals. If anyone expressed an interest in following the Way, he would meet with them afterwards and organize them into a separate group, with a separate meeting time. It was this local group of Christians that was initially referred to as "the Church," for example, the Church of Ephesus, or the Church of Antioch.

The organization of this group typically was modeled on the organization of the synagogue, apparently somewhat similarly to the way synagogues are organized today. Authority was vested in a committee or board of directors. The members of the board were referred to in Greek interchangeably as *presbyteroi*, meaning "elders," or as *episkopoi*, meaning "overseers." Like most board members, they were only part-time. From the beginning the churches recognized a special duty to help Christians who were poor or in distress, and special individuals were appointed to carry out this task, who were called *diakonoi*, meaning "servants" or "messengers."

By the end of the first century it generally came to be felt that someone was needed to run the organization on a full time basis. This individual came to be known as the episkopos, while the part-time members of the board were then called presbyteroi. The English word "priest" comes from *presbyteros*, while "bishop" is derived from *episkopos*, and "deacon" from *diakonos*. Bishops and elders were elected by the local Christian community, or church.

Each local Church had its own bishop, and the various Churches were independent of one another. If a bishop alienated too many of his neighboring bishops, they might get together and declare him and his Church to be outside the true Church. The test of correct belief was whether a person was "in communion" with his bishop, and the bishop with the other bishops. Each Christian Church, that is, each local Christian community, formed part of the Universal Church. To refer to the whole or complete Church, consisting of all the local Churches in communion with one another, the term "Catholic" was used.

The Christian Bible

At the time of Jesus the definitive form of the Hebrew Bible had not yet been agreed on. For the Sadducees the only authoritative scripture was the Five Books of Moses. The Pharisees recognized in addition the books of the Prophets, and after the destruction of the temple in AD 70 the Pharisaical view predominated. The remaining books, called the Writings, such as the Psalms, were added around the end of the first century.

The Christians accepted the Jewish Bible as the "Old Testament." At first, following the Pharisees, this contained only the Law and the Prophets. When the Jews added the Writings, the Christians did too.

In addition the Christians produced their own writings. The first Christian writings to be circulated widely were the letters of Paul to the various churches he founded, which they would pass on to others. The first was the letter to the Church of Thessalonica, written about the year 50. The lives of Jesus which we call the Gospels were written somewhat later, the earliest being the Gospel of Mark, written perhaps around the year 70. The last writing to be accepted as part of the Christian Bible was the Second Letter of Peter, written perhaps around the year 135.

Around AD 180 the list of books was finally settled, after some debate. Christians considered these books authoritative and divinely inspired, and they were called the "New Testament." Since the Church produced the Bible, and decided what books should be recognized as belonging to it, the attitude of the Church at this time was that the Church was superior to the Bible. The rule or criterion of the true faith was not in the first instance the Bible, but the faith of the Church.

The Church and the sacramental system

The Christian participates in the death and resurrection of Jesus, and thus attains to eternal life by the grace of God. How does this participation come about? In the Gospels there are two ceremonies that Jesus enjoins on his followers:

- Baptism, the washing with water as a sign of repentance; and
- the Eucharist, the commemorative meal.

To the early Christians it was clear that these rituals had a very special role to play in the Christian life, according to Jesus' intentions. They were visible signs of the invisible grace of God. But they were not merely signs. The significance given to them by Christ indicated that they actually brought about an objective change in the relationship between the individual and God: they communicated the grace of God to the individual. This is the concept of a sacrament. (The Latin word *sacramentum* meant initially an oath, then an oath of secrecy, and is a translation of the Greek word *mysterion*, which had similar meanings. In the mystery religions the term referred to the secret rituals or "mysteries" carried out at the meetings of the devotees.)

A Catholic priest celebrating Mass (John Smith/Circa Photo Library)

By the time of Peter Lombard in the twelfth century the Church had arrived at the conclusion that five more ceremonies were divinely instituted, based on references in the New Testament:

- Confirmation, derived from the descent of the Holy Spirit at Pentecost;
- Penance, the confession and remission of sin;
- Anointing of the sick;
- Ordination to office in the Church;
- Marriage.

The sacramental system is at the heart of Catholic Christianity.

Theologians developed the theory that the sacraments acted *ex opere operato*, that is, in virtue of the ritual action itself, rather than *ex opere operantis*, in virtue of the subjective piety of the individual. For the sacrament to take effect it was necessary, as a precondition, for the individual to have the right intention, but the individual's intention was not enough by itself to produce the effect of the sacrament.

An Anglican priest baptizing an infant (John Smith/Circa Photo Library)

The Church as authority

In the course of the first few centuries the view developed that the Church is not merely an association of people who happen to believe in Christ, but the only channel by which God communicates grace and salvation to men. It was created by Christ to be his intermediary with the world, uniting man to God and God to man. It is the only source from which we can learn authoritatively the word of God, and it is through the power of the Church that the sacraments are administered (although the view came to be accepted that baptism may be administered by anyone, and that marriage is administered by the couple themselves). Consequently the Church possesses spiritual authority over its members, in the name of God. The voice of the Church is the voice of God.

The Apostolic Succession

Linked with the conception of the authority of the Church is the idea of the apostolic succession. The authority of the Church resides in its bishops. The bishops are the successors of the apostles, Christ's earliest disciples, and in order to share in the authority of the Church a bishop must receive consecration from a bishop who stands in the line of succession from an apostle. Eventually the view came to be accepted that it is the communion of a bishop with the Bishop of Rome that guarantees apostolic succession.

Rome

The Christian church in the city of Rome occupied a special place in a number of ways from fairly early times. The simple fact that Rome was the capital of the Empire gave it much influence on other churches. It was wealthy, and so it could send generous donations to other Christian communities in times of famine, drought, or pestilence. It also developed early on the habit of giving advice to other churches, whether or not it had been requested. However, the church in Rome was apparently one of the last to adopt the "full-time bishop" form of organization. It was probably still being governed by a committee or board of directors well into the second century, making the change to a single bishop from about the middle of the second century.

In the course of the second and third centuries the Church in Rome came to play the role of arbitrator in disputes. If, say, a dispute broke out between the Church in Alexandria and the Church in Antioch, they might appeal to the Church in Rome as an impartial third party to decide the matter for them. The Romans appear to have been good at this, and over time it gave them increasing authority. Although they contributed little to the theory of the Christian faith, they had a practical feel for the safe middle ground which avoided minority or extreme views. Eventually, by about the fourth century, the test of faith came to be whether one was "in communion" with the Bishop of Rome.

Constantine

The attitude of the early Christians towards the Roman Empire was one of distance. All those living in the Roman Empire were expected to worship the image of the emperor, on pain of death for treason. A special exception was made for the Jews, as being what we would call "conscientious objectors." So long as the Christians were part of the Jewish community, the exemption also applied to them. But when they separated themselves from the Jewish community they lost the exemption and became liable to persecution. Until about 250, however, the persecution was sporadic. After 250, with the persecution carried out by the Emperor Decius, it became systematic. Christians, in their turn, wanted nothing to do with government; they lived not for this world, but the next. They were pacifists, for example. The attitude of Christians toward heresy and other religions during this time was one of toleration. No one should be compelled to confess any faith.

In 312, however, a Christian, Constantine, became emperor, and from that time on Christianity underwent a profound change. Constantine ended the persecution and proclaimed Christianity a permitted religion. Further, he regarded himself, and was regarded by the bishops, as the Church's "External Bishop," whose duty it was to protect the Church from its external enemies, and secure its place in civil society.

His successors went further, and in a series of edicts proclaimed Christianity to be not only permitted, but the only religion permitted. Christianity was to

Cross at San Xavier del Bac Mission, Arizona (Photo © David H. Wells/CORBIS)

enjoy a monopoly throughout the empire. It thereupon became intolerant of dissent. The church became an integral part of the Roman Empire and an organ of the civil government. Bishops wore the robes of Roman senators. A close union of the church with civil government persists in parts of Europe to this day.

The status of Jesus

Christians believed that Jesus was the Savior of mankind, which meant that he had a unique relationship to God. There was disagreement, however, as to how to define that relationship. The writings of the New Testament refer to him as the Son of God. Did this mean that he was divine or human? If he was merely human, how could he have the power to save mankind? If he was divine, was there after all more than one God? If not, what was his relationship to the Being he referred to as his father? Again, if he was divine, was his physical body a real body, or merely a convenient appearance taken on for the sake of his mission? And did he then die a real death or merely an apparent death?

These questions divided the Christian community and were debated for centuries. What became the mainstream view was eventually formulated in a series of councils of bishops, beginning with the Council of Nicaea in 325. The eventual conclusion of these councils was:

- that Jesus was both truly God and truly man. This is the doctrine of the Incarnation. It included the doctrine that Jesus' body was a real physical body, and his death a real physical death. On the basis of this doctrine it was possible to say that God suffered and God died, and that Mary was the mother of God.

- that there is only one God, but that in the one God there are three divine persons, the Father, the Son, and the Holy Spirit, of equal power and dignity. This is the doctrine of the Trinity.

These doctrines were expressed in creeds, or statements of faith, the best known of which are the Apostles' Creed, the Nicene Creed, and the Athanasian Creed. Here is a portion of the Athanasian Creed, which is especially noteworthy for its detailed explanation of the Trinity:

> This is the Catholic faith, that we venerate one God in Trinity, and Trinity in unity, neither confusing the Persons with one another, nor dividing up their substance. For the person of the Father is distinct from that of the Son, and the person of the Son is distinct from that of the Holy Spirit. But Father and Son and Holy Spirit have a single divinity, equal glory, and co-equal majesty.
>
> Whatever is true of the Father, is also true of the Son, and also of the Holy Spirit. The Father is uncreated, the Son is uncreated, the Holy Spirit is uncreated . . . the Father is eternal, the Son is eternal, the Holy Spirit is eternal; and yet there are not three eternal beings, but only one, just as there are not three uncreated beings, but only one . . . Similarly, the Father is omnipotent, the Son is omnipotent, the Holy Spirit is omnipotent, and yet there are not three omnipotent beings, but one. Similarly, the Father is God, the Son is God, the Holy Spirit is God, and yet there are not three Gods, but one God . . . For just as we are compelled by the Catholic truth to confess that taken singly each Person is God and Lord, we are forbidden to say that there are three Gods or Lords.
>
> The Father is not made or created or begotten by anyone. The Son is begotten by the Father, but not made or created. The Holy Spirit proceeds from the Father and the Son, but is not made or created or begotten. Therefore there is one Father, not three Fathers; one Son, not three Sons; and one Holy Spirit, not three Holy Spirits. In this Trinity nothing comes earlier or later, nothing is greater or less, but all three Persons are co-eternal and co-equal with one another.

Philosophy and theology

As it became the religion of the European peoples, Christianity inherited the European tradition of philosophical inquiry. The use of philosophical methods to understand and explain religious belief is called theology. This theological tradition, which shows itself in the wrestling over the doctrines of the Incarnation and Trinity, as well as many others, has resulted in an exceptional development of the theoretical side of Christianity by comparison with many other religions, especially Judaism and Islam. For example, it provided Christianity with a philosophical understanding of such concepts as person and nature. Christ, as God incarnate, was one person, namely the divine person of God the Son, but a person with two natures, one divine and one human. The Trinity by contrast was three persons with one nature, namely the divine nature. The nature of a being represents the kind or species of being that it is, while the person represents the acting subject, the individual who is responsible for the being's actions. These concepts were applied to the understanding not only of the divine, but also of human beings.

One of the noteworthy achievements of Christian thought was the philosophical elucidation of the concept of God, carried out especially by St Thomas Aquinas (1224–74). Making use of conceptions developed by Aristotle, Aquinas concluded that God is Pure Actuality, without trace of potentiality, Pure Being, without any element of becoming. Aquinas insisted that there can be no hostility between religion and reason; true religion must be reasonable, because the same God created both. In defense of this view he developed the theory of the Analogy of Being, which explains how it is possible for our human minds and conceptions, which are limited, to attain some knowledge of God by reason. When we say that God is good, for example, there is an infinite gap between God's goodness and anything we can possibly mean by "goodness" on the basis of our limited human experience, and so the word "good" used of God cannot mean precisely what we normally mean by it; yet nonetheless the statement can be meaningful and true because there is an analogy between our meaning and the reality of God. In other words, there can be only one universe: the finite and the infinite do not exist in separate worlds but necessarily stand in some relation.

Christianity and the problem of evil

Our sense of the meaningfulness of life is threatened fundamentally by our experience of evil. This is of two general kinds, physical and moral. On the one hand human beings, like the rest of the animal world, are condemned by the course of nature to eventual death, and often to extremes of suffering during their lives, as the result of illness and accident. On the other, they inflict harm and death on one another, often without cause. If there was a God both all-good and all-powerful, it is often objected, he would not permit this state of affairs, for he would have both the desire and the power to prevent it.

In response to this, Christian theologians have argued that we cannot rule out the possibility that God might have a reason which we do not comprehend for allowing evil, and they have pointed out that faith in a life after death holds out the hope that justice will finally be done. In addition to these lines of reasoning, Christianity offers what might perhaps be called an existential response to the problem, in its conception of the suffering God. The God who made the world, and who by nature was far above all experience of evil, nonetheless, out of love for mankind, took on himself the full burden of human existence, and with it suffering and death. While this does not perhaps solve the problem philosophically, Christians feel that it sets it in a new light.

Purgatory and prayers for the dead

Through Christ God offers us the grace necessary to attain salvation. Whether we accept that grace, however, depends on us. A person who accepts God's grace and leads a good life will acquire merit before God, and will deserve to enter heaven, while one who rejects God's grace and leads an evil life will deserve the eternal punishment of hell. Between the saint, so devoted to God that he enters heaven immediately after death, and the person who deserves hell, there are many who deserve neither the one nor the other. The souls of these at death will enter temporarily an in-between state known as Purgatory, in which they will experience sufferings designed to expiate their guilt, and after a time, when they have been sufficiently purified, they will enter heaven.

On the basis of this doctrine it is possible for the living to help the dead by their prayers. The living can intercede with God to have pity on the souls in Purgatory, and even offer their own present sufferings and merits in this life so that the dead may be released the sooner from their sins. The chief form that this intercession for the dead takes is the offering of the sacrifice of the Eucharist or Mass on their behalf.

The split between East and West

By the end of the third century the Roman Empire had become too big for one emperor to manage. The Emperor Diocletian split it into two: an eastern half, which included Greece, Asia Minor, Palestine, and Egypt, where the predominant language was Greek; and a western half, which included Italy, Spain, and Gaul, where the predominant language was Latin. This political division had a far-reaching effect on the Christian Church.

Gradually the two halves of the Church began to drift apart. Although nominally united, significant differences developed between them. The church in the Eastern Empire came to be more closely identified with the state, becoming in effect a department of the imperial government, a system which has been called Caesaro-papism, where the emperor was practically the head of the Church. In the West the Church retained its independence.

Especially, the Eastern Church had a different conception of the government of the church. It maintained the earlier arrangement of the collegiality of the bishops. While it honored the Bishop of Rome as the chief bishop, it considered his authority to be limited to his own region, and it looked to the Patriarch of Constantinople as its leader. The Western Church, on the other hand, came to attribute to the Bishop of Rome more and more authority. Eventually, in 1054, the two churches excommunicated one another. The Eastern Church is now referred to as the Orthodox Church, the Western Church as the (Roman) Catholic Church.

Although there are many minor differences of spirit and emphasis, the two churches teach essentially the same doctrines. Both adhere to the seven sacraments and to the Nicene Creed (with the exception of one phrase about the

Holy Spirit). The worship of both centers on the Eucharist. The decisive differences are in organization and authority. The split between them is not termed heresy, but schism.

The Germanic tribes and the Middle Ages

Roman Christianity contained elements which emphasized both the merit of the individual and the unmerited grace of God. It could be described as holding a balance between saviorist and pelagian tendencies. In the course of the fourth and fifth centuries, however, the Western Roman Empire collapsed. Northern Europe was inhabited by Germanic tribes, many of whom migrated into the Roman territories, took over the reins of power, and became Christians. This admixture of Germanic culture changed the character of Western Christianity profoundly.

One effect was to emphasize even more strongly the sacramental aspects of Christianity. In addition to the seven Sacraments properly so called, many other rituals of a quasi-sacramental nature, called "sacramentals," were added, such as the veneration of relics, pilgrimages to distant shrines, and the practice of indulgences. (An indulgence is a promise that, in return for certain prayers or good deeds, God will lessen the punishment inflicted after death.) The general effect of this was to give a greater role in the Christian life to the virtuous actions and the merit of the individual, rather than the unmerited grace and mercy of God. In medieval Christianity pelagian tendencies became more manifest.

The Reformation: Luther and Calvin

In 1517 Martin Luther (1483–1546) raised the standard of protest against this development. Inaugurating a movement which was to sweep through northern Europe, he cast off the authority of the Catholic Church. Individuals before him who had attempted to do that had run afoul of the political power of the Catholic Church and typically lost their lives, but Luther succeeded in obtaining the support of a German prince, who protected him. John Calvin (1509–64) developed a related viewpoint in a more systematic fashion, making explicit some assumptions which Luther had made tacitly. Calvin was able to convert the independent Swiss city of Geneva to his views, which gave him the political protection he needed. While there are important differences between the two on secondary matters, their main doctrines are very similar, and amount essentially to a strict interpretation of the faith that it is God who saves us, and not we ourselves.

Salvation by grace alone   We are saved, not by our own actions, however virtuous, nor by the actions of other men, such as the priests of the Church, but only by the grace and mercy of God, which is entirely undeserved. Human beings contribute nothing to their own salvation. This view involves a doctrine of predestination: since the decision as to whether a particular individual will be saved or damned rests entirely with God, and in no way depends on the individual's behavior, his fate must have been decided even before he was born.

Nature and reason are corrupt   No human activity can be of help toward salvation because human nature has been corrupted by Adam's sin. In consequence of this corruption, every human being is condemned by God as a sinner. The corruption extends not only to our moral character but also to our reason, which is of no avail for salvation. Whereas the Catholic tradition has assumed, for example, that we could know through rational argument that God exists, the view of the Reformers was that this is impossible. We can come to know God effectively only through his revelation of himself to us.

The grace of God comes only through Jesus Christ   Because of the incarnation, death, and resurrection of the Son of God, God overlooks the corruption men have inherited from Adam, forgives the sin of those destined for salvation, and bestows righteousness on them. Jesus Christ, and he alone, is the savior of mankind.

Salvation by faith alone   The grace or mercy of God is given to the individual through faith. Our first obligation is to believe in God's mercy. Having faith in God means, for the Reformers, in the first place having confidence in his compassion, and only secondarily signifies an intellectual assent to the doctrines of Christianity – which is what it primarily means for the Catholic tradition.

Certainty of salvation   According to Catholic doctrine, we can never be certain in this life that we will attain salvation, since it is always possible for us to reject God's grace, and to sin. According to Luther and Calvin, by contrast, we cannot reject God's grace once it is given, otherwise God would not be sovereign. While only God knows with certainty who has been destined for salvation and who for damnation, there are powerful signs or indications available to us that we have been saved. The first of these is that we have faith in Christ. Later Puritans saw other signs in the blessings of God bestowed in this life.

Reduction of the sacramental system   The Reformers abolished all sacramentals, because of their pelagian character, and five of the seven sacraments, keeping only the two explicitly mentioned in the New Testament: baptism and the Eucharist. These are effective only through faith.

Different understanding of the church   The church is not the intermediary between God and man, but only the association of those who believe. It exists wherever the word of God is preached sincerely and the sacraments are duly administered. Consequently the church does not possess any absolute authority. The word of God comes to us authoritatively from the Bible, not from the Church.

In principle the Reformers believed in the right of the individual to interpret the Bible as his or her own conscience dictates, but they assumed that all men of

337

good faith would agree with the Reformers, and were extremely distressed to find that this was not the case. The Reformers' doctrine of the right of private interpretation of the Bible made possible the multitude of divisions that have since taken place within Protestant Christianity.

Virtue the consequence of being saved In the view of Catholic and Orthodox Christianity, whether or not a person is saved depends on the kind of life he lives. The Reformers rejected this view. Instead they taught that if a person leads a good life, that is a sign and consequence of the fact that God has decreed his salvation and granted him faith. God does not save us because of our good deeds; instead, he saves us first, which in turn leads us to follow his commandments. For the Catholic, salvation takes place only at death; for Luther and Calvin, however, it takes place essentially during life, though it does not reach completion till death.

The elimination of prayers for the dead Since our salvation is entirely the work of God's grace, and owes nothing whatsoever to human achievements, there is no place for a doctrine of Purgatory, that intermediate state of purification into which, according to Catholic doctrine, the soul enters when it has merited neither heaven nor hell. In the view of the Reformers the individual is either saved or not saved, either chosen by God or not chosen. At death, then, the soul must immediately enter either heaven or hell. Thus there is nothing to be gained by praying for the dead.

The Reformation Churches

In general, the spirit of the Churches of the Reformation is to emphasize the direct relationship of the individual to God, and to eliminate whatever is not strictly necessary to that. The churches that follow Luther (usually called Lutheran or Evangelical) tend to remain somewhat closer to the Catholic tradition, for example, in retaining the office of bishop, and the use of altars, ritual, and pictures, while those that follow Calvin (such as Presbyterians and Congregationalists) tend to be further removed from Catholicism, for example, in having churches bare of all ornament.

In general, the Reformation Churches tend to have more democratic forms of government than the Catholic Church. In the Presbyterian form of government, the supreme authority lies with the presbytery, or assembly of ministers, the ministers themselves being elected by the people. In the Congregational form of government, each local congregation is essentially independent. The Lutheran churches tend to leave more to the local congregation, while retaining an important role for a central government.

Between the Roman Catholic Church and the Churches of the Reformation stands the Church of England, or the Anglican Church, which contains elements of both. Initially, in the reign of Henry VIII, the main question in England was not the reformation of the church in its doctrines or sacramental life, but the

An Anglican priest taking wine at the Eucharist (John Smith/Circa Photo Library)

authority of the Pope. Henry rejected the Pope's authority in England, declaring the monarch to be the head of the English church, but otherwise leaving the church's doctrines unaffected. Although subsequently the Church of England has moved much further in some respects towards the position of the Reformers, especially Calvin, it still retains much of its Catholic inheritance, and has never given up the claim to maintain the Apostolic Succession. Sister churches of the Church of England exist in many countries around the globe, united in the Anglican Communion. In the United States it is represented by the Episcopal Church.

During the eighteenth century, under the leadership of John Wesley, a movement developed within the Church of England which emphasized personal religious experience and man's freedom to respond to God's call, over against the Calvinist doctrine of predestination. This came to be known as Methodism. Eventually it separated from the Church of England and became independent. The Methodist Churches tend to have a centralized form of government, with bishops. In the United States they have been exceptionally active in establishing charitable institutions such as hospitals and homes for children.

In addition to the Reformation Churches, which followed Luther and Calvin, and the Church of England and Methodists, numerous other more radical movements and churches emerged, which believed in a much more extensive right of the individual to follow his own judgement in matters of religion. These include the Anabaptists, the Church of the Brethren or Mennonites (after Menno Simons, an early leader), the Baptists, the Society of Friends, and many others. Churches of this sort have played an especially prominent role in the United States.

Christian Ethics

Christian ethics takes its inspiration above all from the figure on the cross. All Christians look to the Bible, both the Old Testament (for example, the Ten Commandments) and especially the New, the example and teaching of Jesus and the Apostles, for guidance in questions of behavior towards others. The force of the New Testament in ethics is to emphasize the primacy of love and compassion. Beyond that, there are some important differences between Catholics and Protestants.

Catholicism has traditionally placed as much emphasis, if not more, on the tradition of the Church, and that tradition has from early times included an important role for the concept of natural law, as developed in ancient Greek and Roman thought. The doctrine of natural law means that moral values, such as justice, for example, exist in "nature," that is, they have an objective reality, and can be discovered by the right use of reason. Reason thus has a role independent of revelation in ascertaining what is right and wrong. One consequence of this approach has been the acceptance of justice as in certain ways more fundamental than love, and the development of such things as the theory of a just war: under certain specified conditions, such as self-defense, war can be morally justified, but only if those conditions are fulfilled.

The Protestant approach to ethics has been diverse. Luther taught that conscience is always subject to the authority of scripture, but also allowed the possibility of knowing right, and especially wrong, by reason. In his treatise *Whether Soldiers, Too, Can Be Saved*, as well as in later writings on war with the Turks, he develops elements of a just war theory, arguing that a defensive war can be just, otherwise the punishment of criminals would be unjust.

John Calvin also taught that moral right and wrong can be known by reason, and some, such as the Anglican Richard Hooker, taught a doctrine of natural law. The more radical strands of the Protestant tradition tend to draw their ethics entirely from the Bible, and this has not infrequently led them to pacifism.

In modern times Christian ethics has been influenced by the conception of social justice, about which more below.

Modern Developments

It was in the Christian West that science first developed, and it has been expecially Christianity that has felt its intellectual impact. The effect of the rise and success of science has been to cast the shadow of doubt on all beliefs that cannot be established by empirical investigation. This includes, of course, belief in the existence of God, the resurrection of Christ and miracles generally, divine revelation, and life after death. While this doubt was implicit in scientific method from the beginning, it acquired particular force from Darwin's theory of evolution by natural selection, which appears to rule out any need for a supernatural explanation of human existence.

One response to this has been the emergence of Liberal Christianity. Liberal Christians typically support Christianity not as a divine revelation, but because of its moral vision, which if implemented would lead to a profound improvement in human life. Liberal Christianity may keep the traditional Christian liturgy, including the creeds, but allows them to be understood in a symbolic rather than a literal sense. In Liberal Christianity moral concern is typically at the forefront.

Liberal Christianity has achieved a large measure of acceptance in much of the Anglican church and in certain Protestant churches. The Catholic and Orthodox branches of Christianity, as well as conservative Protestants, on the other hand, reject it.

Not unrelated to Liberal Christianity was the emergence of the movement for social justice, which has come to play a large role in the ethical thinking of many Christians. The industrial revolution, which took place towards the end of the eighteenth century in Great Britain, and during the following century in the rest of Europe and the United States, produced a new social class, the working class. Since the new factories were initially few in number, while the pool of workers desiring employment in them was extremely large, wages and working conditions were at first very low, and the inequality between the living standards of the working class and their employers was only too clear to many observers. One response to this situation was the development of the concept of social justice, which views societal inequality not merely as a fact, or even a regrettable fact, but as injustice. In time, as more factories were built and more competition developed for the services of the working class, the inequality would arguably have diminished through the natural operation of the market. Those who argued for social justice, however, found the inequality intolerable in principle and demanded that government take responsibility for eliminating it.

The concept of social justice differs in important ways from traditional conceptions of justice. Traditionally justice and injustice were considered to be features of actions performed by individuals, and therefore involving individual responsibility. The new concept of social justice attributes justice and injustice instead to states of affairs, namely equality or inequality, independent of individual responsibility. Not individuals, but society, is therefore considered responsible for remedying societal inequality. It is not perhaps entirely clear how this can be harmonized with traditional ethical conceptions.

Originally applied to the inequalities between the working and employer classes, the concept of social justice has been extended, under the name of civil rights, to other kinds of inequality, such as those between races, between the

341

sexes, between the generations, or between the hale and the handicapped. Many Christians and Christian churches have now come to view this conception as demanded by Christian principles, though others are more reserved.

Some aspects of social justice, and its relation to socialism and American liberalism, are discussed above, in the chapter on Judaism.

At the same time as these liberalizing tendencies have been at work in Western Christianity, however, movements have also developed in the opposite direction. On the one hand, the more Liberal Christian churches have witnessed a marked decline in membership, while more conservative ones have grown. Among these are the Evangelical churches, which tend to accept the Bible in its literal sense as the word of God, and Pentecostal movements, which take their inspiration from the descriptions in the New Testament of believers speaking in tongues (see Acts 2: 4–12). On the other hand, the Christian churches in the less developed countries, such as those of Africa and Latin America, which tend to be strictly traditional, have experienced remarkable growth, so that there are now more Christians there than in the original Christian nations. At present, therefore, if we view the picture globally, conservative Christians appear to outnumber liberals by a wide margin.

Conclusion

Christianity has inspired an immense body of poetry, including such works as Dante's *Divine Comedy* and Milton's *Paradise Lost*. Here we conclude with a poem by Emily Brontë which expresses the Christian's confidence in God:

> O God within my breast,
> Almighty, ever-present Deity!
> Life – that in me has rest,
> As I – undying Life – have power in Thee!
>
> Vain are the thousand creeds
> That move men's hearts – unutterably vain;
> Worthless as withered reeds,
> Or idlest froth amid the boundless main,
>
> To waken doubt in one
> Holding so fast by Thine infinity;
> So surely anchored on
> The steadfast rock of immortality.
>
> With wide-embracing love
> Thy spirit animates eternal years,
> Pervades and broods above,
> Changes, sustains, dissolves, creates, and rears.

Though earth and man were gone,
And suns and universes ceased to be,
And Thou were left alone,
Every existence would exist in Thee.

There is not room for Death,
Nor atom that his might could render void;
Thou – Thou art Being and Breath,
And what Thou art may never be destroyed.

Summary of Christianity

1 According to the New Testament Jesus preached that:

(a) The Jewish Law was fully kept by loving God and one's fellow-man.

(b) Jesus' teachings inaugurate the kingdom of God on earth, the invisible realm where God's will is obeyed.

(c) To enter it men must repent of their sins and forgive others their offenses.

(d) After death there is a judgement, and there will be a resurrection of the dead.

(e) Jesus will return, bringing the present era to an end, and making the kingdom of God visible and triumphant.

2 Paul preached that:

(a) The human race is thoroughly sinful, having inherited sin from Adam, and so all men are condemned in God's sight.

(b) Jesus has saved mankind from sin and restored man's relationship to God through his death and resurrection.

(c) To become a Christian is to participate in Jesus' death, resurrection, and eternal life. Through faith in Christ we share in his life, which overcomes both the spiritual death of sin, and also the physical death of the body.

Questions for discussion

1 What relationship do you see between Jesus' message and present-day Christianity?

2 Is Paul's message necessarily at odds with Jesus' message?

3 What is your opinion about miracles? Does Christianity depend on belief in them?

Test questions

1 What were the main elements in Jesus' message?

2 What were the main elements in Paul's message?

3 Explain what is meant by the doctrine of the Incarnation.

4 Explain what is meant by the doctrine of the Trinity.

5 Explain what is meant by the sacramental system.

6 What were the goals of the Reformers, Martin Luther and John Calvin?

Additional reading

Bornkamm, Guenther, *Jesus of Nazareth*, New York, Harper, 1960.

Gascoigne, Bamber, *The Christians*, New York, Morrow, 1977.

Kee, Howard Clark, *Jesus in History: An Approach to the Study of the Gospels*, New York, Harcourt, 1970.

Latourette, Kenneth Scott, *A History of Christianity*, New York, Harper, 1975.

Lohse, Bernhard, *Martin Luther: An Introduction to his Life and Work*, Philadelphia, Fortress, 1986.

McGrath, Alister E., *Christian Theology: An Introduction*, Oxford, Blackwell, 1994.

Ratzinger, Joseph, *Introduction to Christianity*, New York, Herder, 1970. A Catholic perspective.

Von Balthasar, Hans Urs, *Who is a Christian?* London, Burns & Oates, 1968. A Catholic perspective.

Weaver, Mary Joe, *Introduction to Christianity*, Belmont, CA, Wadsworth, 1984.

Wendel, François. *Calvin*, London, Collins, 1963.

Wiggins, James B. and Ellwood, Robert S., *Christianity: A Cultural Perspective*, Englewood Cliffs, NJ, Prentice Hall, 1988.

Christianity: Texts

While the Christian scriptures include the Old Testament, and it has played a prominent part especially in Reformed Christianity, the selections given here are all from the New Testament, source portions of the Old Testament have been included in the chapter on Judaism.

The Sermon on the Mount

Although it is presented by Matthew for expository purposes as if it were a single sermon, scholars are agreed that this is a compilation of utterances made by Jesus on several different occasions. Portions of the sermon already included in the text of the chapter above are omitted here.

When he saw the crowds he went up the hill. There he took his seat, and when his disciples had gathered round him he began to address them. And this is the teaching he gave:

> "How blest are those who know that they are poor;
>   the kingdom of Heaven is theirs.
> How blest are the sorrowful;
>   they shall find consolation.
> How blest are those of a gentle spirit;
>   they shall have the earth for their possession.
> How blest are those who hunger and thirst to see right prevail;
>   they shall be satisfied.

> How blest are those who show mercy;
>> mercy shall be shown to them.
> How blest are those whose hearts are pure;
>> they shall see God.
> How blest are the peacemakers;
>> God shall call them his sons.
> How blest are those who have suffered persecution for the cause of right;
>> the kingdom of Heaven is theirs.

"How blest you are, when you suffer insults and persecution and every kind of calumny for my sake. Accept it with gladness and exultation, for you have a rich reward in heaven; in the same way they persecuted the prophets before you.

"You are salt to the world. And if salt becomes tasteless, how is its saltness to be restored? It is now good for nothing but to be thrown away and trodden underfoot.

"You are light for all the world. A town that stands on a hill cannot be hidden. When a lamp is lit, it is not put under the meal-tub, but on the lamp-stand, where it gives light to everyone in the house. And you, like the lamp, must shed light among your fellows, so that, when they see the good you do, they may give praise to your Father in heaven . . .

"If, when you are bringing your gift to the altar, you suddenly remember that your brother has a grievance against you, leave your gift where it is before the altar. First go and make your peace with your brother, and only then come back and offer your gift.

"If someone sues you, come to terms with him promptly while you are both on your way to court; otherwise he may hand you over to the judge, and the judge to the constable, and you will be put in jail. I tell you, once you are there you will not be let out till you have paid the last farthing . . .

"If your right eye leads you astray, tear it out and fling it away; it is better for you to lose one part of your body than for the whole of it to be thrown into hell. And if your right hand is your undoing, cut it off and fling it away; it is better for you to lose one part of your body than for the whole of it to go to hell.

"They were told, 'A man who divorces his wife must give her a note of dismissal.' But what I tell you is this: If a man divorces his wife for any cause other than unchastity he involves her in adultery; and anyone who marries a woman so divorced commits adultery.

"Again, you have learned that they were told, 'Do not break your oath,' and, 'Oaths sworn to the Lord must be kept.' But what I tell you is this: You are not to swear at all – not by heaven, for it is God's throne, nor by earth, for it is his footstool, nor by Jerusalem, for it is the city of the great King, nor by your own head, because you cannot turn one hair of it white or black. Plain 'Yes' or 'No' is all you need to say; anything beyond that comes from the devil.

"You have learned that they were told, 'An eye for an eye, and a tooth for a tooth.' But what I tell you is this: Do not set yourself against the man who wrongs you. If someone slaps you on the right cheek, turn and offer him your left. If a man wants to sue you for your shirt, let him have your coat as well. If a man in authority makes you go one mile, go with him two. Give when you are asked to give; and do not turn your back on a man who wants to borrow.

"You have learned that they were told, 'Love your neighbour, hate your enemy.' But what I tell you is this: Love your enemies and pray for your persecutors; only so can you be children of your heavenly Father, who makes his sun rise on good and bad alike, and sends the rain on the honest and the dishonest. If you love only those who love you, what reward can you expect? Surely the tax-gatherers do as much as that. And if you greet only your brothers, what is there extraordinary about that? Even the heathen do as much. You must therefore be all goodness, just as your heavenly Father is all good.

"Be careful not to make a show of your religion before men; if you do, no reward awaits you in your Father's house in heaven.

"Thus, when you do some act of charity, do not announce it with a flourish of trumpets, as the hypocrites do in synagogue and in the streets to win admiration from men. I tell you this: they have their reward already. No; when you do some act of charity, do not let your left hand know what your right is doing; your good deed must be secret, and your Father who sees what is done in secret will reward you.

"Again, when you pray, do not be like the hypocrites; they love to say their prayers standing up in synagogue and at the street-corners, for everyone to see them. I tell you this: they have their reward already. But when you pray, go into a room by yourself, shut the door, and pray to your Father who is there in the secret place; and your Father who sees what is secret will reward you.

"In your prayers do not go babbling on like the heathen, who imagine that the more they say the more likely they are to be heard. Do not imitate them. Your Father knows what your needs are before you ask him.

"This is how you should pray:

> Our Father in heaven,
> Thy name be hallowed;
> Thy kingdom come,
> Thy will be done,
> On earth as in heaven.
> Give us today our daily bread.
> Forgive us the wrong we have done,
> As we have forgiven those who have wronged us.
> And do not bring us to the test,
> But save us from the evil one.

For if you forgive others the wrongs they have done, your heavenly Father will also forgive you; but if you do not forgive others, then the wrongs you have done will not be forgiven by your Father.

"So too when you fast, do not look gloomy like the hypocrites; they make their faces unsightly so that other people may see that they are fasting. I tell you this: they have their reward already. But when you fast, anoint your head and wash your face, so that men may not see that you are fasting, but only your Father who is in the secret place; and your Father who sees what is secret will give you your reward.

"Do not store up for yourselves treasure on earth, where it grows rusty and moth-eaten, and thieves break in to steal it. Store up treasure in heaven, where there is no moth and no rust to spoil it, no thieves to break in and steal. For where your wealth is, there will your heart be also.

"The lamp of the body is the eye. If your eyes are sound, you will have light for your whole body; if the eyes are bad, your whole body will be in darkness. If then the only light you have is darkness, the darkness is doubly dark.

"No servant can be slave to two masters; for either he will hate the first and love the second, or he will be devoted to the first and think nothing of the second. You cannot serve God and Money.

"Therefore I bid you put away anxious thoughts about food and drink to keep you alive, and clothes to cover your body. Surely life is more than food, the body more than clothes. Look at the birds of the air; they do not sow and reap and store in barns, yet your heavenly Father feeds them. You are worth more than the birds! Is there a man of you who by anxious thought can add a foot to his height? And why be anxious about clothes? Consider how the lilies grow in the fields; they do not work, they do not spin; and yet, I tell you, even Solomon in all his splendour was not attired like one of these. But if that is how God clothes the grass in the fields, which is there today, and tomorrow is thrown on the stove, will he not all the more clothe you? How little faith you have! No, do not ask anxiously, "What are we to eat? What are we to drink? What shall we wear?" All these things are for the heathen to run after, not for you, because your heavenly Father knows that you need them all. Set your mind on God's kingdom and his justice before everything else, and all the rest will come to you as well. So do not be anxious about tomorrow; tomorrow will look after itself. Each day has troubles enough of its own.

"Pass no judgement, and you will not be judged. For as you judge others, so you will yourselves be judged, and whatever measure you deal out to others will be dealt back to you. Why do you look at the speck of sawdust in your brother's eye, with never a thought for the great plank in your own? Or how can you say to your brother, 'Let me take the speck out of your eye,' when all the time there is that plank in your own? You hypocrite! First take the plank out of your own eye, and then you will see clearly to take the speck out of your brother's.

"Do not give dogs what is holy; do not feed your pearls to pigs: they will only trample on them, and turn and tear you to pieces.

"Ask, and you will receive; seek, and you will find; knock, and the door will be opened. For everyone who asks receives, he who seeks finds, and to him who knocks, the door will be opened.

"Is there a man among you who will offer his son a stone when he asks for bread, or a snake when he asks for fish? If you, then, bad as you are, know how to give your children what is good for them, how much more will your heavenly Father give good things to those who ask him!

348

"Always treat others as you would like them to treat you: that is the Law and the prophets.

"Enter by the narrow gate. The gate is wide that leads to perdition, there is plenty of room on the road, and many go that way; but the gate that leads to life is small and the road is narrow, and those who find it are few.

"Beware of false prophets, men who come to you dressed up as sheep while underneath they are savage wolves. You will recognize them by the fruits they bear. Can grapes be picked from briars, or figs from thistles? In the same way, a good tree always yields good fruit, and a poor tree bad fruit. A good tree cannot bear bad fruit, or a poor tree good fruit. And when a tree does not yield good fruit it is cut down and burnt. That is why I say you will recognize them by their fruits.

"Not everyone who calls me 'Lord, Lord' will enter the kingdom of Heaven, but only those who do the will of my heavenly Father. When that day comes, many will say to me, 'Lord, Lord, did we not prophesy in your name, cast out devils in your name, and in your name perform many miracles?' Then I will tell them to their face, 'I never knew you: out of my sight, you and your wicked ways!'

"What then of the man who hears these words of mine and acts upon them? He is like a man who had the sense to build his house on rock. The rain came down, the floods rose, the wind blew, and beat upon that house; but it did not fall, because its foundations were on rock. But what of the man who hears these words of mine and does not act upon them? He is like a man who was foolish enough to build his house on sand. The rain came down, the floods rose, the wind blew, and beat upon that house; down it fell with a great crash."

When Jesus had finished this discourse the people were astounded at his teaching; unlike their own teachers he taught with a note of authority.

(Matthew 5: 1–7: 29, *The New English Bible with the Apocrypha*, Oxford, Oxford University Press, 1971)

The Good Samaritan

On one occasion a lawyer came forward to put this test question to him: "Master, what must I do to inherit eternal life?"

Jesus said, "What is written in the Law? What is your reading of it?"

He replied, "Love the Lord your God with all your heart, with all your soul, with all your strength, and with all your mind; and your neighbour as yourself."

"That is the right answer," said Jesus; "do that and you will live."

But he wanted to vindicate himself, so he said to Jesus, "And who is my neighbour?"

Jesus replied, "A man was on his way from Jerusalem to Jericho when he fell in with robbers, who stripped him, beat him, and went off leaving him half dead. It so happened that a priest was going down by the same road; but when he saw him, he went past on the other side. So too a Levite came to the place, and when he saw him went past on the other side. But a Samaritan who was making the journey came upon him, and when he saw him was moved to pity. He went up and bandaged his wounds, bathing them with oil and wine. Then he lifted him onto his own beast, brought him to an inn, and looked after him there. Next day he produced two silver pieces and gave them to the inn-keeper, and said, 'Look after him; and if you spend any more, I will repay you on my way back.' Which of these three do you think was neighbour to the man who fell into the hands of the robbers?" He answered, "The one who showed him kindness." Jesus said, "Go and do as he did."

(Luke 10: 25–37)

The Prodigal Son

Another time, the tax-gatherers and other bad characters were all crowding in to listen to [Jesus]; and the Pharisees and the doctors of the law began grumbling among themselves: "This fellow," they said, "welcomes sinners and eats with them." He answered them . . . :

"There was once a man who had two sons; and the younger said to his father, 'Father, give me my share of the property.' So he divided his estate between them. A few days later the younger son turned the whole of his share into cash and left home for a distant country, where he squandered it in reckless living. He had spent it all, when a severe famine fell upon that country and he began to feel the pinch. So he went and attached himself to one of the local landowners, who sent him onto his farm to mind the pigs. He would have been glad to fill his belly with the pods that the pigs were eating; and no one gave him anything. Then he came to his senses and said, 'How many of my father's paid servants have more food than they can eat, and here am I, starving to death! I will set off and go to my father, and say to him, "Father, I have sinned, against God and against you; I am no longer fit to be called your son; treat me as one of your paid servants."' So he set out for his father's house. But while he was still a long way off his father saw him, and his heart went out to him. He ran to meet him, flung his arms round him, and kissed him. The son said, 'Father, I have sinned, against God and against you; I am no longer fit to be called your son.' But the father said to his servants, 'Quick! fetch a robe, my best one, and put it on him; put a ring on his finger and shoes on his feet. Bring the fatted calf and kill it, and let us have a feast to celebrate the day. For this son of mine was dead and has come back to life; he was lost and is found.' And the festivities began.

"Now the elder son was out on the farm; and on his way back, as he approached the house, he heard music and dancing. He called one of the servants and asked what it meant. The servant told him, 'Your brother has come home, and your father has killed the fatted calf because he has him back safe and sound.' But he was angry and refused to go in. His father came out and pleaded with him; but he retorted, 'You know how I have slaved for you all these years; I never once disobeyed your orders; and you never gave me so much as a kid, for a feast with my friends. But now that this son of yours turns up, after running through your money with his women, you kill the fatted calf for him.'

"'My boy,' said the father, 'you are always with me, and everything I have is yours. How could we help celebrating this happy day? Your brother here was dead and has come back to life, was lost and is found.'"

(Luke 15: 1–32)

The Gospel according to John

The Gospel of John presents Jesus in terms of dramatic images reflecting his role as savior: Jesus is the bread of life, the light of the world, the good shepherd, the life of the world.

The bread of life

Some time later Jesus withdrew to the farther shore of the Sea of Galilee (or Tiberias), and a large crowd of people followed who had seen the signs he performed in healing the sick. Then Jesus went up the hill-side and sat down with his disciples. It was near the time of Passover, the great Jewish festival. Raising his eyes and seeing a large crowd coming towards him, Jesus said to Philip, "Where are we to buy bread to feed these people?" This he said to test him; Jesus himself knew what he meant to do. Philip replied, "Twenty pounds would not buy enough bread for every one of them to have a little." One of his disciples, Andrew, the brother of Simon Peter, said to him, "There is a boy here who has five barley loaves and two fishes; but what is that among so many?" Jesus said, "Make the people sit down." There was plenty of grass there, so the men sat down, about five thousand of them. Then Jesus took the loaves, gave thanks, and distributed them to the people as they sat there. He did the same with the fishes, and they had as much as they wanted. When everyone had had enough, he said to his disciples, "Collect the pieces left over, so that nothing may be lost." This they did, and filled twelve baskets with the pieces left uneaten of the five barley loaves.

When the people saw the sign Jesus had performed, the word went round, "Surely this must be the prophet that was to come into the world." Jesus, aware that they meant to come and seize him to proclaim him king, withdrew again to the hills by himself.

At nightfall his disciples went down to the sea, got into their boat, and pushed off to cross the water to Capernaum. Darkness had already fallen, and Jesus had not yet joined them. By now a strong wind was blowing and the sea grew rough. When they had rowed about three or four miles they saw Jesus walking on the sea and approaching the boat. They were terrified, but he called out, "It is I; do not be afraid." Then they were ready to take him aboard, and immediately the boat reached the land they were making for.

Next morning the crowd was standing on the opposite shore. They had seen only one boat there, and Jesus, they knew, had not embarked with his disciples, who had gone away without him. Boats from Tiberias, however, came ashore near the place where the people had eaten the bread over which the Lord gave thanks. When the people saw that neither Jesus nor his disciples were any longer there, they themselves went aboard these boats and made for Capernaum in search of Jesus. They found him on the other side. "Rabbi," they said, "When did you come here?" Jesus replied, "In very truth I know that you have come looking for me because your hunger was satisfied with the loaves you ate, not because you saw signs. You must work, not for this perishable food, but for the food that lasts, the food of eternal life.

"This food the Son of Man will give you, for he it is upon whom the Father has set the seal of his authority." "Then what must we do," they asked him, "if we are to work as God would have us work?" Jesus replied, "This is the work that God requires: believe in the one whom he has sent."

They said, "What sign can you give us to see, so that we may believe you? What is the work you do? Our ancestors had manna to eat in the desert; as Scripture says, 'He gave them bread from heaven to eat.'" Jesus answered, "I tell you this: the truth is, not that Moses gave you the bread from heaven, but that my Father gives you the real bread from heaven. The bread that God gives comes down from heaven and brings life to the world." They said to him, "Sir, give us this bread now and always." Jesus said to them, "I am the bread of life. Whoever comes to me shall never be hungry, and whoever believes in me shall never be thirsty. But you, as I said, do not believe although you have seen. All that the Father gives me will come to me, and the man who comes to me I will never turn away. I have come down from heaven, not to do my own will, but the will of him who sent me. It is his will that I should not lose even one of all that he has given me, but raise them all up on the last day. For it is my Father's will that everyone who looks upon the Son and puts his faith in him shall possess eternal life; and I will raise him up on the last day."

At this the Jews began to murmur disapprovingly because he said, "I am the bread which came down from heaven." They said, "Surely this is Jesus son of Joseph; we know his father and mother. How can he now say, 'I have come down from heaven?'" Jesus answered, "Stop murmuring among yourselves. No man can come to me unless he is drawn by the Father who sent me; and I will raise him up on the last day. It is written in the prophets: 'And they shall all be taught by God.' Everyone who has listened to the Father and learned from him comes to me.

"I do not mean that anyone has seen the Father. He who has come from God has seen the Father, and he alone. In truth, in very truth I tell you, the believer possesses eternal life. I am the bread of life. Your forefathers ate the manna in the desert and they are dead. I am speaking of the bread that comes down from heaven, which a man may eat, and never die. I am that living bread which has come down from heaven: if anyone eats this bread he shall live for ever. Moreover, the bread which I will give is my own flesh; I give it for the life of the world."

This led to a fierce dispute among the Jews. "How can this man give us his flesh to eat?" they said. Jesus replied, "In truth, in very truth I tell you, unless you eat the flesh of the Son of Man and drink his blood you can have no life in you. Whoever eats my flesh and drinks my blood possesses eternal life, and I will raise him up on the last day. My flesh is real food; my blood is real drink. Whoever eats my flesh and drinks my blood dwells continually in me and I dwell in him. As the living Father sent me, and I live because of the Father, so he who eats me shall live because of me. This is the bread which came down from heaven; and it is not like the bread which our fathers ate: they are dead, but whoever eats this bread shall live for ever."

(John 6: 1–58)

The light of the world

As he went on his way Jesus saw a man blind from his birth. His disciples put the question, "Rabbi, who sinned, this man or his parents? Why was he born blind?" "It is not that this man or his parents sinned," Jesus answered; "he was born blind that God's power might be displayed in curing him. While daylight lasts we must carry on the work of him who sent me; night comes, when no one can work. While I am in the world I am the light of the world."

With these words he spat on the ground and made a paste with the spittle; he spread it on the man's eyes, and said to him, "Go and wash in the pool of Siloam." (The name means "sent.") The man went away and washed, and when he returned he could see.

His neighbours and those who were accustomed to see him begging said, "Is not this the man who used to sit and beg?" Others said, "Yes, this is the man." Others again said, "No, but it is someone like him." The man himself said, "I am the man." They asked him, "How were your eyes opened?" He replied, "The man called Jesus made a paste and smeared my eyes with it, and told me to go to Siloam and wash. I went and washed, and gained my sight." "Where is he?" they asked. He answered, "I do not know."

The man who had been blind was brought before the Pharisees. As it was a Sabbath day when Jesus made the paste and opened his eyes, the Pharisees now asked him by what means he had gained his sight. The man told them, "He spread a paste on my eyes; then I washed, and now I can see." Some of the Pharisees said, "This fellow is no man of God; he does not keep the Sabbath." Others said, "How could such signs come from a sinful man?" So they took different sides.

Then they continued to question him: "What have you to say about him? It was your eyes he opened." He answered, "He is a prophet." The Jews would not believe that the man had been blind and had gained his sight, until they had summoned his parents and questioned them: "Is this man your son? Do you say that he was born blind? How is it that he can see now?" The parents replied, "We know that he is our son, and that he was born blind. But how it is that he can now see, or who opened his eyes, we do not know. Ask him; he is of age;

he will speak for himself." His parents gave this answer because they were afraid of the Jews; for the Jewish authorities had already agreed that anyone who acknowledged Jesus as Messiah should be banned from the synagogue. That is why the parents said, "He is of age; ask him."

So for the second time they summoned the man who had been blind, and said, "Speak the truth before God. We know that this fellow is a sinner." "Whether or not he is a sinner, I do not know," the man replied. "All I know is this: once I was blind, now I can see." "What did he do to you?" they asked. "How did he open your eyes?" "I have told you already," he retorted, "but you took no notice. Why do you want to hear it again? Do you also want to become his disciples?" Then they became abusive. "You are that man's disciple," they said, "but we are disciples of Moses. We know that God spoke to Moses, but as for this fellow, we do not know where he comes from."

The man replied, "What an extraordinary thing! Here is a man who has opened my eyes, yet you do not know where he comes from! It is common knowledge that God does not listen to sinners; he listens to anyone who is devout and obeys his will. To open the eyes of a man born blind – it is unheard of since time began. If that man had not come from God he could have done nothing." "Who are you to give us lessons," they retorted, "born and bred in sin as you are?" Then they expelled him from the synagogue.

Jesus heard that they had expelled him. When he found him he asked, "Have you faith in the Son of Man?" The man answered, "Tell me who he is, sir, that I should put my faith in him." "You have seen him," said Jesus; "indeed, it is he who is speaking to you." "Lord, I believe," he said, and bowed before him.

Jesus said, "It is for judgement that I have come into this world – to give sight to the sightless and to make blind those who see." Some Pharisees in his company asked, "Do you mean that we are blind?" "If you were blind," said Jesus, "you would not be guilty, but because you say 'We see,' your guilt remains."

(John 9)

The good shepherd

"In truth I tell you, in very truth, the man who does not enter the sheepfold by the door, but climbs in some other way, is nothing but a thief or a robber. The man who enters by the door is the shepherd in charge of the sheep. The door-keeper admits him, and the sheep hear his voice; he calls his own sheep by name, and leads them out. When he has brought them all out, he goes ahead and the sheep follow, because they know his voice. They will not follow a stranger; they will run away from him, because they do not recognize the voice of strangers."

This was a parable that Jesus told them, but they did not understand what he meant by it.

So Jesus spoke again: "In truth, in very truth I tell you, I am the door of the sheepfold. The sheep paid no heed to any who came before me, for these were all thieves and robbers. I am the door; anyone who comes into the fold through me shall be safe. He shall go in and out and shall find pasturage.

"The thief comes only to steal, to kill, to destroy; I have come that men may have life and may have it in all its fullness. I am the good shepherd; the good shepherd lays down his life for the sheep. The hireling, when he sees the wolf coming, abandons the sheep and runs away, because he is no shepherd and the sheep are not his. Then the wolf harries the flock and scatters the sheep. The man runs away because he is a hireling and cares nothing for the sheep.

"I am the good shepherd; I know my own sheep and my sheep know me – as the Father knows me and I know the Father – and I lay down my life for the sheep. But there are other sheep of mine, not belonging to this fold, whom I must bring in; and they too will listen to my voice. There will then be one flock, one shepherd. "The Father loves me because I lay down my life, to receive it back again. No one has robbed me of it; I am laying it down of my own free will. I have the right to lay it down, and I have the right to receive it back again; this charge I have received from my Father."

These words once again caused a split among the Jews. Many of them said, "He is possessed, he is raving. Why listen to him?" Others said, "No one possessed by an evil spirit could speak like this. Could an evil spirit open blind men's eyes?"

(John 10: 1–21)

The life of the world

There was a man named Lazarus who had fallen ill. His home was at Bethany, the village of Mary and her sister Martha. (This Mary, whose brother Lazarus had fallen ill, was the woman who anointed the Lord with ointment and wiped his feet with her hair.) The sisters sent a message to him: "Sir, you should know that your friend lies ill." When Jesus heard this he said, "This sickness will not end in death; it has come for the glory of God, to bring glory to the Son of God." And therefore, though he loved Martha and her sister and Lazarus, after hearing of his illness Jesus waited for two days in the place where he was.

After this, he said to his disciples, "Let us go back to Judaea." "Rabbi," his disciples said, "it is not long since the Jews there were wanting to stone you. Are you going there again?" Jesus replied, "Are there not twelve hours of daylight? Anyone can walk in day-time without stumbling, because he sees the light of this world. But if he walks after nightfall he stumbles, because the light fails him." After saying this he added, "Our friend Lazarus has fallen asleep, but I shall go and wake him." The disciples said, "Master, if he has fallen asleep he will recover." Jesus, however, had been speaking of his death, but they thought that he meant natural sleep. Then Jesus spoke out plainly: "Lazarus is dead. I am glad not to have been there; it will be for your good and for the good of your faith. But let us go to him." Thomas, called "the Twin", said to his fellow-disciples, "Let us also go, that we may die with him."

On his arrival Jesus found that Lazarus had already been four days in the tomb. Bethany was just under two miles from Jerusalem, and many of the people had come from the city to Martha and Mary to condole with them on their brother's death. As soon as she heard that Jesus was on his way. Martha went to meet him, while Mary stayed at home.

Martha said to Jesus, "If you had been here, sir, my brother would not have died. Even now I know that whatever you ask of God, God will grant you."

Jesus said, "Your brother will rise again." "I know that he will rise again," said Martha, "at the resurrection on the last day." Jesus said, "I am the resurrection and I am life. If a man has faith in me, even though he die, he shall come to life; and no one who is alive and has faith shall ever die. Do you believe this?" "Lord, I do," she answered; "I now believe that you are the Messiah, the Son of God who was to come into the world."

With these words she went to call her sister Mary, and taking her aside, she said, "The Master is here; he is asking for you." When Mary heard this she rose up quickly and went to him. Jesus had not yet reached the village, but was still at the place where Martha left him. The Jews who were in the house condoling with Mary, when they saw her start up and leave the house, went after her, for they supposed that she was going to the tomb to weep there.

So Mary came to the place where Jesus was. As soon as she caught sight of him she fell at his feet and said, "O sir, if you had only been here my brother would not have died." When Jesus saw her weeping and the Jews her companions weeping, he sighed heavily and was deeply moved. "Where have you laid him?" he asked. They replied, "Come and see, sir." Jesus wept. The Jews said, "How dearly he must have loved him!" But some of them said, "Could not this man, who opened the blind man's eyes, have done something to keep Lazarus from dying?"

Jesus again sighed deeply; then he went over to the tomb. It was a cave, with a stone placed against it. Jesus said, "Take away the stone." Martha, the dead man's sister, said to him, "Sir, by now there will be a stench; he has been there four days." Jesus said, "Did I not tell you that if you have faith you will see the glory of God?" So they removed the stone.

Then Jesus looked upwards and said, "Father, I thank thee: thou hast heard me. I knew already that thou always hearest me, but I spoke for the sake of the people standing round, that they might believe that thou didst send me."

Then he raised his voice in a great cry: "Lazarus, come forth." The dead man came out, his hands and feet swathed in linen bands, his face wrapped in a cloth. Jesus said, "Loose him; let him go."

Now many of the Jews who had come to visit Mary and had seen what Jesus did, put their faith in him. But some of them went off to the Pharisees and reported what he had done.

Thereupon the chief priests and the Pharisees convened a meeting of the Council. "What action are we taking?" they said. "This man is performing many signs. If we leave him alone like this the whole populace will believe in him. Then the Romans will come and sweep away our temple and our nation." But one of them, Caiaphas, who was High Priest that year, said, "You know nothing whatever; you do not use your judgement; it is more to your interest that one man should die for the people, than that the whole nation should be destroyed." He did not say this of his own accord, but as the High Priest in office that year, he was prophesying that Jesus would die for the nation – die not for the nation alone but to gather together the scattered children of God. So from that day on they plotted his death.

Accordingly Jesus no longer went about publicly in Judaea, but left that region for the country bordering on the desert, and came to a town called Ephraim, where he stayed with his disciples.

(John 11: 1–54)

Questions for discussion

1   What does Jesus save us from? How are things different for the human race, in the Christian view, since Jesus came?

2   How did Jesus' death constitute a sacrifice, since it was brought about by others?

3   If God decided to save the human race, why could he not have done that directly, simply by a decree of his will? What necessity could there have been to send a Savior?

4   How would you compare and contrast Christianity with Mahayana Buddhism?

Paul's First Letter to the Corinthians

Paul preached the Christian message in Corinth with much success for 18 months. By the time he left, the Christian community there had already grown quite large. Some time later they wrote to him in Ephesus asking his advice on a variety of problems, and this letter was his response. It was written between AD 54 and 58.

Love

I may speak in tongues of men or of angels, but if I am without love, I am a sounding gong or a clanging cymbal. I may have the gift of prophecy, and know every hidden truth; I may have faith strong enough to move mountains; but if I have no love, I am nothing. I may dole out all I possess, or even give my body to be burnt, but if I have no love, I am none the better.

Love is patient; love is kind and envies no one. Love is never boastful, nor conceited, nor rude; never selfish, not quick to take offense. Love keeps no score of wrongs; does not gloat over other men's sins, but delights in the truth.

357

There is nothing love cannot face; there is no limit to its faith, its hope, and its endurance.

Love will never come to an end. Are there prophets? their work will be over. Are there tongues of ecstasy? they will cease. Is there knowledge? it will vanish away; for our knowledge and our prophecy alike are partial, and the partial vanishes when wholeness comes. When I was a child, my speech, my outlook, and my thoughts were all childish. When I grew up, I had finished with childish things. Now we see only puzzling reflections in a mirror, but then we shall see face to face. My knowledge now is partial; then it will be whole, like God's knowledge of me. In a word, there are three things that last for ever: faith, hope, and love; but the greatest of them all is love.

(1 Corinthians 13: 1–13)

Resurrection

First and foremost, I handed on to you the facts which had been imparted to me: that Christ died for our sins, in accordance with the scriptures; that he was buried; that he was raised to life on the third day, according to the scriptures; and that he appeared to Cephas, and afterwards to the Twelve. Then he appeared to over five hundred of our brothers at once, most of whom are still alive, though some have died. Then he appeared to James, and afterwards to all the apostles.

In the end he appeared even to me; though this birth of mine was monstrous, for I had persecuted the church of God and am therefore inferior to all other apostles – indeed not fit to be called an apostle. However, by God's grace I am what I am, nor has his grace been given to me in vain; on the contrary, in my labours I have outdone them all – not I, indeed, but the grace of God working with me. But what matter, I or they? This is what we all proclaim, and this is what you believed.

Now if this is what we proclaim, that Christ was raised from the dead, how can some of you say there is no resurrection of the dead? If there be no resurrection, then Christ was not raised; and if Christ was not raised, then our gospel is null and void, and so is your faith; and we turn out to be lying witnesses for God, because we bore witness that he raised Christ to life, whereas, if the dead are not raised, he did not raise him. For if the dead are not raised, it follows that Christ was not raised; and if Christ was not raised, your faith has nothing in it and you are still in your old state of sin. It follows also that those who have died within Christ's fellowship are utterly lost. If it is for this life only that Christ has given us hope, we of all men are most to be pitied.

But the truth is, Christ was raised to life – the first fruits of the harvest of the dead. For since it was a man who brought death into the world, a man also brought resurrection of the dead. As in Adam all men die, so in Christ all will be brought to life; but each in his own proper place: Christ the first fruits, and afterwards, at his coming, those who belong to Christ. Then comes the end, when he delivers up the kingdom to God the Father, after abolishing every kind of domination, authority, and power. For he is destined to reign until God has put all enemies under his feet; and the last enemy to be abolished is death. Scripture says, "He has put all things in subjection under his feet." But in saying "all things", it clearly means to exclude God who subordinates them; and when all things are thus subject to him, then the Son himself will also be made subordinate to God who made all things subject to him, and thus God will be all in all.

Again, there are those who receive baptism on behalf of the dead. Why should they do this? If the dead are not raised to life at all, what do they mean by being baptized on their behalf?

And we ourselves – why do we face these dangers hour by hour? Every day I die: I swear it by my pride in you, my brothers – for in Christ Jesus our Lord I am proud of you. If, as the saying is, I "fought wild beasts" at Ephesus, what have I gained by it? If the dead are never raised to life, "let us eat and drink, for tomorrow we die."

Make no mistake: "Bad company is the ruin of a good character." Come back to a sober and upright life and leave your sinful ways. There are some who know nothing of God; to your shame I say it.

But, you may ask, how are the dead raised? In what kind of body? A senseless question! The seed you sow does not come to life unless it has first died; and what you sow is not the body that shall be, but a naked grain, perhaps of wheat, or of some other kind; and God clothes it with the body of his choice, each seed with its own particular body. All flesh is not the same flesh: there is flesh of men, flesh of beasts, of birds, and of fishes – all different. There are heavenly bodies and earthly bodies; and the splendour of the heavenly bodies is one thing, the splendour of the earthly, another. The sun has a splendour of its own, the moon another splendour, and the stars another, for star differs from star in brightness. So it is with the resurrection of the dead. What is sown in the earth as a perishable thing is raised imperishable. Sown in humiliation, it is raised in glory; sown in weakness, it is raised in power; sown as an animal body, it is raised as a spiritual body.

If there is such a thing as an animal body, there is also a spiritual body. It is in this sense that Scripture says, "The first man, Adam, became an animate being," whereas the last Adam has become a life-giving spirit. Observe, the spiritual does not come first; the animal body comes first, and then the spiritual. The first man was made "of the dust of the earth": the second man is from heaven. The man made of dust is the pattern of all men of dust, and the heavenly man is the pattern of all the heavenly. As we have worn the likeness of the man made of dust, so we shall wear the likeness of the heavenly man.

What I mean, my brothers, is this: flesh and blood can never possess the kingdom of God, and the perishable cannot possess immortality. Listen! I will unfold a mystery: we shall not all die, but we shall all be changed in a flash, in the twinkling of an eye, at the last trumpet-call. For the trumpet will sound, and the dead will rise immortal, and we shall be changed. This perishable being must be clothed with the imperishable, and what is mortal must be clothed with immortality. And when our mortality has been clothed with immortality, then the saying of Scripture will come true: "Death is swallowed up; victory is won!" "O Death, where is your victory? O Death, where is your sting?" The sting of death is sin, and sin gains its power from the law; but, God be praised, he gives us the victory through our Lord Jesus Christ.

Therefore, my beloved brothers, stand firm and immovable, and work for the Lord always, work without limit, since you know that in the Lord your labour cannot be lost.

(1 Corinthians 15: 3–58)

Questions for discussion

1 How do Paul's remarks on love relate to his overall message?

2 To what extent does Christianity depend on belief in the bodily resurrection of Jesus?

Glossary

In brackets after each explanation the religious tradition to which the term belongs is indicated, where it is not clear from the explanation itself. The traditions are designated as follows:

B: Buddhism
CB: Chinese Buddhism
Ch: Christianity
Cn: Confucianism
H: Hinduism
I: Islam
J: Judaism
S: Sikhism
T: Taoism

A Mi T'o, the Chinese name for the Buddha Amitabha (q.v.)
Aberah, sin (J)
Abhidamma, Pali form of Sanskrit "Abhidharma," the third section of the Buddhist scriptures
Achariya, a title of respect (H)
Adhan, the call to prayer (I)
Adonai, a name of God (J)
Agni, the Vedic god of fire, and so of the fire-sacrifice, the hearth, and the priestly caste (H)
Ahimsa, non-violence, the principle that one ought not to cause harm (B)
Allah, God, from "al-ilah," "the God" (I)
Amitabha, the Buddha who brings his devotees to the Pure Land
Amoraim, commentators on the Mishnah (J)
Analects, the chief collection of Confucius's sayings

Anatta, (Pali form of Sanskrit "Anatman") the doctrine of No Self or No Soul (B)

Anicca, (Pali form of Sanskrit "Anitya") the doctrine of impermanence (B)

Anointing of the Sick, one of the seven Sacraments accepted by Catholic and Eastern Orthodox Christians

Apocrypha, books not properly to be included in the Bible (Ch)

Arhant, one who has attained nirvana (B)

Arjuna, the hero of the Bhagavad-Gita (H)

Artha, one of the recognized goals of life (H)

Aryan, noble; a term applied to the Indo-European tribes that migrated into India around 1500 B.C. (H)

Asana, a posture in the practice of yoga (H)

Ashkenazim, Jews who lived in northern Europe, or their descendants

Atharva Veda, one of the Vedas (H)

Atman, the Self (H)

Avalokiteshvara, a Bodhisattva (B)

Avatara, incarnation of a god, esp. Vishnu (H)

Ayat Allah (Arabic) or **Ayatollah** (Persian), "Sign of God." Title of an especially eminent religious scholar (I)

Baptism, the ceremony of washing, one of the Christian Sacraments. In Sikhism, the ceremony of induction into the Khalsa (q.v.)

Bar Mitzvah, a ceremony of entrance into adulthood (J)

Bat Mitzvah, a similar ceremony to the Bar Mitzvah, for girls

Berakhah, blessing (J)

Bhagavad-Gita, the Song of God, part of the epic poem, the Mahabharata (H)

Bhakti, devotion (H)

Bhikkhu, a monk (B)

Bible, the sacred scriptures of Judaism and Christianity; from the Greek, "ta biblia," "the books"

Bishop, an official of the Christian Church, from the Greek "episkopos," an overseer (Ch)

B'nai B'rith, "Sons of the Covenant," a Jewish organization

Bodhi, enlightenment (B)

Brahma, the creator god (H)

Brahmacarin, a celibate student, the first stage of life (H)

Brahman, power, the Absolute Reality (H)

Brahmin, a member of the priestly class (H)

B'rit Milah, circumcision (J)

B'rit, Covenant (J)

Buddha, the Enlightened One

Caliph, Mohammed's successor as ruler of the faithful (I)

Christ, the Messiah, from the Greek meaning "the Anointed One" (Ch)

Ch'un Ch'iu, the Spring and Autumn Annals, one of the Confucian classics

Chun-Tzu, the Noble Man, the Princely Man, the gentleman (Cn)
Chung, sincerity (Cn)
Church, from the Greek "kyriake," meaning "belonging to the Lord" (Ch)
Confirmation, a Sacrament recognized by Catholic and Eastern Orthodox churches (Ch)

Deva, divinity (H)
Devi, the Mother Goddess (H)
Dhamma, the teachings of the Buddha (Pali)
Dharma, duty, esp. class duty (H)
Dharma, the teachings of the Buddha (Sanskrit)
Dhyana, meditation (B)
Diaspora, the Jewish community outside of Palestine
Doctrine of the Mean, one of the Confucian "Four Books"
Dukkha, suffering, sorrow, discontent. The first Noble Truth **(B)**
Durga, goddess, wife of Shiva (H)

El, a name of God (J)
Elohim, a name of God (J)
Emancipation, the liberation of the Jews in Europe from civil disabilities
Emunah, faith (J)
Eschatology, the doctrine of the Last Things (Ch)
Eucharist, the Christian celebration of the communal meal, one of the Sacraments

Ganesha, son of Shiva and Parvati, the god who prospers undertakings, has the head of an elephant (H)
Gehenna, Greek form of Gehinnom used in New Testament (Ch)
Gehinnom, place of punishment, named after a waste disposal site near Jerusalem
Gemara, "Completion," a portion of the Talmud containing comments on the Mishnah (J)
Gentile, a non-Jew
Gita, song, abbreviation for Bhagavad-Gita (H)
Gospel, in general, "Good News;" as a document, an early life of Jesus with some claim to be considered part of Scripture
Granth, also **Adi Granth**, **Guru Granth Sahib**, the sacred book of the Sikh community
Great Learning, one of the Confucian "Four Books"
Grihastha, householder (H)
Guru, an authority; title of the leader of the Sikh community.

Hadath, a form of uncleanness (I)
Hadith, the sayings and deeds of Mohammed (I)
Haggadah, the sermons of the rabbis, part of the Talmud (J)
Hajj, the pilgrimage to Mecca (I)
Halakhah, part of the Talmud relating to the observance of the Law (J)

Hallel, praise of God (J)

Hanukah, Jewish festival celebrating the victory of the Maccabees

Hasidism, a form of Jewish mysticism

Haumai, self-love (S)

Heresy, a doctrine considered not correct or orthodox

Het, sin (J)

Hijra, Hegira, Mohammed's journey from Mecca to Medina in A.D. 622 (I)

Hinayana, the "Narrow Vehicle," one of the chief forms of Buddhism

Ho, harmony (Cn)

Hsiao, filial piety (Cn)

Hukam, the divine will (S)

I, justice, righteousness (Cn)

I Ching, the Book of Changes (Cn)

Imam, leader, especially the leader of prayer in the Salat. In Shiite Islam, the divinely appointed guide of the whole Moslem community (I)

Indra, Vedic god of thunder and lightning, god of warriors (H)

Islam, "surrender," "submission"

Jati, birth, caste (H)

Jihad, "striving," "battle." Can be either the internal and spiritual battle against oneself, or the external holy war against unbelievers (I)

Jiva, soul (H)

Jivatman, soul (H)

Jnana, intellect (H)

Kabbalah, a form of Jewish mysticism

Kach, short trousers, worn by members of the Khalsa (S)

Kaddish, a prayer of blessing (J)

Kali, goddess, wife of Shiva (H)

Kalimah, the name of the statement witnessed to in the Shahadah (I)

Kama, desire, love, craving (B)

Kama, love, desire; one of the recognized goals of life (H)

Kamma, Pali word for Karma

Kangha, comb, worn in the hair by members of the Khalsa (S)

Kara, steel wrist band worn by members of the Khalsa (S)

Karma, action (H and B)

Karuna, compassion (B)

Kashrut, the dietary laws of Judaism

Kaur, "princess," surname given to female members of the Khalsa (S)

Kes, uncut hair, a mark of the Khalsa (S)

Khalsa, the Pure, an elite group within the Sikh community

Kippah, a skullcap, worn out of reverence for the presence of God (J)

Kirpan, sword, a dagger worn by members of the Khalsa (S)

Kirtan, hymn-singing (S)
Koran, the sacred scripture of Islam (see **Qur'an**) (I)
Kosher, belonging to Kashrut (J)
Krishna, incarnation of Vishnu (H)
Kshatriya, warrior class (H)
Kuan Yin, the Chinese name for the Bodhisattva Avalokiteshvara (q.v.) (B)
Kuei, a bad spirit (Cn)

Langar, "kitchen," the common meal of the Sikh community
Li, appropriate action, ritual (Cn)
Li Chi, one of the Confucian classics, the Book of Ritual
Limbo, a state after death for those worthy neither of heaven nor of hell (Ch)
Lin Chi, a branch of Ch'an Buddhism
Lingam, stylized representation of phallus, symbol of Shiva (H)

Magga, Pali form of Sanskrit "Marga," the Path. The fourth Noble Truth (B)
Mahayana, one of the chief forms of Buddhism
Mantra, a verbal formula used in meditation (B)
Marga, the Path (H, B)
Masjid, mosque (I)
Mass, a Catholic term for the Eucharist, considered especially as a sacramental sacrifice (Ch)
Maya, magician's trick, a term for the empirical world in Hindu thought
Mencius, one of the Confucian "Four Books," named after one of Confucius's chief followers
Messiah, from the Hebrew, meaning the "Anointed One," a term applied to the expected savior (J and Ch)
Metta, friendship, love, universal love (B)
Mezuzah, a small container placed on the frame of the door, holding a portion of the scriptures (J)
Mihrab, the niche in the wall of a mosque indicating the direction of Mecca (I)
Mishnah, "Repetition," a portion of the Talmud composed by Rabbi Judah, containing the opinions of the Tannaim (J)
Moksha, liberation (H)
Muezzin, mu'adhdhin, the one who calls to prayer (I)
Mullah, Iranian form of "mawla," a religious teacher (I)
Muslim, one who has surrendered to God (I)

Nadar, the grace of God (S)
Najasa, a substance causing pollution (I)
Nam, "name", a title of God (S)
Nirguna, without attributes, a term applied to Brahman (H)
Nirodha, the cessation of Dukkha, the third Noble Truth (B)
Nirvana, the state of final release, especially from the ego (H and B)

Orthodoxy, a doctrine held to be officially correct; a branch of the Christian Church

Paramartha (Pali: **paramattha)**, Absolute Truth, Ultimate Reality (B)
Parinirvana, final or ultimate nirvana attained after death (B)
Parvati, the wife of Shiva (H)
Penance, the Sacrament of the confession and forgiveness of sins, accepted by Catholic and Eastern Orthodox Christians
Pesach, Passover (J)
Prajna (Pali: **Panna)**, wisdom (B)
Priest, from the Greek "presbyteros," an elder
Puja, worship (H)
Purgatory, a state of purification after death for those not yet ready to enter heaven (Ch)
Purim, a Jewish festival celebrating the triumph of Esther

Qadi, a religious judge (I)
Qibla, the direction of Mecca (I)
Qur'an, "recitation", the sacred scripture of Islam (I)

Raja, "king," also name of a form of yoga (H)
Rama, an incarnation of Vishnu, hero of the Ramayana (H)
Ramadan, the month of fasting (I)
Ren, human-heartedness, compassion (Cn)
Rig Veda, one of the Vedas (H)
Rinzai, the Japanese name for Lin Chi (q.v.)
Rosh Hashanah, the New Year, one of the chief Jewish festivals
Rta, the natural law (H)

Sabad, "Word," God as revealed in the human heart (S)
Sach, "truth," a title of God
Sacrament, a visible sign of an invisible grace, from the Latin "sacramentum" (Ch)
Saguna, with attributes, a designation of Brahman (H)
Salat, ritual prayer (I)
Sama Veda, one of the Vedas (H)
Samadhi, concentration attained through meditation; mental discipline (B)
Samsara, the cycle of birth, death and rebirth (H and B)
Samudaya, the origin of Dukkha, the second Noble Truth (B)
Sangha, the Buddhist community
Sannyasin, the fourth stage of life, complete renunciation (H)
Sartori, enlightenment (B)
Satguru, the highest Guru, a title of God (S)
Sati, mindfulness, the practice of being aware of one's thoughts, actions and feelings (B)
Sawm, fasting (I)

Schism, an organizational split or rupture of a religious body

Sephardim, Jews who lived in Spain, or their descendants

Shaddai, a name of God (J)

Shahada, the confession of faith that there is no God but God or Allah (I)

Shakti, power or force, used as name of the wife of Shiva (H)

Shang Ti, the supreme ancestor worshipped by the Shang (Cn)

Shari'ah, the divine law (I)

Shastra, "Instruction," a class of non-scriptural treatises (H)

Shavuot, the feast of Pentecost, celebrating the giving of the Law to Moses on Mount Sinai (J)

Shekinah, the presence of God (J)

Shen, a good spirit (Cn)

Shia, a branch of Islam

Shih Ching, the Book of Poetry (Cn)

Shirk, the sin of placing a created thing on the same level as Allah (I)

Shiva, mourning for the dead (J)

Shiva, one of the principal gods of classical Hinduism

Shraddha (Pali: **Saddha**) faith, belief, confidence (B)

Shu, concern for others, altruism (Cn)

Shu Ching, the Book of History (Cn)

Sikh, a disciple or follower (S)

Sila, ethics (B)

Simhat Torah, the Joy of Torah, a festival, the last day of Sukkot (J)

Singh, "lion," surname given to male members of the Khalsa (S)

Skandha (Pali: Khandha), aggregate (B)

Smrti, "Remembered," authoritative texts not part of the scripture (H)

Soma, a plant with narcotic qualities, the god associated with this, and by extension the moon (H)

Soto, the Japanese name for Tsao Tung (q.v.)

Sruti, "Heard," sacred scripture (H)

Stupa, a shrine containing relies of the Buddha

Sudra, a laborer, the lowest of the four classic classes of Hindu society

Sufi, a mystic (I)

Sukhavati-vyuha Sutra, the Buddhist writing describing the Pure Land of Amitabha

Sukkot, the festival of Tabernacles (J)

Sunna, custom, especially of Mohammed (I)

Sunni, one of the chief branches of Islam

Sutra, "Discourse." In Hinduism, a class of non-scriptural writings. In Buddhism, the second section of the Buddhist scriptures

Sutta, the Pali form of "Sutra"

Tallit, a prayer-shawl (J)

Tanha, desire, craving (B)

Tao, in Confucianism, the right way to live; the teachings of Confucius

Tao, in Taoism, the ultimate principle of the universe

Tathagata, the "Thus-Come," a title of the Buddha

Te, originally power, subsequently moral power (Cn)

Tefillin, leather straps containing portions of the Hebrew scriptures, worn on the arms and forehead during prayer (J)

Theravada, the Way of the Elders, one of the chief branches of Buddhism

Ti, a divinity of the Shang (Cn)

T'i, brotherly love (Cn)

T'ien, Heaven (Cn and T)

T'ien Ming, the Mandate of Heaven (Cn)

T'ien Tzu, the Son of Heaven (Cn)

Torah, the divine Law (J)

Tripitaka, the "Three Baskets," the scriptures of Buddhism

Tsao Tung, a branch of Ch'an Buddhism

Ulama, the group of religious experts (I)

Umma, the Muslim community

Upadana, grasping, attachment (B)

Upanishad, a document appended to the Vedas (H)

Vaisya, a trader or peasant, the third class of Hindu society

Vanaprastha, a forest-dweller, the third stage of life (H)

Varna, class (H)

Veda, one of the sacred books of Hinduism

Vinaya, "Conduct," the first section of the Buddhist scriptures

Vishnu, one of the chief gods of classical Hinduism

Wu, enlightenment, sartori (B)

Wu wei, inactive action, laissez-faire, benign neglect, dealing with things according to their natures (T)

Yahweh, a name of God in Judaism

Yajur Veda, one of the Vedas, the sacred books of Hinduism

Yang and Yin, the complementary forces operating in nature (Cn and T)

Yoga, a path to spiritual liberation (H)

Yom Kippur, the Day of Atonement (J)

Yoni, the symbol of the female sexual organs, representing Shakti (H)

Zakat, obligatory almsgiving (I)

Some Technical Terms Used in the Discussion of Religions

Agnosticism is the view that it is impossible to know with any certainty whether some belief is true or not, for example, whether there is a God or not.

Animism is the belief that physical objects such as mountains or trees are inhabited by spiritual beings.

Atheism is the rejection of belief in God.

Deism is the belief that God created the world at the beginning of time, but does not further intervene in its operations in miraculous ways such as special revelations.

Dualism is the view that there are two primordial realities, for example, that the principle of evil is just as eternal and independent as the principle of good, or the view that reality is divided into two fundamental parts or halves.

Henotheism. It sometimes happens that the followers of a religion recognize the existence of many gods, but worship only one. The ancient Israelites, for example, appear to have believed that the gods worshipped by their neighboring peoples really existed, but they confined their own worship to their own national divinity, Yahweh. This state of affairs is called henotheism, from the Greek "hen," meaning "one."

Kathenotheism. It also sometimes happens that the followers of a religion recognize the existence of more than one god, and also worship them, but at the time they are worshipping any one particular god, they speak as if the god they are worshipping at that time is the only existing god. We find evidence of this, for example, in portions of the Vedas, the scriptures of Hinduism. This is called kathenotheism, from the Greek "kath-" meaning "as it were."

Monism is the view that fundamentally there is only one reality, only one existing being. If this reality or being is divine, the view is pantheism.

Monotheism, from the Greek "monos," meaning "alone, single," is the belief that there is only one personal God.

Mysticism is the search for an experiential oneness with the supreme reality.

Naturalism is the belief that there are no supernatural realities, but only natural ones.

Panentheism is the view that God is present in everything, without being simply identical with everything.

Pantheism is the belief that God is everything, and everything is God. It implies monism.

Polytheism is belief in the existence of more than one God (poly = many).

Skepticism is doubt, especially doubt whether there is a God or whether religious belief is valid.

Theism, from the Greek "theos," God, is belief in the existence of God, usually understanding "God" to mean a personal being rather than an impersonal force. In practice it is largely synonymous with monotheism.

Index